D1490360

Scribbles at an Exhibition

Other *Baby Blues*® Books from Andrews McMeel Publishing

Guess Who Didn't Take a Nap?

I Thought Labor Ended When the Baby Was Born

We Are Experiencing Parental Difficulties . . . Please Stand By

Night of the Living Dad

I Saw Elvis in My Ultrasound

One More and We're Outnumbered!

Check, Please . . .

threats, bribes & videotape

If I'm a Stay-at-Home Mom, Why Am I Always in the Car?

Lift and Separate

I Shouldn't Have to Scream More Than Once!

Motherhood Is Not for Wimps

Baby Blues®: Unplugged

Dad to the Bone

Never a Dry Moment

Two Plus One Is Enough

Playdate: Category 5

Our Server Is Down

Something Chocolate This Way Comes

Briefcase Full of Baby Blues®

Night Shift

The Day Phonics Kicked In

My Space

The Natural Disorder of Things

We Were Here First

Ambushed! In the Family Room

Cut!

Eat, Cry, Poop

Treasuries

The Super-Absorbent Biodegradable Family-Size Baby Blues®

Baby Blues®: Ten Years and Still in Diapers

Butt-Naked Baby Blues®

Wall-to-Wall Baby Blues®

Driving Under the Influence of Children

Framed!

X-Treme Parenting

Gift Books

It's a Boy

It's a Girl

BABY BLUES®

Scribbles At An Exhibition

Scrapbook 29

by Rick Kirkman & Jerry Scott

**Andrews McMeel
Publishing, LLC**

Kansas City • Sydney • London

Baby Blues® is syndicated internationally by King Features Syndicate, Inc. For information, write King Features Syndicate, Inc., 300 West Fifty-Seventh Street, New York, New York 10019.

Scribbles at an Exhibition copyright © 2012 by Baby Blues Partnership. All rights reserved. Printed in China. No part of this book may be used or reproduced in any manner whatsoever without written permission except in the case of reprints in the context of reviews.

Andrews McMeel Publishing, LLC
an Andrews McMeel Universal company
1130 Walnut Street, Kansas City, Missouri 64106

www.andrewsmcmeel.com

12 13 14 15 16 SHO 10 9 8 7 6 5 4 3 2 1

ISBN: 978-1-4494-0972-2

Library of Congress Control Number: 2011932643

Find *Baby Blues*® on the Web at
www.babyblues.com.

Front cover credits
Oil painting by Jerry Scott
Design and drawing by Rick Kirkman
Framed drawings and paintings (from left to right):
Taylor Kirkman, Brandon Denton, Brooke Denton, Cady Scott
Painting photograph by Madison Kirkman

Back cover credits
Jerry's oil palette photograph by Jerry Scott

─── **ATTENTION: SCHOOLS AND BUSINESSES** ───

Andrews McMeel books are available at quantity discounts with bulk purchase for educational, business, or sales promotional use. For information, please e-mail the Andrews McMeel Publishing Special Sales Department: specialsales@amuniversal.com

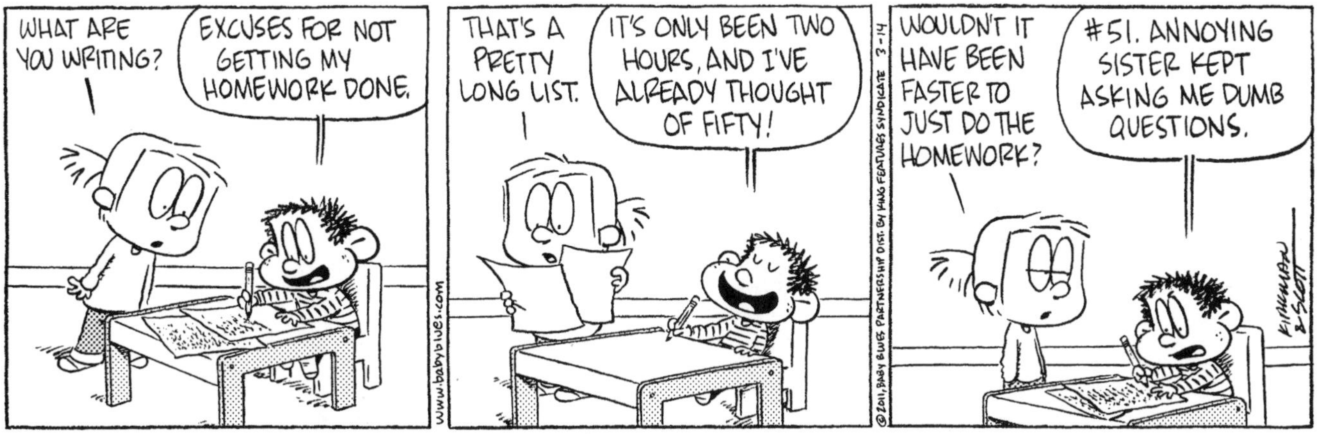
WHAT ARE YOU WRITING?
EXCUSES FOR NOT GETTING MY HOMEWORK DONE.
www.babyblues.com
THAT'S A PRETTY LONG LIST.
IT'S ONLY BEEN TWO HOURS, AND I'VE ALREADY THOUGHT OF FIFTY!
©2011, BABY BLUES PARTNERSHIP DIST. BY KING FEATURES SYNDICATE 3-14
WOULDN'T IT HAVE BEEN FASTER TO JUST DO THE HOMEWORK?
#51. ANNOYING SISTER KEPT ASKING ME DUMB QUESTIONS.
KIRKMAN & SCOTT

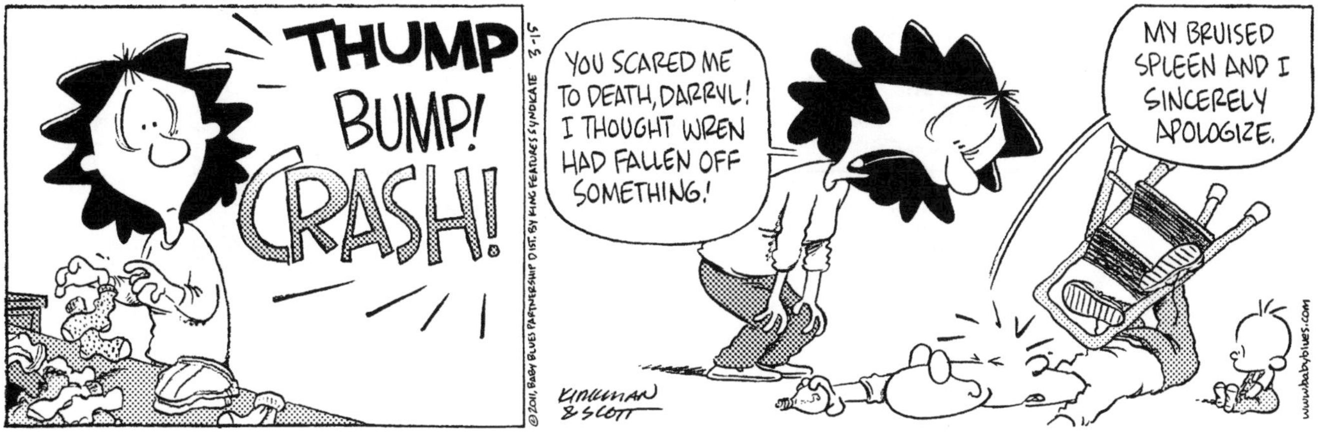
THUMP
BUMP!
CRASH!
3-15
©2011, BABY BLUES PARTNERSHIP DIST. BY KING FEATURES SYNDICATE
KIRKMAN & SCOTT
YOU SCARED ME TO DEATH, DARRYL! I THOUGHT WREN HAD FALLEN OFF SOMETHING!
MY BRUISED SPLEEN AND I SINCERELY APOLOGIZE.
www.babyblues.com

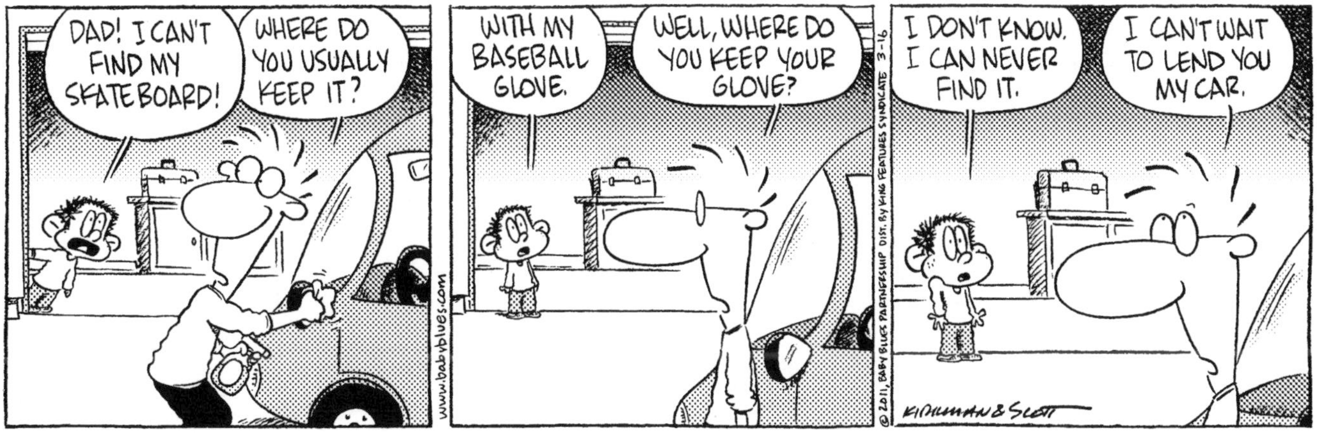
DAD! I CAN'T FIND MY SKATEBOARD!
WHERE DO YOU USUALLY KEEP IT?
www.babyblues.com
WITH MY BASEBALL GLOVE.
WELL, WHERE DO YOU KEEP YOUR GLOVE?
©2011, BABY BLUES PARTNERSHIP DIST. BY KING FEATURES SYNDICATE 3-16
I DON'T KNOW. I CAN NEVER FIND IT.
I CAN'T WAIT TO LEND YOU MY CAR.
KIRKMAN & SCOTT

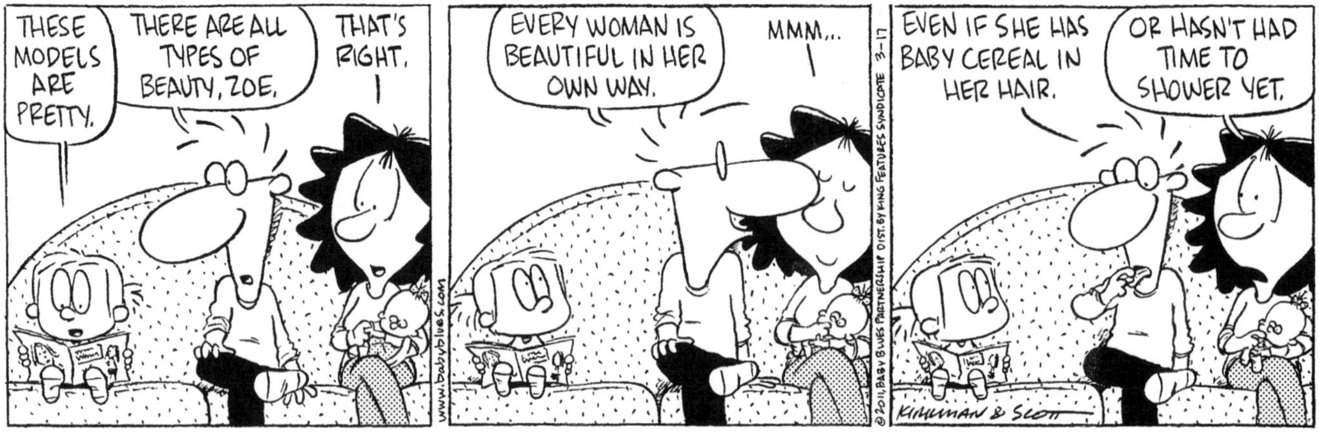
THESE MODELS ARE PRETTY.
THERE ARE ALL TYPES OF BEAUTY, ZOE.
THAT'S RIGHT.
www.babyblues.com
EVERY WOMAN IS BEAUTIFUL IN HER OWN WAY.
MMM...
© 2011, BABY BLUES PARTNERSHIP DIST. BY KING FEATURES SYNDICATE 3-17
EVEN IF SHE HAS BABY CEREAL IN HER HAIR.
OR HASN'T HAD TIME TO SHOWER YET.
KIRKMAN & SCOTT

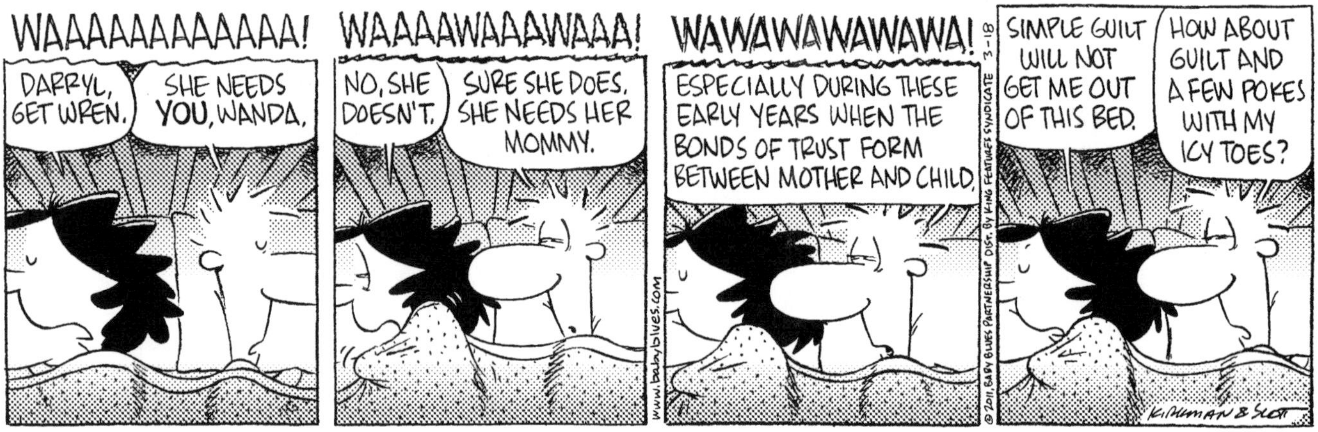
WAAAAAAAAAAAA!
DARRYL, GET WREN.
SHE NEEDS YOU, WANDA.
WAAAAWAAAWAAA!
NO, SHE DOESN'T.
SURE SHE DOES. SHE NEEDS HER MOMMY.
www.babyblues.com
WAWAWAWAWAWA!
ESPECIALLY DURING THESE EARLY YEARS WHEN THE BONDS OF TRUST FORM BETWEEN MOTHER AND CHILD.
© 2011, BABY BLUES PARTNERSHIP DIST. BY KING FEATURES SYNDICATE 3-18
SIMPLE GUILT WILL NOT GET ME OUT OF THIS BED.
HOW ABOUT GUILT AND A FEW POKES WITH MY ICY TOES?
KIRKMAN & SCOTT

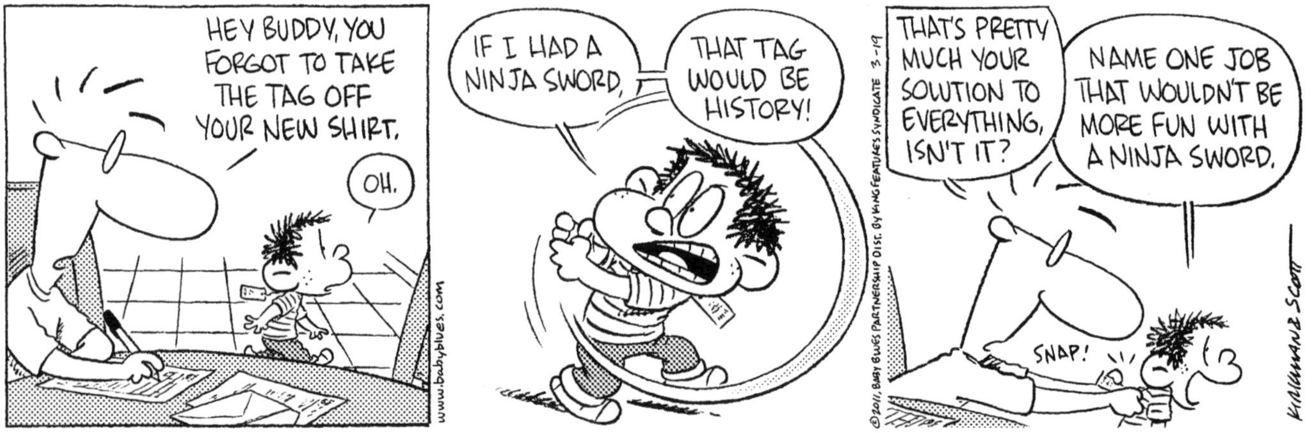
HEY BUDDY, YOU FORGOT TO TAKE THE TAG OFF YOUR NEW SHIRT.
OH.
www.babyblues.com
IF I HAD A NINJA SWORD,
THAT TAG WOULD BE HISTORY!
© 2011, BABY BLUES PARTNERSHIP DIST. BY KING FEATURES SYNDICATE 3-19
THAT'S PRETTY MUCH YOUR SOLUTION TO EVERYTHING, ISN'T IT?
NAME ONE JOB THAT WOULDN'T BE MORE FUN WITH A NINJA SWORD.
SNAP!
KIRKMAN & SCOTT

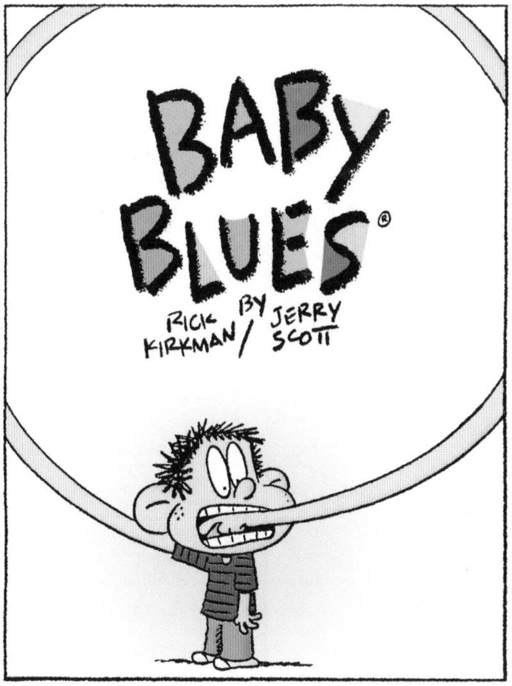
BABY BLUES®
RICK KIRKMAN / BY JERRY SCOTT

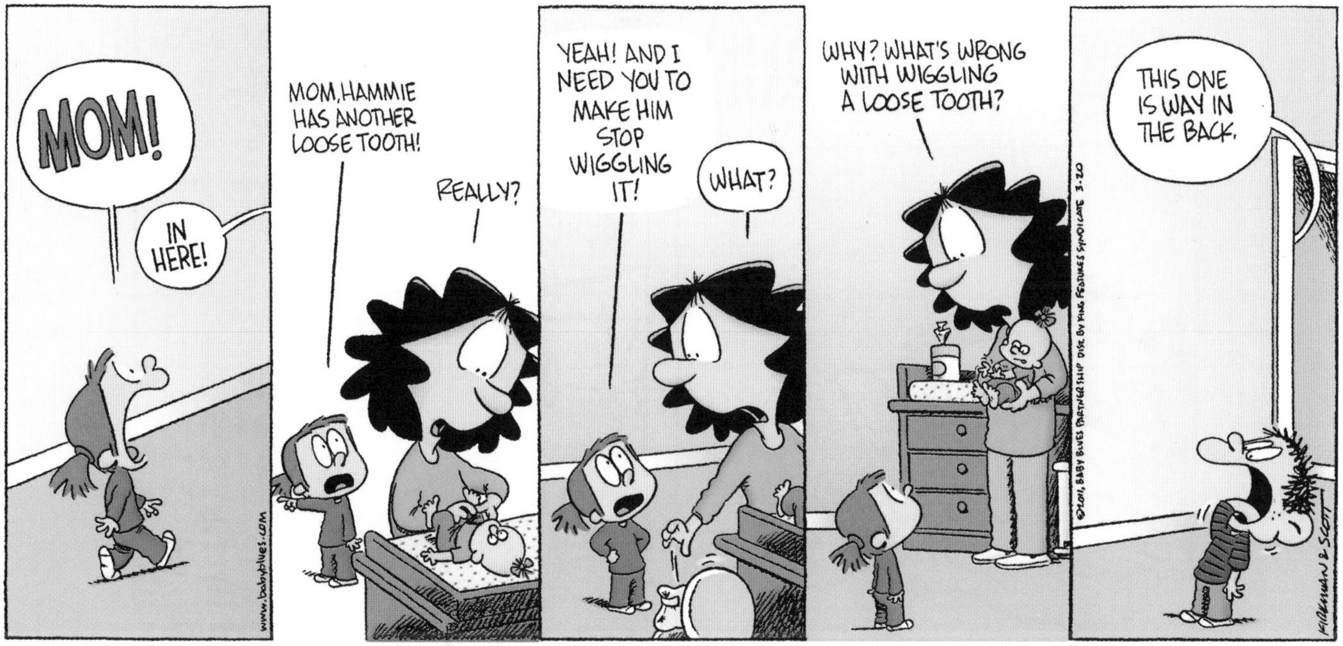
MOM!
IN HERE!
www.babyblues.com
MOM, HAMMIE HAS ANOTHER LOOSE TOOTH!
REALLY?
YEAH! AND I NEED YOU TO MAKE HIM STOP WIGGLING IT!
WHAT?
WHY? WHAT'S WRONG WITH WIGGLING A LOOSE TOOTH?
©2011, BABY BLUES PARTNERSHIP DIST. BY KING FEATURES SYNDICATE 3-20
THIS ONE IS WAY IN THE BACK.
KIRKMAN & SCOTT

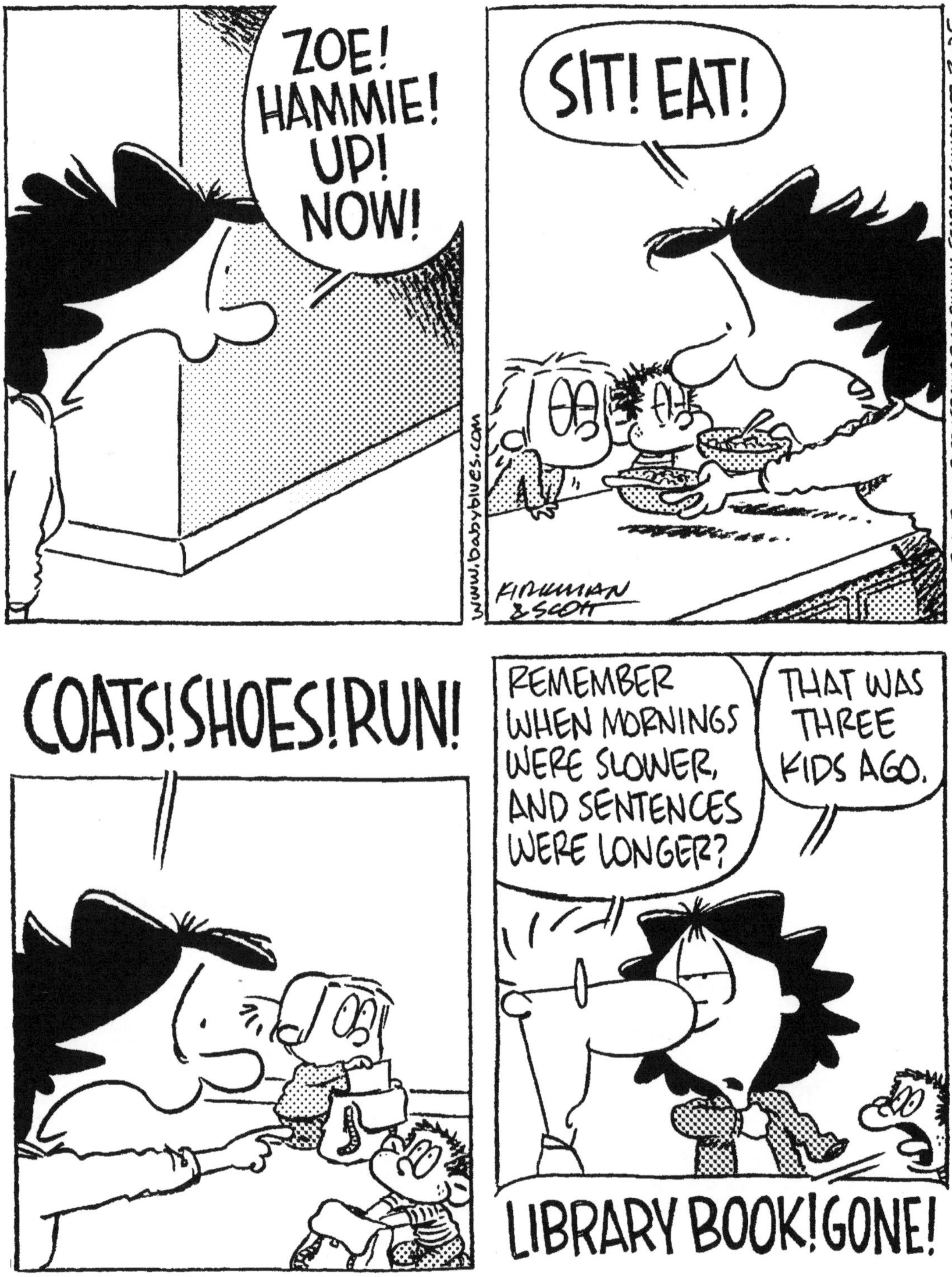
ZOE! HAMMIE! UP! NOW!
SIT! EAT!
COATS! SHOES! RUN!
REMEMBER WHEN MORNINGS WERE SLOWER, AND SENTENCES WERE LONGER?
THAT WAS THREE KIDS AGO.
LIBRARY BOOK! GONE!
www.babyblues.com
KIRKMAN & SCOTT
©2011, BABY BLUES PARTNERSHIP DIST. BY KING FEATURES SYNDICATE 3-25

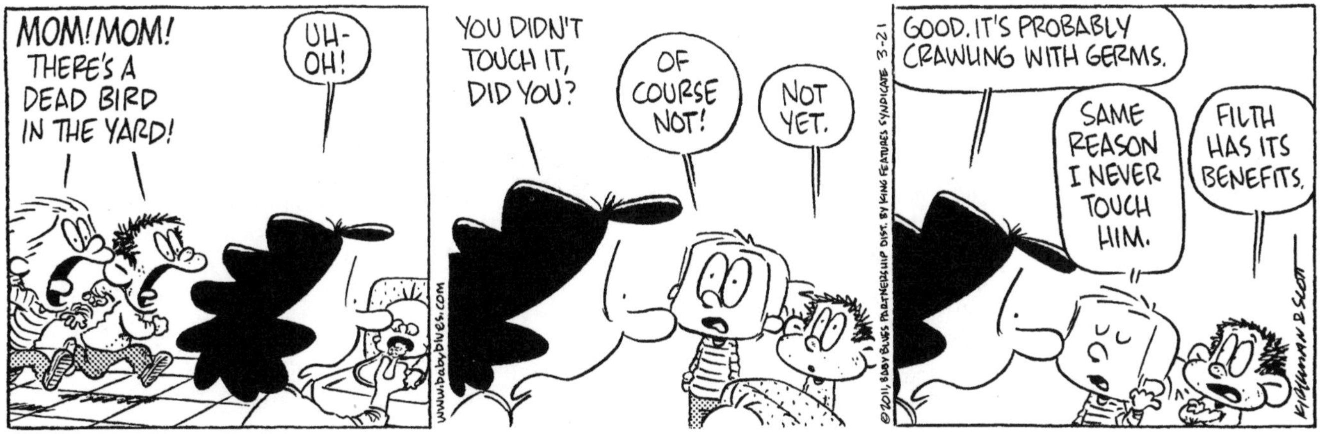
MOM! MOM! THERE'S A DEAD BIRD IN THE YARD!
UH-OH!
YOU DIDN'T TOUCH IT, DID YOU?
OF COURSE NOT!
NOT YET.
GOOD. IT'S PROBABLY CRAWLING WITH GERMS.
SAME REASON I NEVER TOUCH HIM.
FILTH HAS ITS BENEFITS.
www.babyblues.com
© 2011, BABY BLUES PARTNERSHIP DIST. BY KING FEATURES SYNDICATE 3-21
KIRKMAN & SCOTT

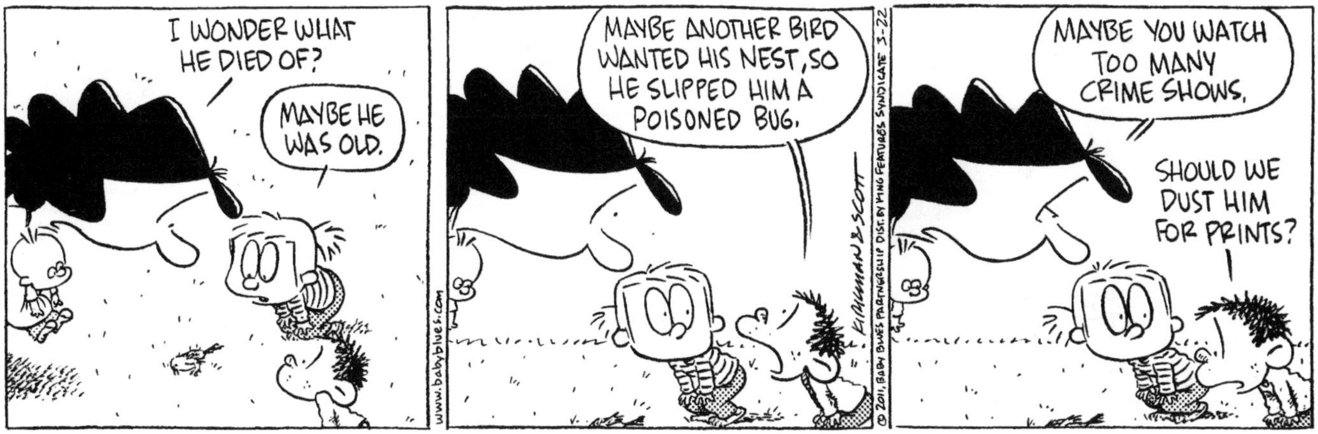
I WONDER WHAT HE DIED OF?
MAYBE HE WAS OLD.
MAYBE ANOTHER BIRD WANTED HIS NEST, SO HE SLIPPED HIM A POISONED BUG.
MAYBE YOU WATCH TOO MANY CRIME SHOWS.
SHOULD WE DUST HIM FOR PRINTS?
www.babyblues.com
© 2011, BABY BLUES PARTNERSHIP DIST. BY KING FEATURES SYNDICATE 3-22
KIRKMAN & SCOTT

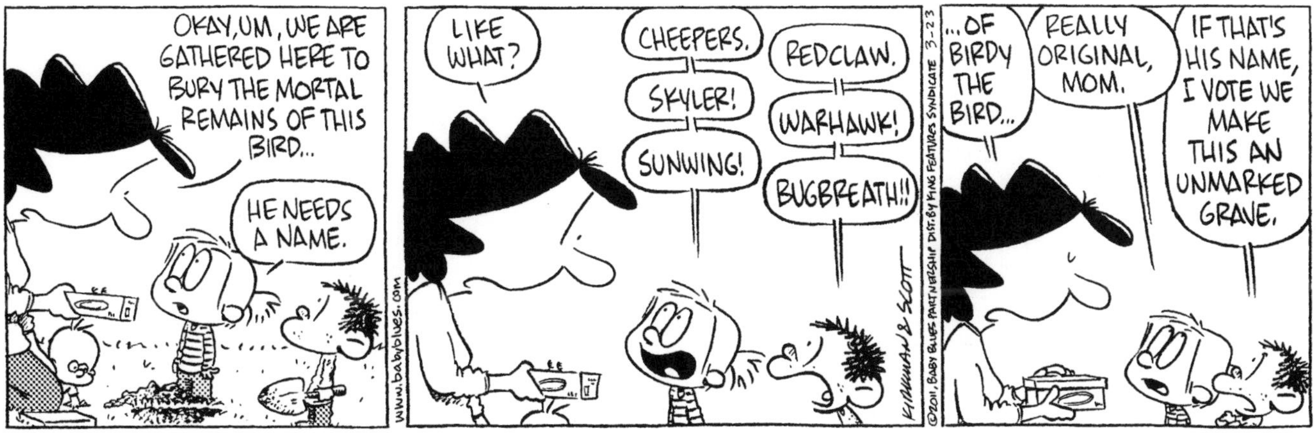
OKAY, UM, WE ARE GATHERED HERE TO BURY THE MORTAL REMAINS OF THIS BIRD...
HE NEEDS A NAME.
LIKE WHAT?
CHEEPERS.
SKYLER!
SUNWING!
REDCLAW.
WARHAWK!
BUGBREATH!!
...OF BIRDY THE BIRD...
REALLY ORIGINAL, MOM.
IF THAT'S HIS NAME, I VOTE WE MAKE THIS AN UNMARKED GRAVE.
www.babyblues.com
© 2011, BABY BLUES PARTNERSHIP DIST. BY KING FEATURES SYNDICATE 3-23
KIRKMAN & SCOTT

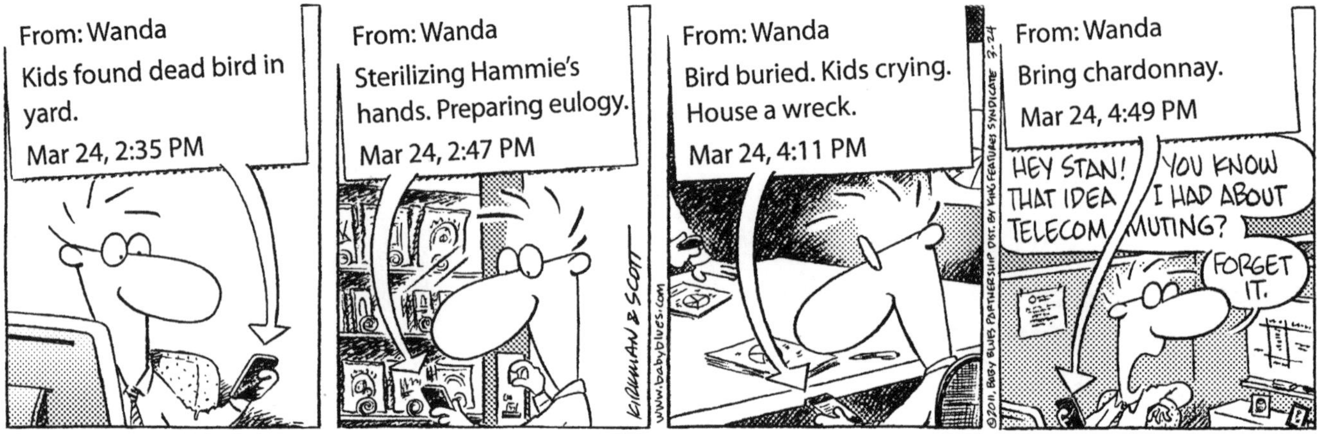
From: Wanda
Kids found dead bird in yard.
Mar 24, 2:35 PM
From: Wanda
Sterilizing Hammie's hands. Preparing eulogy.
Mar 24, 2:47 PM
KIRKMAN & SCOTT
www.babyblues.com
From: Wanda
Bird buried. Kids crying. House a wreck.
Mar 24, 4:11 PM
©2011, BABY BLUES PARTNERSHIP DIST. BY KING FEATURES SYNDICATE 3-24
From: Wanda
Bring chardonnay.
Mar 24, 4:49 PM
HEY STAN! THAT IDEA TELECOM
YOU KNOW I HAD ABOUT MUTING?
FORGET IT.

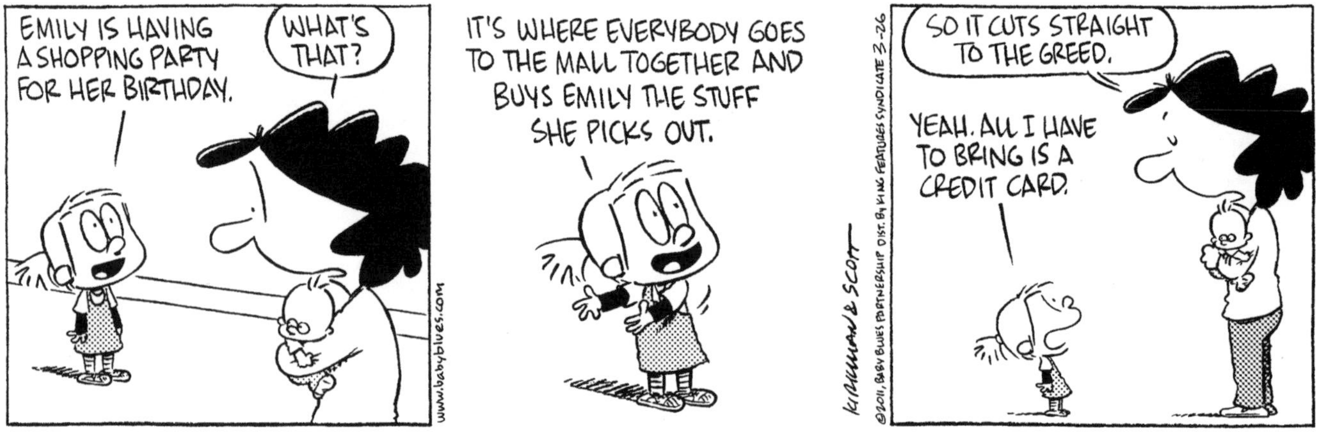
EMILY IS HAVING A SHOPPING PARTY FOR HER BIRTHDAY.
WHAT'S THAT?
www.babyblues.com
IT'S WHERE EVERYBODY GOES TO THE MALL TOGETHER AND BUYS EMILY THE STUFF SHE PICKS OUT.
KIRKMAN & SCOTT
©2011, BABY BLUES PARTNERSHIP DIST. BY KING FEATURES SYNDICATE 3-26
SO IT CUTS STRAIGHT TO THE GREED.
YEAH. ALL I HAVE TO BRING IS A CREDIT CARD.

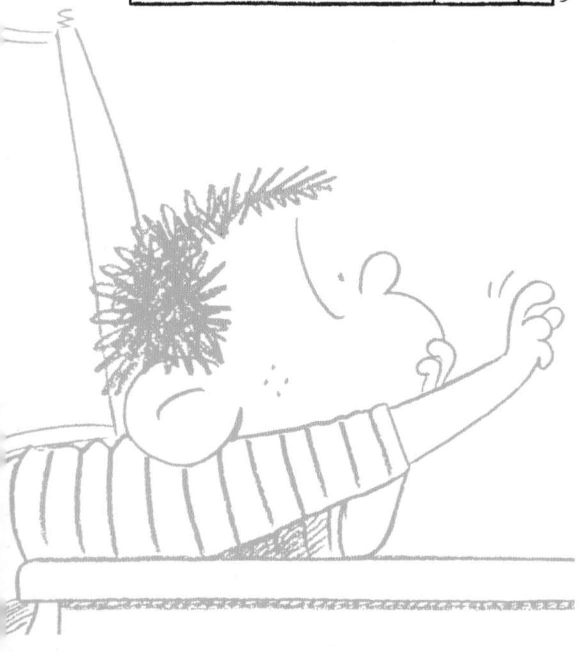

1000mL
BABY BLUES®
RICK KIRKMAN / BY / JERRY SCOTT
MILK CHOCOLATE

I'M SURE YOU HAD A HARD DAY, BUT I DON'T THINK THERE IS SUCH A THING AS A CHOCOLATE I.V.
WELL, THERE SHOULD BE.
www.babyblues.com
KIRKMAN / SCOTT
©2011, BABY BLUES PARTNERSHIP DIST. BY KING FEATURES SYNDICATE 3-27

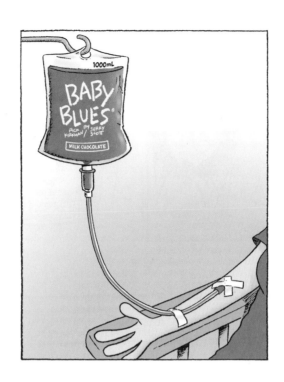

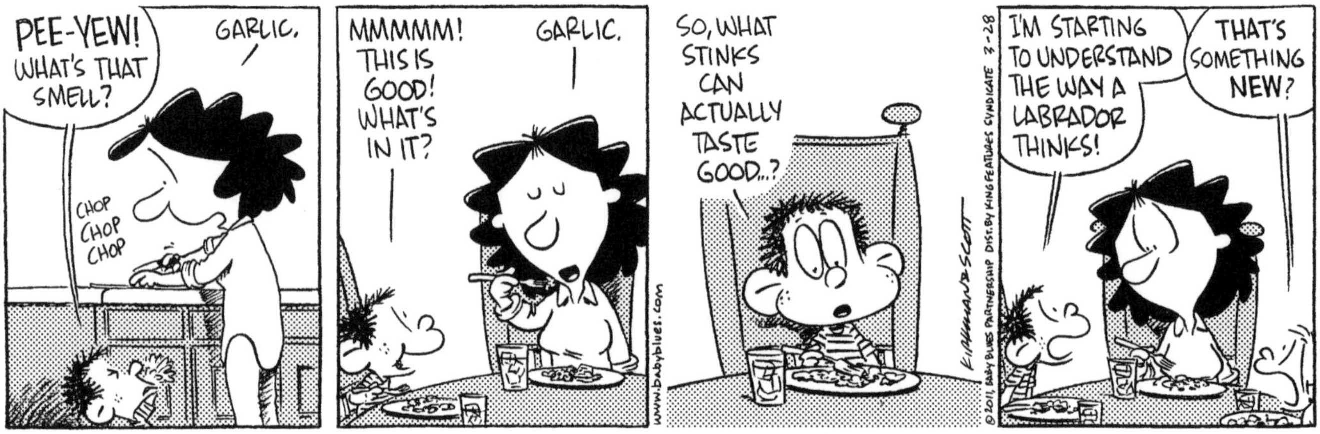
PEE-YEW! WHAT'S THAT SMELL?
GARLIC.
CHOP CHOP CHOP
MMMMM! THIS IS GOOD! WHAT'S IN IT?
GARLIC.
www.babyblues.com
SO, WHAT STINKS CAN ACTUALLY TASTE GOOD...?
KIRKMAN & SCOTT
© 2011, BABY BLUES PARTNERSHIP DIST. BY KING FEATURES SYNDICATE 3-28
I'M STARTING TO UNDERSTAND THE WAY A LABRADOR THINKS!
THAT'S SOMETHING NEW?

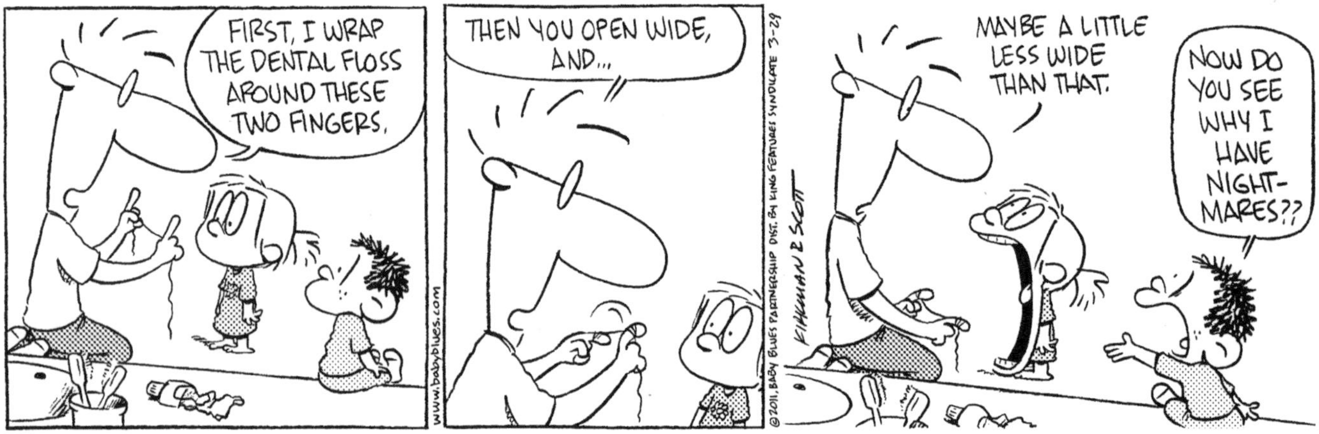
FIRST, I WRAP THE DENTAL FLOSS AROUND THESE TWO FINGERS.
www.babyblues.com
THEN YOU OPEN WIDE, AND...
© 2011, BABY BLUES PARTNERSHIP DIST. BY KING FEATURES SYNDICATE 3-29
KIRKMAN & SCOTT
MAYBE A LITTLE LESS WIDE THAN THAT.
NOW DO YOU SEE WHY I HAVE NIGHT-MARES??

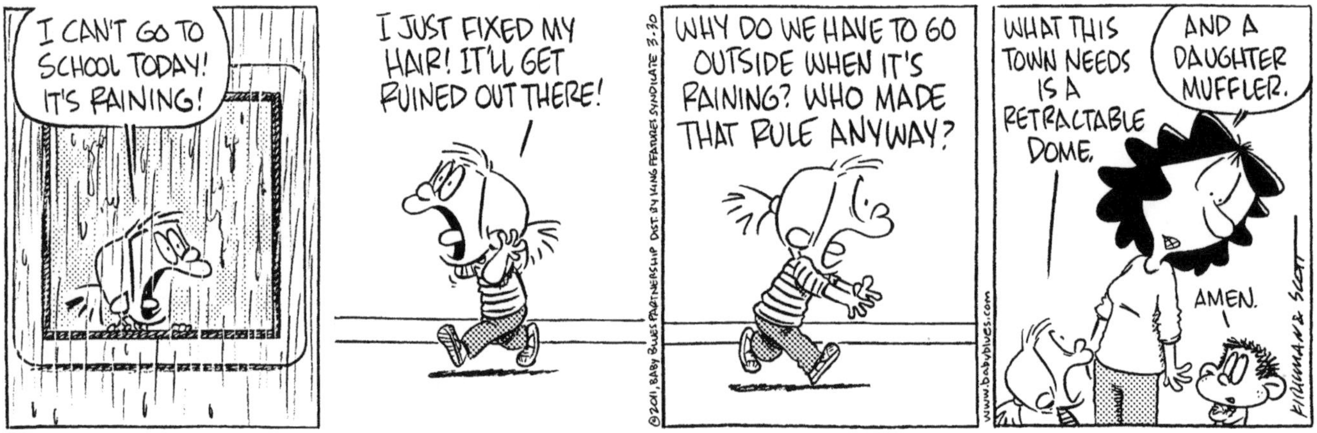
I CAN'T GO TO SCHOOL TODAY! IT'S RAINING!
I JUST FIXED MY HAIR! IT'LL GET RUINED OUT THERE!
© 2011, BABY BLUES PARTNERSHIP DIST. BY KING FEATURES SYNDICATE 3-30
WHY DO WE HAVE TO GO OUTSIDE WHEN IT'S RAINING? WHO MADE THAT RULE ANYWAY?
www.babyblues.com
WHAT THIS TOWN NEEDS IS A RETRACTABLE DOME.
AND A DAUGHTER MUFFLER.
AMEN.
KIRKMAN & SCOTT

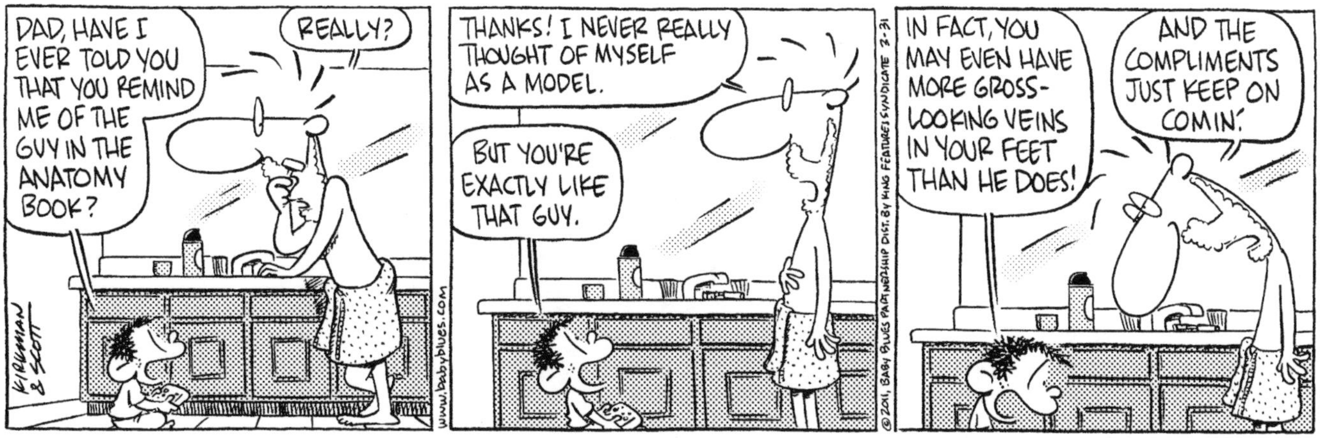
DAD, HAVE I EVER TOLD YOU THAT YOU REMIND ME OF THE GUY IN THE ANATOMY BOOK?
REALLY?
THANKS! I NEVER REALLY THOUGHT OF MYSELF AS A MODEL.
BUT YOU'RE EXACTLY LIKE THAT GUY.
IN FACT, YOU MAY EVEN HAVE MORE GROSS-LOOKING VEINS IN YOUR FEET THAN HE DOES!
AND THE COMPLIMENTS JUST KEEP ON COMIN'.
KIRKMAN & SCOTT
www.babyblues.com
© 2011, BABY BLUES PARTNERSHIP DIST. BY KING FEATURES SYNDICATE 3-31

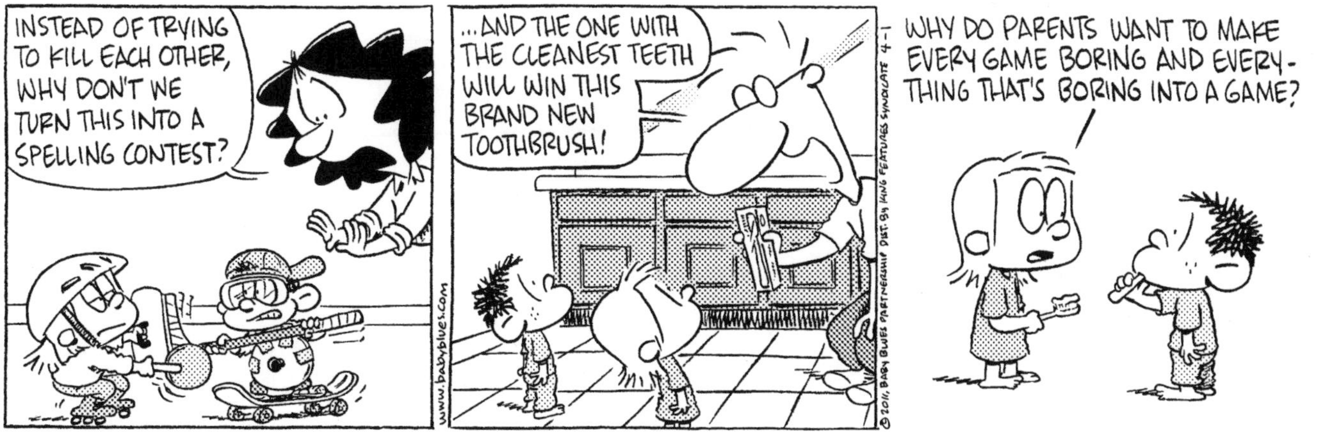
INSTEAD OF TRYING TO KILL EACH OTHER, WHY DON'T WE TURN THIS INTO A SPELLING CONTEST?
...AND THE ONE WITH THE CLEANEST TEETH WILL WIN THIS BRAND NEW TOOTHBRUSH!
WHY DO PARENTS WANT TO MAKE EVERY GAME BORING AND EVERYTHING THAT'S BORING INTO A GAME?
www.babyblues.com
© 2011, BABY BLUES PARTNERSHIP DIST. BY KING FEATURES SYNDICATE 4-1

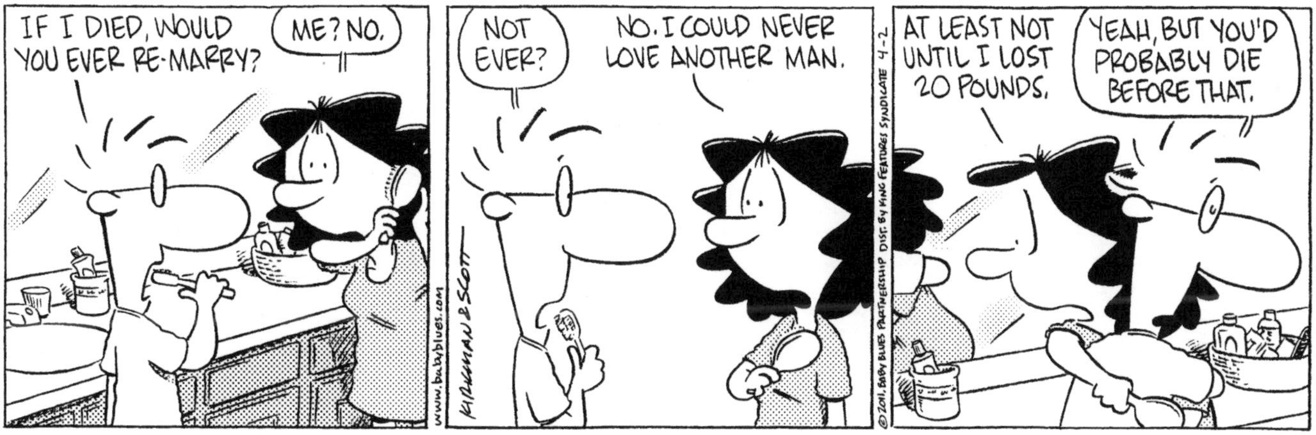
IF I DIED, WOULD YOU EVER RE-MARRY?
ME? NO.
NOT EVER?
NO. I COULD NEVER LOVE ANOTHER MAN.
AT LEAST NOT UNTIL I LOST 20 POUNDS.
YEAH, BUT YOU'D PROBABLY DIE BEFORE THAT.
www.babyblues.com
KIRKMAN & SCOTT
© 2011, BABY BLUES PARTNERSHIP DIST. BY KING FEATURES SYNDICATE 4-2

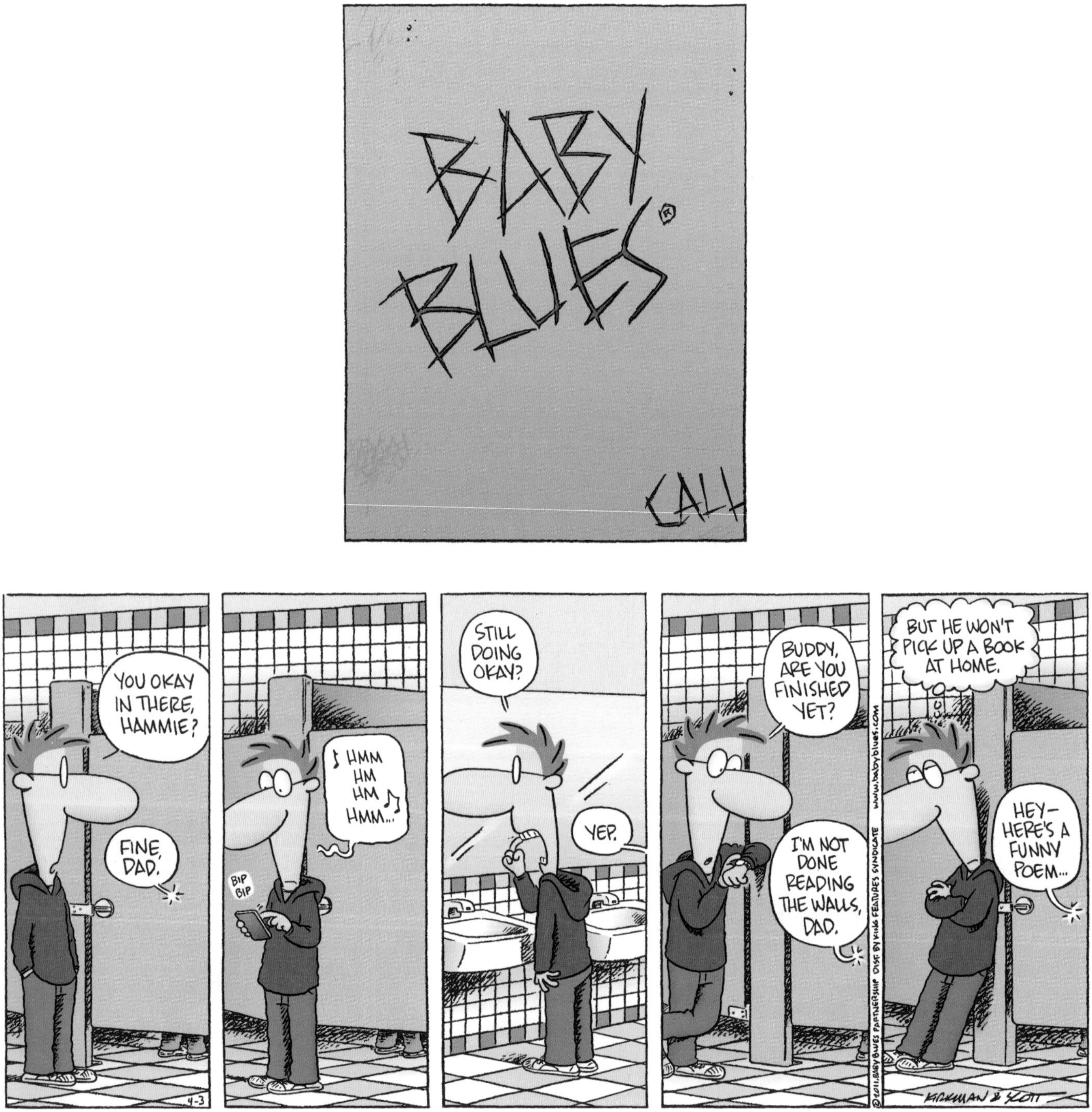
BABY BLUES®
CALL
YOU OKAY IN THERE, HAMMIE?
FINE, DAD.
4-3
♪ HMM HM HM HMM... ♪
BIP BIP
STILL DOING OKAY?
YEP.
BUDDY, ARE YOU FINISHED YET?
I'M NOT DONE READING THE WALLS, DAD.
©2011, BABY BLUES PARTNERSHIP DIST. BY KING FEATURES SYNDICATE www.babyblues.com
BUT HE WON'T PICK UP A BOOK AT HOME.
HEY— HERE'S A FUNNY POEM...
KIRKMAN & SCOTT

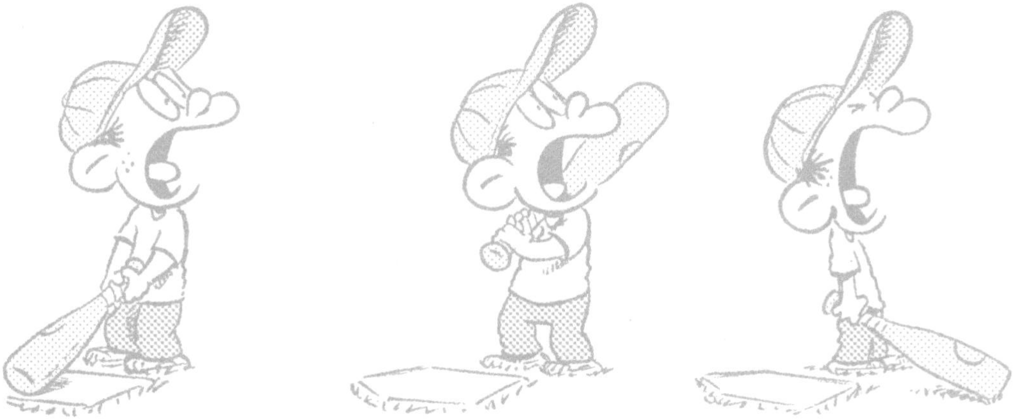

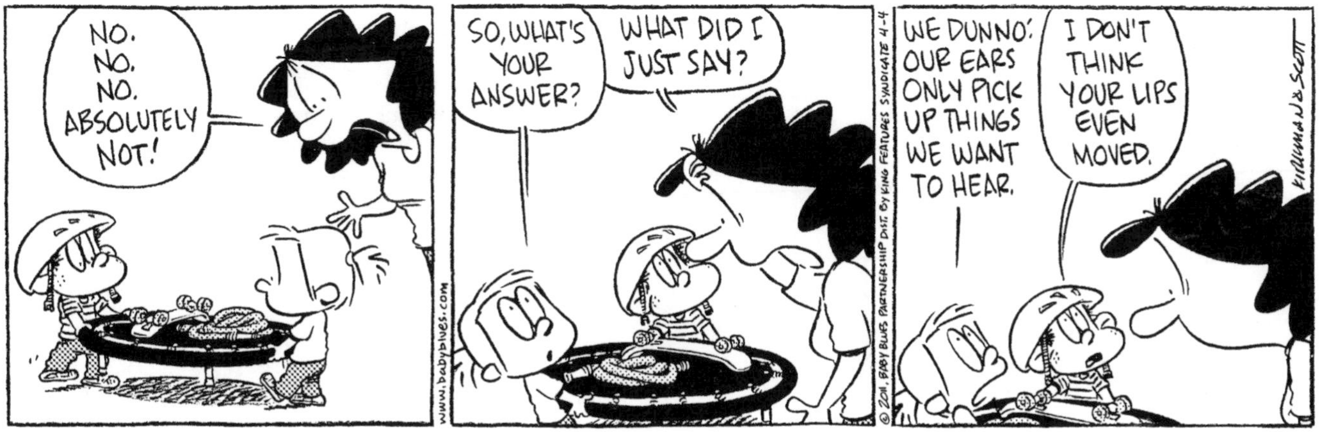
NO. NO. NO. ABSOLUTELY NOT!
www.babyblues.com
SO, WHAT'S YOUR ANSWER?
WHAT DID I JUST SAY?
© 2011, BABY BLUES PARTNERSHIP DIST. BY KING FEATURES SYNDICATE 4-4
WE DUNNO. OUR EARS ONLY PICK UP THINGS WE WANT TO HEAR.
I DON'T THINK YOUR LIPS EVEN MOVED.
KIRKMAN & SCOTT

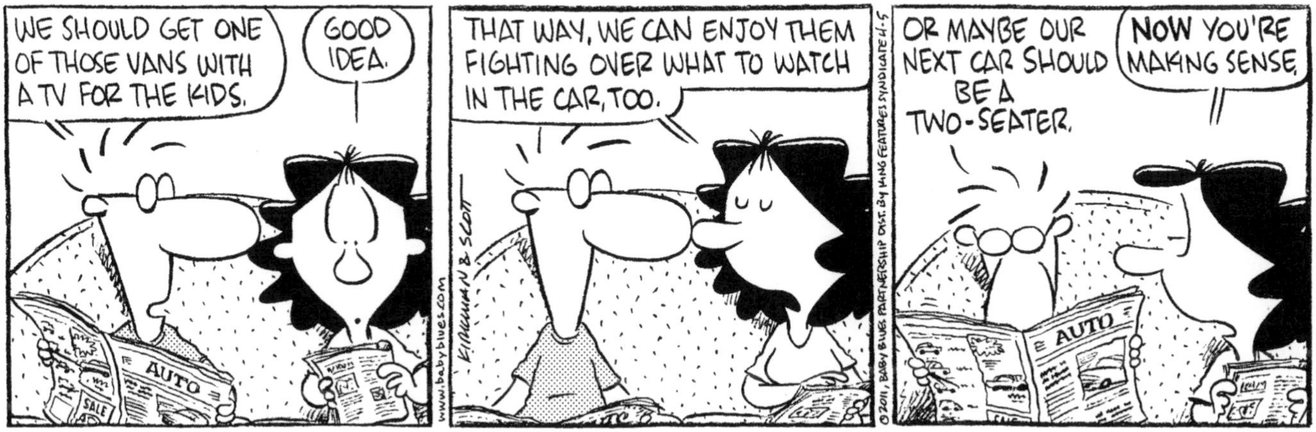
WE SHOULD GET ONE OF THOSE VANS WITH A TV FOR THE KIDS.
GOOD IDEA.
AUTO
SALE
www.babyblues.com
KIRKMAN & SCOTT
THAT WAY, WE CAN ENJOY THEM FIGHTING OVER WHAT TO WATCH IN THE CAR, TOO.
© 2011, BABY BLUES PARTNERSHIP DIST. BY KING FEATURES SYNDICATE 4-5
OR MAYBE OUR NEXT CAR SHOULD BE A TWO-SEATER.
NOW YOU'RE MAKING SENSE.
AUTO

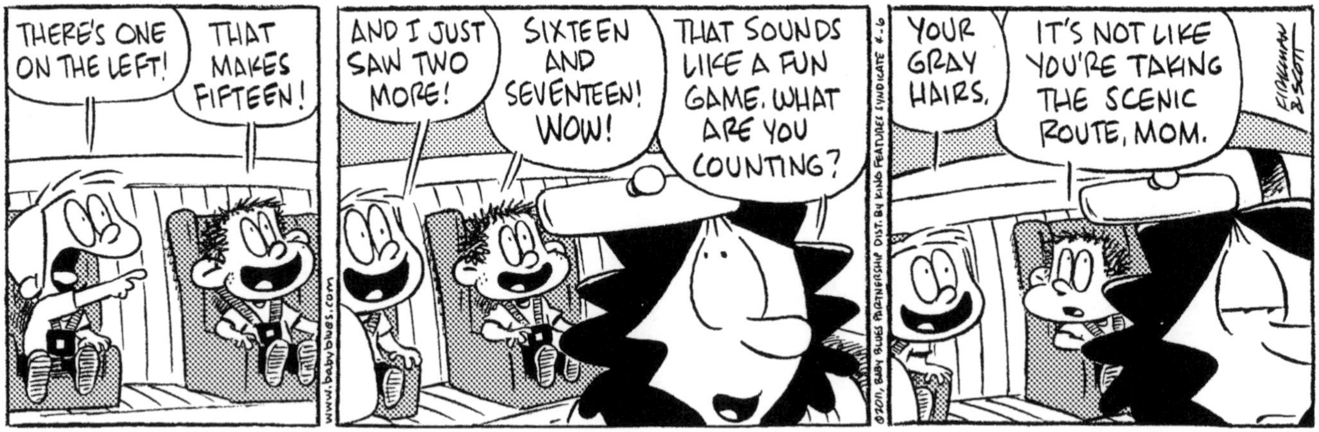
THERE'S ONE ON THE LEFT!
THAT MAKES FIFTEEN!
www.babyblues.com
AND I JUST SAW TWO MORE!
SIXTEEN AND SEVENTEEN! WOW!
THAT SOUNDS LIKE A FUN GAME. WHAT ARE YOU COUNTING?
© 2011, BABY BLUES PARTNERSHIP DIST. BY KING FEATURES SYNDICATE 4-6
YOUR GRAY HAIRS.
IT'S NOT LIKE YOU'RE TAKING THE SCENIC ROUTE, MOM.
KIRKMAN & SCOTT

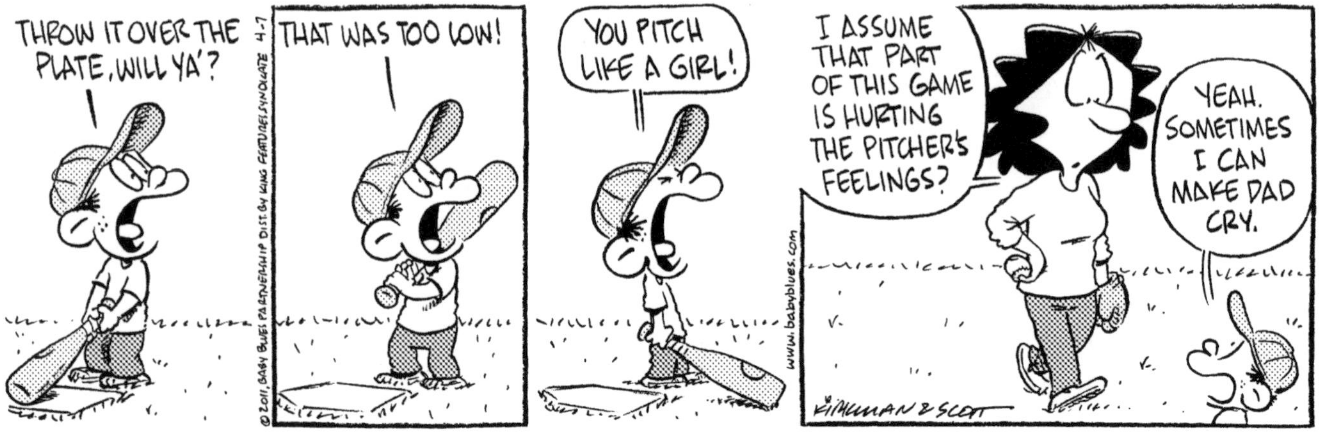
THROW IT OVER THE PLATE, WILL YA'?
© 2011, BABY BLUES PARTNERSHIP DIST. BY KING FEATURES SYNDICATE 4-7
THAT WAS TOO LOW!
YOU PITCH LIKE A GIRL!
www.babyblues.com
I ASSUME THAT PART OF THIS GAME IS HURTING THE PITCHER'S FEELINGS?
YEAH. SOMETIMES I CAN MAKE DAD CRY.
KIRKMAN & SCOTT

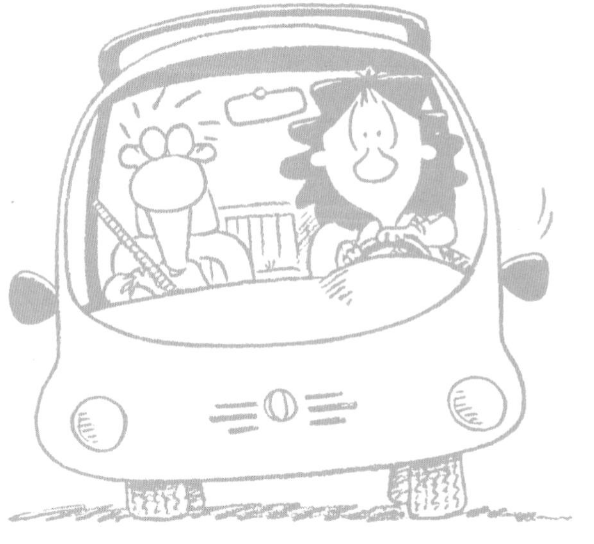

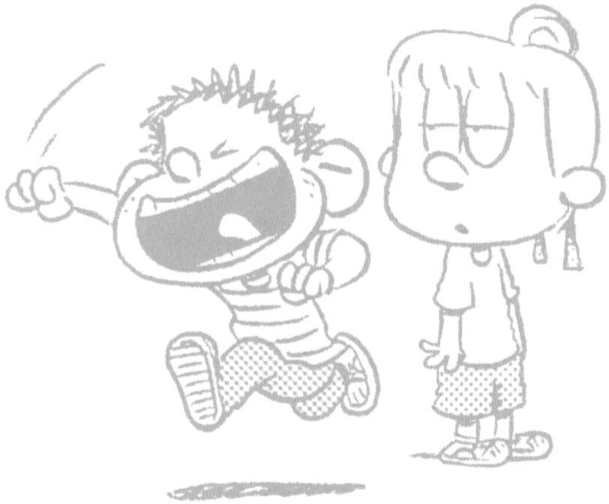

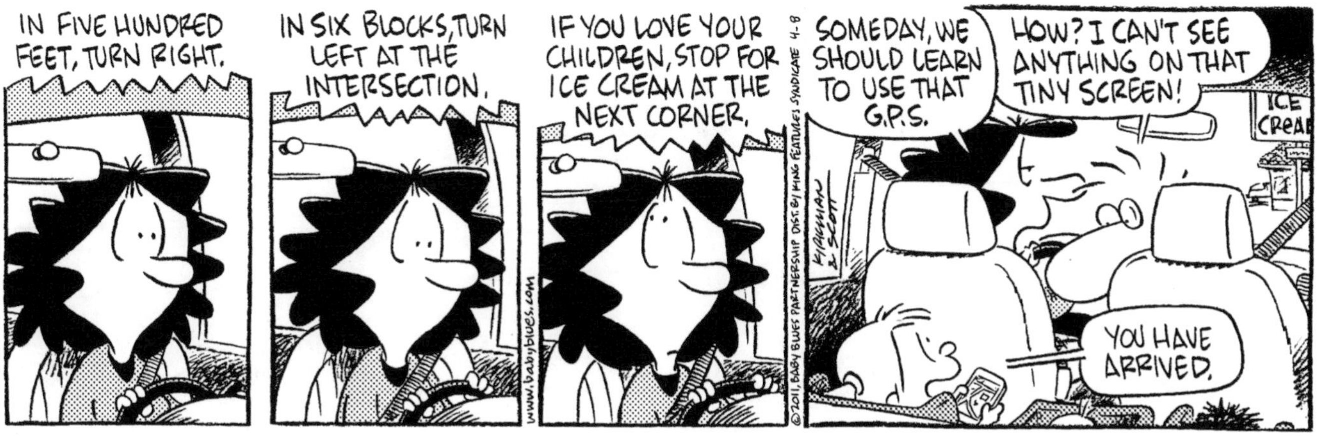
IN FIVE HUNDRED FEET, TURN RIGHT.
IN SIX BLOCKS, TURN LEFT AT THE INTERSECTION.
IF YOU LOVE YOUR CHILDREN, STOP FOR ICE CREAM AT THE NEXT CORNER.
SOMEDAY, WE SHOULD LEARN TO USE THAT G.P.S.
HOW? I CAN'T SEE ANYTHING ON THAT TINY SCREEN!
YOU HAVE ARRIVED.
ICE CREA
www.babyblues.com
© 2011, BABY BLUES PARTNERSHIP DIST. BY KING FEATURES SYNDICATE 4-8
KIRKMAN & SCOTT

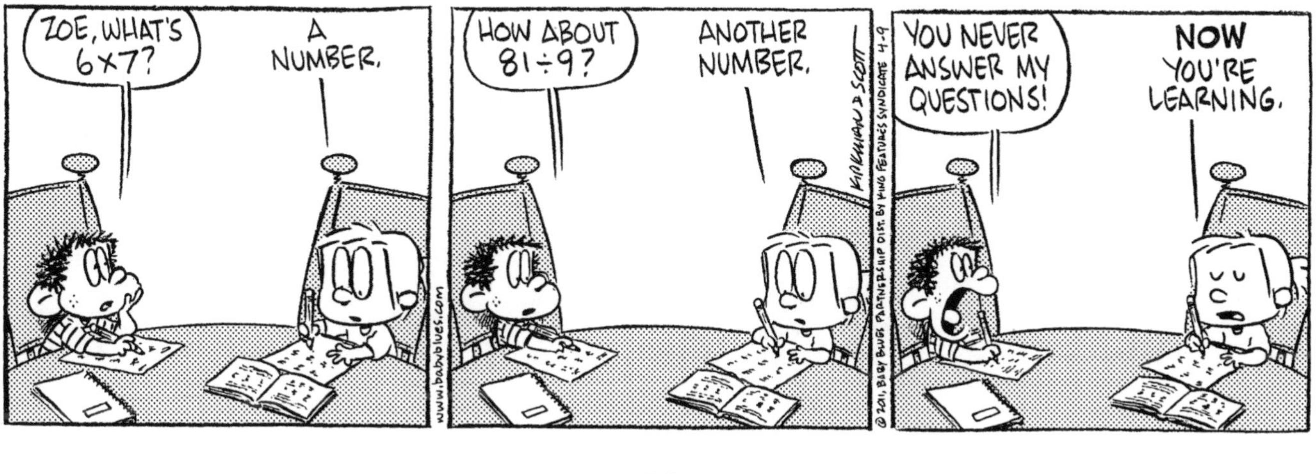
ZOE, WHAT'S 6×7?
A NUMBER.
HOW ABOUT 81÷9?
ANOTHER NUMBER.
YOU NEVER ANSWER MY QUESTIONS!
NOW YOU'RE LEARNING.
www.babyblues.com
© 2011, BABY BLUES PARTNERSHIP DIST. BY KING FEATURES SYNDICATE 4-9
KIRKMAN & SCOTT

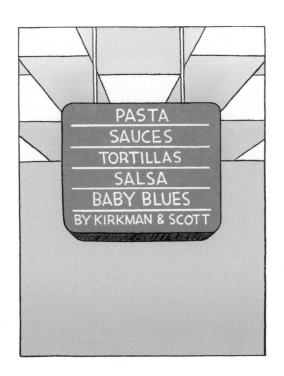

PASTA
SAUCES
TORTILLAS
SALSA
BABY BLUES
BY KIRKMAN & SCOTT

WHAT'S NEXT ON THE LIST?
SPAGHETTI.
I'LL GET IT!
WATCH IT!
OOPS!
AAAAGH!
www.babyblues.com
THEY HAVE ABOUT A MILLION KINDS OF PICKLES, SO I CHOSE FOUR.
©2011, BABY BLUES PARTNERSHIP DIST. BY KING FEATURES SYNDICATE
HEY, DAD, DO WE NEED APPLES?
OH, WOW. THAT OPENED EASY.
GROAN!
CLEANUP ON AISLES 3, 4, 5, 6 AND WHEREVER THE GUY IN THE GREEN SWEATPANTS IS HEADED NEXT.
WHENEVER WE SHOP WITH DAD, I FEEL LIKE I'M SHOPPING WITH A CELEBRITY.
4-10
KIRKMAN & SCOTT

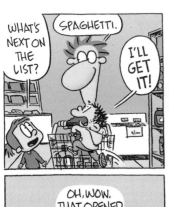

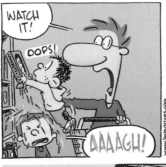

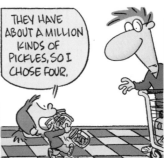

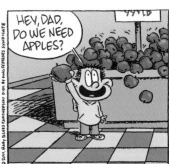

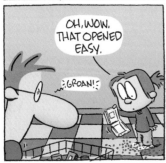

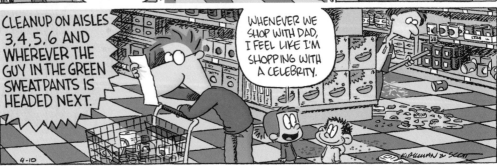

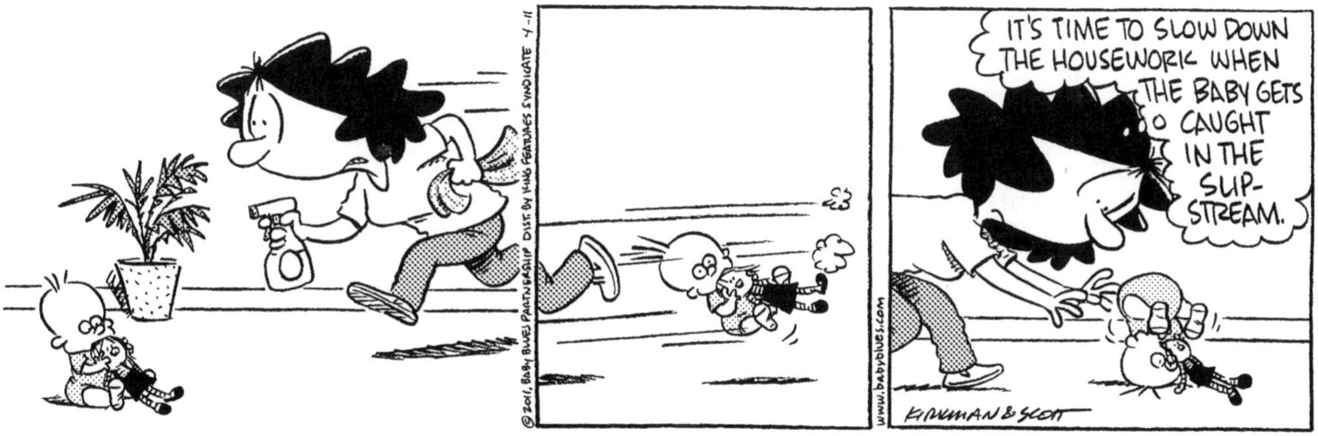
©2011, BABY BLUES PARTNERSHIP DIST. BY KING FEATURES SYNDICATE 4-11
IT'S TIME TO SLOW DOWN THE HOUSEWORK WHEN THE BABY GETS CAUGHT IN THE SLIP-STREAM.
www.babyblues.com
KIRKMAN & SCOTT

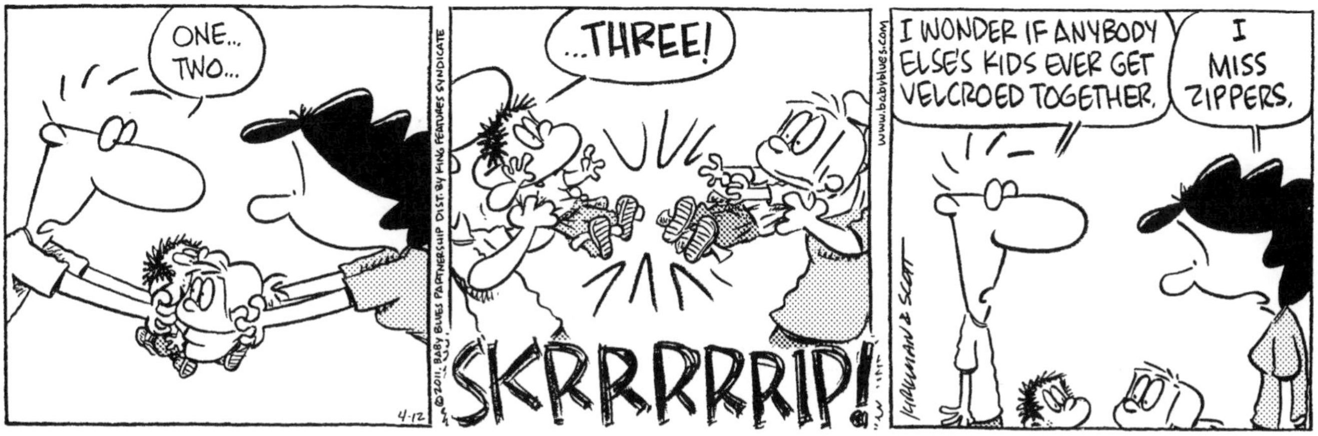
ONE... TWO...
4-12
©2011, BABY BLUES PARTNERSHIP DIST. BY KING FEATURES SYNDICATE
...THREE!
SKRRRRRRIP!
www.babyblues.com
I WONDER IF ANYBODY ELSE'S KIDS EVER GET VELCROED TOGETHER.
I MISS ZIPPERS.
KIRKMAN & SCOTT

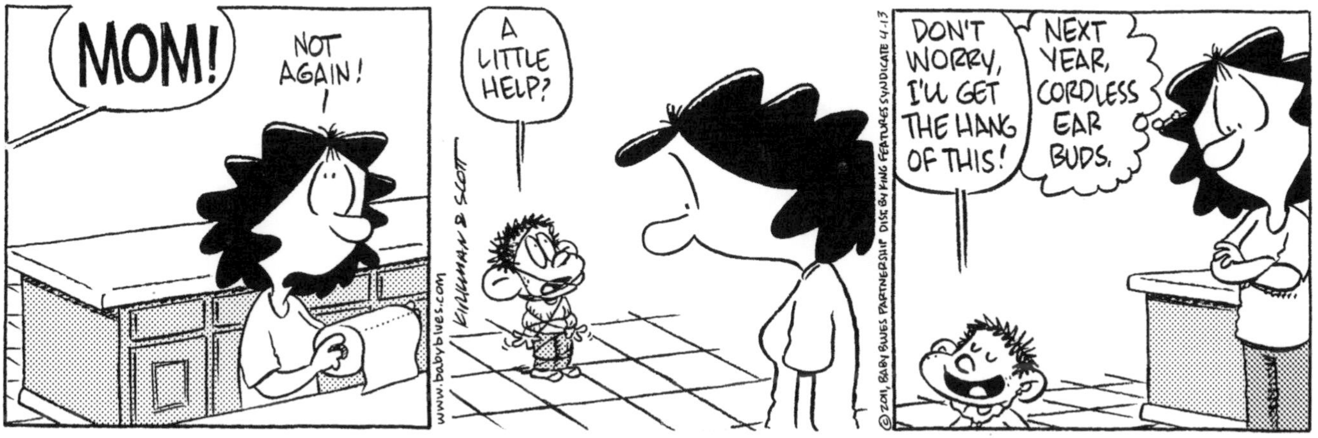
MOM!
NOT AGAIN!
www.babyblues.com
A LITTLE HELP?
KIRKMAN & SCOTT
©2011, BABY BLUES PARTNERSHIP DIST. BY KING FEATURES SYNDICATE 4-13
DON'T WORRY, I'LL GET THE HANG OF THIS!
NEXT YEAR, CORDLESS EAR BUDS.

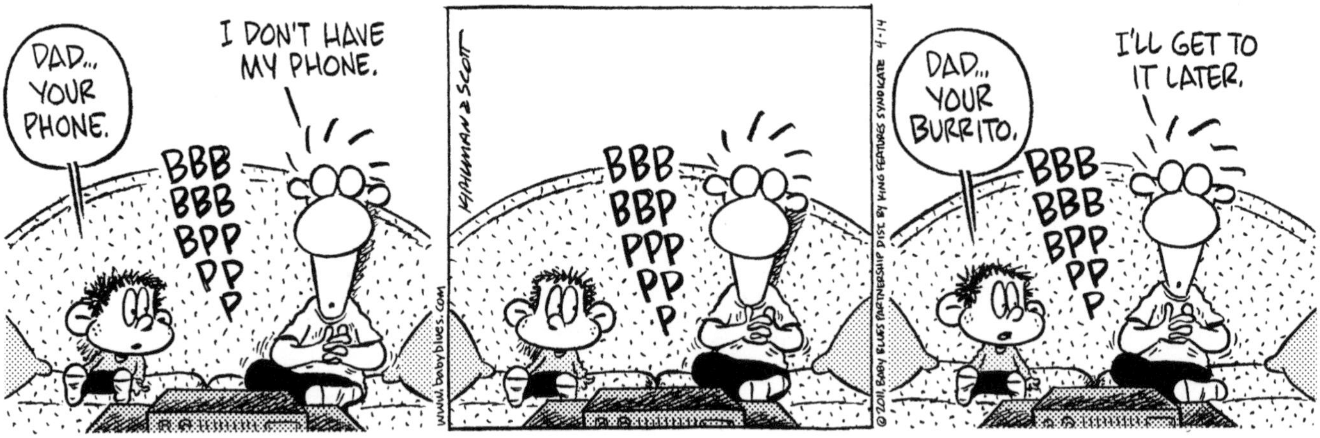
DAD... YOUR PHONE.
BBB BBB BPP PP P
I DON'T HAVE MY PHONE.
www.babyblues.com
KIRKMAN & SCOTT
BBB BBP PPP PP P
© 2011, BABY BLUES PARTNERSHIP DIST. BY KING FEATURES SYNDICATE 4-14
DAD... YOUR BURRITO.
BBB BBB BPP PP P
I'LL GET TO IT LATER.

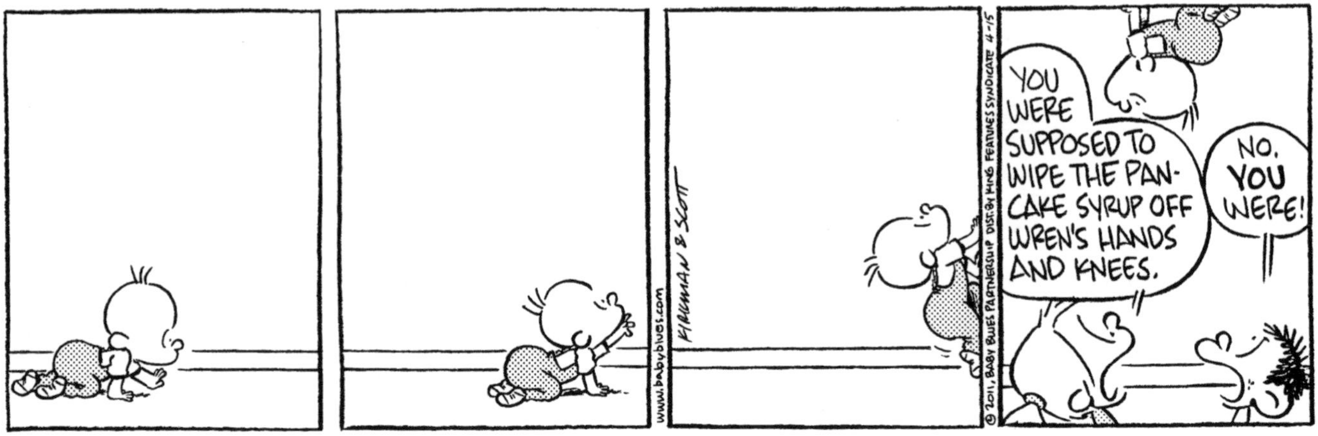
www.babyblues.com
KIRKMAN & SCOTT
© 2011, BABY BLUES PARTNERSHIP DIST. BY KING FEATURES SYNDICATE 4-15
YOU WERE SUPPOSED TO WIPE THE PAN-CAKE SYRUP OFF WREN'S HANDS AND KNEES.
NO. **YOU** WERE!

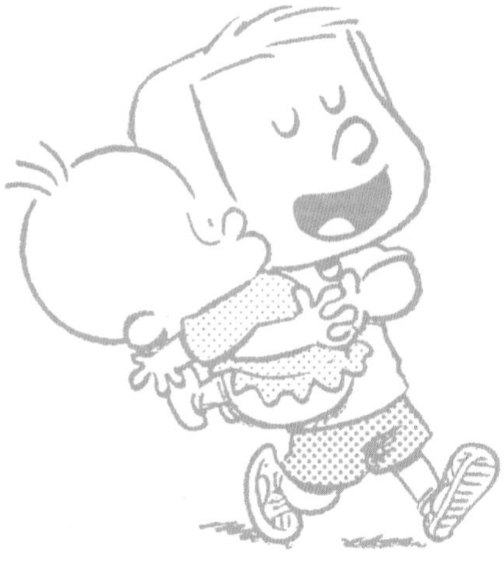

BABY BLUES®
BY RICK KIRKMAN / JERRY SCOTT
COOKIES

BROWNIE TIME!
YAY!
ME FIRST!
HEY! I WAS GONNA PICK THAT ONE!
THERE'S PLENTY FOR EVERYBODY!
www.babyblues.com
MMMMM— WAIT.
YEAH...
WHAT'S IN THESE BROWNIES?
NOTHING! EAT UP! MMMM!
GAH! IT'S GREEN STUFF!
I THINK I'M GONNA' BARF!
SIGH! MAYBE I SHOULD JUST GIVE UP.
YEAH, THEY DON'T FOOL EASILY.
HOW ARE THE BROCCOLI BROWNIES, ANYWAY?
ABOUT AS GOOD AS YOUR CABBAGE COOKIES.
KIRKMAN & SCOTT 4-17

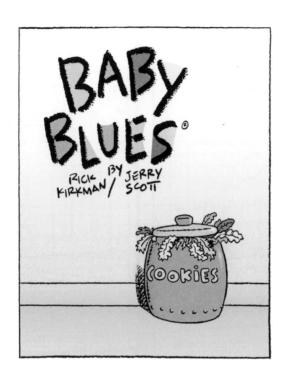

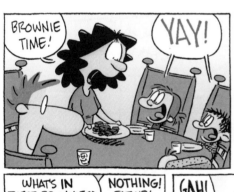

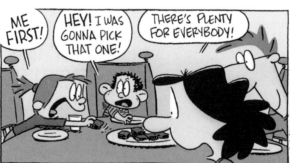

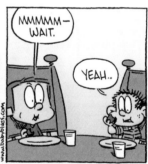

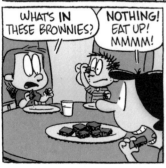

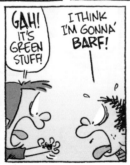

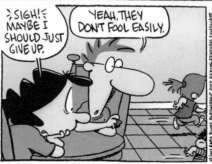

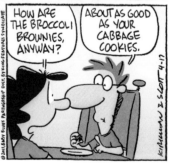

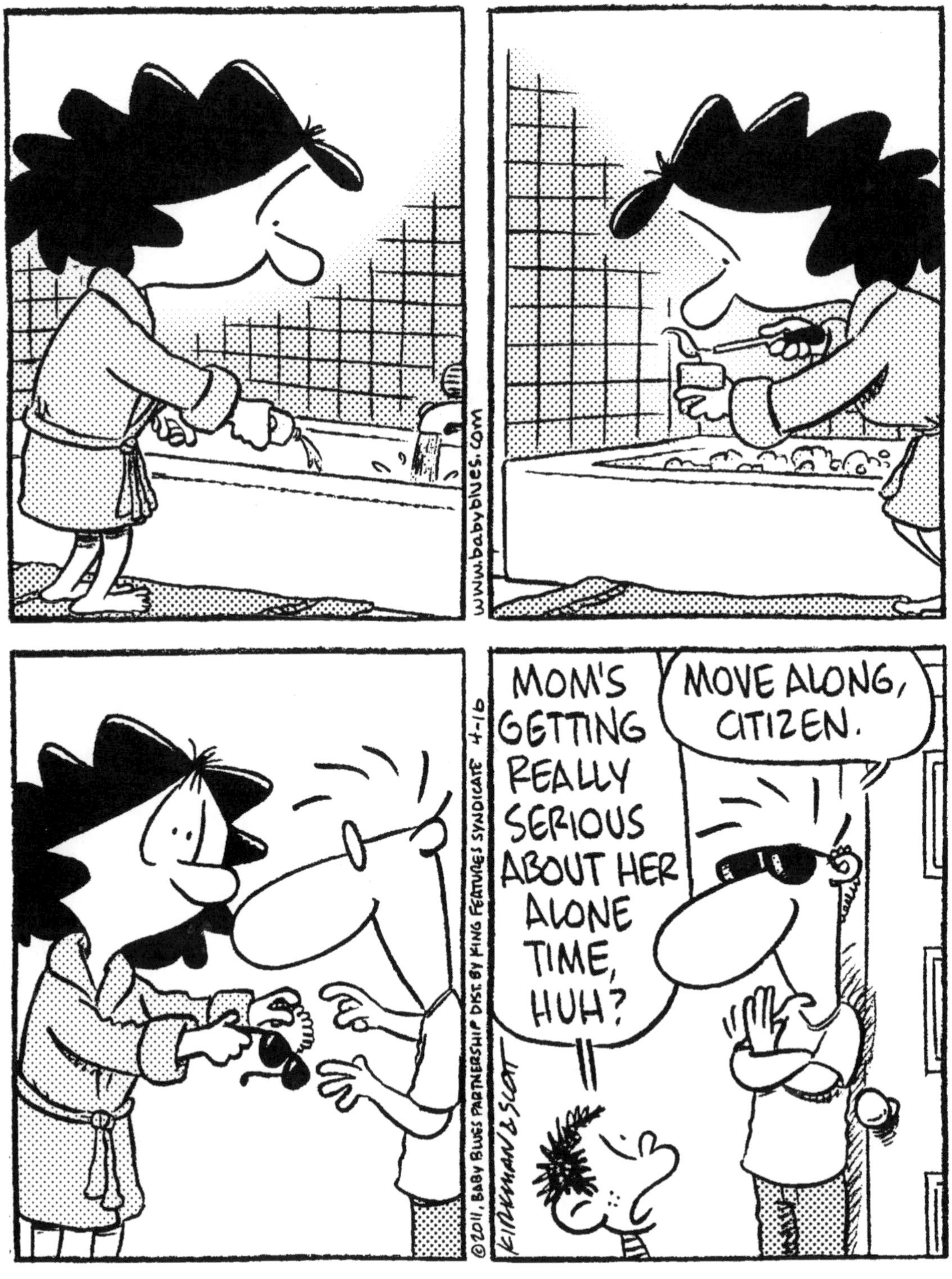
www.babyblues.com
©2011, BABY BLUES PARTNERSHIP DIST. BY KING FEATURES SYNDICATE 4-16
KIRKMAN & SCOTT
MOM'S GETTING REALLY SERIOUS ABOUT HER ALONE TIME, HUH?
MOVE ALONG, CITIZEN.

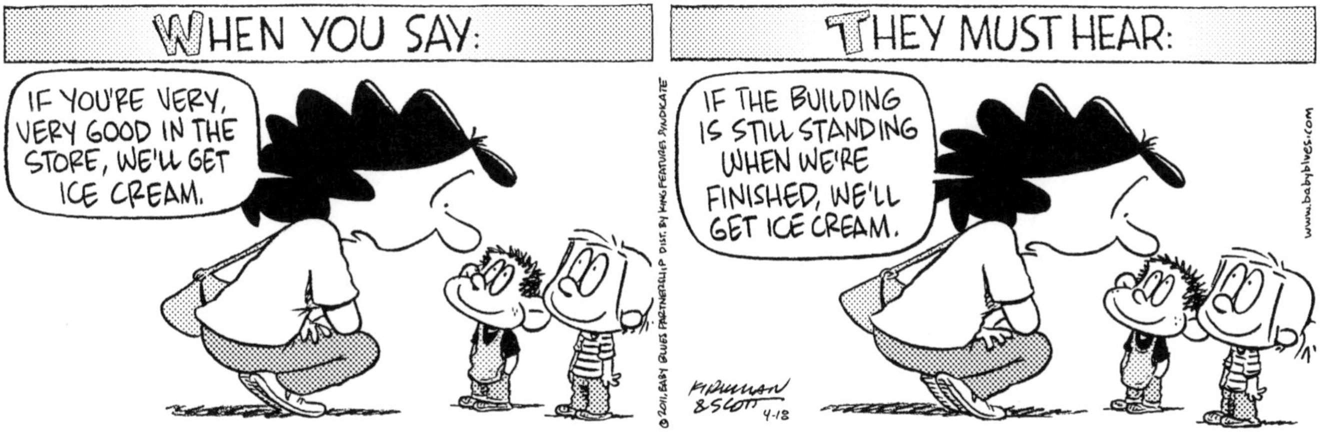
WHEN YOU SAY:
IF YOU'RE VERY, VERY GOOD IN THE STORE, WE'LL GET ICE CREAM.
THEY MUST HEAR:
IF THE BUILDING IS STILL STANDING WHEN WE'RE FINISHED, WE'LL GET ICE CREAM.
© 2011, BABY BLUES PARTNERSHIP DIST. BY KING FEATURES SYNDICATE
KIRKMAN & SCOTT 4-18
www.babyblues.com

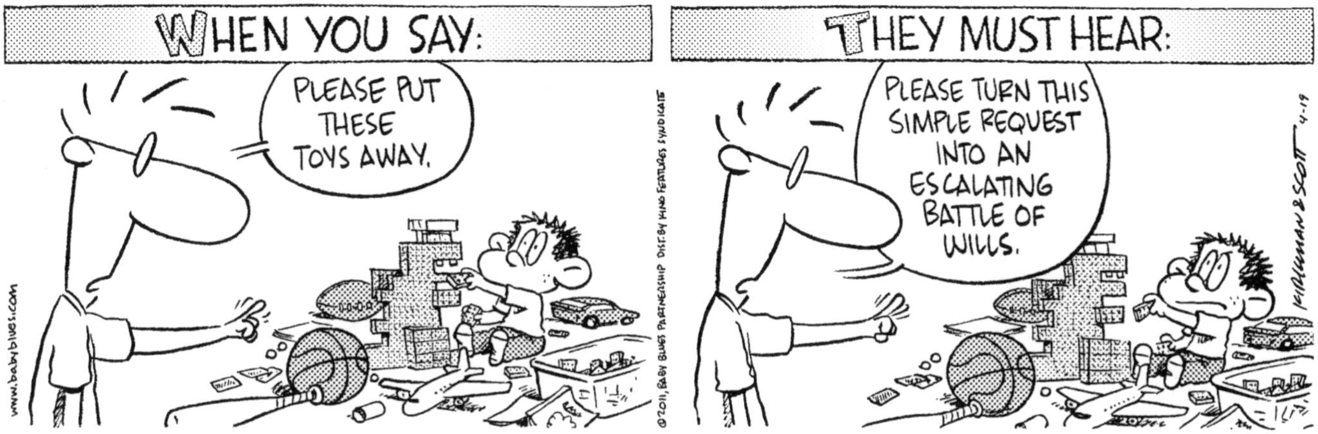
WHEN YOU SAY:
PLEASE PUT THESE TOYS AWAY.
THEY MUST HEAR:
PLEASE TURN THIS SIMPLE REQUEST INTO AN ESCALATING BATTLE OF WILLS.
www.babyblues.com
© 2011, BABY BLUES PARTNERSHIP DIST. BY KING FEATURES SYNDICATE
KIRKMAN & SCOTT 4-19

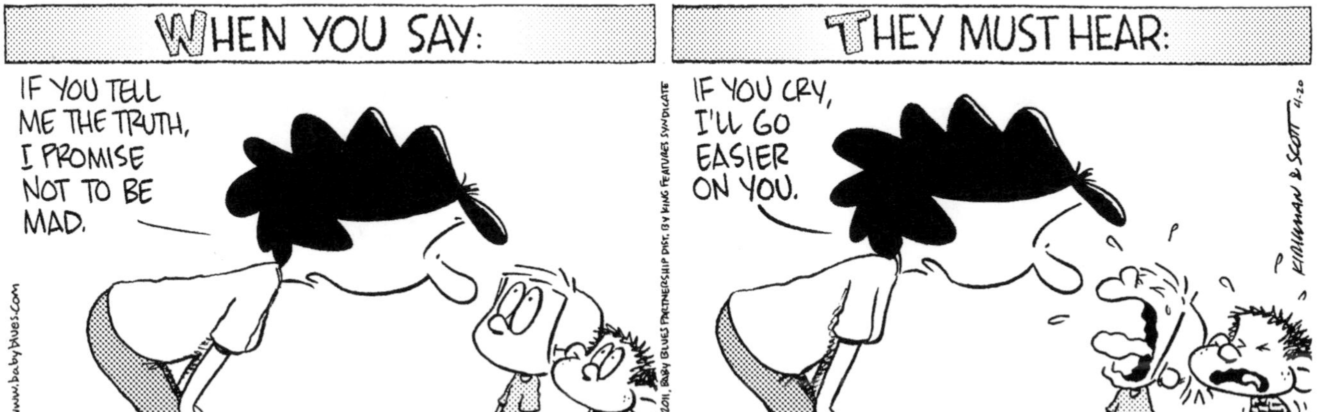
WHEN YOU SAY:
IF YOU TELL ME THE TRUTH, I PROMISE NOT TO BE MAD.
THEY MUST HEAR:
IF YOU CRY, I'LL GO EASIER ON YOU.
www.babyblues.com
© 2011, BABY BLUES PARTNERSHIP DIST. BY KING FEATURES SYNDICATE
KIRKMAN & SCOTT 4-20

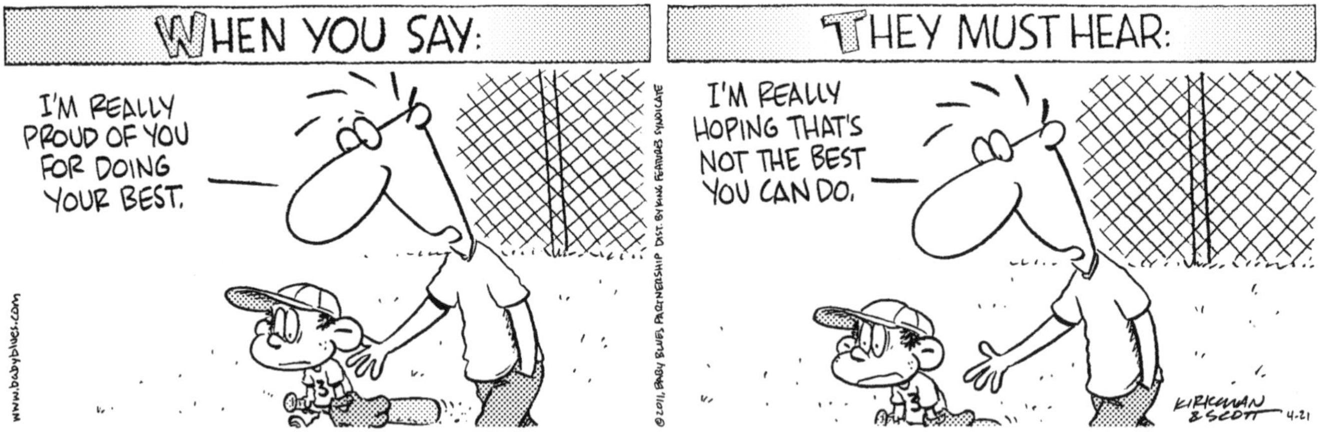
WHEN YOU SAY:
I'M REALLY PROUD OF YOU FOR DOING YOUR BEST.
THEY MUST HEAR:
I'M REALLY HOPING THAT'S NOT THE BEST YOU CAN DO.

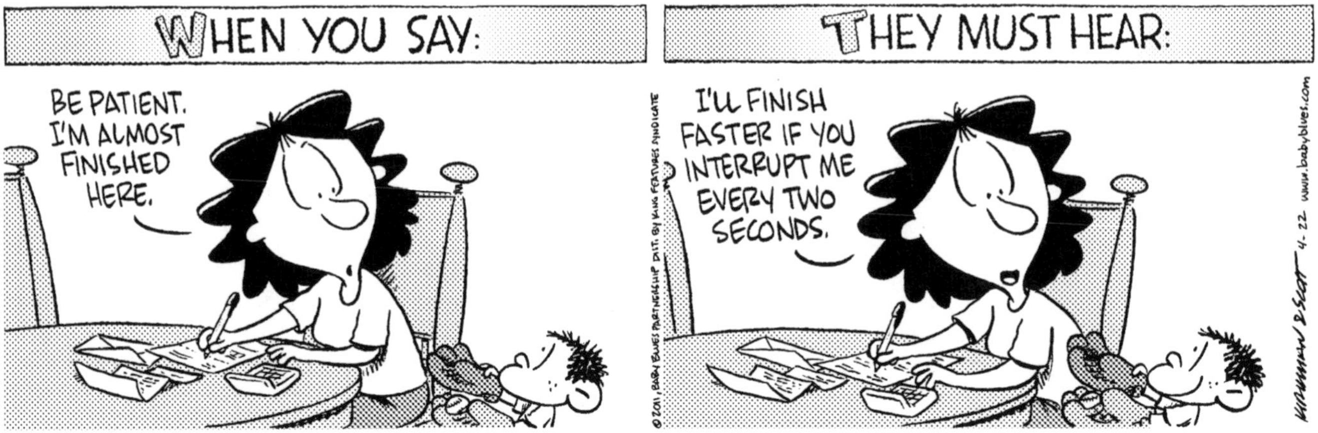
WHEN YOU SAY:
BE PATIENT. I'M ALMOST FINISHED HERE.
THEY MUST HEAR:
I'LL FINISH FASTER IF YOU INTERRUPT ME EVERY TWO SECONDS.

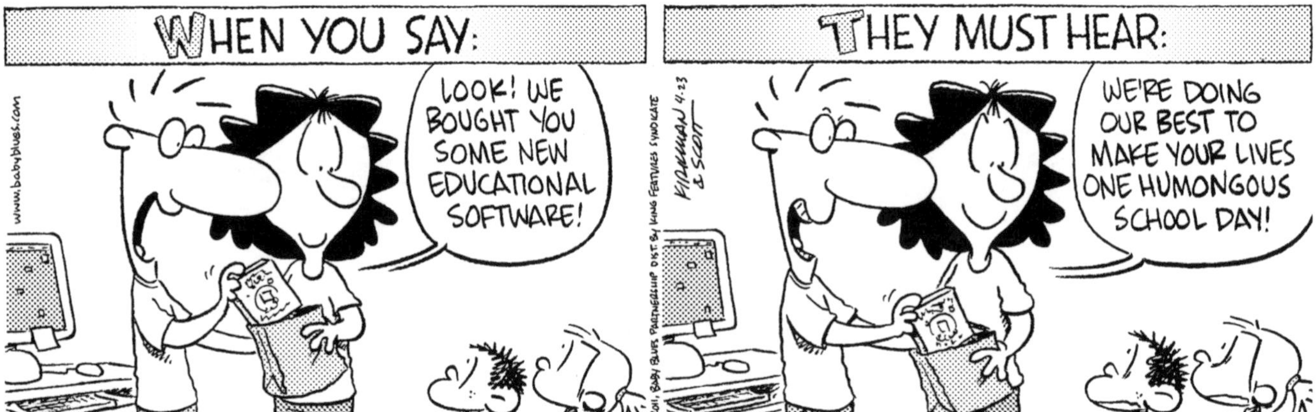
WHEN YOU SAY:
LOOK! WE BOUGHT YOU SOME NEW EDUCATIONAL SOFTWARE!
THEY MUST HEAR:
WE'RE DOING OUR BEST TO MAKE YOUR LIVES ONE HUMONGOUS SCHOOL DAY!

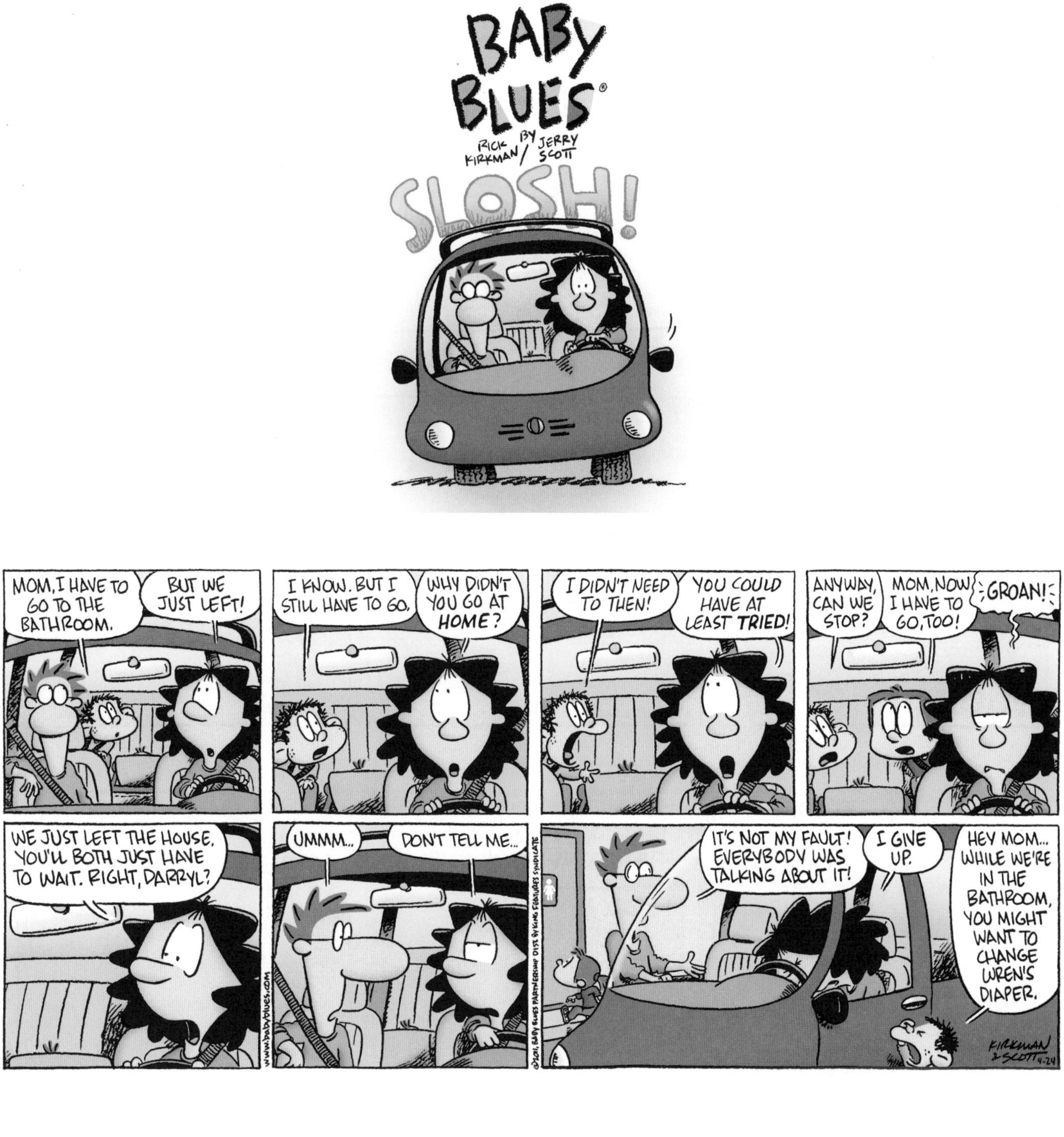
BABY BLUES®
BY RICK KIRKMAN / JERRY SCOTT
SLOSH!
MOM, I HAVE TO GO TO THE BATHROOM.
BUT WE JUST LEFT!
I KNOW. BUT I STILL HAVE TO GO.
WHY DIDN'T YOU GO AT **HOME**?
I DIDN'T NEED TO THEN!
YOU COULD HAVE AT LEAST **TRIED**!
ANYWAY, CAN WE STOP?
MOM, NOW I HAVE TO GO, TOO!
GROAN!
WE JUST LEFT THE HOUSE. YOU'LL BOTH JUST HAVE TO WAIT. RIGHT, DARRYL?
www.babyblues.com
UMMM...
DON'T TELL ME...
©2011, BABY BLUES PARTNERSHIP DIST. BY KING FEATURES SYNDICATE
IT'S NOT MY FAULT! EVERYBODY WAS TALKING ABOUT IT!
I GIVE UP.
HEY MOM... WHILE WE'RE IN THE BATHROOM, YOU MIGHT WANT TO CHANGE WREN'S DIAPER.
KIRKMAN & SCOTT 4-24

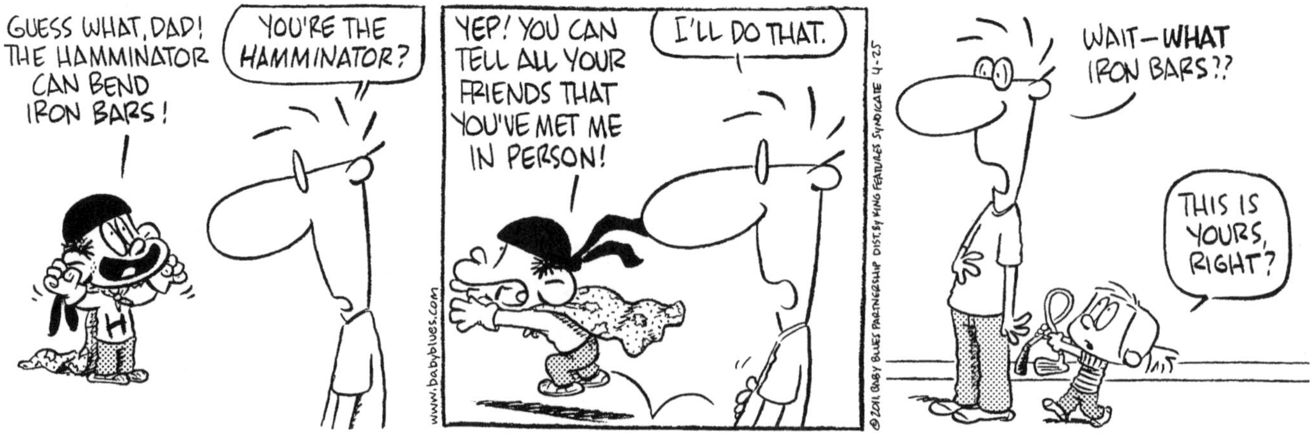
GUESS WHAT, DAD! THE HAMMINATOR CAN BEND IRON BARS!
YOU'RE THE HAMMINATOR?
www.babyblues.com
YEP! YOU CAN TELL ALL YOUR FRIENDS THAT YOU'VE MET ME IN PERSON!
I'LL DO THAT.
©2011 BABY BLUES PARTNERSHIP DIST. BY KING FEATURES SYNDICATE 4-25
WAIT—WHAT IRON BARS??
THIS IS YOURS, RIGHT?

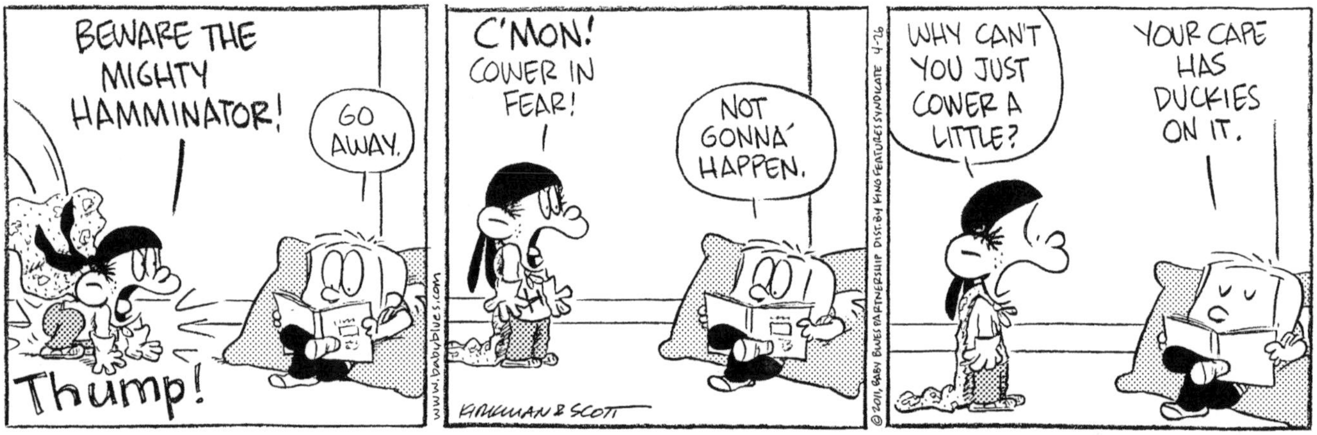
BEWARE THE MIGHTY HAMMINATOR!
GO AWAY.
Thump!
www.babyblues.com
C'MON! COWER IN FEAR!
NOT GONNA' HAPPEN.
KIRKMAN & SCOTT
©2011, BABY BLUES PARTNERSHIP DIST. BY KING FEATURES SYNDICATE 4-26
WHY CAN'T YOU JUST COWER A LITTLE?
YOUR CAPE HAS DUCKIES ON IT.

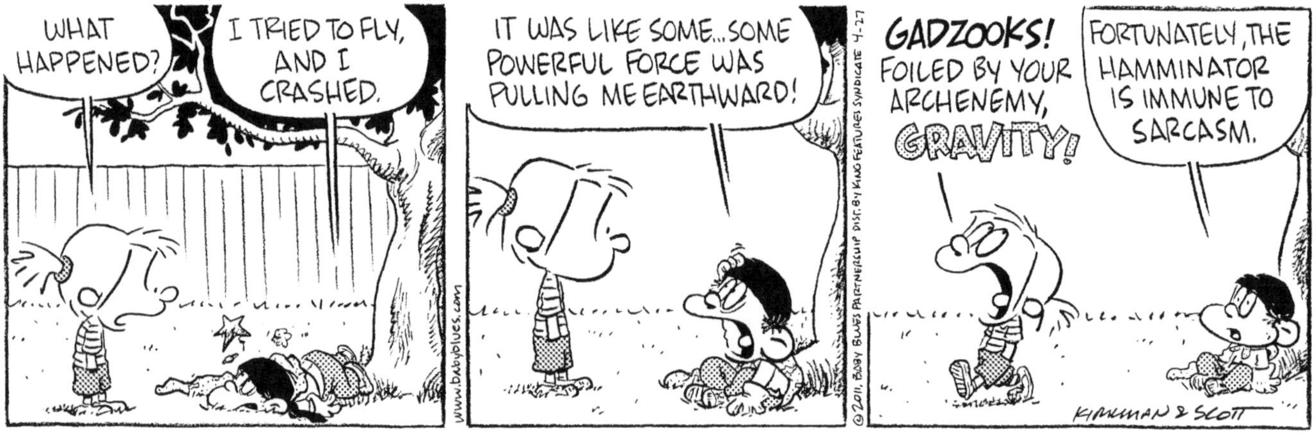
WHAT HAPPENED?
I TRIED TO FLY, AND I CRASHED.
www.babyblues.com
IT WAS LIKE SOME...SOME POWERFUL FORCE WAS PULLING ME EARTHWARD!
©2011, BABY BLUES PARTNERSHIP DIST. BY KING FEATURES SYNDICATE 4-27
GADZOOKS! FOILED BY YOUR ARCHENEMY, GRAVITY!
FORTUNATELY, THE HAMMINATOR IS IMMUNE TO SARCASM.
KIRKMAN & SCOTT

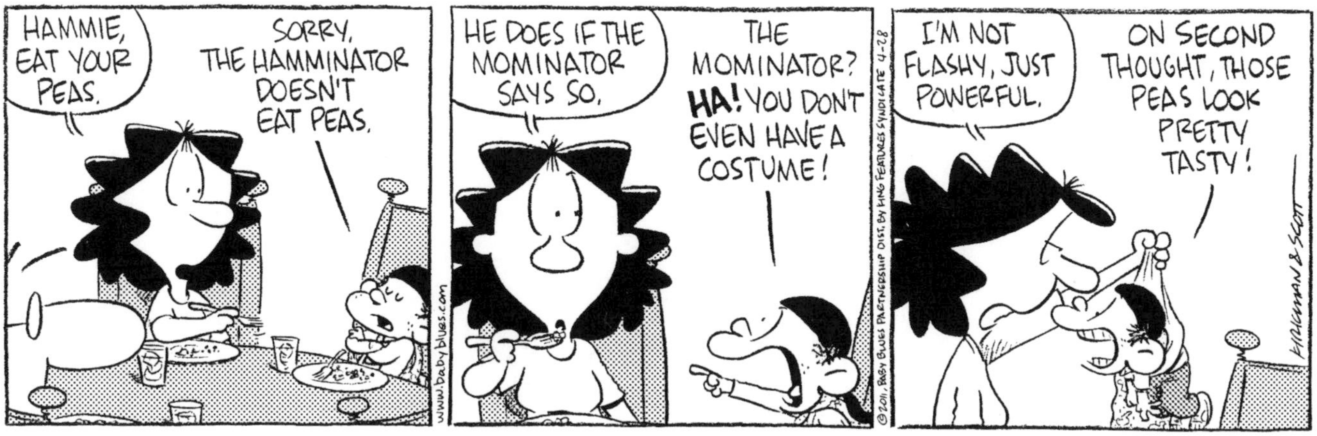
HAMMIE, EAT YOUR PEAS.
SORRY. THE HAMMINATOR DOESN'T EAT PEAS.
HE DOES IF THE MOMINATOR SAYS SO.
THE MOMINATOR? HA! YOU DON'T EVEN HAVE A COSTUME!
I'M NOT FLASHY, JUST POWERFUL.
ON SECOND THOUGHT, THOSE PEAS LOOK PRETTY TASTY!

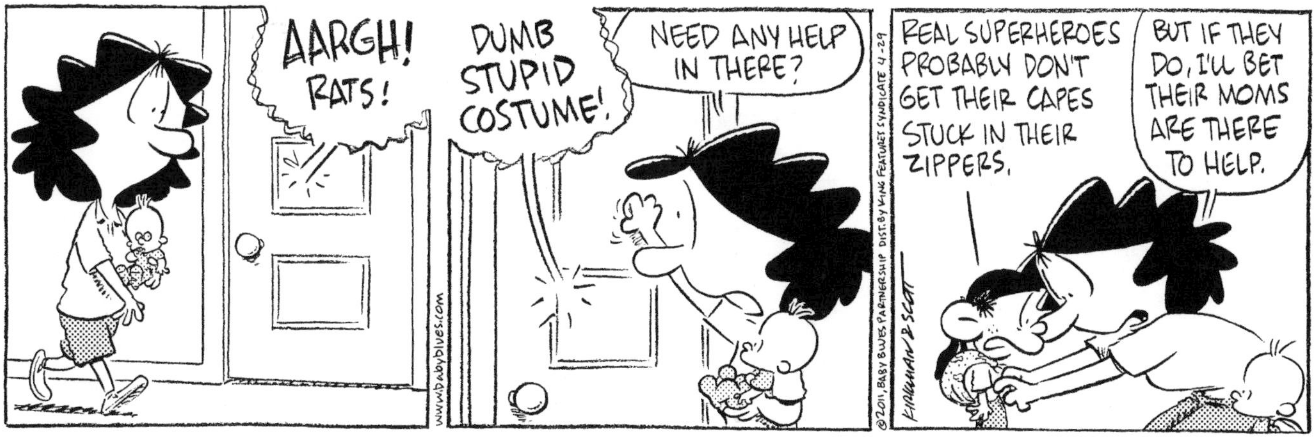
AARGH! RATS!
DUMB STUPID COSTUME!
NEED ANY HELP IN THERE?
REAL SUPERHEROES PROBABLY DON'T GET THEIR CAPES STUCK IN THEIR ZIPPERS.
BUT IF THEY DO, I'LL BET THEIR MOMS ARE THERE TO HELP.

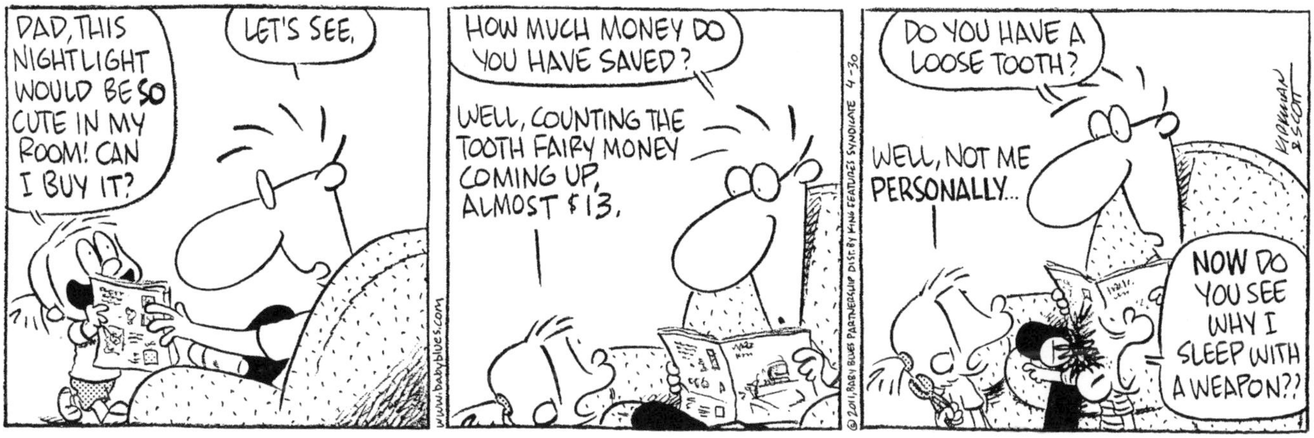
DAD, THIS NIGHTLIGHT WOULD BE SO CUTE IN MY ROOM! CAN I BUY IT?
LET'S SEE.
HOW MUCH MONEY DO YOU HAVE SAVED?
WELL, COUNTING THE TOOTH FAIRY MONEY COMING UP, ALMOST $13.
DO YOU HAVE A LOOSE TOOTH?
WELL, NOT ME PERSONALLY...
NOW DO YOU SEE WHY I SLEEP WITH A WEAPON??

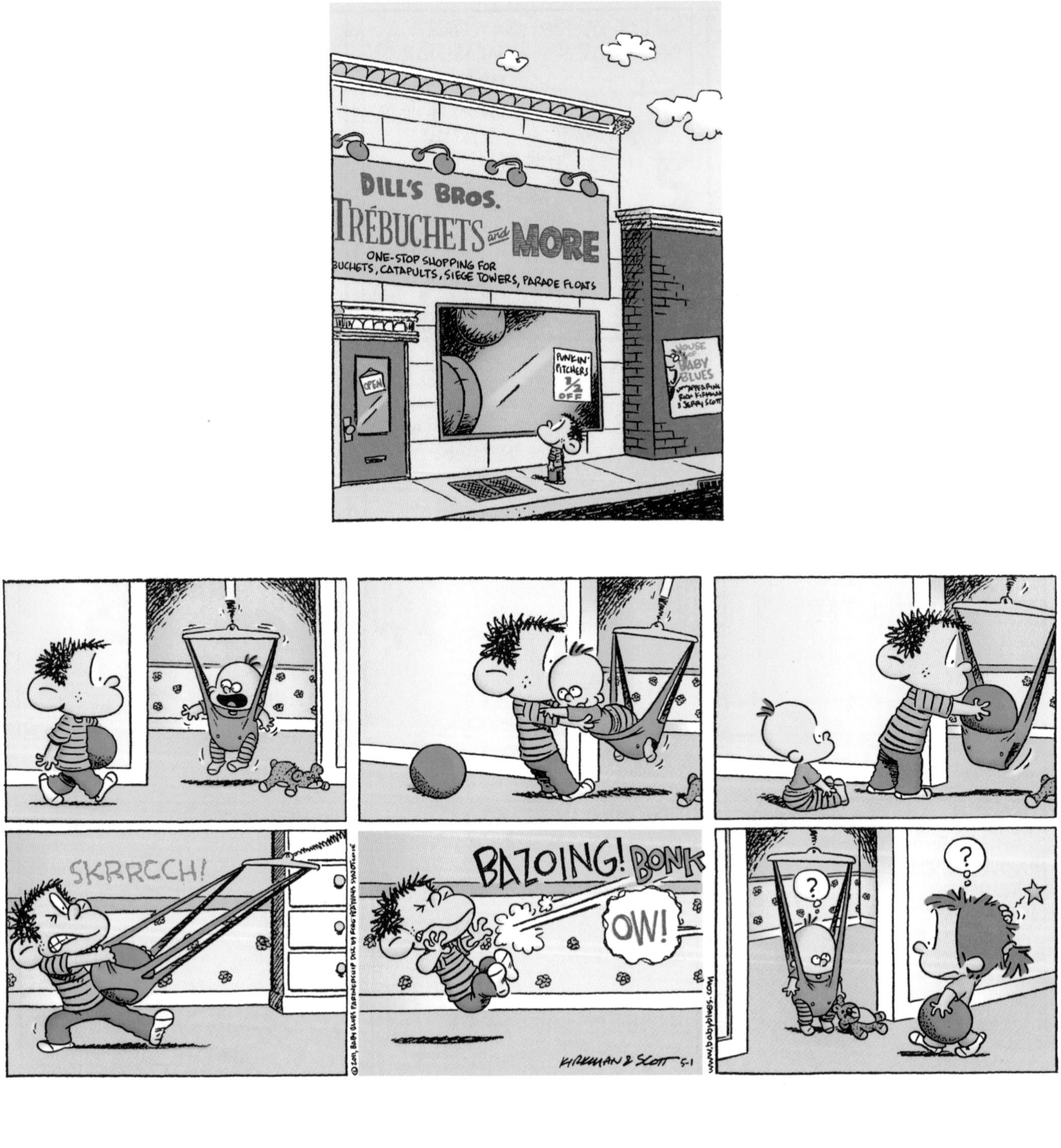
DILL'S BROS.
TRÉBUCHETS and MORE
ONE-STOP SHOPPING FOR
BUCHETS, CATAPULTS, SIEGE TOWERS, PARADE FLOATS
OPEN
PUNKIN' PITCHERS 1/2 OFF
SKRRCCH!
BAZOING!
BONK
OW!
?
?
KIRKMAN & SCOTT 5-1
www.babyblues.com

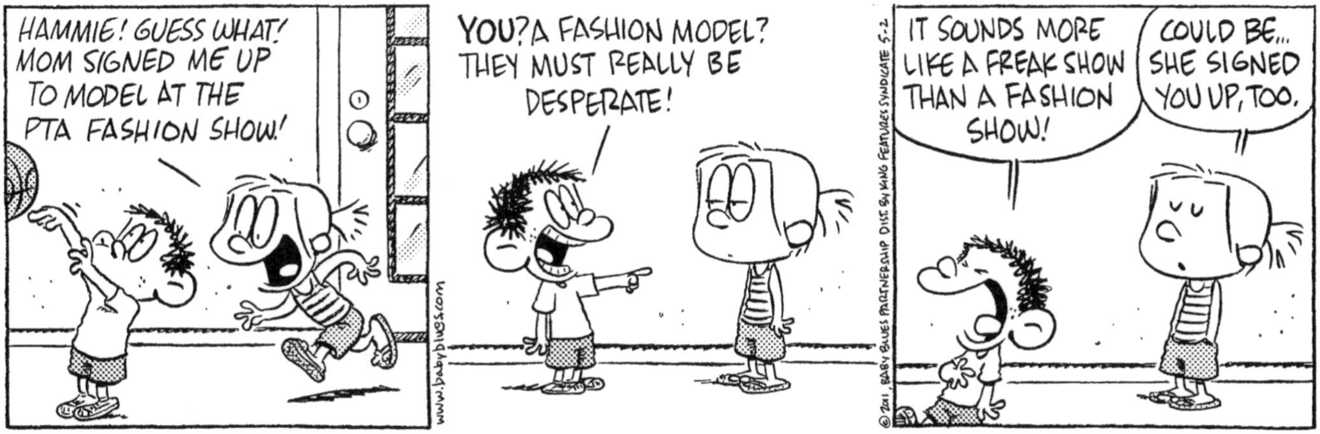
HAMMIE! GUESS WHAT! MOM SIGNED ME UP TO MODEL AT THE PTA FASHION SHOW!
YOU? A FASHION MODEL? THEY MUST REALLY BE DESPERATE!
IT SOUNDS MORE LIKE A FREAK SHOW THAN A FASHION SHOW!
COULD BE... SHE SIGNED YOU UP, TOO.
www.babyblues.com
© 2011, BABY BLUES PARTNERSHIP DIST. BY KING FEATURES SYNDICATE 5-2

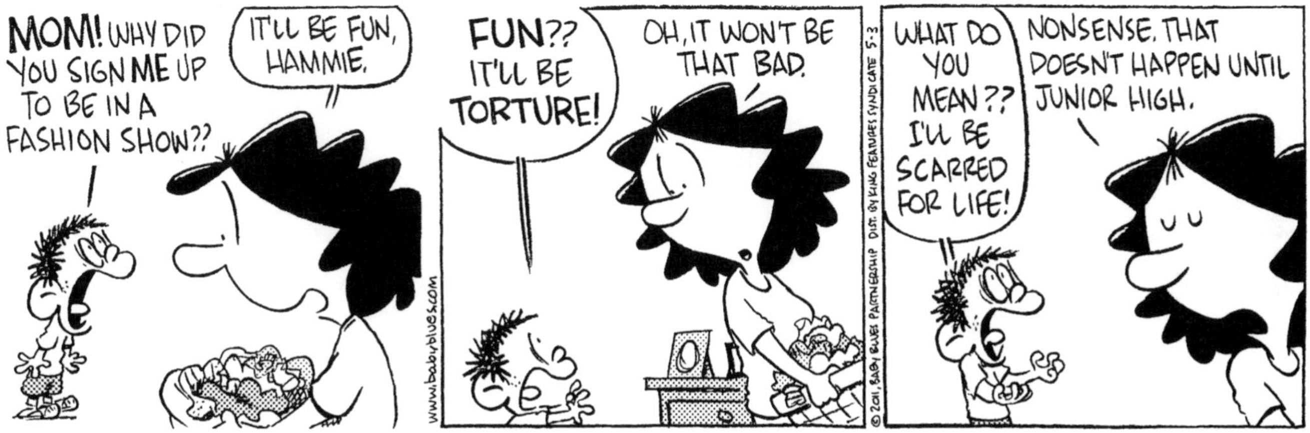
MOM! WHY DID YOU SIGN ME UP TO BE IN A FASHION SHOW??
IT'LL BE FUN, HAMMIE.
FUN?? IT'LL BE TORTURE!
OH, IT WON'T BE THAT BAD.
WHAT DO YOU MEAN?? I'LL BE SCARRED FOR LIFE!
NONSENSE. THAT DOESN'T HAPPEN UNTIL JUNIOR HIGH.
www.babyblues.com
© 2011, BABY BLUES PARTNERSHIP DIST. BY KING FEATURES SYNDICATE 5-3

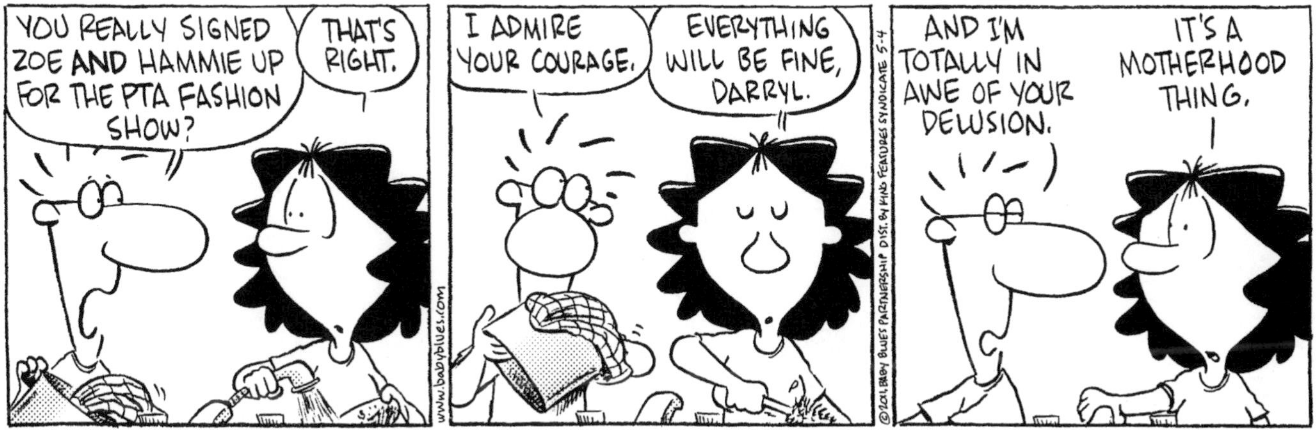
YOU REALLY SIGNED ZOE AND HAMMIE UP FOR THE PTA FASHION SHOW?
THAT'S RIGHT.
I ADMIRE YOUR COURAGE.
EVERYTHING WILL BE FINE, DARRYL.
AND I'M TOTALLY IN AWE OF YOUR DELUSION.
IT'S A MOTHERHOOD THING.
www.babyblues.com
© 2011, BABY BLUES PARTNERSHIP DIST. BY KING FEATURES SYNDICATE 5-4

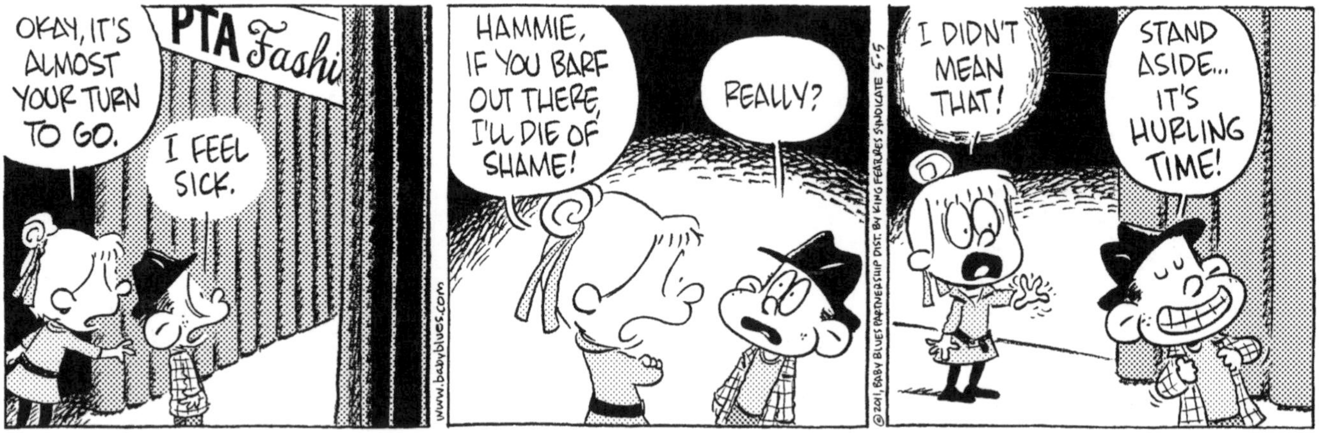
OKAY, IT'S ALMOST YOUR TURN TO GO.
I FEEL SICK.
PTA Fashi
HAMMIE, IF YOU BARF OUT THERE, I'LL DIE OF SHAME!
REALLY?
I DIDN'T MEAN THAT!
STAND ASIDE... IT'S HURLING TIME!
www.babyblues.com
© 2011, BABY BLUES PARTNERSHIP DIST. BY KING FEATURES SYNDICATE 5-5

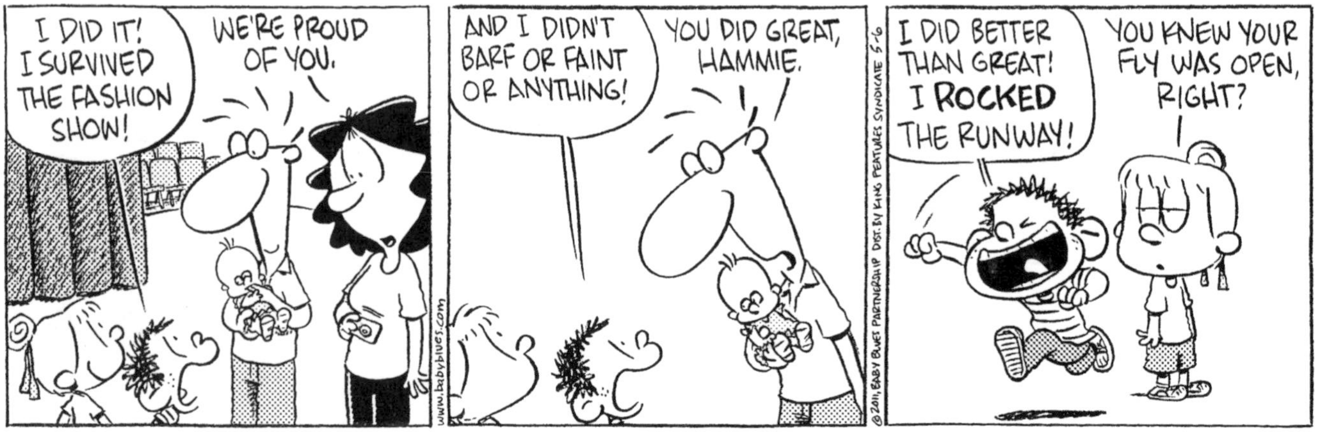
I DID IT! I SURVIVED THE FASHION SHOW!
WE'RE PROUD OF YOU.
AND I DIDN'T BARF OR FAINT OR ANYTHING!
YOU DID GREAT, HAMMIE.
I DID BETTER THAN GREAT! I **ROCKED** THE RUNWAY!
YOU KNEW YOUR FLY WAS OPEN, RIGHT?
www.babyblues.com
© 2011, BABY BLUES PARTNERSHIP DIST. BY KING FEATURES SYNDICATE 5-6

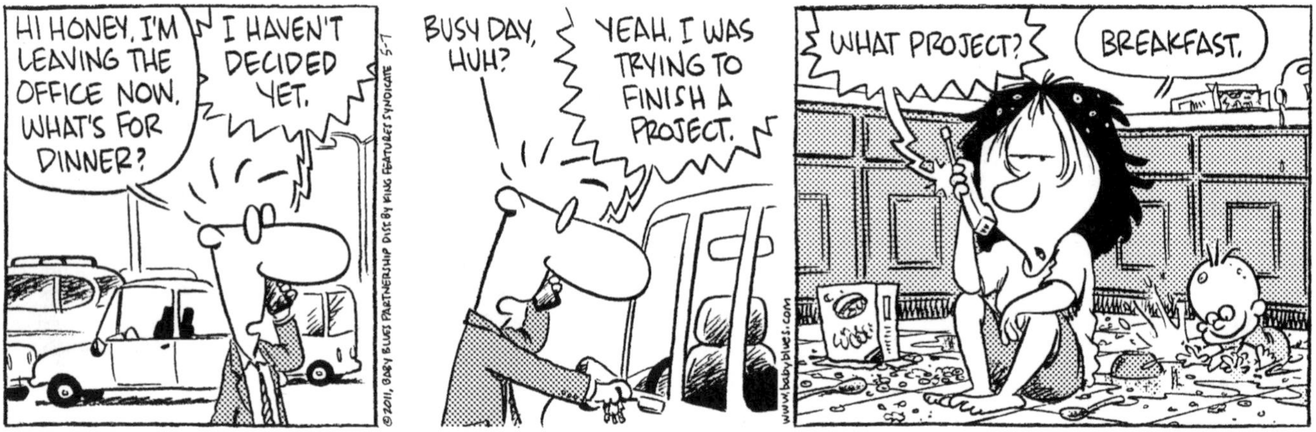
HI HONEY, I'M LEAVING THE OFFICE NOW. WHAT'S FOR DINNER?
I HAVEN'T DECIDED YET.
BUSY DAY, HUH?
YEAH. I WAS TRYING TO FINISH A PROJECT.
WHAT PROJECT?
BREAKFAST.
© 2011, BABY BLUES PARTNERSHIP DIST. BY KING FEATURES SYNDICATE 5-7
www.babyblues.com

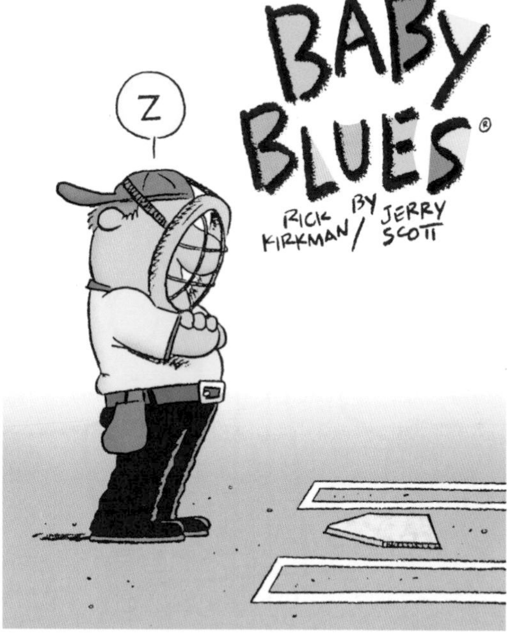
Z
BABY BLUES®
RICK KIRKMAN / BY JERRY SCOTT

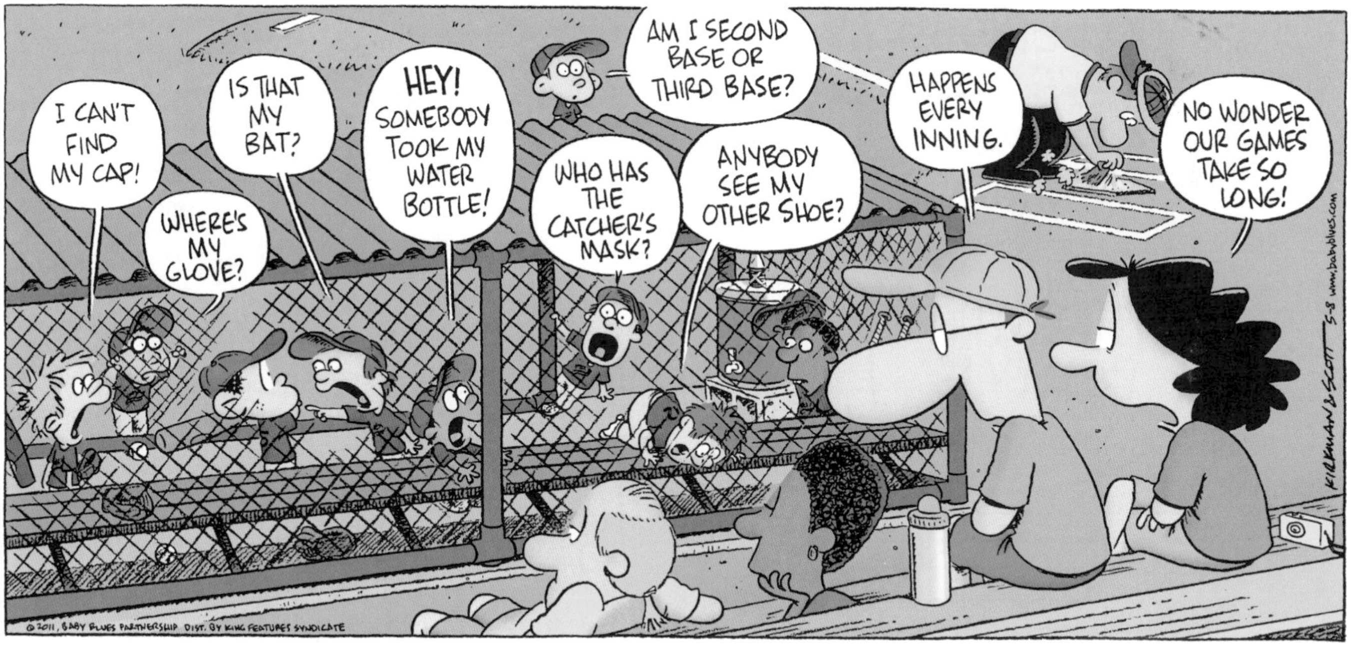
I CAN'T FIND MY CAP!
WHERE'S MY GLOVE?
IS THAT MY BAT?
HEY! SOMEBODY TOOK MY WATER BOTTLE!
AM I SECOND BASE OR THIRD BASE?
WHO HAS THE CATCHER'S MASK?
ANYBODY SEE MY OTHER SHOE?
HAPPENS EVERY INNING.
NO WONDER OUR GAMES TAKE SO LONG!
KIRKMAN & SCOTT 5-8 www.babyblues.com
© 2011, BABY BLUES PARTNERSHIP DIST. BY KING FEATURES SYNDICATE

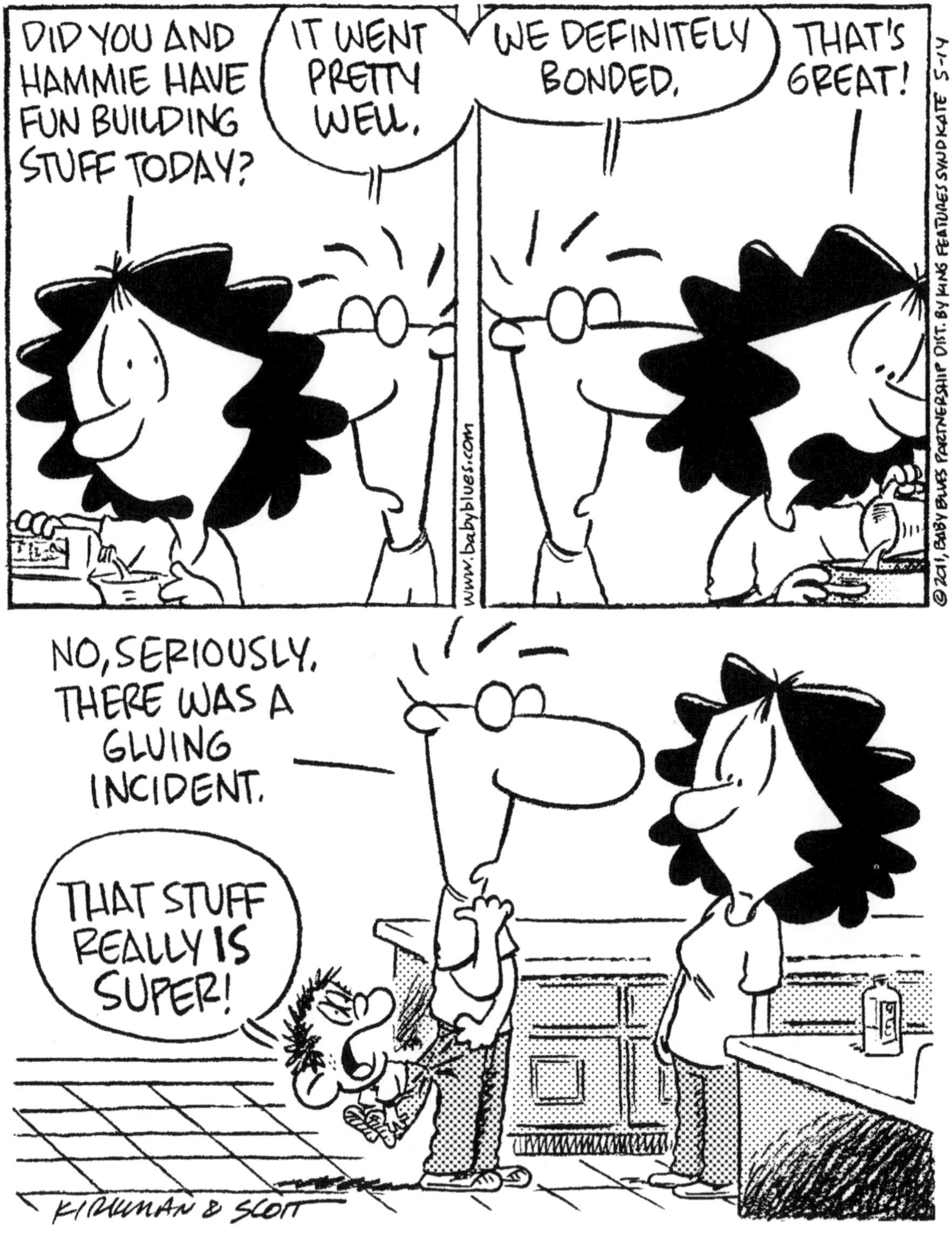
DID YOU AND HAMMIE HAVE FUN BUILDING STUFF TODAY?
IT WENT PRETTY WELL.
WE DEFINITELY BONDED.
THAT'S GREAT!
www.babyblues.com
© 2011, BABY BLUES PARTNERSHIP DIST. BY KING FEATURES SYNDICATE 5-14
NO, SERIOUSLY. THERE WAS A GLUING INCIDENT.
THAT STUFF REALLY IS SUPER!
KIRKMAN & SCOTT

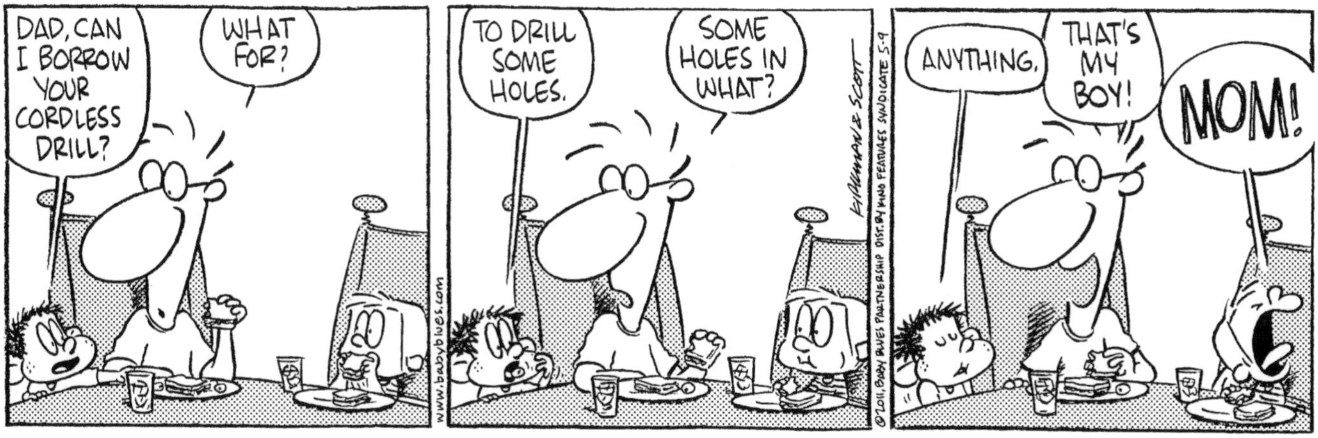
DAD, CAN I BORROW YOUR CORDLESS DRILL?
WHAT FOR?
www.babyblues.com
TO DRILL SOME HOLES.
SOME HOLES IN WHAT?
KIRKMAN & SCOTT
©2011, BABY BLUES PARTNERSHIP DIST. BY KING FEATURES SYNDICATE 5-9
ANYTHING.
THAT'S MY BOY!
MOM!

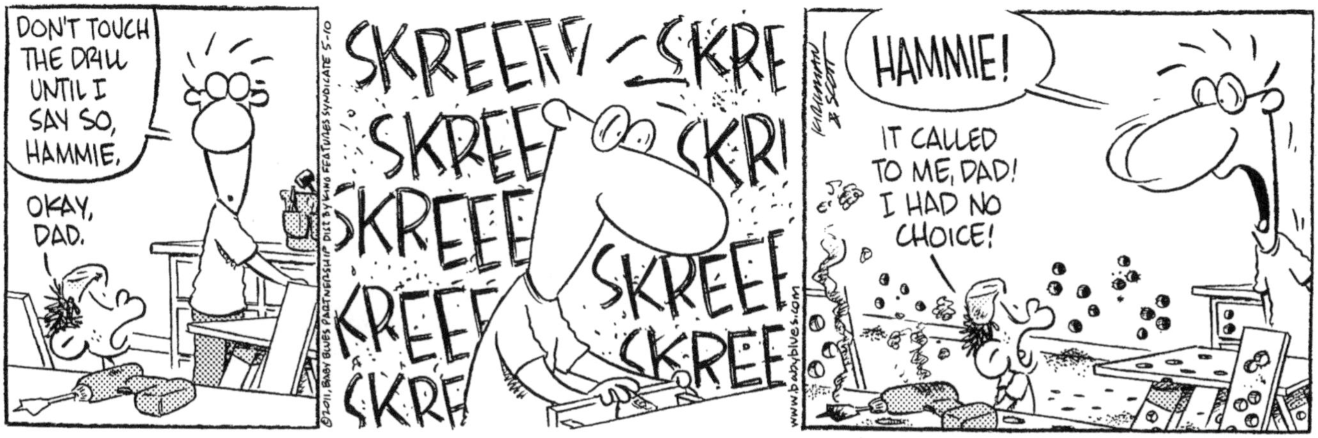
DON'T TOUCH THE DRILL UNTIL I SAY SO, HAMMIE.
OKAY, DAD.
©2011, BABY BLUES PARTNERSHIP DIST. BY KING FEATURES SYNDICATE 5-10
SKREEE
SKREE
SKREEE
www.babyblues.com
KIRKMAN & SCOTT
HAMMIE!
IT CALLED TO ME, DAD! I HAD NO CHOICE!

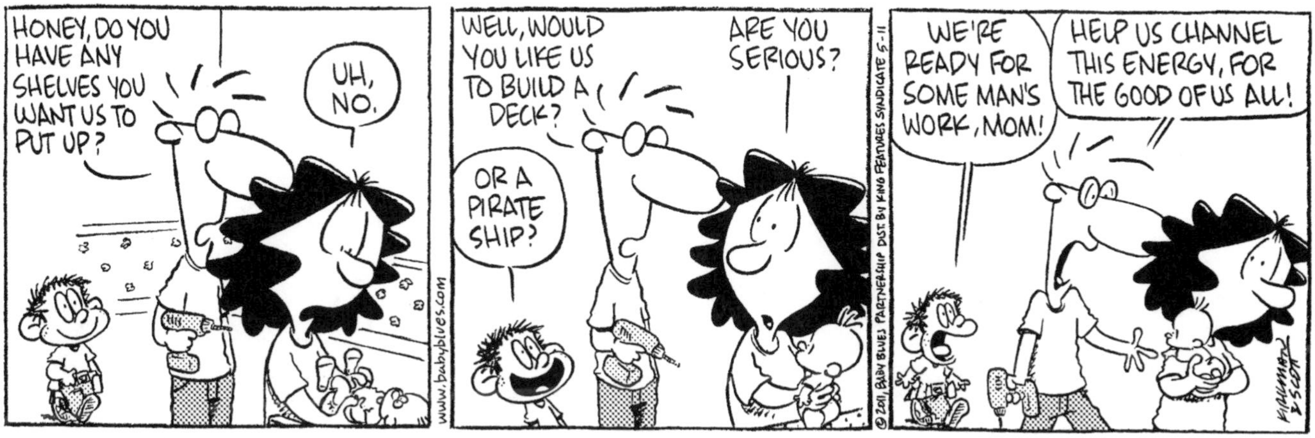
HONEY, DO YOU HAVE ANY SHELVES YOU WANT US TO PUT UP?
UH, NO.
www.babyblues.com
WELL, WOULD YOU LIKE US TO BUILD A DECK?
ARE YOU SERIOUS?
OR A PIRATE SHIP?
©2011, BABY BLUES PARTNERSHIP DIST. BY KING FEATURES SYNDICATE 5-11
WE'RE READY FOR SOME MAN'S WORK, MOM!
HELP US CHANNEL THIS ENERGY, FOR THE GOOD OF US ALL!
KIRKMAN & SCOTT

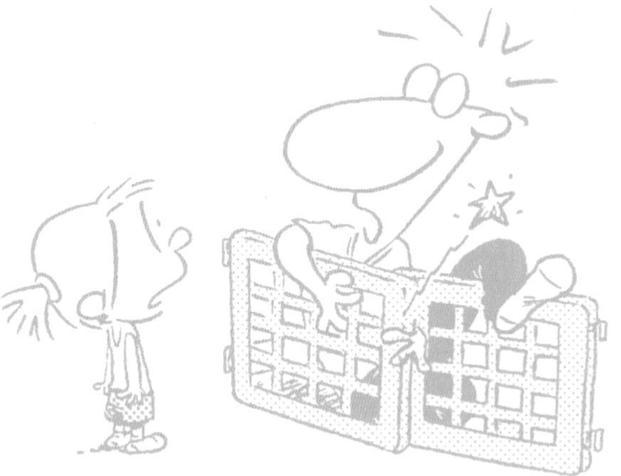

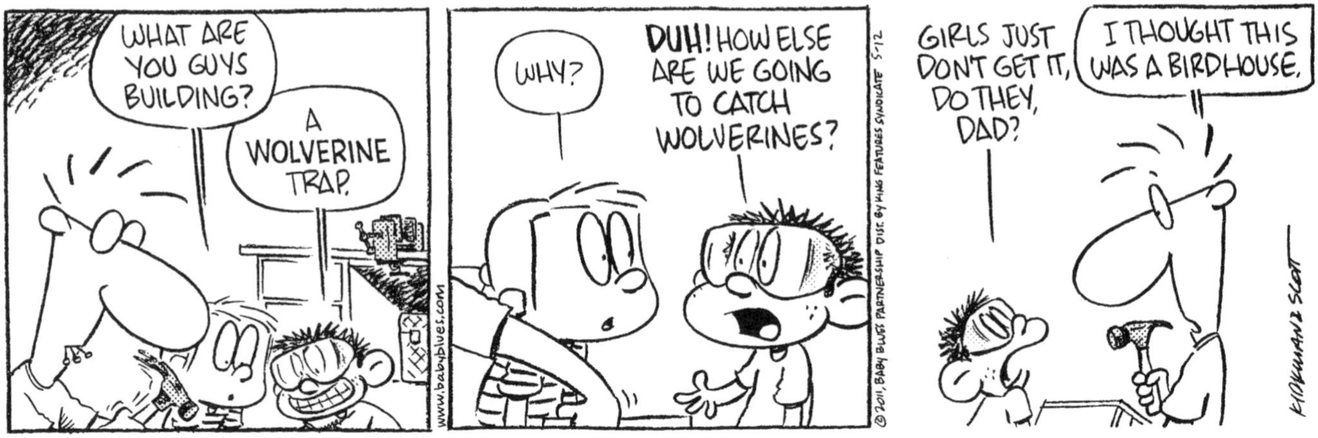

WHAT ARE YOU GUYS BUILDING?
A WOLVERINE TRAP.
www.babyblues.com
WHY?
DUH! HOW ELSE ARE WE GOING TO CATCH WOLVERINES?
© 2011, BABY BLUES PARTNERSHIP DIST. BY KING FEATURES SYNDICATE 5-12
GIRLS JUST DON'T GET IT, DO THEY, DAD?
I THOUGHT THIS WAS A BIRDHOUSE.
KIRKMAN & SCOTT

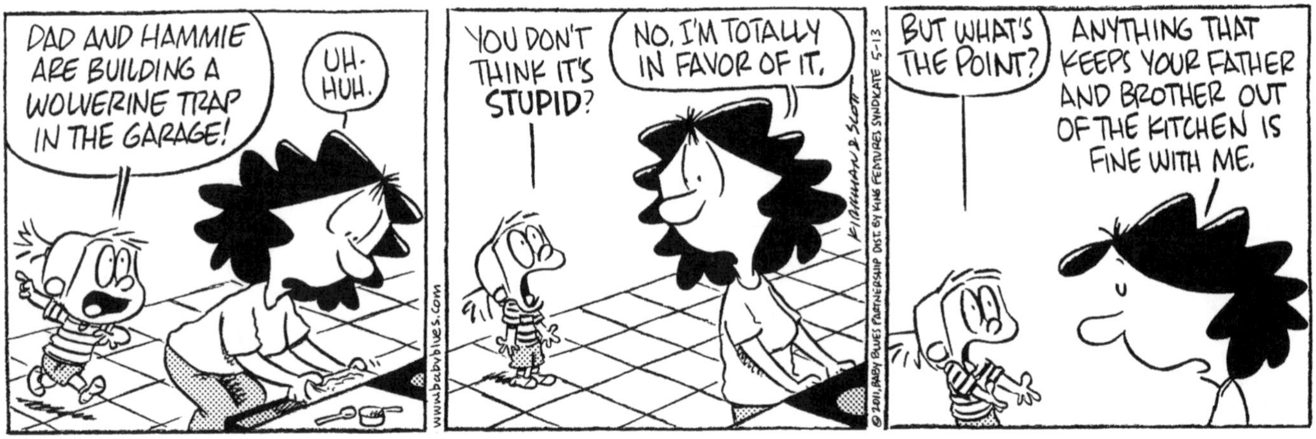

DAD AND HAMMIE ARE BUILDING A WOLVERINE TRAP IN THE GARAGE!
UH-HUH.
www.babyblues.com
YOU DON'T THINK IT'S STUPID?
NO, I'M TOTALLY IN FAVOR OF IT.
KIRKMAN & SCOTT
© 2011, BABY BLUES PARTNERSHIP DIST. BY KING FEATURES SYNDICATE 5-13
BUT WHAT'S THE POINT?
ANYTHING THAT KEEPS YOUR FATHER AND BROTHER OUT OF THE KITCHEN IS FINE WITH ME.

PROD
BABY BLUES®
DIR
RICK KIRKMAN & JERRY SCOTT
SCENE
BEDTIME
TAKE
∞

BEDTIME: Take 1
MISSION ACCOMPLISHED!
HEY DAD, YOU FORGOT TO TURN ON MY NIGHT-LIGHT.
BEDTIME: Take 2
FINALLY!
I NEED A REFILL.
BEDTIME: Take 7
WAAAAAAAA!
I'LL GET HER.
NOT AGAIN!
BEDTIME: Take 12
THERE'S A FLY IN MY ROOM.
DIBS!
GROAN!
BEDTIME: CUT. PRINT. IT'S A WRAP!
Z
Z
Z
Z
Z
©2011, BABY BLUES PARTNERSHIP DIST. BY KING FEATURES SYNDICATE
KIRKMAN & SCOTT 5-15

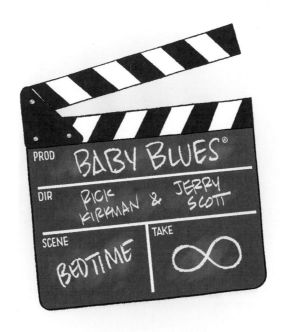

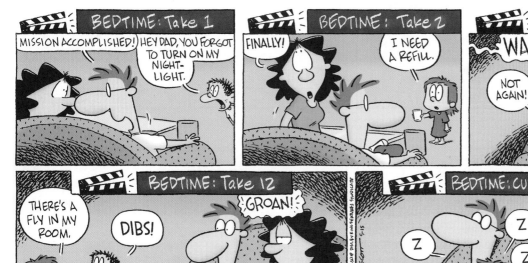

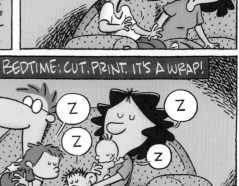

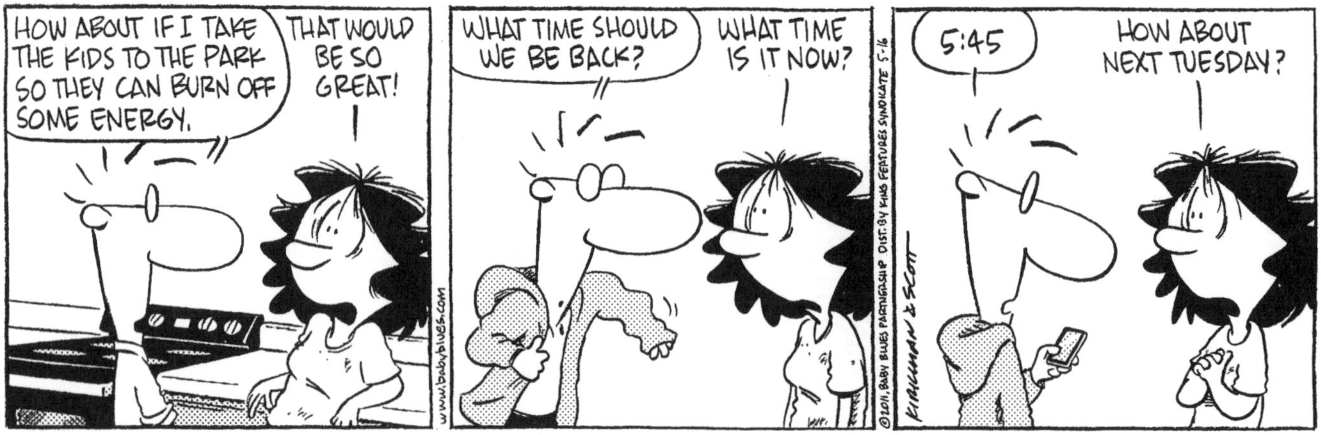
HOW ABOUT IF I TAKE THE KIDS TO THE PARK SO THEY CAN BURN OFF SOME ENERGY.
THAT WOULD BE SO GREAT!
WHAT TIME SHOULD WE BE BACK?
WHAT TIME IS IT NOW?
5:45
HOW ABOUT NEXT TUESDAY?
www.babyblues.com
© 2011, BABY BLUES PARTNERSHIP DIST. BY KING FEATURES SYNDICATE 5-16
KIRKMAN & SCOTT

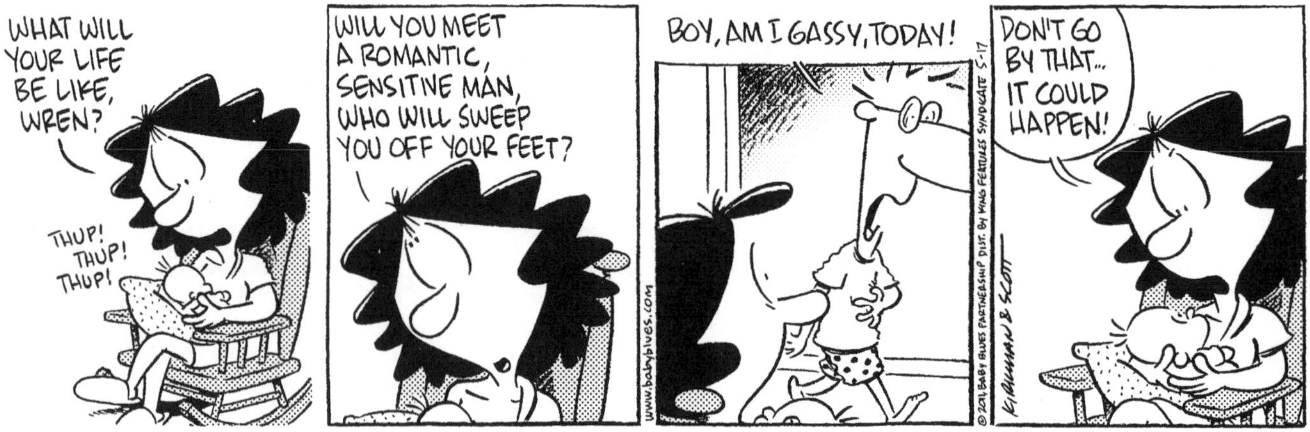
WHAT WILL YOUR LIFE BE LIKE, WREN?
THUP! THUP! THUP!
WILL YOU MEET A ROMANTIC, SENSITIVE MAN, WHO WILL SWEEP YOU OFF YOUR FEET?
www.babyblues.com
BOY, AM I GASSY, TODAY!
DON'T GO BY THAT... IT COULD HAPPEN!
© 2011, BABY BLUES PARTNERSHIP DIST. BY KING FEATURES SYNDICATE 5-17
KIRKMAN & SCOTT

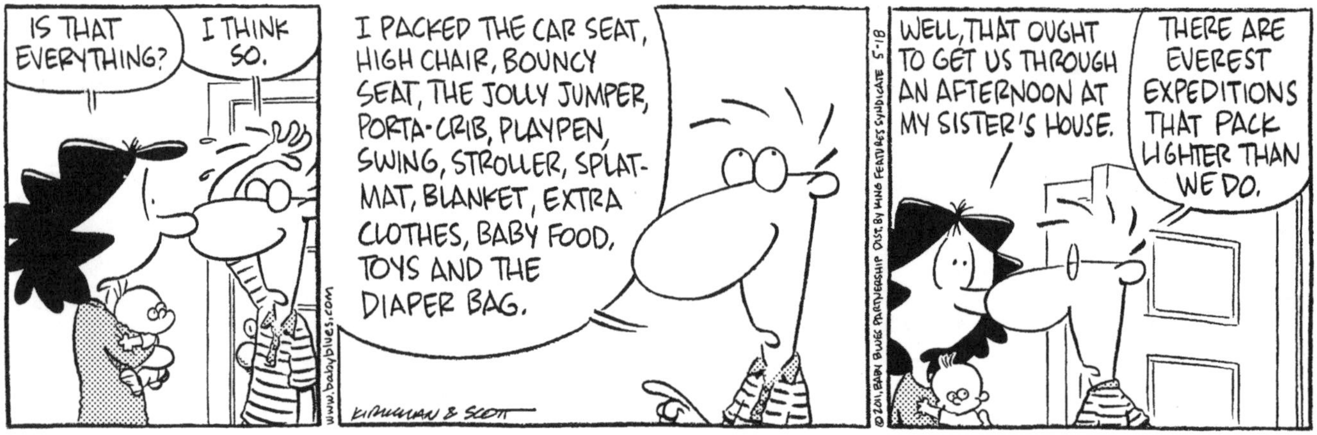
IS THAT EVERYTHING?
I THINK SO.
www.babyblues.com
I PACKED THE CAR SEAT, HIGH CHAIR, BOUNCY SEAT, THE JOLLY JUMPER, PORTA-CRIB, PLAYPEN, SWING, STROLLER, SPLAT-MAT, BLANKET, EXTRA CLOTHES, BABY FOOD, TOYS AND THE DIAPER BAG.
KIRKMAN & SCOTT
WELL, THAT OUGHT TO GET US THROUGH AN AFTERNOON AT MY SISTER'S HOUSE.
THERE ARE EVEREST EXPEDITIONS THAT PACK LIGHTER THAN WE DO.
© 2011, BABY BLUES PARTNERSHIP DIST. BY KING FEATURES SYNDICATE 5-18

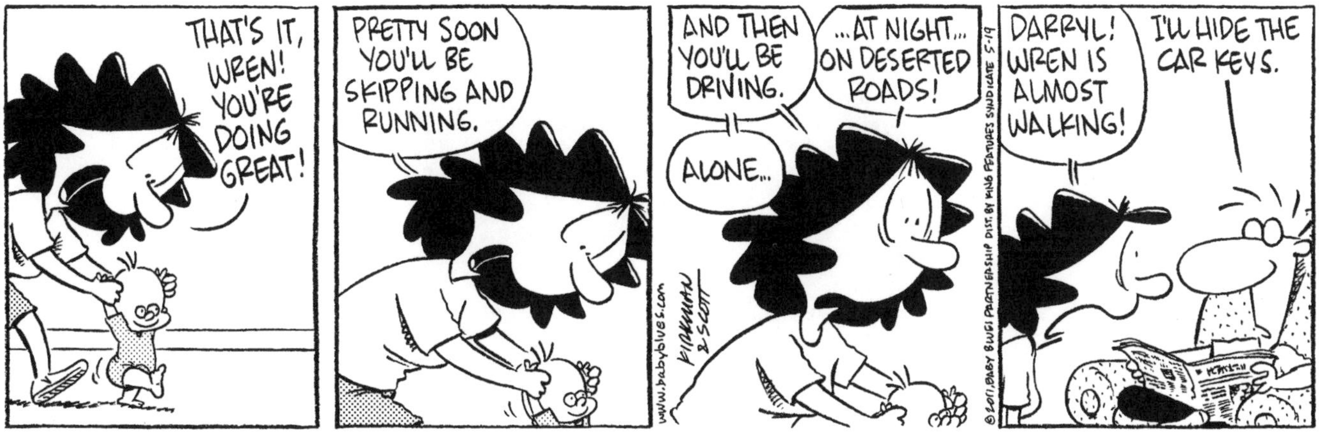
THAT'S IT, WREN! YOU'RE DOING GREAT!
PRETTY SOON YOU'LL BE SKIPPING AND RUNNING.
www.babyblues.com
KIRKMAN & SCOTT
AND THEN YOU'LL BE DRIVING.
...AT NIGHT... ON DESERTED ROADS!
ALONE...
©2011, BABY BLUES PARTNERSHIP DIST. BY KING FEATURES SYNDICATE 5-19
DARRYL! WREN IS ALMOST WALKING!
I'LL HIDE THE CAR KEYS.

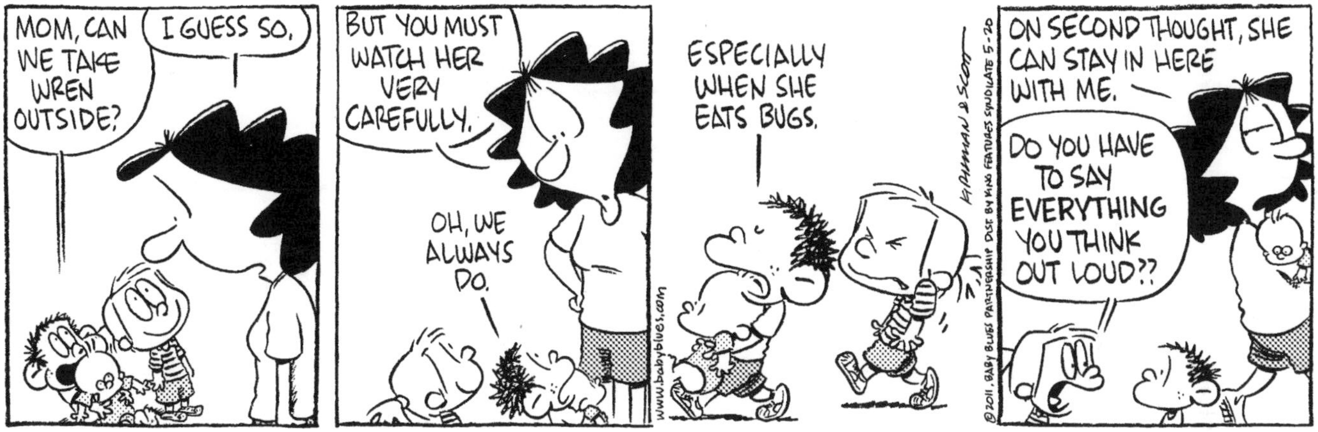
MOM, CAN WE TAKE WREN OUTSIDE?
I GUESS SO.
BUT YOU MUST WATCH HER VERY CAREFULLY.
OH, WE ALWAYS DO.
www.babyblues.com
ESPECIALLY WHEN SHE EATS BUGS.
KIRKMAN & SCOTT
©2011, BABY BLUES PARTNERSHIP DIST. BY KING FEATURES SYNDICATE 5-20
ON SECOND THOUGHT, SHE CAN STAY IN HERE WITH ME.
DO YOU HAVE TO SAY EVERYTHING YOU THINK OUT LOUD??

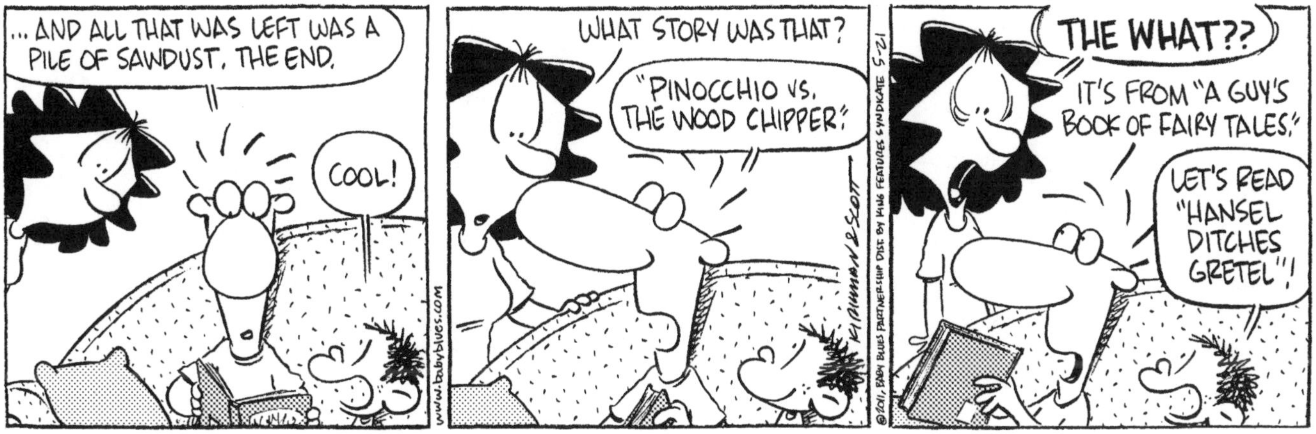
...AND ALL THAT WAS LEFT WAS A PILE OF SAWDUST. THE END.
COOL!
www.babyblues.com
WHAT STORY WAS THAT?
"PINOCCHIO VS. THE WOOD CHIPPER."
KIRKMAN & SCOTT
©2011, BABY BLUES PARTNERSHIP DIST. BY KING FEATURES SYNDICATE 5-21
THE WHAT??
IT'S FROM "A GUY'S BOOK OF FAIRY TALES."
LET'S READ "HANSEL DITCHES GRETEL"!

BABY BLUES®
BY RICK KIRKMAN / JERRY SCOTT

OOF! I'M EXHAUSTED!
I'M SO GLAD IT'S FRIDAY!
I'M GOING TO SLEEP LIKE A LOG.
YOU AND ME, BOTH.
OF COURSE, WREN WILL BE UP AT SIX TOMORROW.
CLICK!
AND I PROMISED ZOE THAT I'D MAKE PANCAKES FOR BREAKFAST.
OH, AND HAMMIE HAS A GAME AT EIGHT.
BUT FIRST WE HAVE TO TAKE YOUR CAR IN FOR SERVICE.
www.babyblues.com
GROAN!
GROAN!
KIRKMAN & SCOTT
© 2011, BABY BLUES PARTNERSHIP DIST. BY KING FEATURES SYNDICATE
WELL, LET'S JUST GET AS MUCH REST AS WE CAN.
WAY AHEAD OF YOU.
MY POOP IS BLUE.

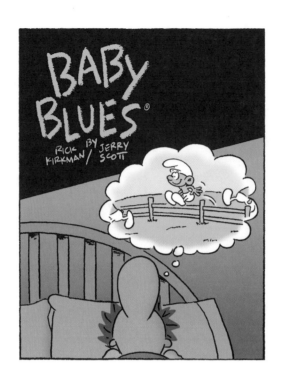

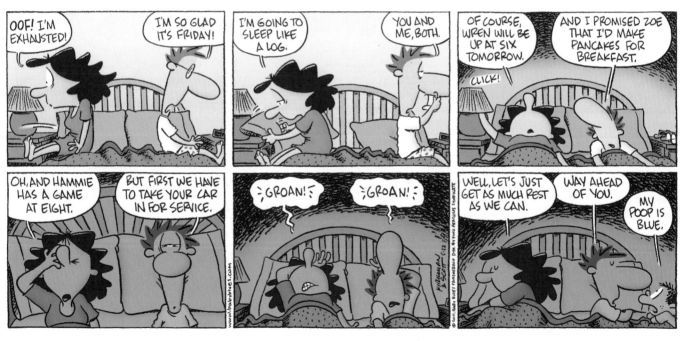

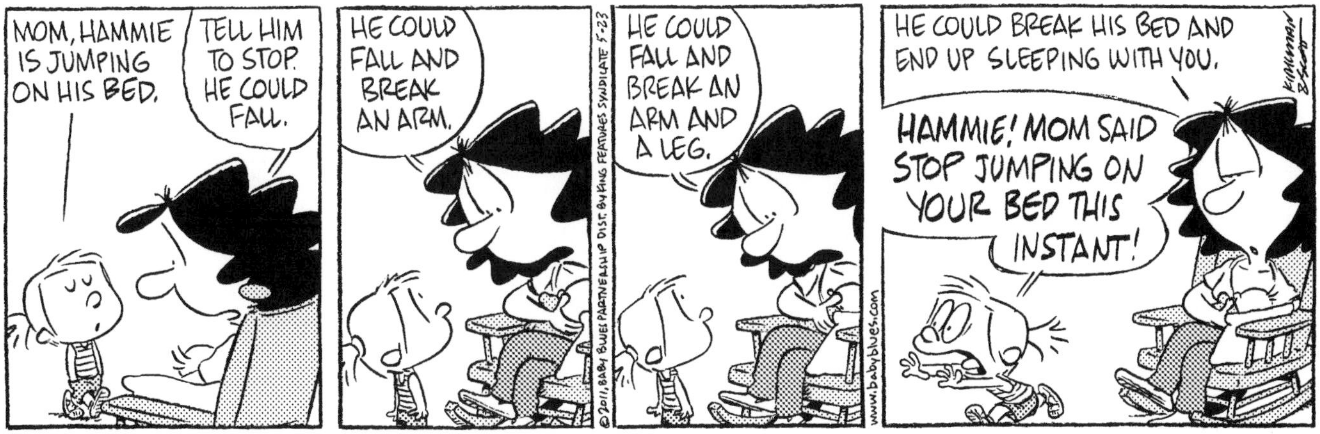
MOM, HAMMIE IS JUMPING ON HIS BED.
TELL HIM TO STOP. HE COULD FALL.
HE COULD FALL AND BREAK AN ARM.
©2011, BABY BLUES PARTNERSHIP DIST. BY KING FEATURES SYNDICATE 5-23
HE COULD FALL AND BREAK AN ARM AND A LEG.
www.babyblues.com
HE COULD BREAK HIS BED AND END UP SLEEPING WITH YOU.
HAMMIE! MOM SAID STOP JUMPING ON YOUR BED THIS INSTANT!
KIRKMAN & SCOTT

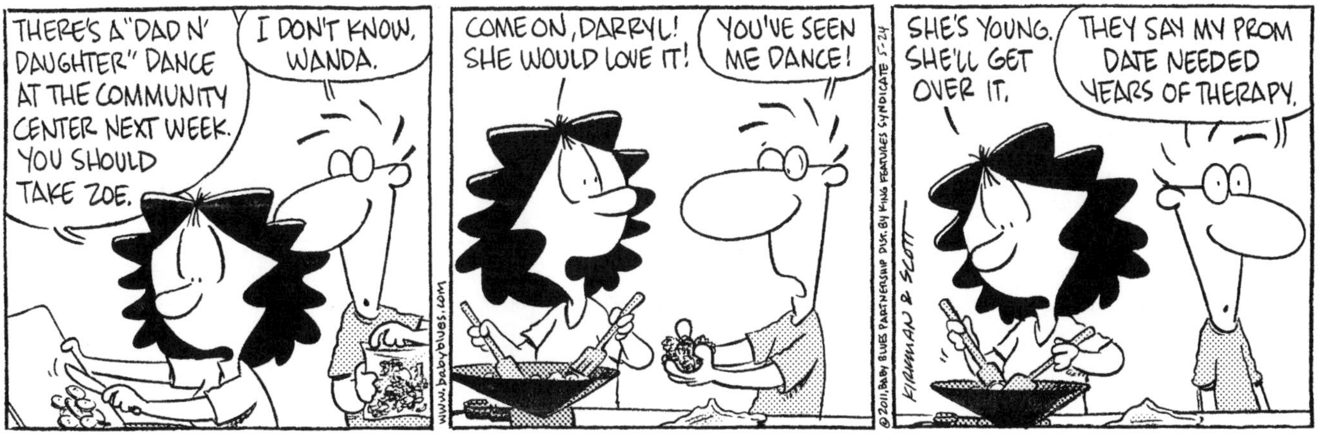
THERE'S A "DAD N' DAUGHTER" DANCE AT THE COMMUNITY CENTER NEXT WEEK. YOU SHOULD TAKE ZOE.
I DON'T KNOW, WANDA.
www.babyblues.com
COME ON, DARRYL! SHE WOULD LOVE IT!
YOU'VE SEEN ME DANCE!
©2011, BABY BLUES PARTNERSHIP DIST. BY KING FEATURES SYNDICATE 5-24
KIRKMAN & SCOTT
SHE'S YOUNG. SHE'LL GET OVER IT.
THEY SAY MY PROM DATE NEEDED YEARS OF THERAPY.

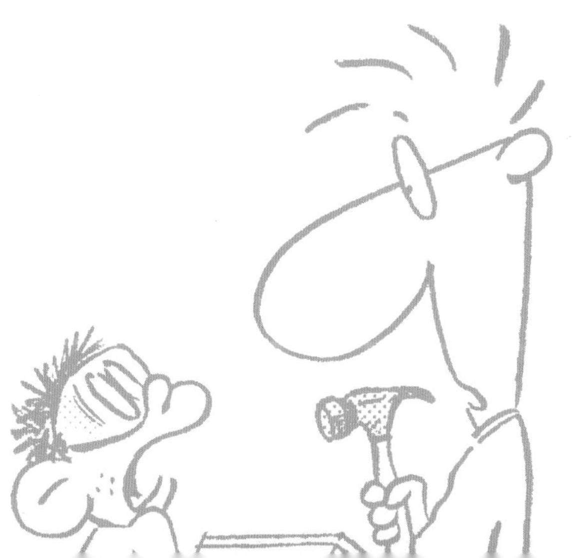

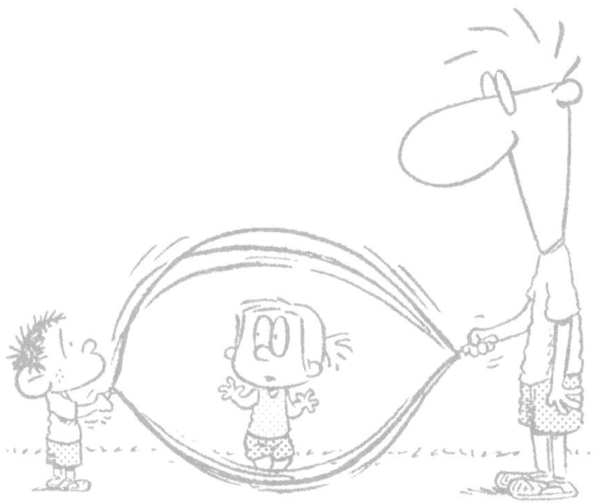

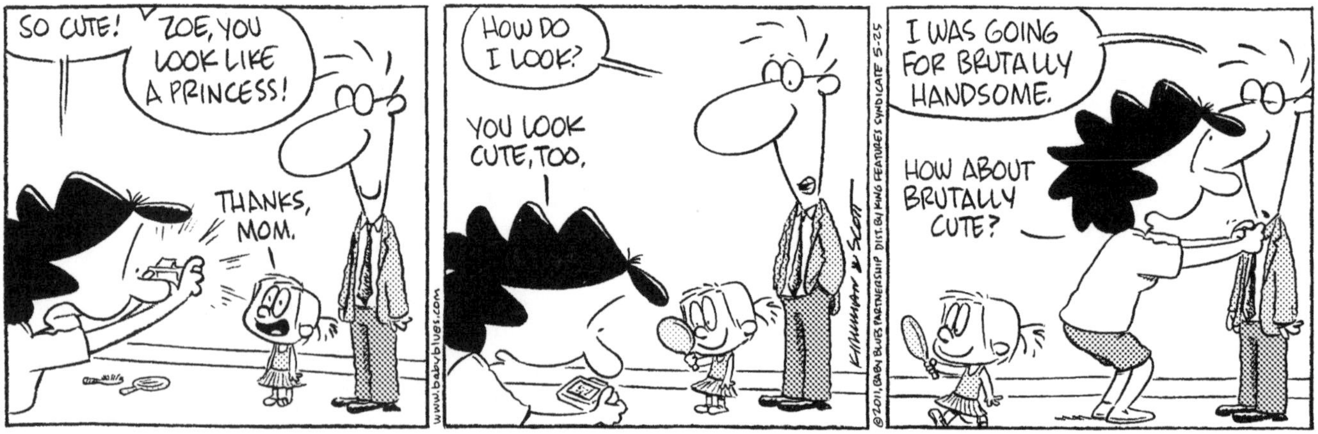
SO CUTE!
ZOE, YOU LOOK LIKE A PRINCESS!
THANKS, MOM.
www.babyblues.com
HOW DO I LOOK?
YOU LOOK CUTE, TOO.
KIRKMAN & SCOTT
©2011, BABY BLUES PARTNERSHIP DIST. BY KING FEATURES SYNDICATE 5-25
I WAS GOING FOR BRUTALLY HANDSOME.
HOW ABOUT BRUTALLY CUTE?

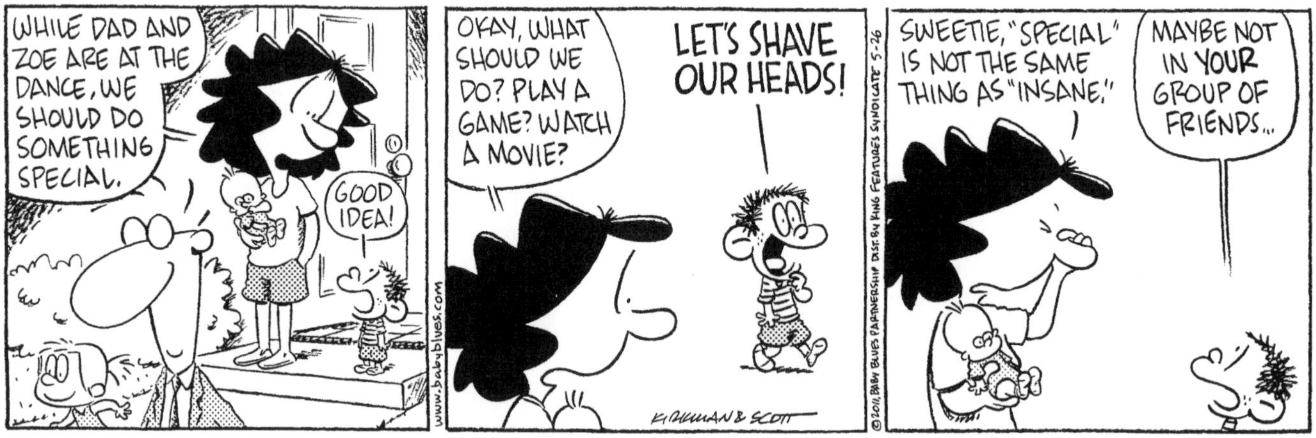
WHILE DAD AND ZOE ARE AT THE DANCE, WE SHOULD DO SOMETHING SPECIAL.
GOOD IDEA!
www.babyblues.com
OKAY, WHAT SHOULD WE DO? PLAY A GAME? WATCH A MOVIE?
LET'S SHAVE OUR HEADS!
KIRKMAN & SCOTT
©2011, BABY BLUES PARTNERSHIP DIST. BY KING FEATURES SYNDICATE 5-26
SWEETIE, "SPECIAL" IS NOT THE SAME THING AS "INSANE."
MAYBE NOT IN YOUR GROUP OF FRIENDS...

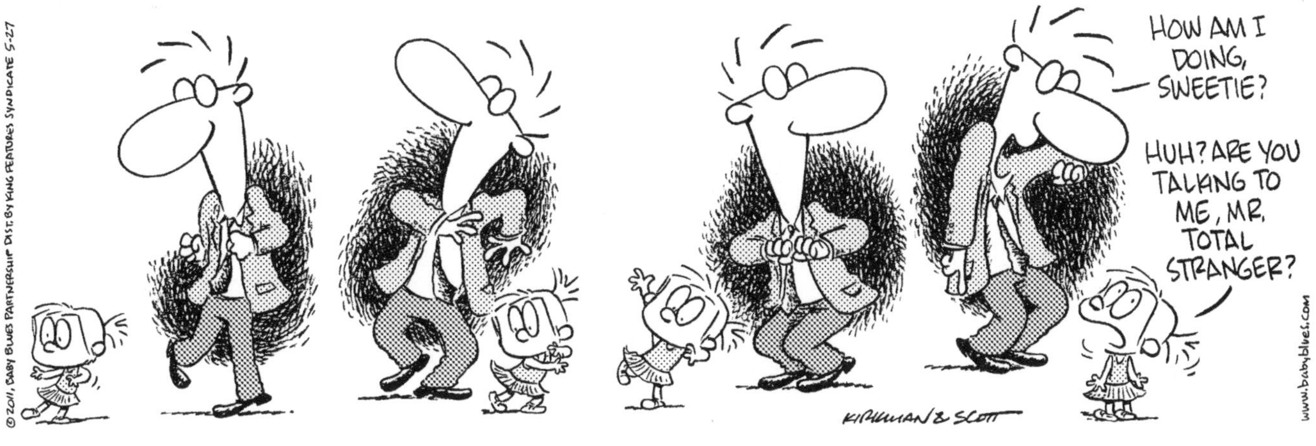
© 2011, BABY BLUES PARTNERSHIP DIST. BY KING FEATURES SYNDICATE 5-27
HOW AM I DOING, SWEETIE?
HUH? ARE YOU TALKING TO ME, MR. TOTAL STRANGER?
KIRKMAN & SCOTT
www.babyblues.com

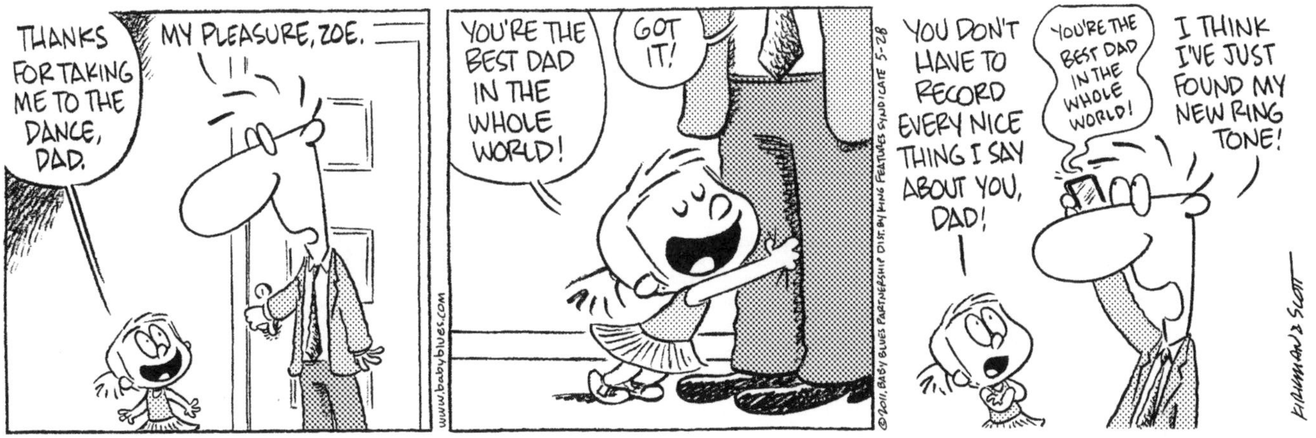
THANKS FOR TAKING ME TO THE DANCE, DAD.
MY PLEASURE, ZOE.
www.babyblues.com
YOU'RE THE BEST DAD IN THE WHOLE WORLD!
GOT IT!
© 2011, BABY BLUES PARTNERSHIP DIST. BY KING FEATURES SYNDICATE 5-28
YOU DON'T HAVE TO RECORD EVERY NICE THING I SAY ABOUT YOU, DAD!
YOU'RE THE BEST DAD IN THE WHOLE WORLD!
I THINK I'VE JUST FOUND MY NEW RING TONE!
KIRKMAN & SCOTT

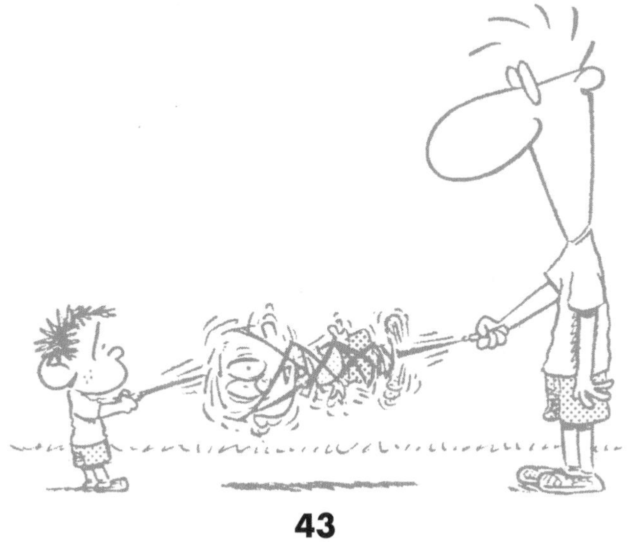

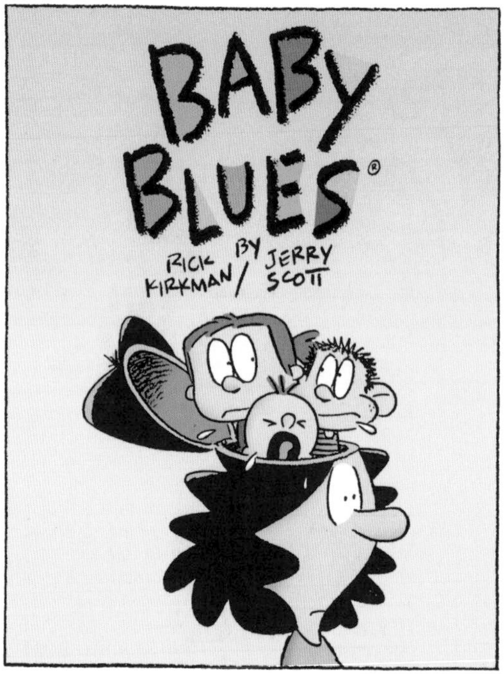
BABY BLUES®
BY
RICK KIRKMAN / JERRY SCOTT

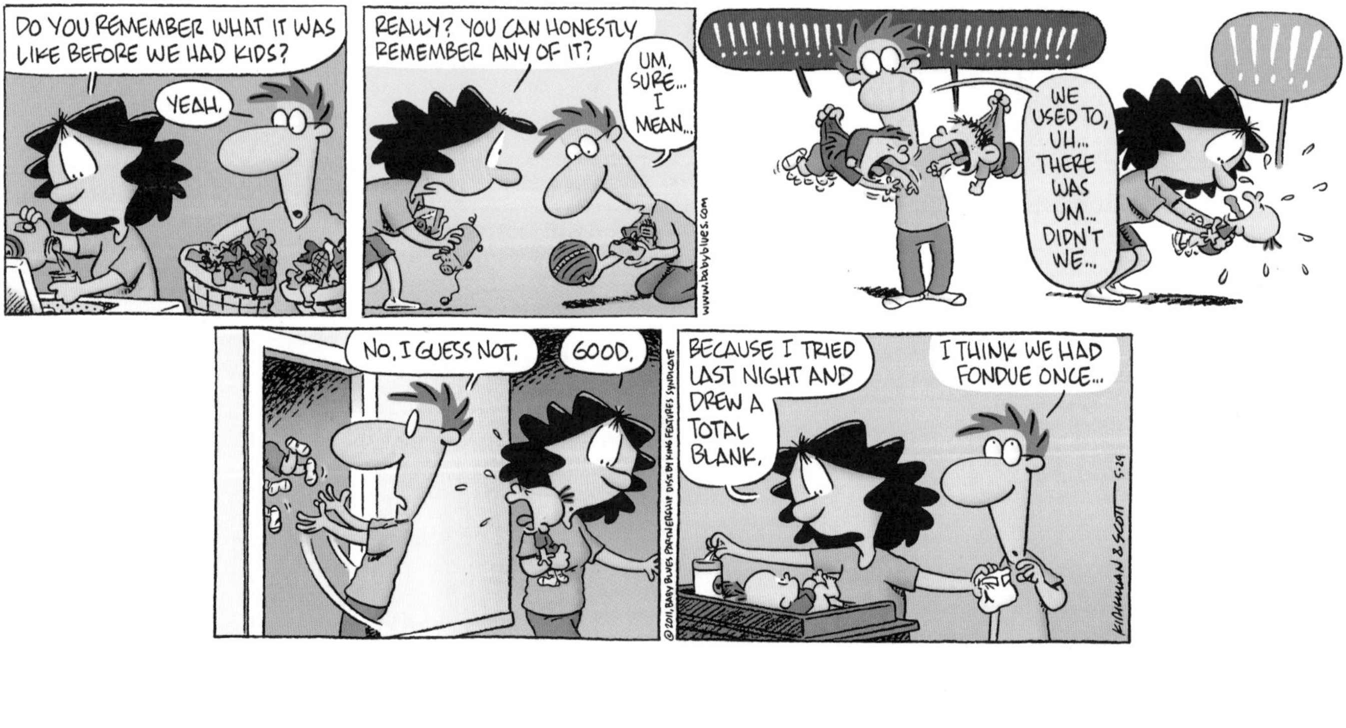
DO YOU REMEMBER WHAT IT WAS LIKE BEFORE WE HAD KIDS?
YEAH.
REALLY? YOU CAN HONESTLY REMEMBER ANY OF IT?
UM, SURE... I MEAN...
www.babyblues.com
!!!!!!!!!!!!!!!!!!!!!!!!
!!!!
WE USED TO, UH... THERE WAS UM... DIDN'T WE...
NO, I GUESS NOT.
GOOD.
BECAUSE I TRIED LAST NIGHT AND DREW A TOTAL BLANK.
I THINK WE HAD FONDUE ONCE...
©2011, BABY BLUES PARTNERSHIP DIST. BY KING FEATURES SYNDICATE
5-29
KIRKMAN & SCOTT

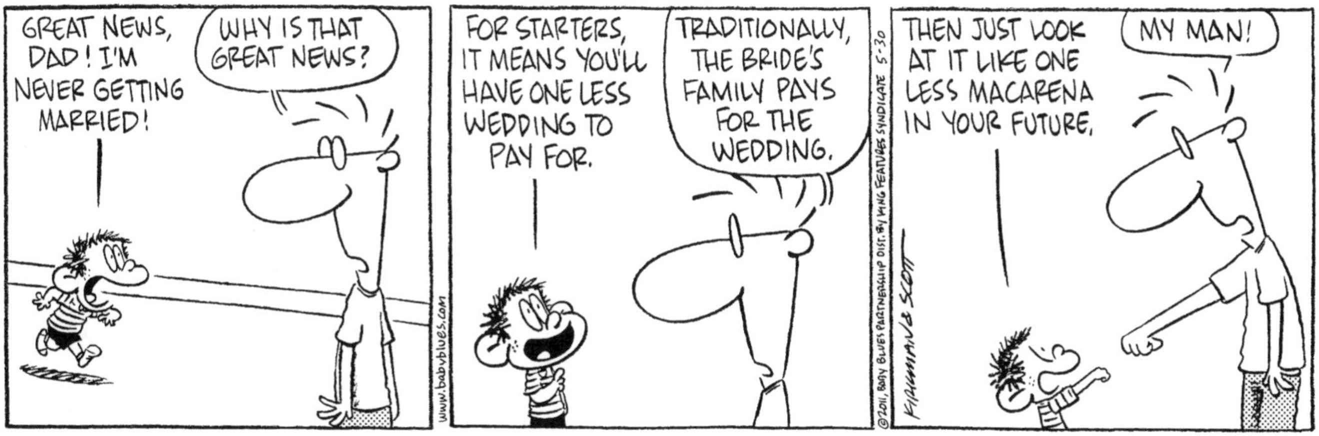
GREAT NEWS, DAD! I'M NEVER GETTING MARRIED!
WHY IS THAT GREAT NEWS?
FOR STARTERS, IT MEANS YOU'LL HAVE ONE LESS WEDDING TO PAY FOR.
TRADITIONALLY, THE BRIDE'S FAMILY PAYS FOR THE WEDDING.
THEN JUST LOOK AT IT LIKE ONE LESS MACARENA IN YOUR FUTURE.
MY MAN!
www.babyblues.com
©2011, BABY BLUES PARTNERSHIP DIST. BY KING FEATURES SYNDICATE 5-30
KIRKMAN & SCOTT

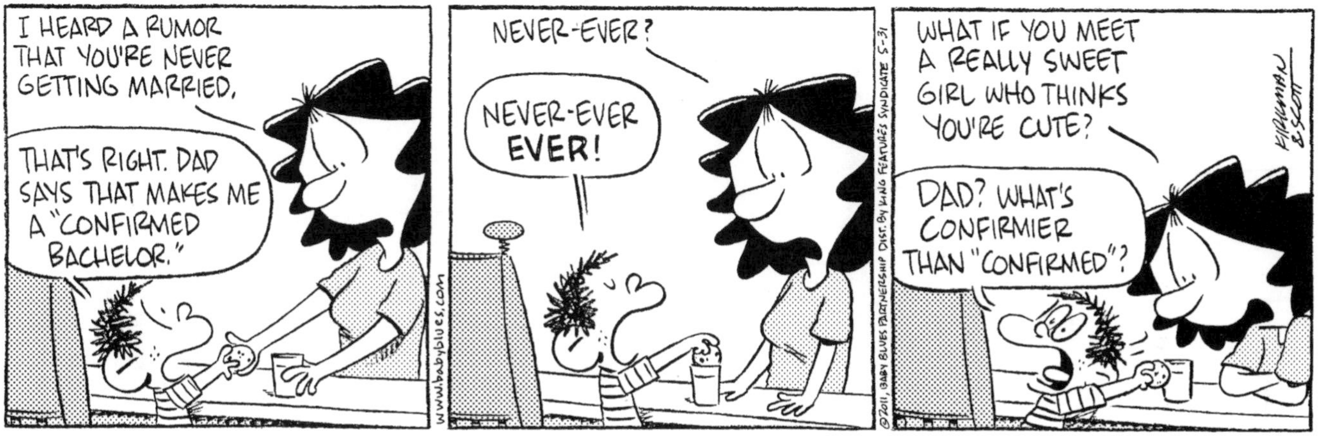
I HEARD A RUMOR THAT YOU'RE NEVER GETTING MARRIED.
THAT'S RIGHT. DAD SAYS THAT MAKES ME A "CONFIRMED BACHELOR."
NEVER-EVER?
NEVER-EVER **EVER**!
WHAT IF YOU MEET A REALLY SWEET GIRL WHO THINKS YOU'RE CUTE?
DAD? WHAT'S CONFIRMIER THAN "CONFIRMED"?
www.babyblues.com
©2011, BABY BLUES PARTNERSHIP DIST. BY KING FEATURES SYNDICATE 5-31
KIRKMAN & SCOTT

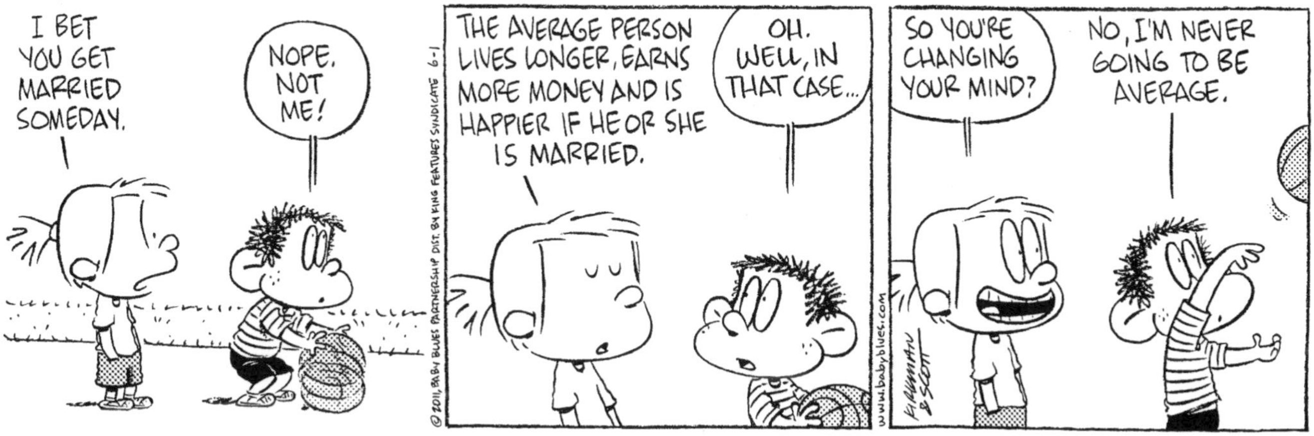
I BET YOU GET MARRIED SOMEDAY.
NOPE. NOT ME!
THE AVERAGE PERSON LIVES LONGER, EARNS MORE MONEY AND IS HAPPIER IF HE OR SHE IS MARRIED.
OH. WELL, IN THAT CASE...
SO YOU'RE CHANGING YOUR MIND?
NO, I'M NEVER GOING TO BE AVERAGE.
©2011, BABY BLUES PARTNERSHIP DIST. BY KING FEATURES SYNDICATE 6-1
www.babyblues.com
KIRKMAN & SCOTT

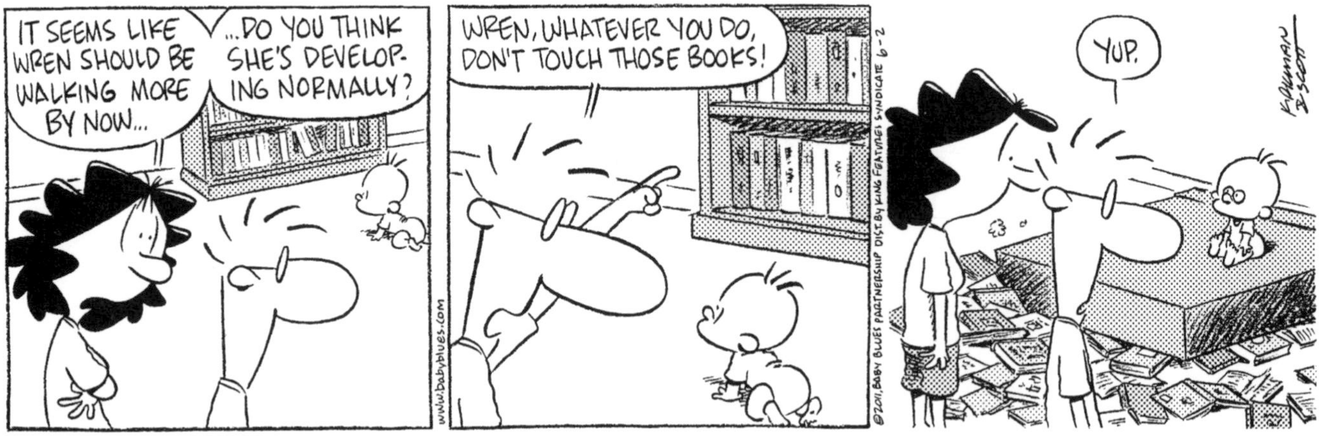
IT SEEMS LIKE WREN SHOULD BE WALKING MORE BY NOW...
...DO YOU THINK SHE'S DEVELOPING NORMALLY?
www.babyblues.com
WREN, WHATEVER YOU DO, DON'T TOUCH THOSE BOOKS!
©2011, BABY BLUES PARTNERSHIP DIST. BY KING FEATURES SYNDICATE 6-2
YUP.
KIRKMAN & SCOTT

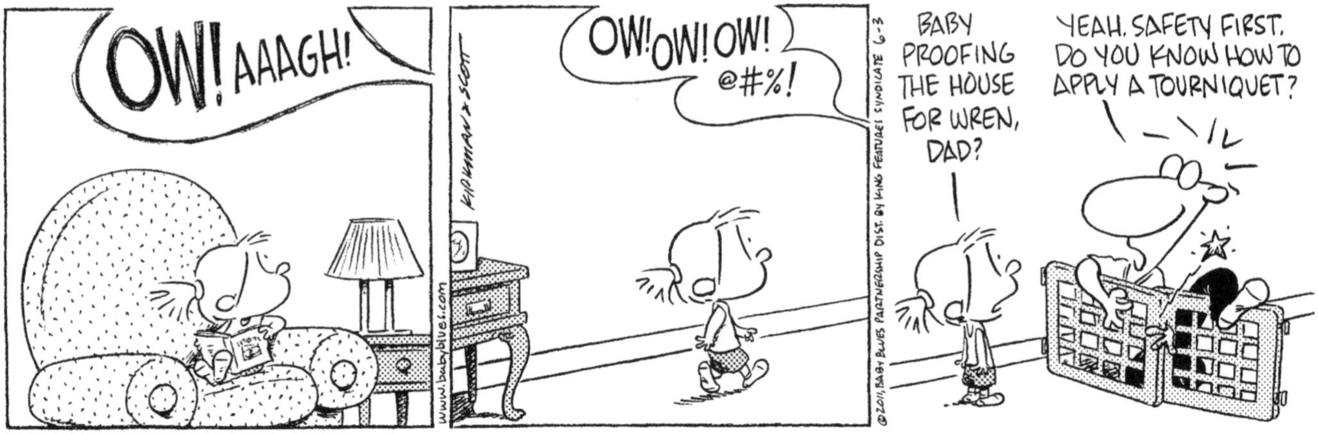
OW! AAAGH!
KIRKMAN & SCOTT
www.babyblues.com
OW! OW! OW! @#%!
©2011, BABY BLUES PARTNERSHIP DIST. BY KING FEATURES SYNDICATE 6-3
BABY PROOFING THE HOUSE FOR WREN, DAD?
YEAH. SAFETY FIRST. DO YOU KNOW HOW TO APPLY A TOURNIQUET?

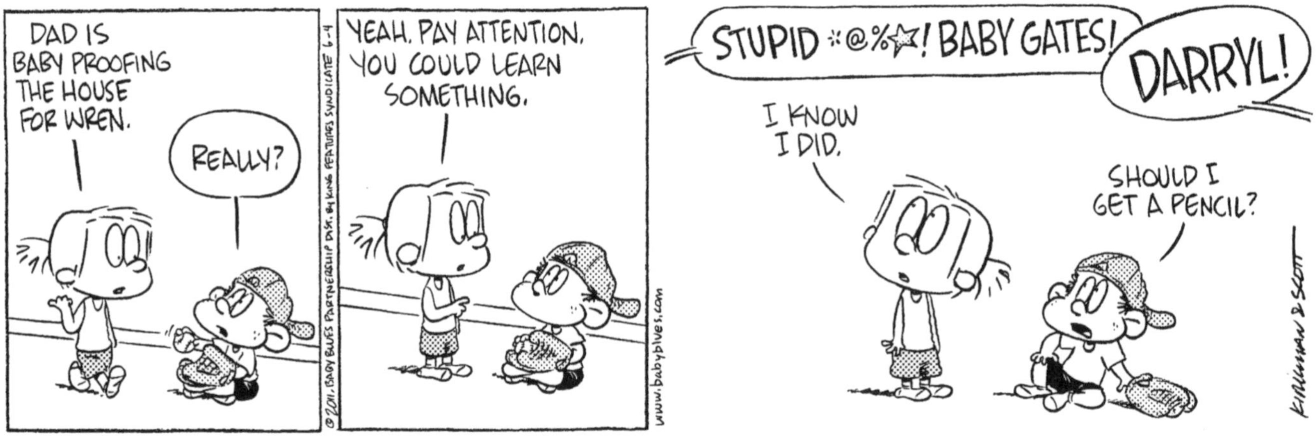
DAD IS BABY PROOFING THE HOUSE FOR WREN.
REALLY?
©2011, BABY BLUES PARTNERSHIP DIST. BY KING FEATURES SYNDICATE 6-4
YEAH. PAY ATTENTION. YOU COULD LEARN SOMETHING.
www.babyblues.com
STUPID *@%☆! BABY GATES!
DARRYL!
I KNOW I DID.
SHOULD I GET A PENCIL?
KIRKMAN & SCOTT

BABY BLUES®
BY RICK KIRKMAN / JERRY SCOTT
SALMON PINK
CORAL PINK
SUNRISE PINK
TONGUE PINK
SUNSET PINK

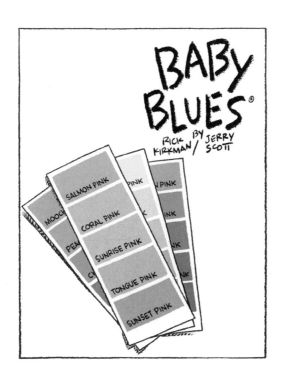

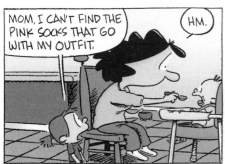

MOM, I CAN'T FIND THE PINK SOCKS THAT GO WITH MY OUTFIT.
HM.
IT'S REALLY A PROBLEM. I'M NOT SURE HOW TO HANDLE THIS.
JUST WEAR THE PURPLE ONES.
© 2011, BABY BLUES PARTNERSHIP DIST. BY KING FEATURES SYNDICATE
PURPLE?
PURPLE??
www.thecartoonistsstudio.com
OH MY GOSH!
YOU'RE SERIOUS!!
6-5
KIRKMAN & SCOTT
WHERE DO MOMS KEEP THEIR SENSE OF FASHION??
MAYBE IT'S IN THE POCKETS OF THEIR SWEAT-PANTS!!
www.babyblues.com

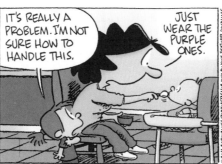

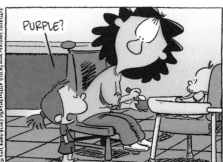

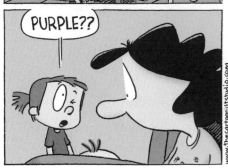

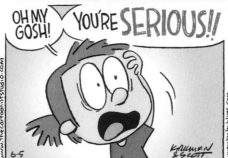

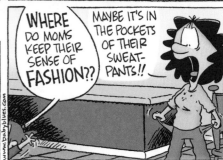

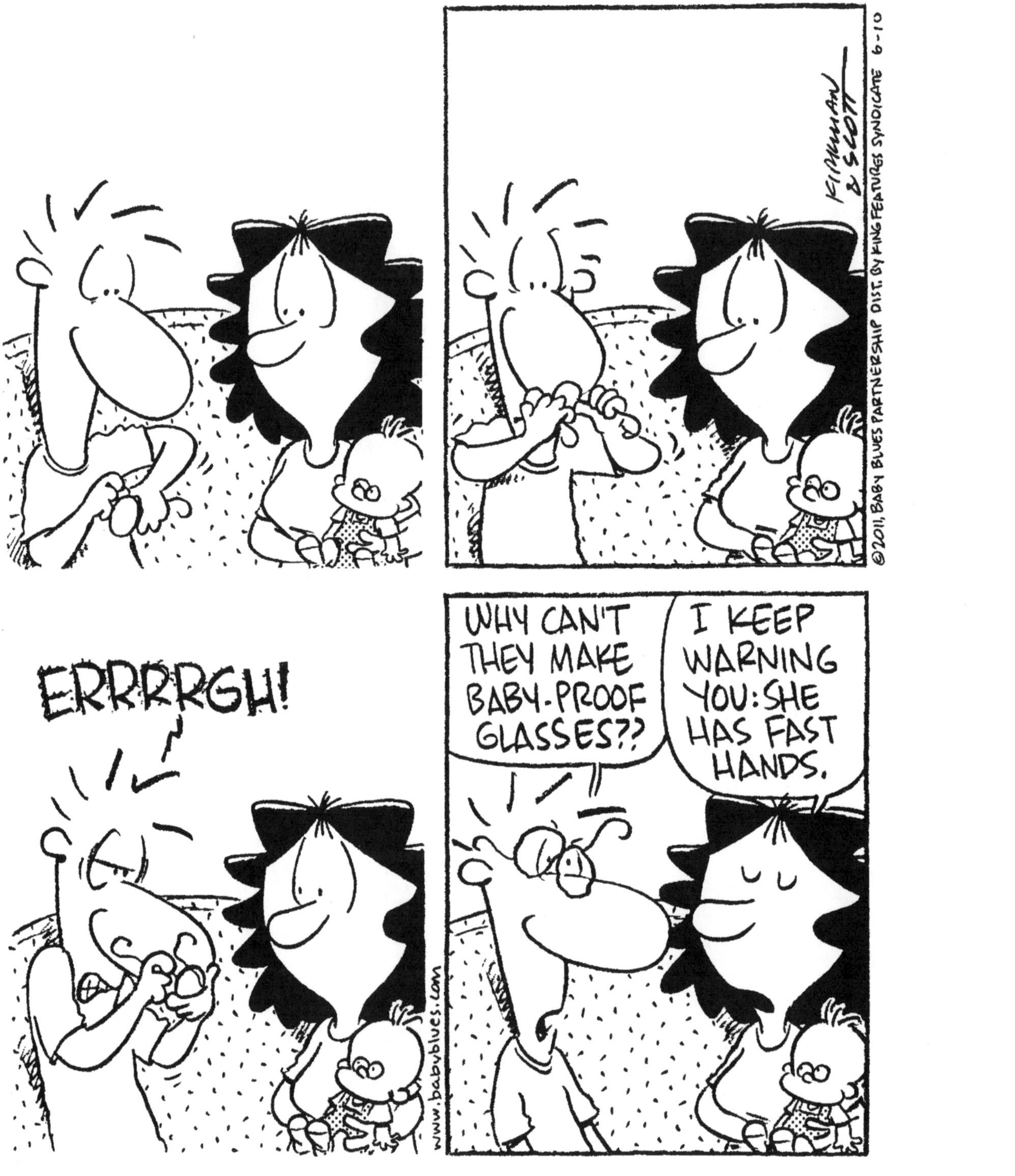
KIRKMAN & SCOTT
©2011, BABY BLUES PARTNERSHIP DIST. BY KING FEATURES SYNDICATE 6-10
ERRRRGH!
www.babyblues.com
WHY CAN'T THEY MAKE BABY-PROOF GLASSES??
I KEEP WARNING YOU: SHE HAS FAST HANDS.

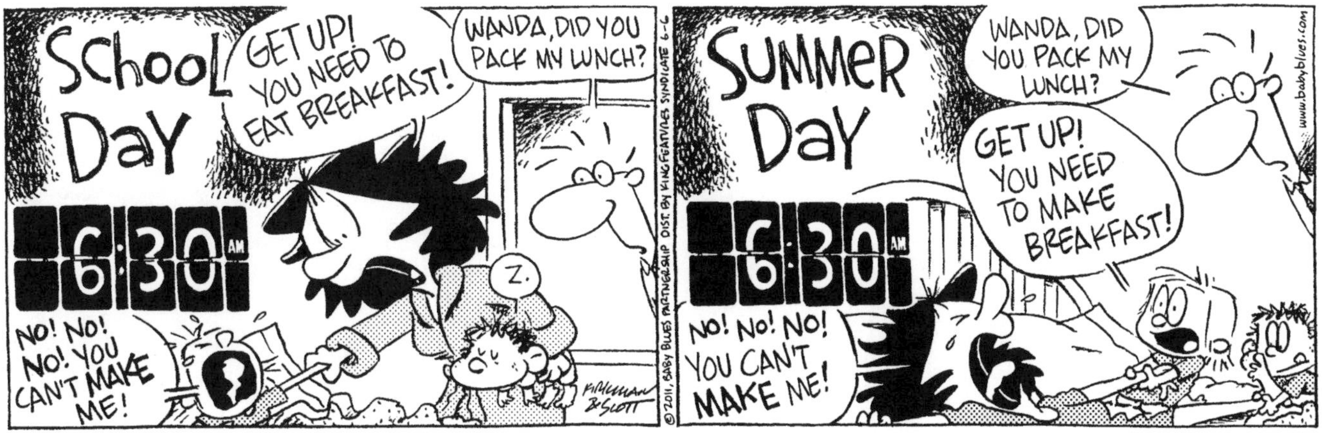
School Day
6:30 AM
GET UP! YOU NEED TO EAT BREAKFAST!
WANDA, DID YOU PACK MY LUNCH?
Z.
NO! NO! NO! YOU CAN'T MAKE ME!
KIRKMAN & SCOTT
© 2011, BABY BLUES PARTNERSHIP DIST. BY KING FEATURES SYNDICATE 6-6
Summer Day
6:30 AM
WANDA, DID YOU PACK MY LUNCH?
GET UP! YOU NEED TO MAKE BREAKFAST!
NO! NO! NO! YOU CAN'T MAKE ME!
www.babyblues.com

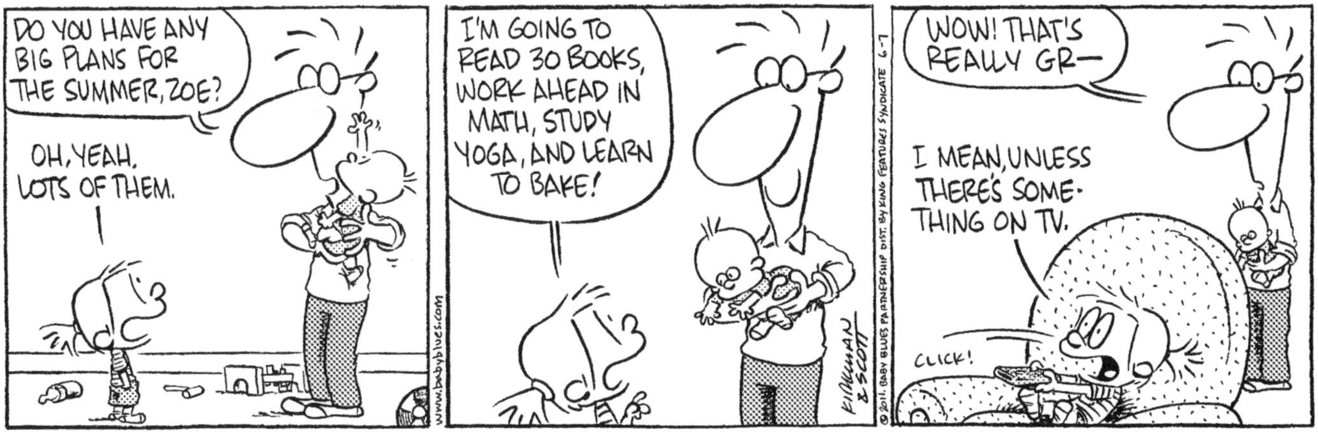
DO YOU HAVE ANY BIG PLANS FOR THE SUMMER, ZOE?
OH, YEAH. LOTS OF THEM.
www.babyblues.com
I'M GOING TO READ 30 BOOKS, WORK AHEAD IN MATH, STUDY YOGA, AND LEARN TO BAKE!
KIRKMAN & SCOTT
© 2011, BABY BLUES PARTNERSHIP DIST. BY KING FEATURES SYNDICATE 6-7
WOW! THAT'S REALLY GR—
I MEAN, UNLESS THERE'S SOME-THING ON TV.
CLICK!

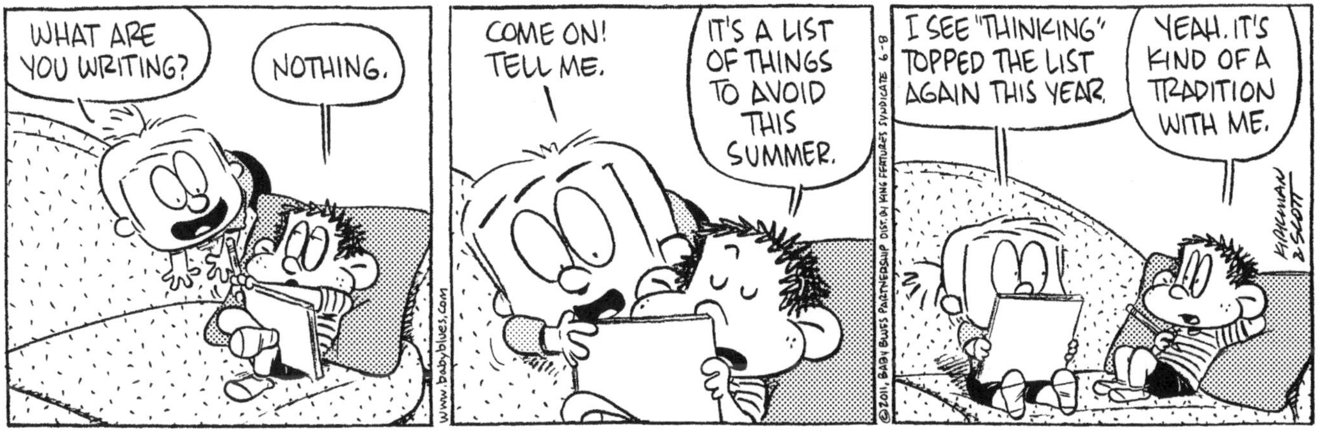
WHAT ARE YOU WRITING?
NOTHING.
www.babyblues.com
COME ON! TELL ME.
IT'S A LIST OF THINGS TO AVOID THIS SUMMER.
© 2011, BABY BLUES PARTNERSHIP DIST. BY KING FEATURES SYNDICATE 6-8
I SEE "THINKING" TOPPED THE LIST AGAIN THIS YEAR.
YEAH. IT'S KIND OF A TRADITION WITH ME.
KIRKMAN & SCOTT

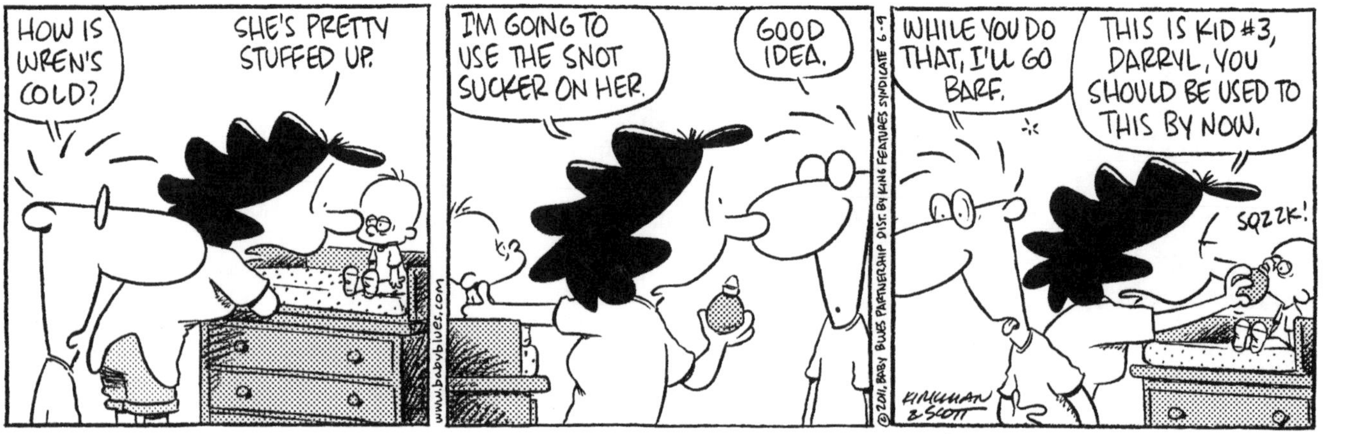
HOW IS WREN'S COLD?
SHE'S PRETTY STUFFED UP.
I'M GOING TO USE THE SNOT SUCKER ON HER.
GOOD IDEA.
WHILE YOU DO THAT, I'LL GO BARF.
THIS IS KID #3, DARRYL, YOU SHOULD BE USED TO THIS BY NOW.
SQZZK!
www.babyblues.com
©2011, BABY BLUES PARTNERSHIP DIST. BY KING FEATURES SYNDICATE 6-9
KIRKMAN & SCOTT

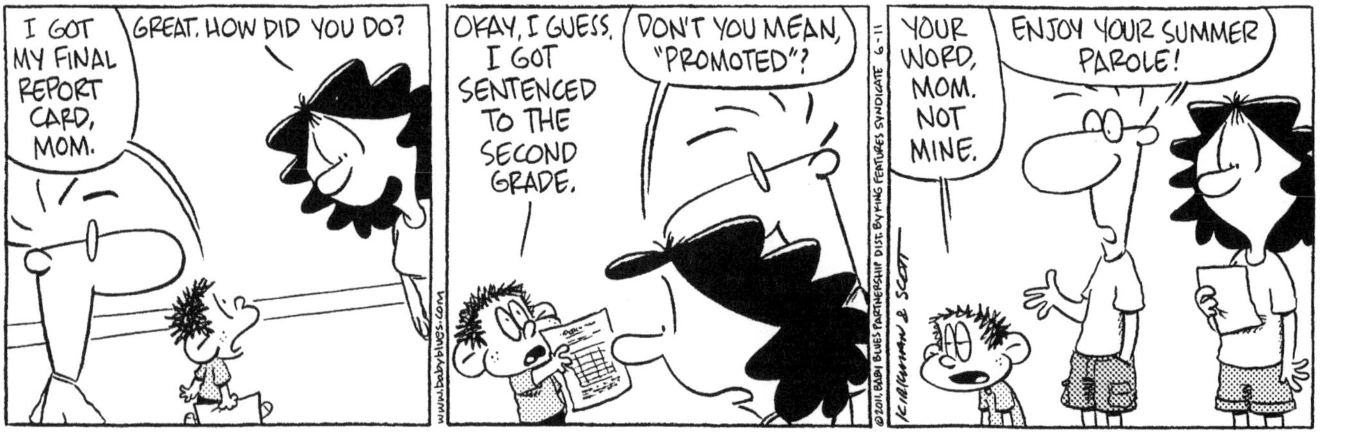
I GOT MY FINAL REPORT CARD, MOM.
GREAT. HOW DID YOU DO?
OKAY, I GUESS. I GOT SENTENCED TO THE SECOND GRADE.
DON'T YOU MEAN, "PROMOTED"?
YOUR WORD, MOM. NOT MINE.
ENJOY YOUR SUMMER PAROLE!
www.babyblues.com
©2011, BABY BLUES PARTNERSHIP DIST. BY KING FEATURES SYNDICATE 6-11
KIRKMAN & SCOTT

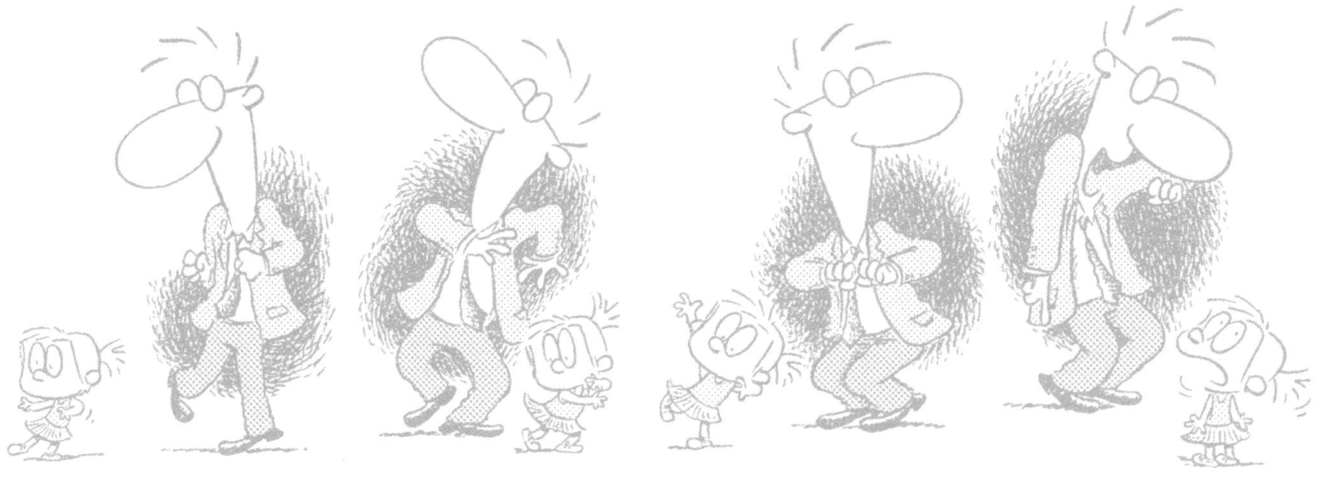

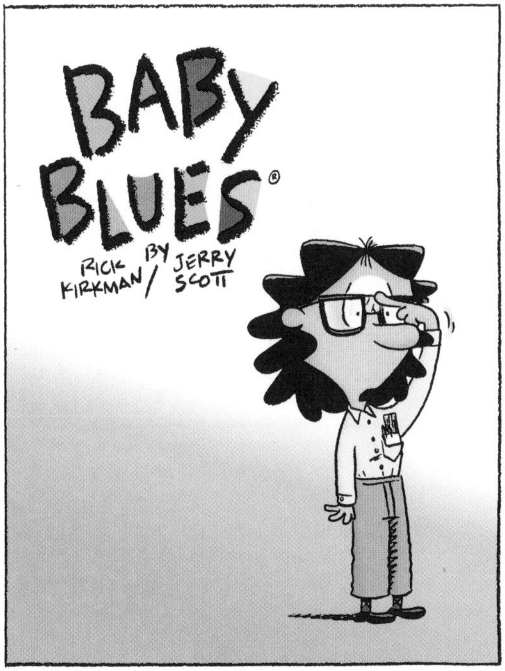
BABY BLUES®
BY RICK KIRKMAN / JERRY SCOTT

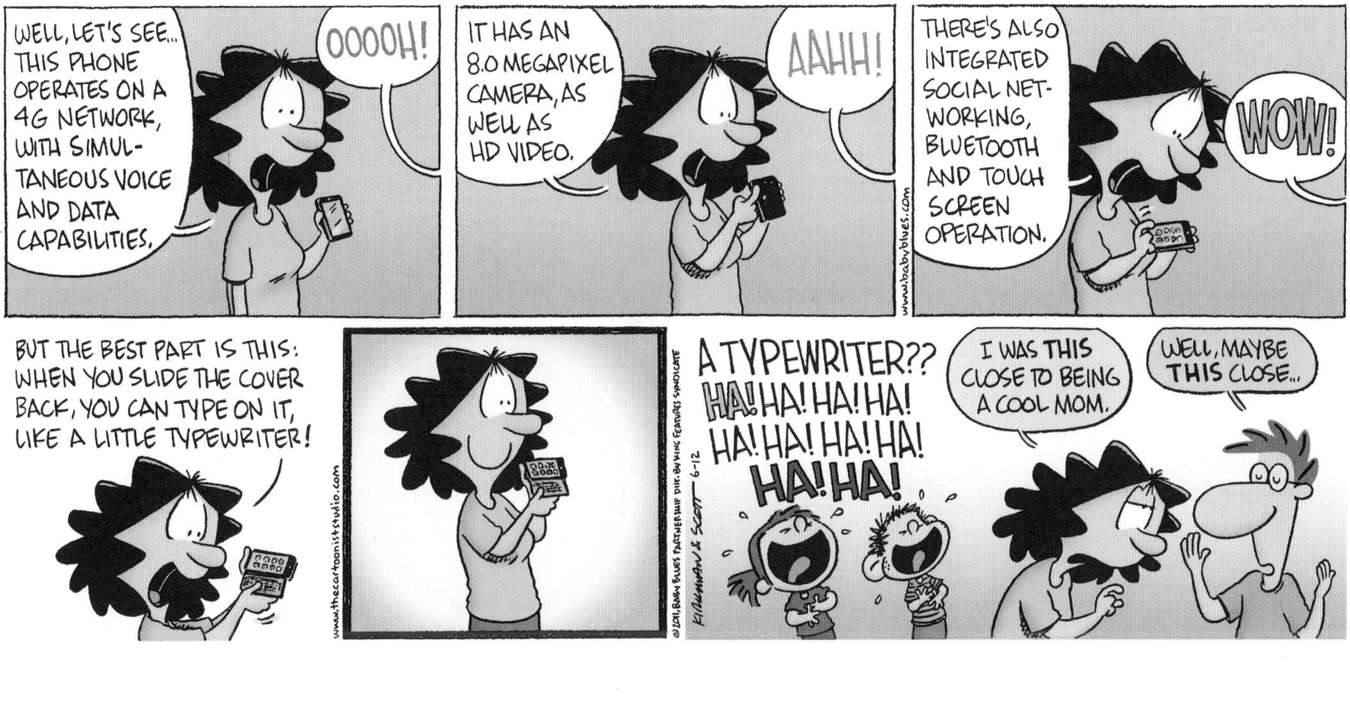
WELL, LET'S SEE... THIS PHONE OPERATES ON A 4G NETWORK, WITH SIMUL-TANEOUS VOICE AND DATA CAPABILITIES.
OOOOH!
IT HAS AN 8.0 MEGAPIXEL CAMERA, AS WELL AS HD VIDEO.
AAHH!
THERE'S ALSO INTEGRATED SOCIAL NET-WORKING, BLUETOOTH AND TOUCH SCREEN OPERATION.
WOW!
www.babyblues.com
BUT THE BEST PART IS THIS: WHEN YOU SLIDE THE COVER BACK, YOU CAN TYPE ON IT, LIKE A LITTLE TYPEWRITER!
www.thecartoonniststudio.com
©2011, BABY BLUES PARTNERSHIP DIST. BY KING FEATURES SYNDICATE
KIRKMAN & SCOTT 6-12
A TYPEWRITER?? HA! HA! HA! HA! HA! HA! HA! HA! HA! HA!
I WAS THIS CLOSE TO BEING A COOL MOM.
WELL, MAYBE THIS CLOSE...

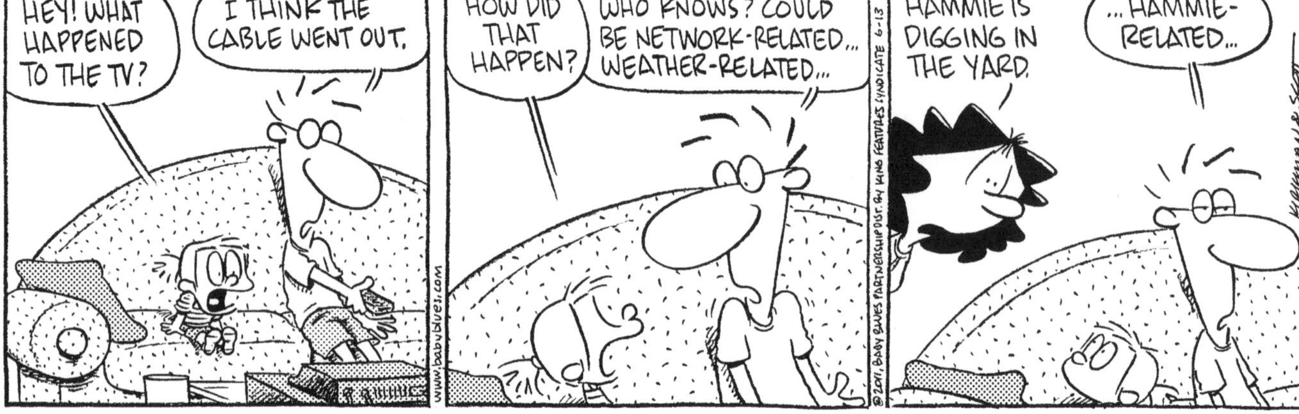
HEY! WHAT HAPPENED TO THE TV?
I THINK THE CABLE WENT OUT.
HOW DID THAT HAPPEN?
WHO KNOWS? COULD BE NETWORK-RELATED... WEATHER-RELATED...
HAMMIE IS DIGGING IN THE YARD.
...HAMMIE-RELATED...
www.babyblues.com
©2011, BABY BLUES PARTNERSHIP DIST. BY KING FEATURES SYNDICATE 6-13
KIRKMAN & SCOTT

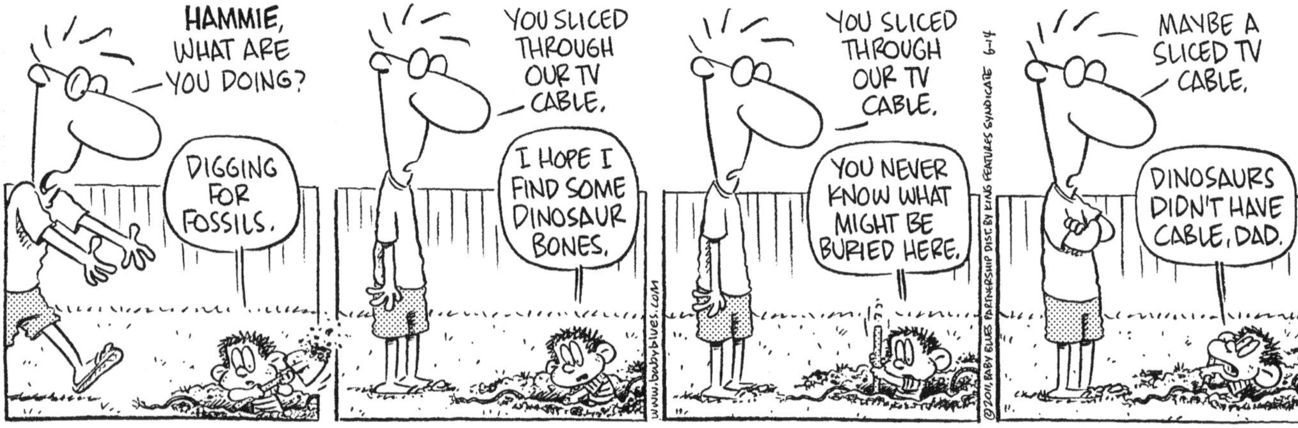
HAMMIE, WHAT ARE YOU DOING?
DIGGING FOR FOSSILS.
YOU SLICED THROUGH OUR TV CABLE.
I HOPE I FIND SOME DINOSAUR BONES.
www.babyblues.com
YOU SLICED THROUGH OUR TV CABLE.
YOU NEVER KNOW WHAT MIGHT BE BURIED HERE.
©2011, BABY BLUES PARTNERSHIP DIST. BY KING FEATURES SYNDICATE 6-14
MAYBE A SLICED TV CABLE.
DINOSAURS DIDN'T HAVE CABLE, DAD.

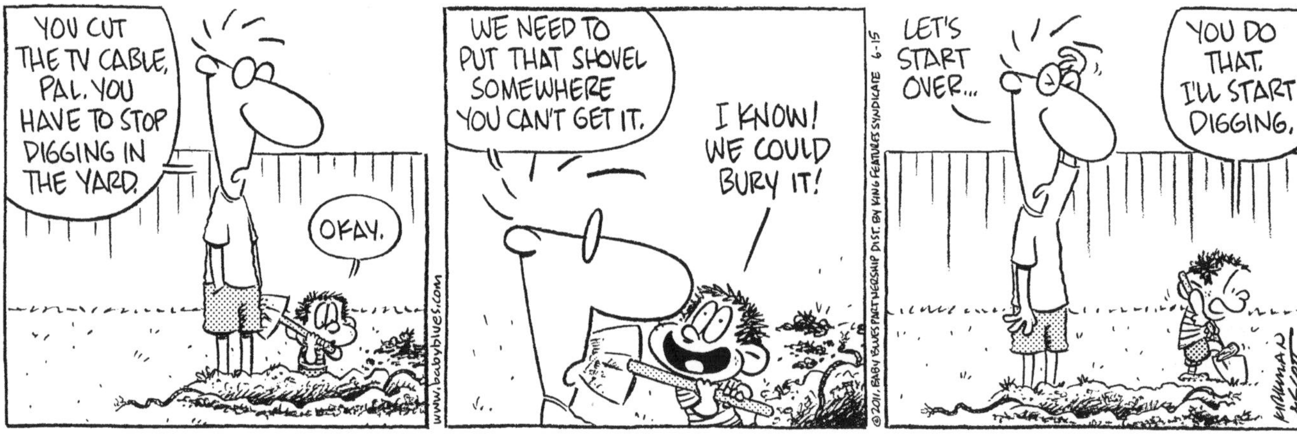
YOU CUT THE TV CABLE, PAL. YOU HAVE TO STOP DIGGING IN THE YARD.
OKAY.
www.babyblues.com
WE NEED TO PUT THAT SHOVEL SOMEWHERE YOU CAN'T GET IT.
I KNOW! WE COULD BURY IT!
©2011, BABY BLUES PARTNERSHIP DIST. BY KING FEATURES SYNDICATE 6-15
LET'S START OVER...
YOU DO THAT. I'LL START DIGGING.
KIRKMAN & SCOTT

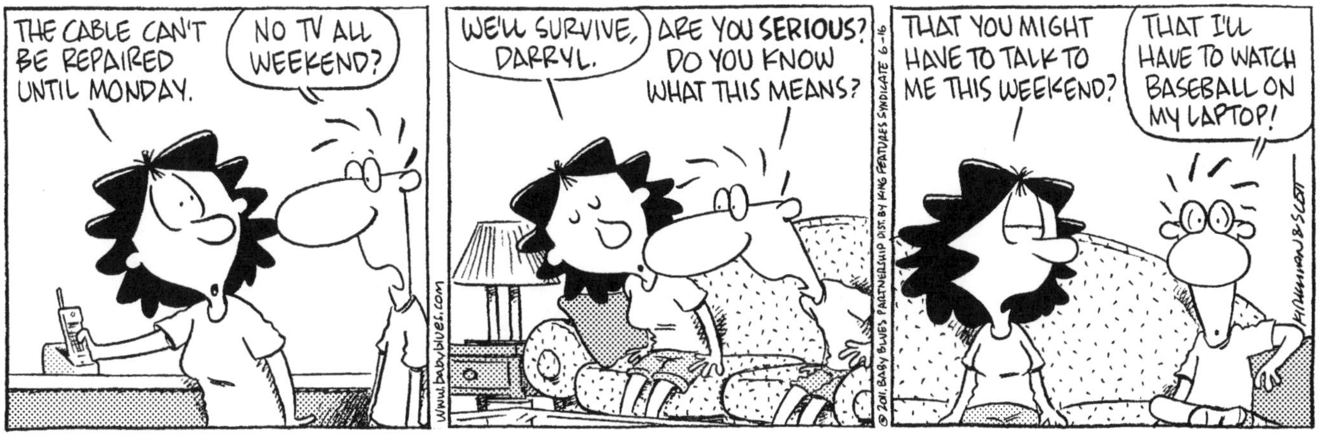
THE CABLE CAN'T BE REPAIRED UNTIL MONDAY.
NO TV ALL WEEKEND?
WE'LL SURVIVE, DARRYL.
ARE YOU SERIOUS? DO YOU KNOW WHAT THIS MEANS?
THAT YOU MIGHT HAVE TO TALK TO ME THIS WEEKEND?
THAT I'LL HAVE TO WATCH BASEBALL ON MY LAPTOP!
www.babyblues.com
© 2011, BABY BLUES PARTNERSHIP DIST. BY KING FEATURES SYNDICATE 6-16
KIRKMAN & SCOTT

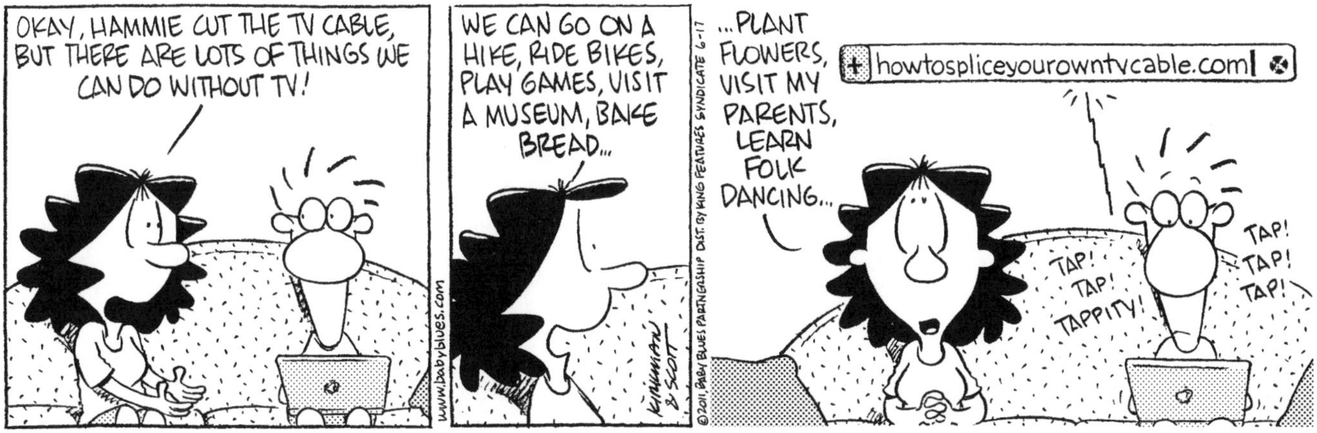
OKAY, HAMMIE CUT THE TV CABLE, BUT THERE ARE LOTS OF THINGS WE CAN DO WITHOUT TV!
WE CAN GO ON A HIKE, RIDE BIKES, PLAY GAMES, VISIT A MUSEUM, BAKE BREAD...
...PLANT FLOWERS, VISIT MY PARENTS, LEARN FOLK DANCING...
howtospliceyourowntvcable.com
TAP! TAP! TAPPITY!
TAP! TAP! TAP!
www.babyblues.com
KIRKMAN & SCOTT
© 2011, BABY BLUES PARTNERSHIP DIST. BY KING FEATURES SYNDICATE 6-17

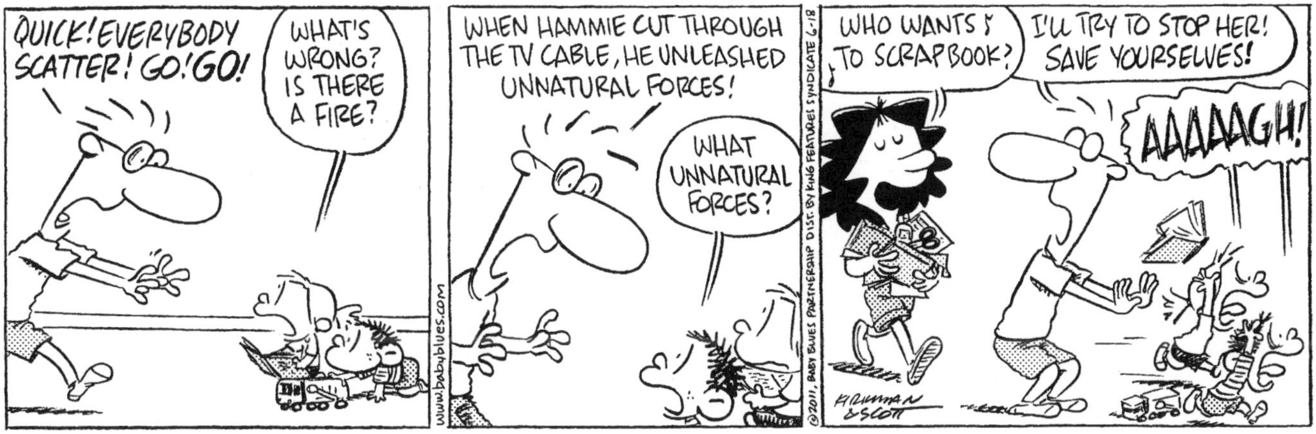
QUICK! EVERYBODY SCATTER! GO! GO!
WHAT'S WRONG? IS THERE A FIRE?
WHEN HAMMIE CUT THROUGH THE TV CABLE, HE UNLEASHED UNNATURAL FORCES!
WHAT UNNATURAL FORCES?
WHO WANTS TO SCRAPBOOK?
I'LL TRY TO STOP HER! SAVE YOURSELVES!
AAAAAGH!
www.babyblues.com
© 2011, BABY BLUES PARTNERSHIP DIST. BY KING FEATURES SYNDICATE 6-18
KIRKMAN & SCOTT

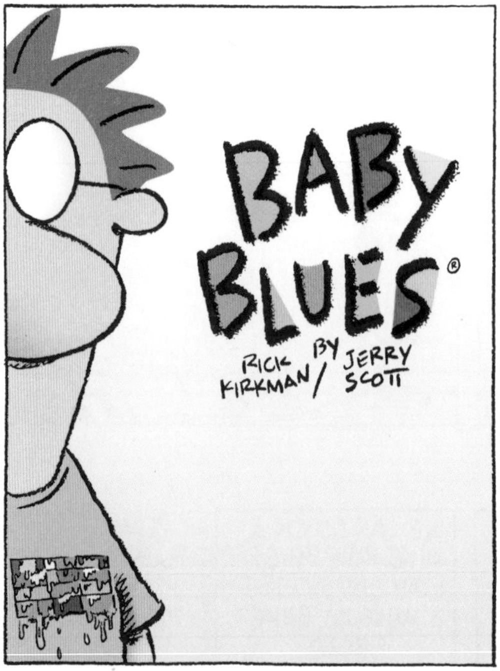
BABY BLUES®
BY RICK KIRKMAN / JERRY SCOTT

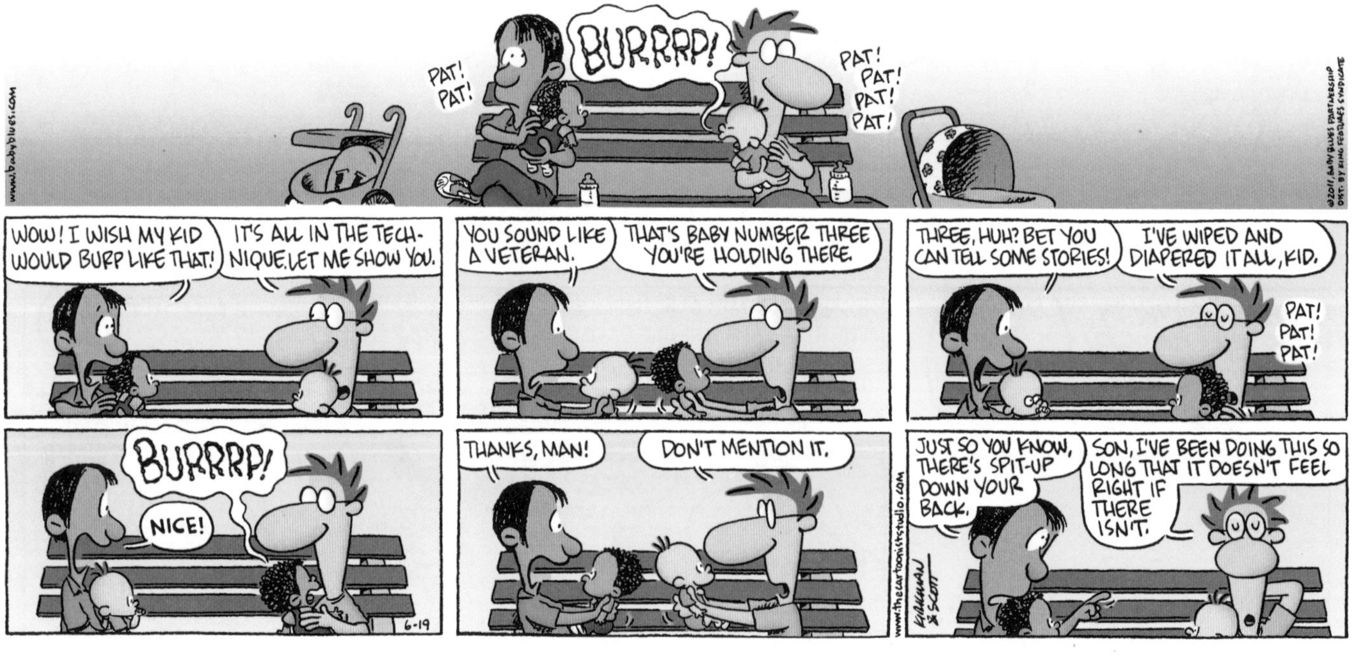
www.babyblues.com
PAT! PAT!
BURRRP!
PAT! PAT! PAT! PAT!
©2011, BABY BLUES PARTNERSHIP
DIST. BY KING FEATURES SYNDICATE
WOW! I WISH MY KID WOULD BURP LIKE THAT!
IT'S ALL IN THE TECH-NIQUE. LET ME SHOW YOU.
YOU SOUND LIKE A VETERAN.
THAT'S BABY NUMBER THREE YOU'RE HOLDING THERE.
THREE, HUH? BET YOU CAN TELL SOME STORIES!
I'VE WIPED AND DIAPERED IT ALL, KID.
PAT! PAT! PAT!
BURRRP!
NICE!
6-19
THANKS, MAN!
DON'T MENTION IT.
www.thecartooniststudio.com
KIRKMAN & SCOTT
JUST SO YOU KNOW, THERE'S SPIT-UP DOWN YOUR BACK.
SON, I'VE BEEN DOING THIS SO LONG THAT IT DOESN'T FEEL RIGHT IF THERE ISN'T.

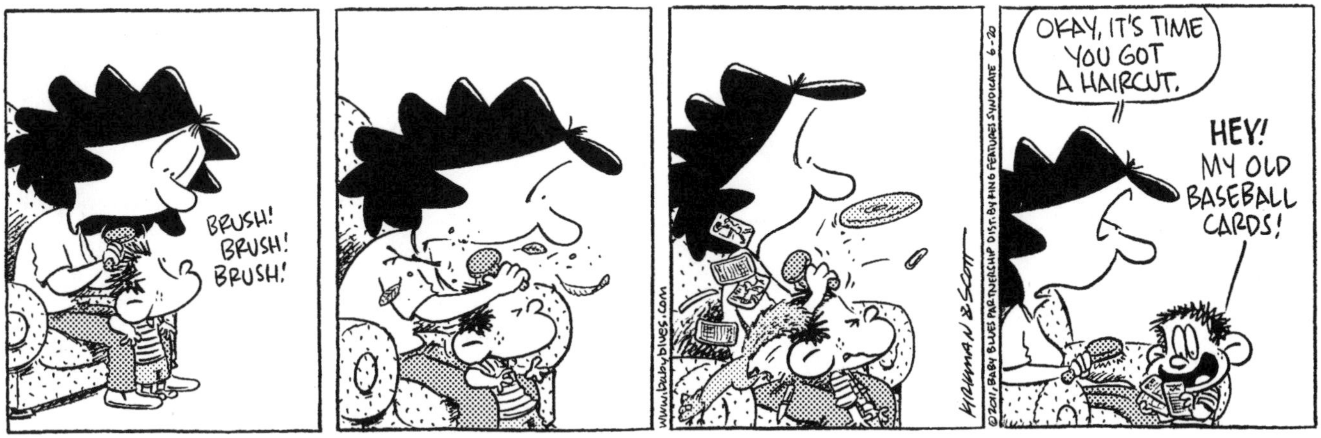
BRUSH! BRUSH! BRUSH!
www.babyblues.com
KIRKMAN & SCOTT
©2011, BABY BLUES PARTNERSHIP DIST. BY KING FEATURES SYNDICATE 6-20
OKAY, IT'S TIME YOU GOT A HAIRCUT.
HEY! MY OLD BASEBALL CARDS!

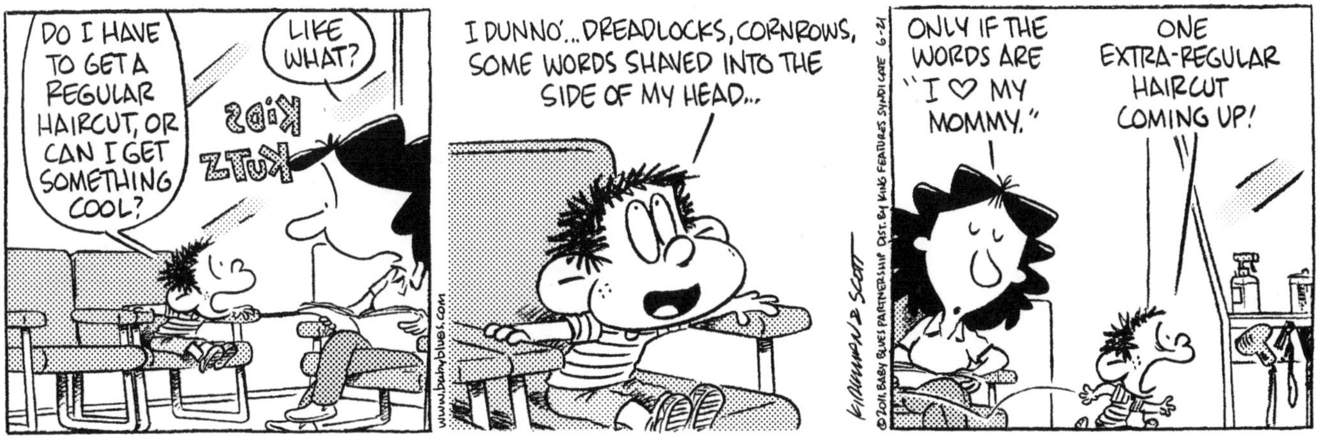
DO I HAVE TO GET A REGULAR HAIRCUT, OR CAN I GET SOMETHING COOL?
LIKE WHAT?
KIDS KUTZ
www.babyblues.com
I DUNNO'... DREADLOCKS, CORNROWS, SOME WORDS SHAVED INTO THE SIDE OF MY HEAD...
KIRKMAN & SCOTT
©2011, BABY BLUES PARTNERSHIP DIST. BY KING FEATURES SYNDICATE 6-21
ONLY IF THE WORDS ARE "I ♡ MY MOMMY."
ONE EXTRA-REGULAR HAIRCUT COMING UP!

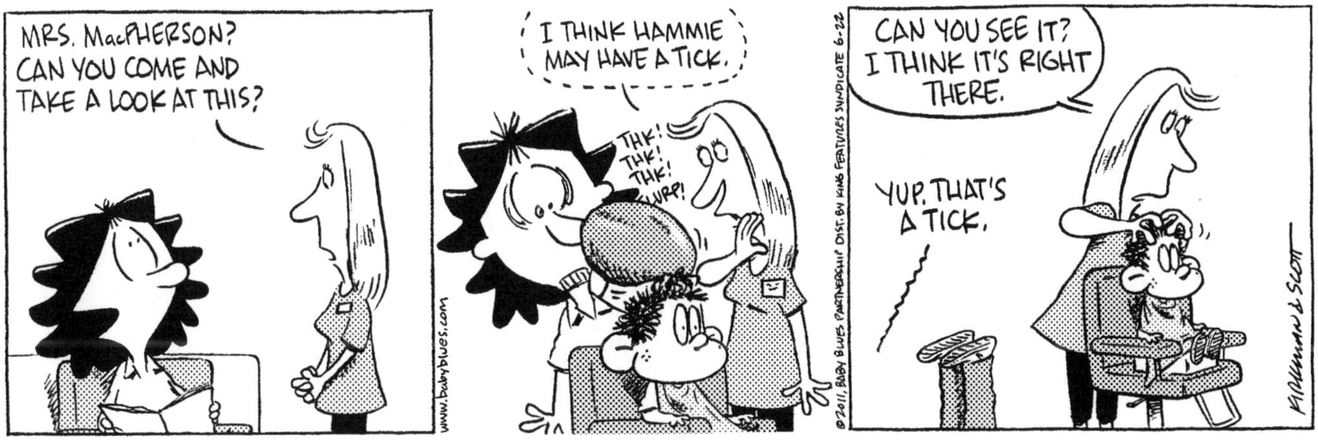
MRS. MacPHERSON? CAN YOU COME AND TAKE A LOOK AT THIS?
www.babyblues.com
I THINK HAMMIE MAY HAVE A TICK.
THK! THK! THK! SLURP!
©2011, BABY BLUES PARTNERSHIP DIST. BY KING FEATURES SYNDICATE 6-22
CAN YOU SEE IT? I THINK IT'S RIGHT THERE.
YUP. THAT'S A TICK.
KIRKMAN & SCOTT

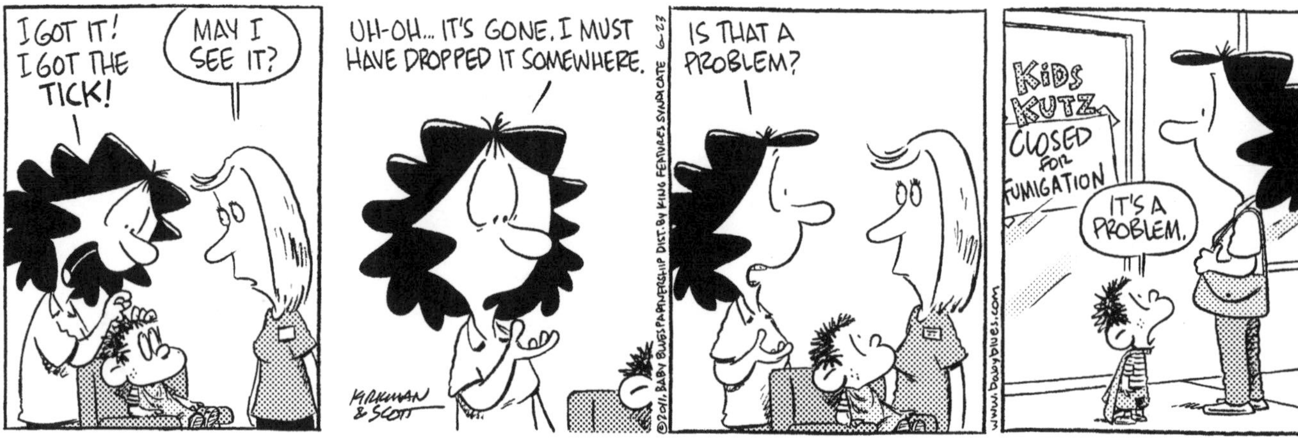
I GOT IT! I GOT THE TICK!
MAY I SEE IT?
UH-OH... IT'S GONE. I MUST HAVE DROPPED IT SOMEWHERE.
KIRKMAN & SCOTT
©2011, BABY BLUES PARTNERSHIP DIST. BY KING FEATURES SYNDICATE 6-23
IS THAT A PROBLEM?
KIDS KUTZ
CLOSED FOR FUMIGATION
IT'S A PROBLEM.
www.babyblues.com

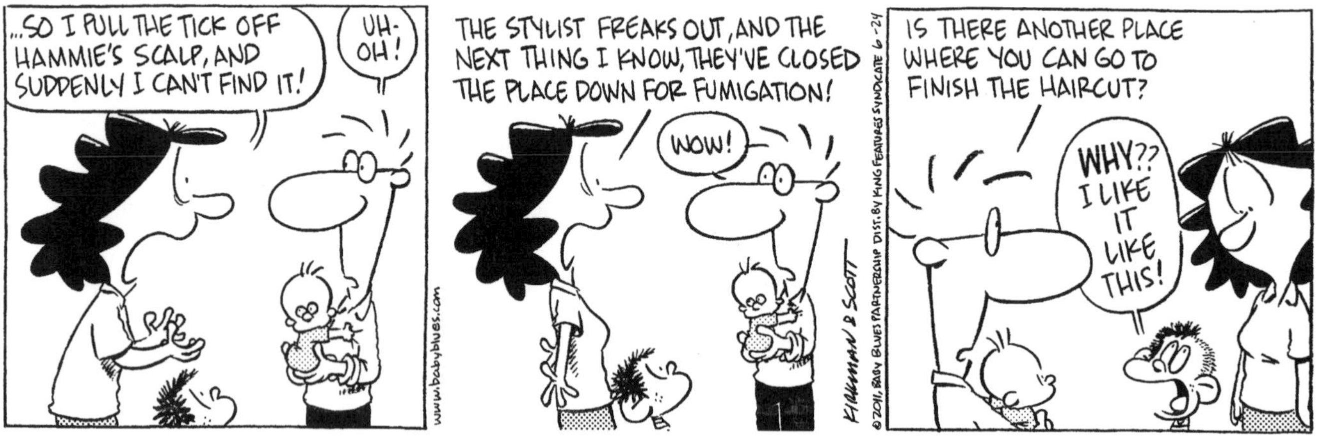
...SO I PULL THE TICK OFF HAMMIE'S SCALP, AND SUDDENLY I CAN'T FIND IT!
UH-OH!
www.babyblues.com
THE STYLIST FREAKS OUT, AND THE NEXT THING I KNOW, THEY'VE CLOSED THE PLACE DOWN FOR FUMIGATION!
WOW!
KIRKMAN & SCOTT
©2011, BABY BLUES PARTNERSHIP DIST. BY KING FEATURES SYNDICATE 6-24
IS THERE ANOTHER PLACE WHERE YOU CAN GO TO FINISH THE HAIRCUT?
WHY?? I LIKE IT LIKE THIS!

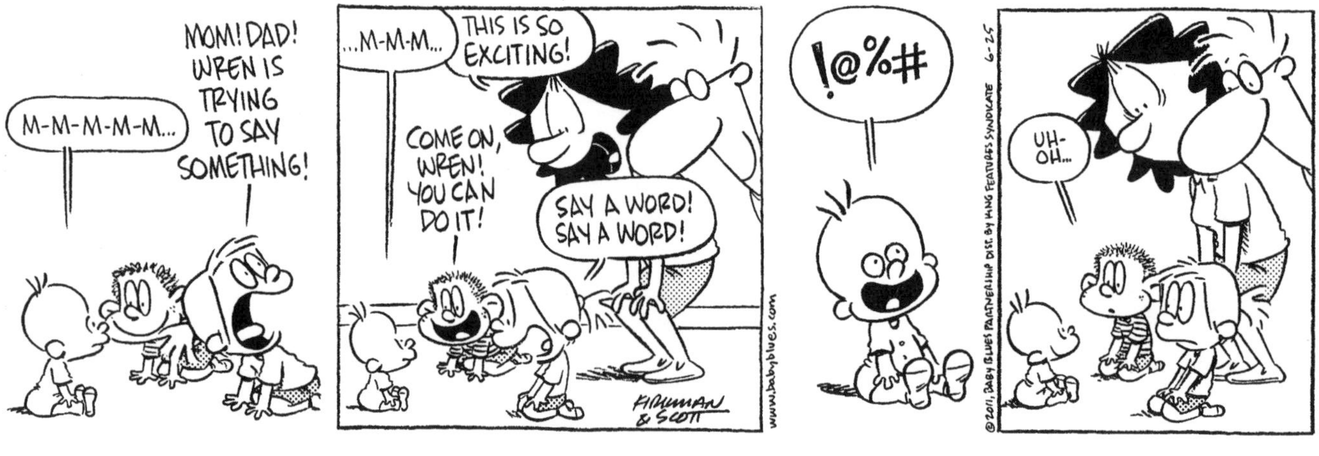
M-M-M-M-M...
MOM! DAD! WREN IS TRYING TO SAY SOMETHING!
...M-M-M...
THIS IS SO EXCITING!
COME ON, WREN! YOU CAN DO IT!
SAY A WORD! SAY A WORD!
KIRKMAN & SCOTT
www.babyblues.com
!@%#
©2011, BABY BLUES PARTNERSHIP DIST. BY KING FEATURES SYNDICATE 6-25
UH-OH...

BABY BLUES

BY RICK KIRKMAN & JERRY SCOTT

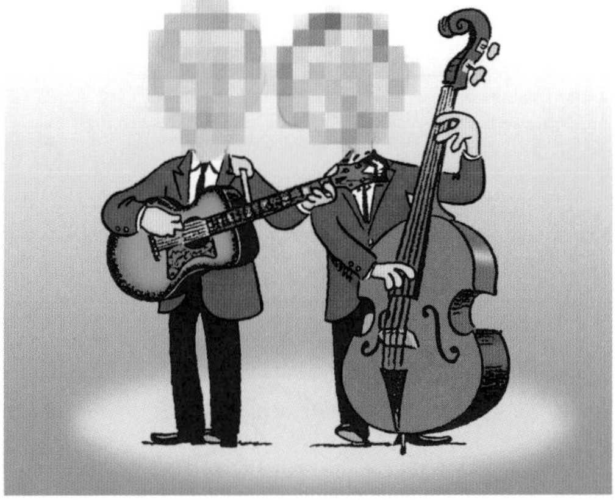

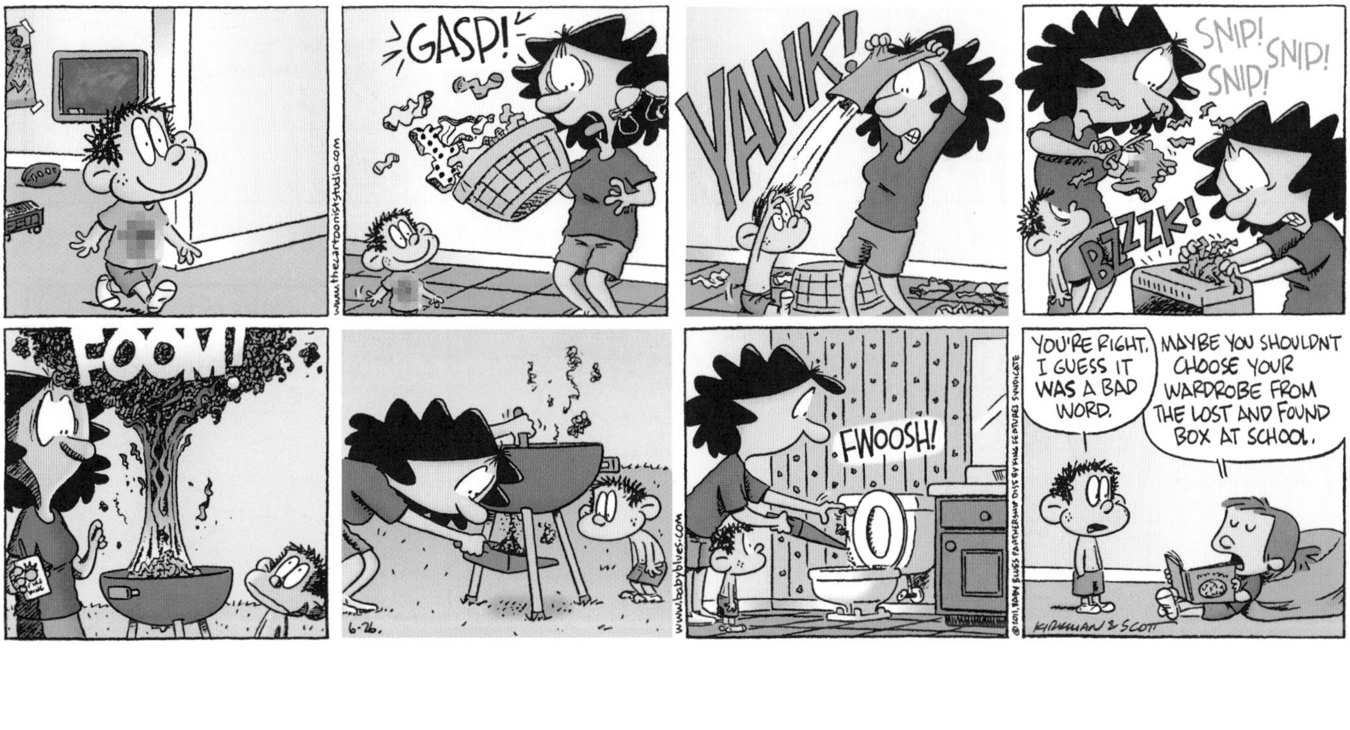
www.thecartoonistsstudio.com
GASP!
YANK!
SNIP! SNIP! SNIP!
BZZZK!
FOOM!
6-26.
www.babyblues.com
FWOOSH!
© 2011 BABY BLUES PARTNERSHIP DIST BY KING FEATURES SYNDICATE
YOU'RE RIGHT. I GUESS IT WAS A BAD WORD.
MAYBE YOU SHOULDN'T CHOOSE YOUR WARDROBE FROM THE LOST AND FOUND BOX AT SCHOOL.
KIRKMAN & SCOTT

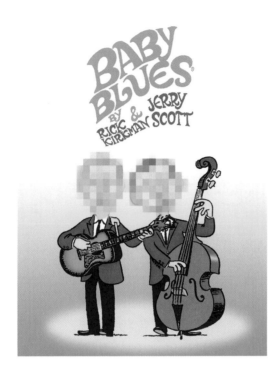

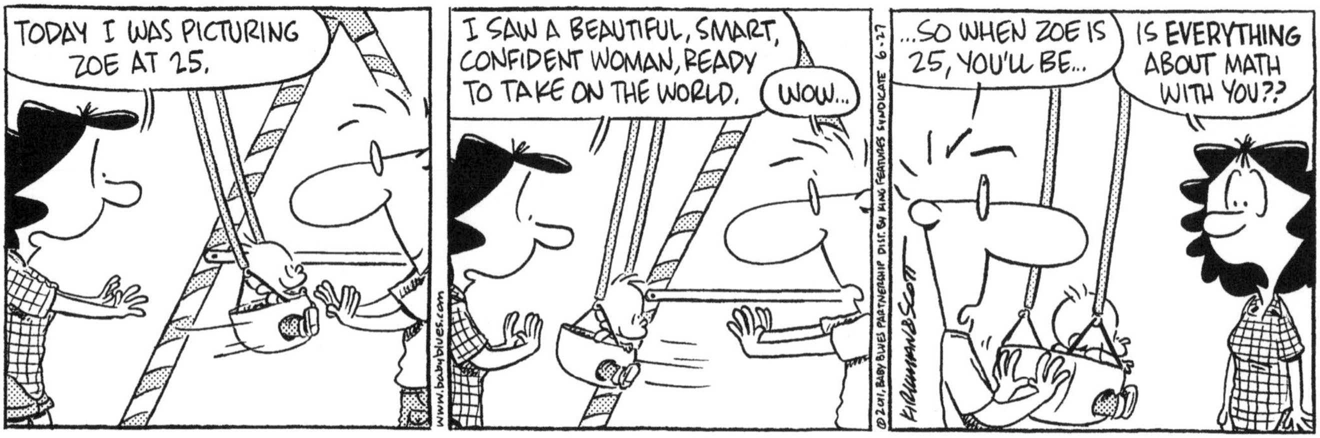
TODAY I WAS PICTURING ZOE AT 25.
I SAW A BEAUTIFUL, SMART, CONFIDENT WOMAN, READY TO TAKE ON THE WORLD.
WOW...
...SO WHEN ZOE IS 25, YOU'LL BE...
IS EVERYTHING ABOUT MATH WITH YOU??
www.babyblues.com
© 2011, BABY BLUES PARTNERSHIP DIST. BY KING FEATURES SYNDICATE 6-27
KIRKMAN & SCOTT

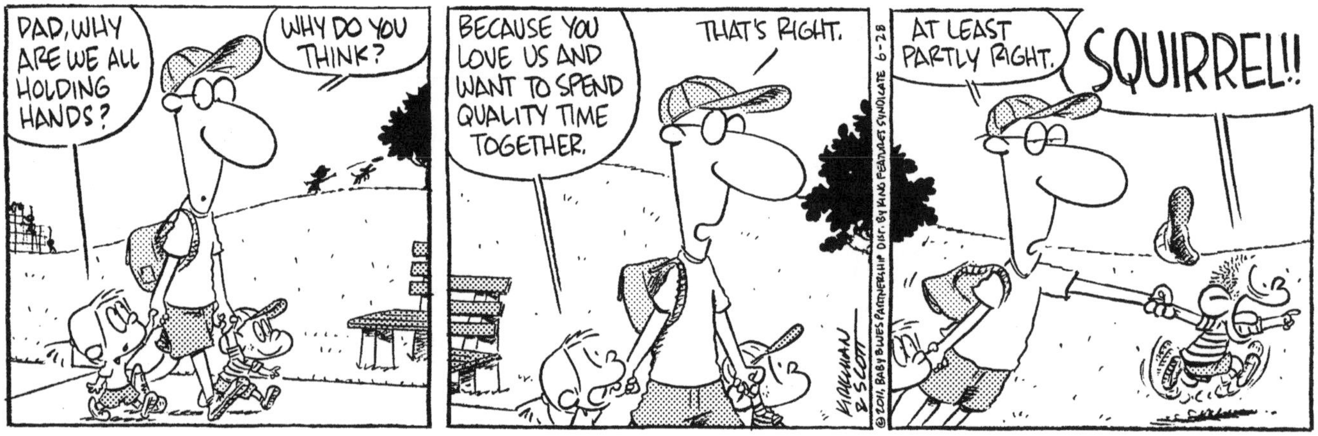
DAD, WHY ARE WE ALL HOLDING HANDS?
WHY DO YOU THINK?
BECAUSE YOU LOVE US AND WANT TO SPEND QUALITY TIME TOGETHER.
THAT'S RIGHT.
AT LEAST PARTLY RIGHT.
SQUIRREL!!
KIRKMAN & SCOTT
© 2011, BABY BLUES PARTNERSHIP DIST. BY KING FEATURES SYNDICATE 6-28

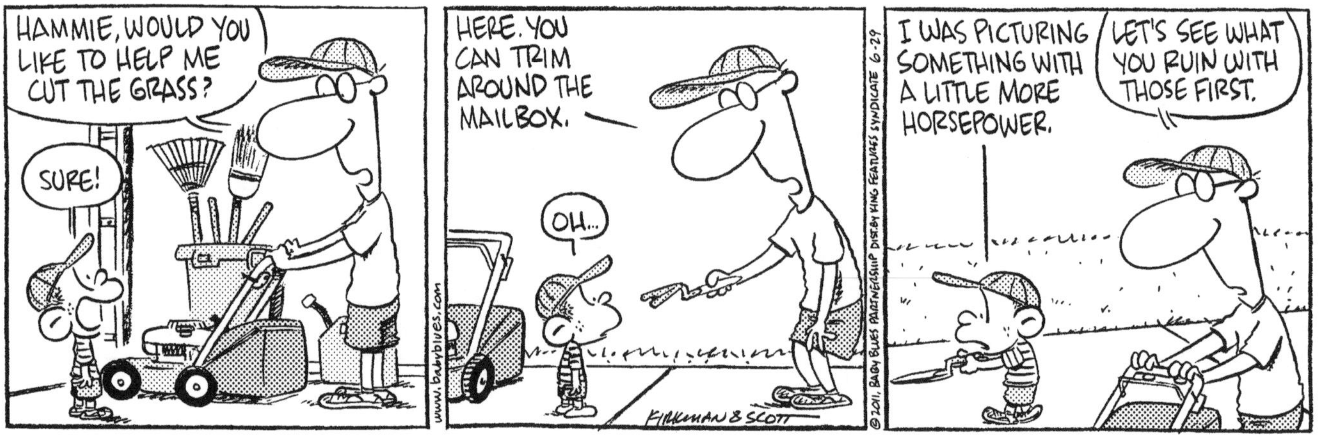
HAMMIE, WOULD YOU LIKE TO HELP ME CUT THE GRASS?
SURE!
HERE. YOU CAN TRIM AROUND THE MAILBOX.
OH...
I WAS PICTURING SOMETHING WITH A LITTLE MORE HORSEPOWER.
LET'S SEE WHAT YOU RUIN WITH THOSE FIRST.
www.babyblues.com
KIRKMAN & SCOTT
© 2011, BABY BLUES PARTNERSHIP DIST. BY KING FEATURES SYNDICATE 6-29

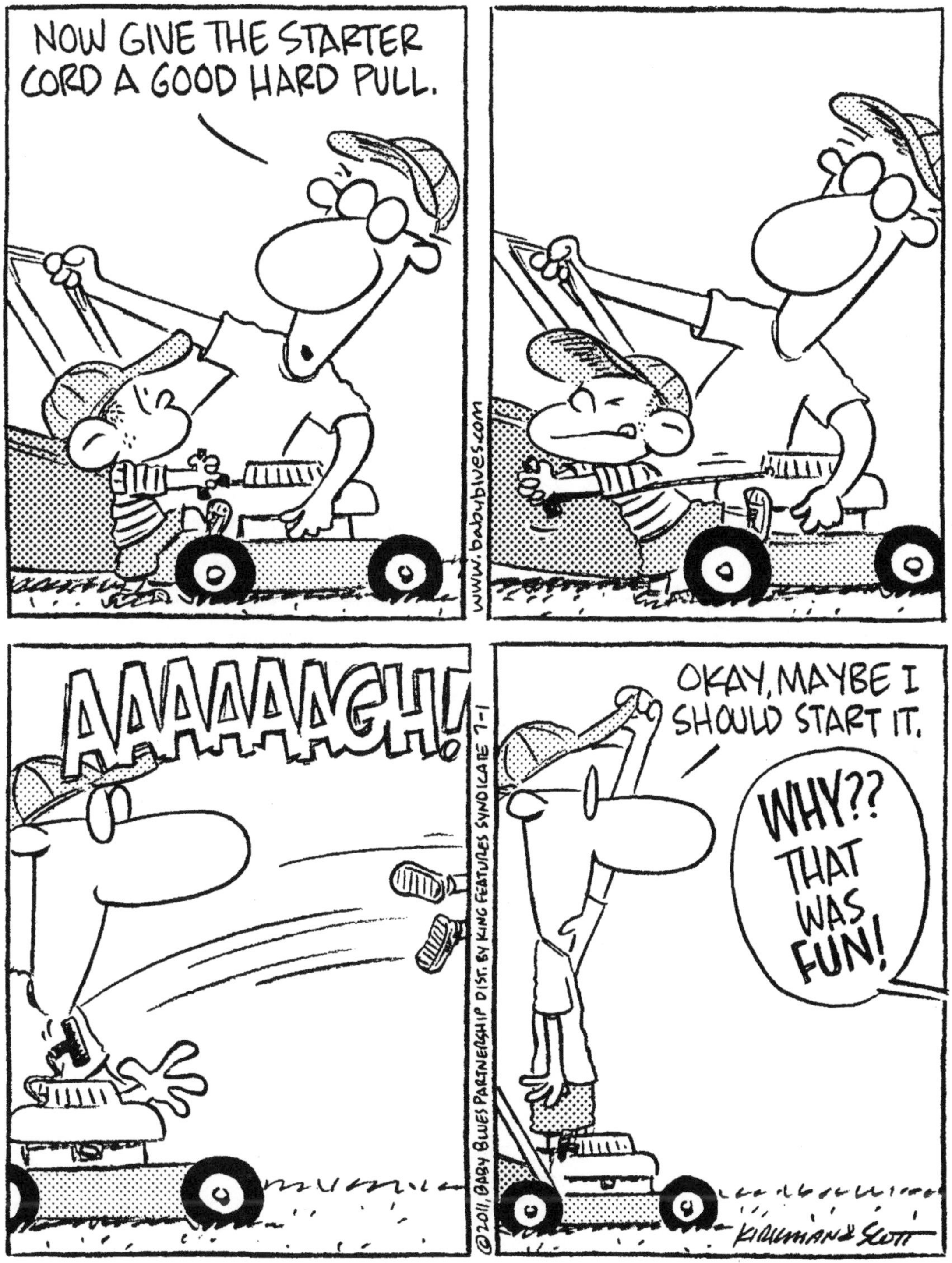
NOW GIVE THE STARTER CORD A GOOD HARD PULL.
www.babyblues.com
AAAAAAGH!
©2011, BABY BLUES PARTNERSHIP DIST. BY KING FEATURES SYNDICATE 7-1
OKAY, MAYBE I SHOULD START IT.
WHY?? THAT WAS FUN!
KIRKMAN & SCOTT

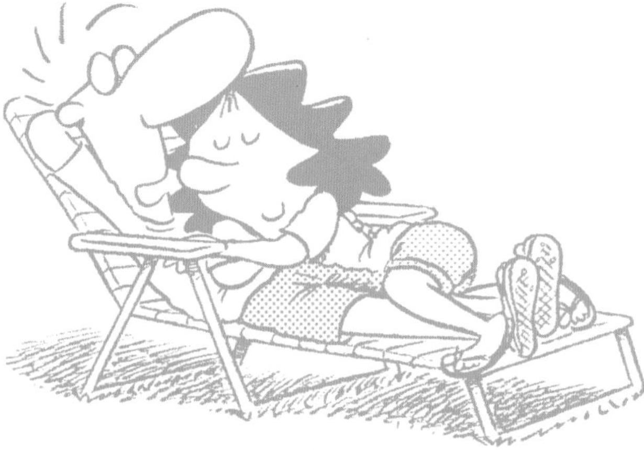

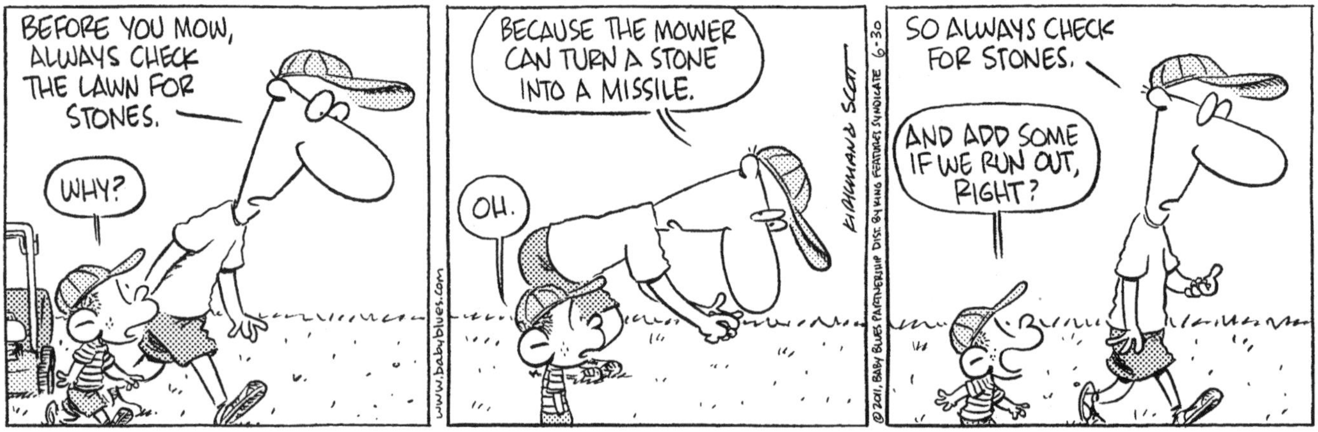
BEFORE YOU MOW, ALWAYS CHECK THE LAWN FOR STONES.
WHY?
BECAUSE THE MOWER CAN TURN A STONE INTO A MISSILE.
OH.
SO ALWAYS CHECK FOR STONES.
AND ADD SOME IF WE RUN OUT, RIGHT?
www.babyblues.com
KIRKMAN & SCOTT
©2011, BABY BLUES PARTNERSHIP DIST. BY KING FEATURES SYNDICATE 6-30

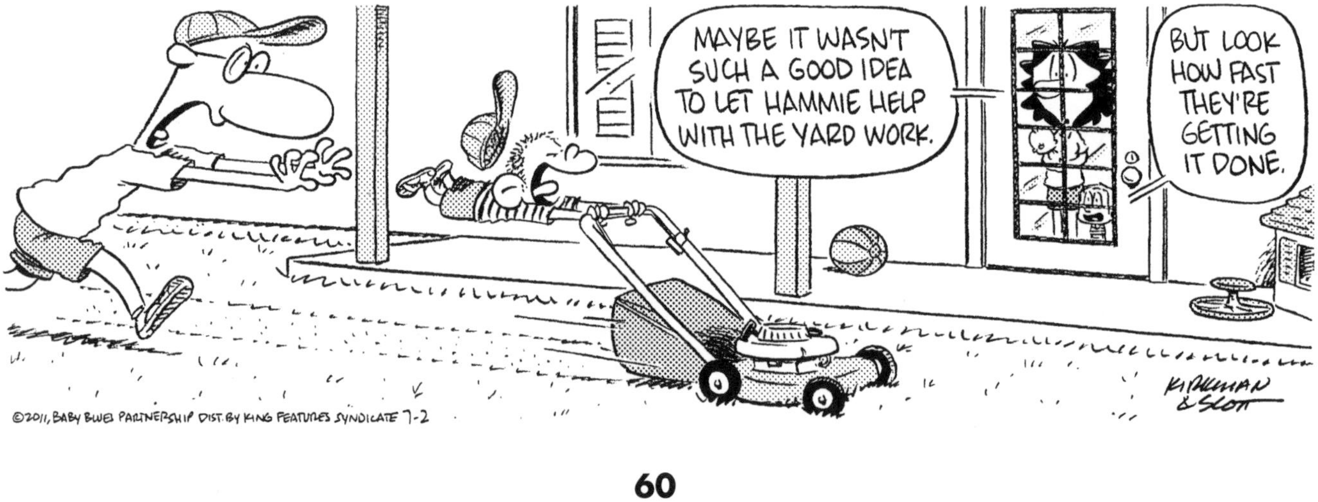
MAYBE IT WASN'T SUCH A GOOD IDEA TO LET HAMMIE HELP WITH THE YARD WORK.
BUT LOOK HOW FAST THEY'RE GETTING IT DONE.
KIRKMAN & SCOTT
©2011, BABY BLUES PARTNERSHIP DIST. BY KING FEATURES SYNDICATE 7-2

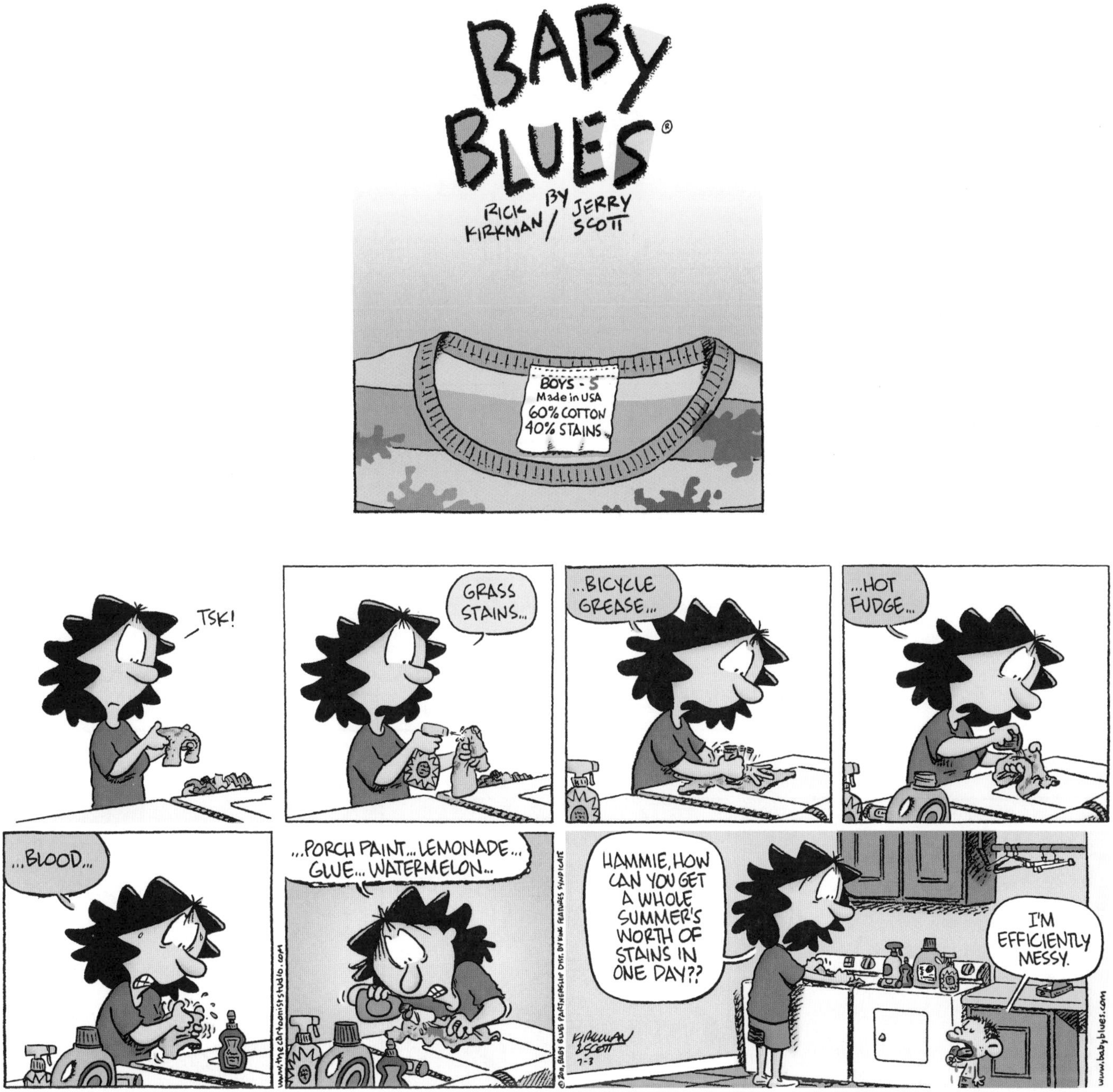
BABY BLUES®
BY RICK KIRKMAN / JERRY SCOTT
BOYS - 5
Made in USA
60% COTTON
40% STAINS
TSK!
GRASS STAINS...
...BICYCLE GREASE...
...HOT FUDGE...
...BLOOD...
...PORCH PAINT... LEMONADE... GLUE... WATERMELON...
HAMMIE, HOW CAN YOU GET A WHOLE SUMMER'S WORTH OF STAINS IN ONE DAY??
I'M EFFICIENTLY MESSY.
KIRKMAN & SCOTT 7-3
www.thecartoonistsstudio.com
© 2011, BABY BLUES PARTNERSHIP DIST. BY KING FEATURES SYNDICATE
www.babyblues.com

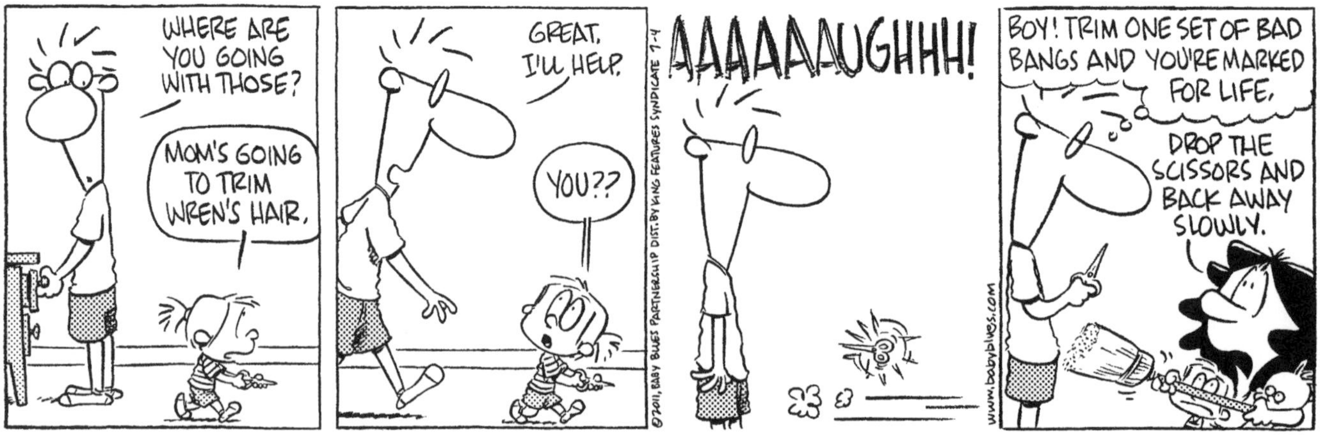
WHERE ARE YOU GOING WITH THOSE?
MOM'S GOING TO TRIM WREN'S HAIR.
GREAT. I'LL HELP.
YOU??
© 2011, BABY BLUES PARTNERSHIP DIST. BY KING FEATURES SYNDICATE 7-4
AAAAAAUGHHH!
BOY! TRIM ONE SET OF BAD BANGS AND YOU'RE MARKED FOR LIFE.
DROP THE SCISSORS AND BACK AWAY SLOWLY.
www.babyblues.com

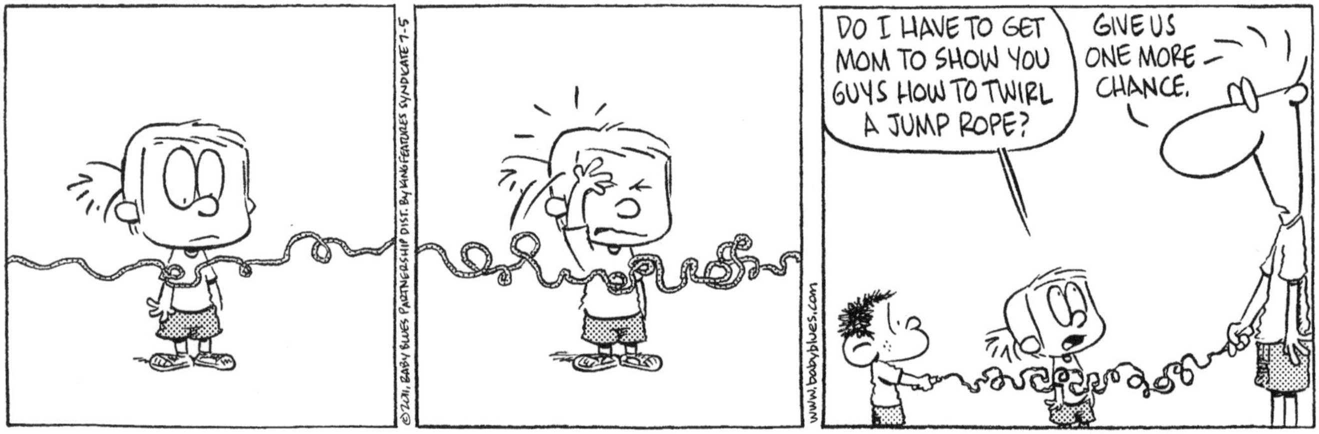
© 2011, BABY BLUES PARTNERSHIP DIST. BY KING FEATURES SYNDICATE 7-5
www.babyblues.com
DO I HAVE TO GET MOM TO SHOW YOU GUYS HOW TO TWIRL A JUMP ROPE?
GIVE US ONE MORE CHANCE.

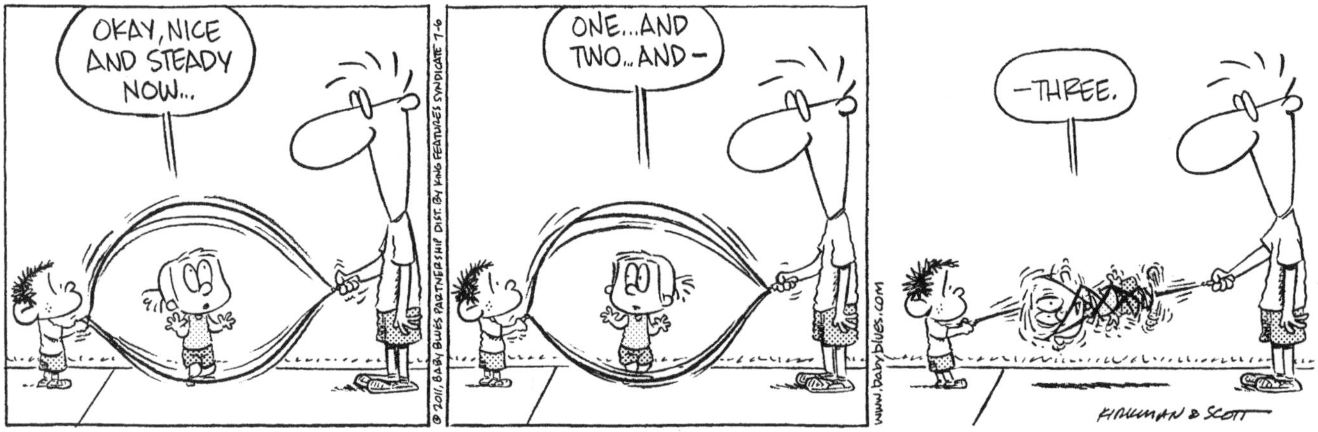
OKAY, NICE AND STEADY NOW...
© 2011, BABY BLUES PARTNERSHIP DIST. BY KING FEATURES SYNDICATE 7-6
ONE...AND TWO...AND–
www.babyblues.com
–THREE.
KIRKMAN & SCOTT

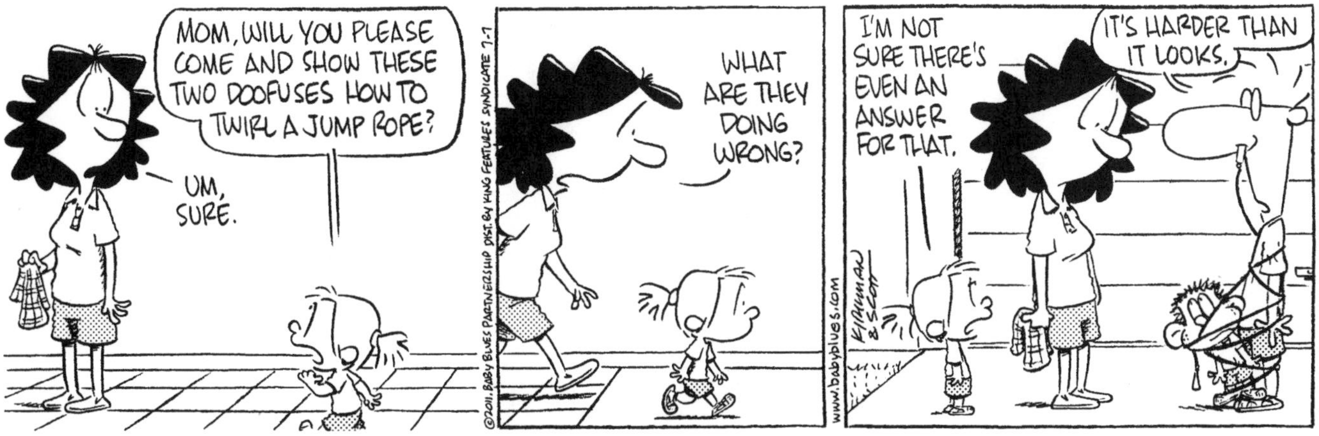
MOM, WILL YOU PLEASE COME AND SHOW THESE TWO DOOFUSES HOW TO TWIRL A JUMP ROPE?
UM, SURE.
WHAT ARE THEY DOING WRONG?
I'M NOT SURE THERE'S EVEN AN ANSWER FOR THAT.
IT'S HARDER THAN IT LOOKS.
©2011, BABY BLUES PARTNERSHIP DIST. BY KING FEATURES SYNDICATE 7-7
KIRKMAN & SCOTT
www.babyblues.com

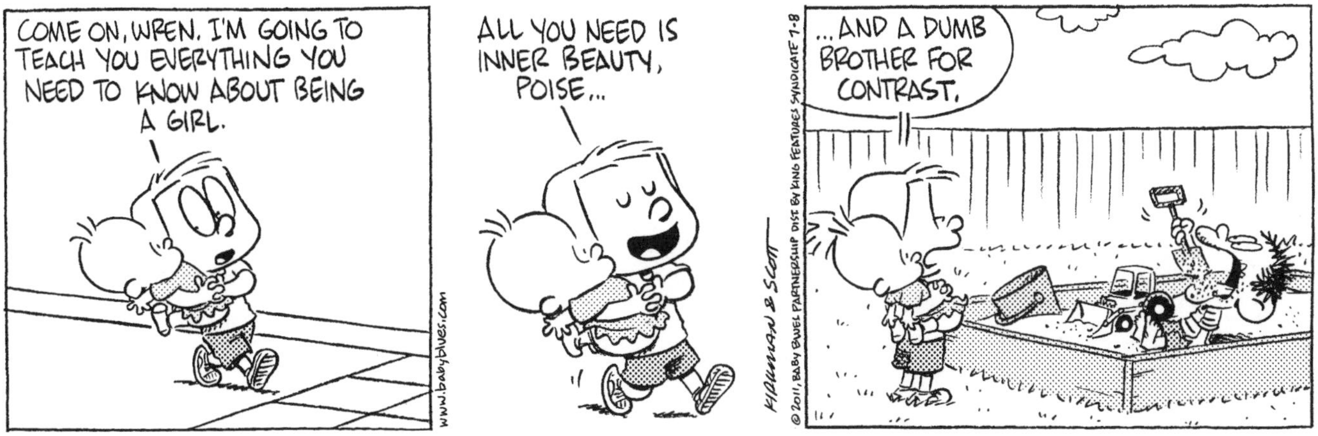
COME ON, WREN. I'M GOING TO TEACH YOU EVERYTHING YOU NEED TO KNOW ABOUT BEING A GIRL.
ALL YOU NEED IS INNER BEAUTY, POISE...
...AND A DUMB BROTHER FOR CONTRAST.
www.babyblues.com
KIRKMAN & SCOTT
©2011, BABY BLUES PARTNERSHIP DIST. BY KING FEATURES SYNDICATE 7-8

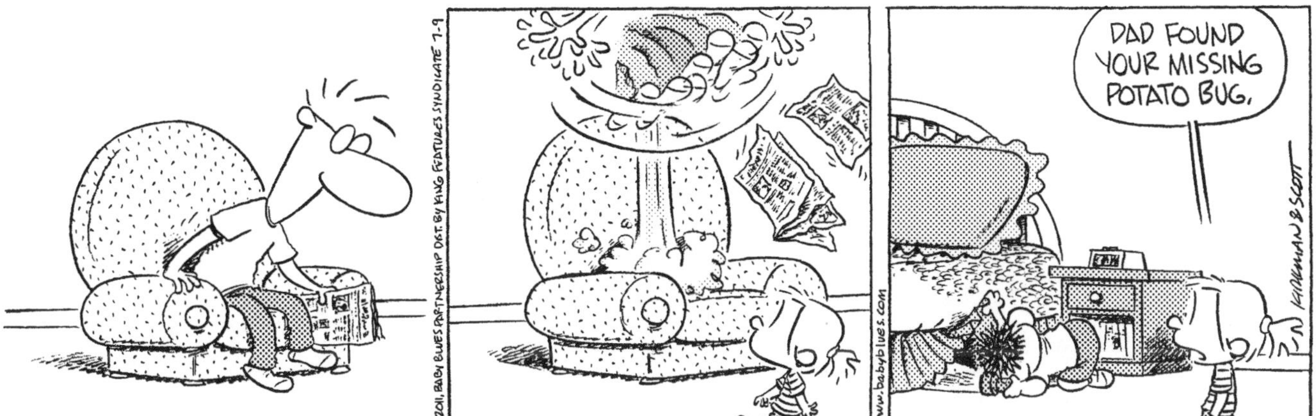
©2011, BABY BLUES PARTNERSHIP DIST. BY KING FEATURES SYNDICATE 7-9
www.babyblues.com
DAD FOUND YOUR MISSING POTATO BUG.
KIRKMAN & SCOTT

BABY BLUES®
BY RICK KIRKMAN / JERRY SCOTT

ARRGH!
WHOOSH!
OOF!
WELL, THAT DAY AT THE BEACH WAS NO DAY AT THE BEACH.
KIRKMAN & SCOTT 7-10
©2011 BABY BLUES PARTNERSHIP DIST. BY KING FEATURES SYNDICATE
www.babyblues.com
thecartoonistsstudio.com

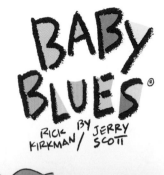

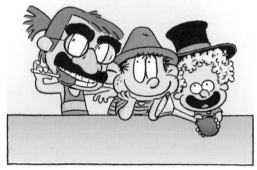

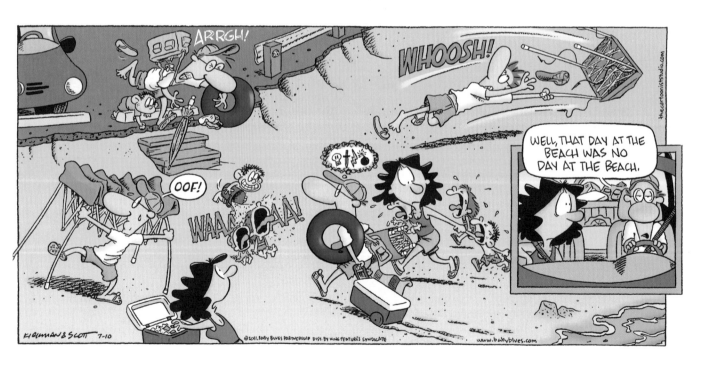

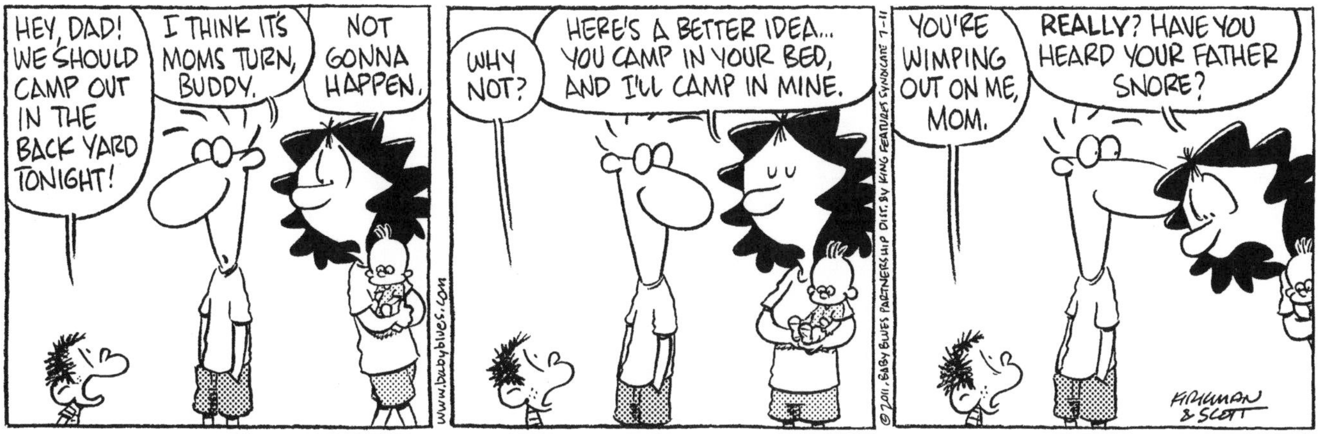
HEY, DAD! WE SHOULD CAMP OUT IN THE BACK YARD TONIGHT!
I THINK IT'S MOMS TURN, BUDDY.
NOT GONNA HAPPEN.
www.babyblues.com
WHY NOT?
HERE'S A BETTER IDEA... YOU CAMP IN YOUR BED, AND I'LL CAMP IN MINE.
©2011, BABY BLUES PARTNERSHIP DIST. BY KING FEATURES SYNDICATE 7-11
YOU'RE WIMPING OUT ON ME, MOM.
REALLY? HAVE YOU HEARD YOUR FATHER SNORE?
KIRKMAN & SCOTT

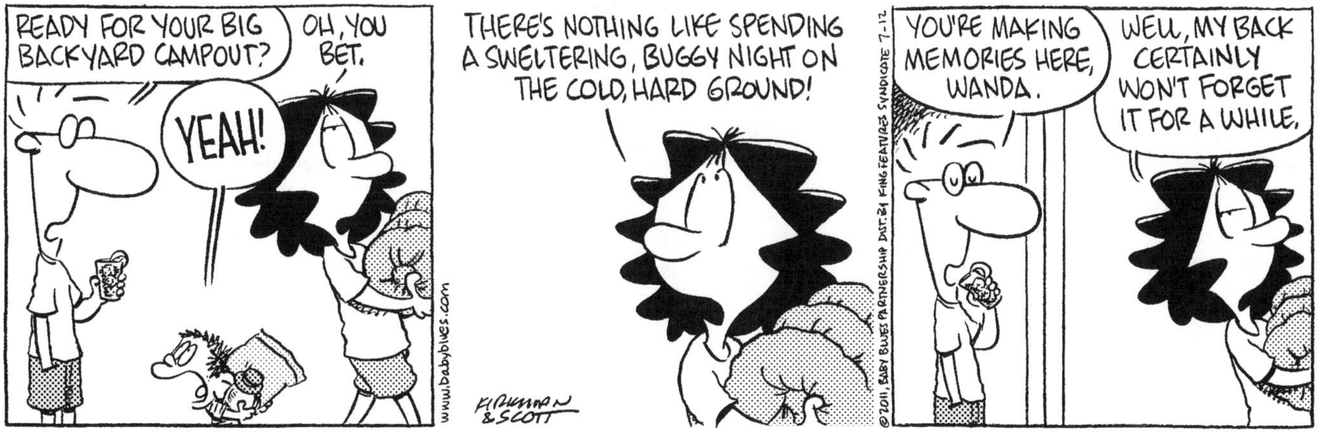
READY FOR YOUR BIG BACKYARD CAMPOUT?
OH, YOU BET.
YEAH!
www.babyblues.com
THERE'S NOTHING LIKE SPENDING A SWELTERING, BUGGY NIGHT ON THE COLD, HARD GROUND!
KIRKMAN & SCOTT
©2011, BABY BLUES PARTNERSHIP DIST. BY KING FEATURES SYNDICATE 7-12
YOU'RE MAKING MEMORIES HERE, WANDA.
WELL, MY BACK CERTAINLY WON'T FORGET IT FOR A WHILE.

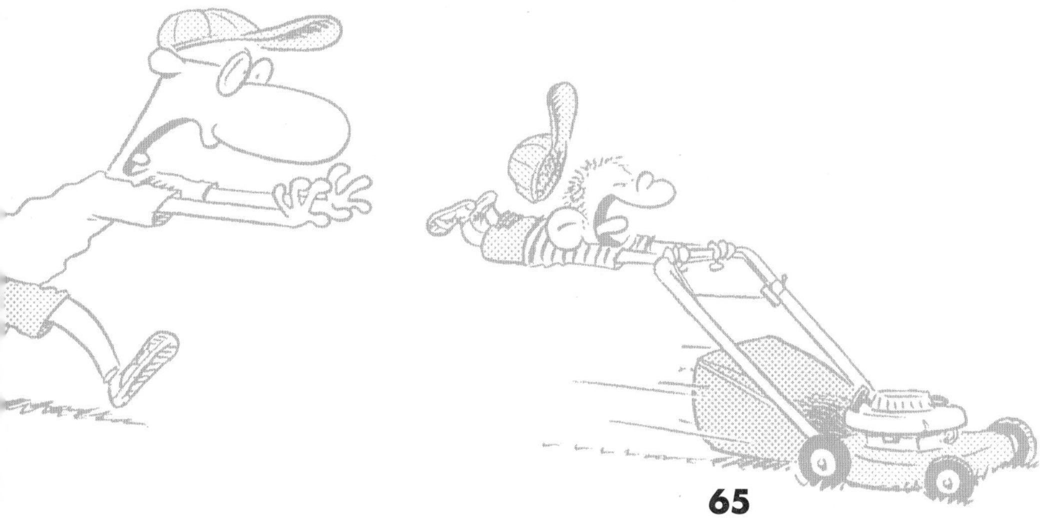

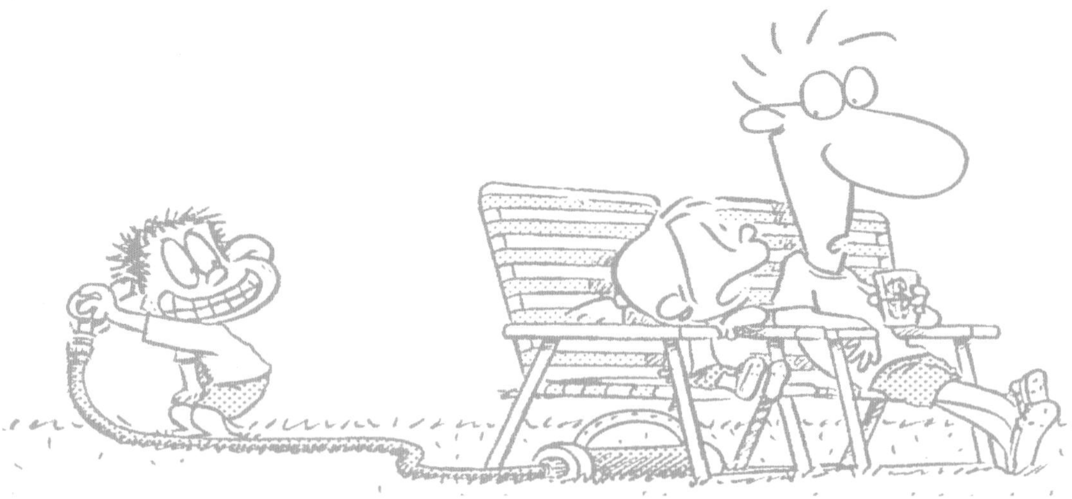

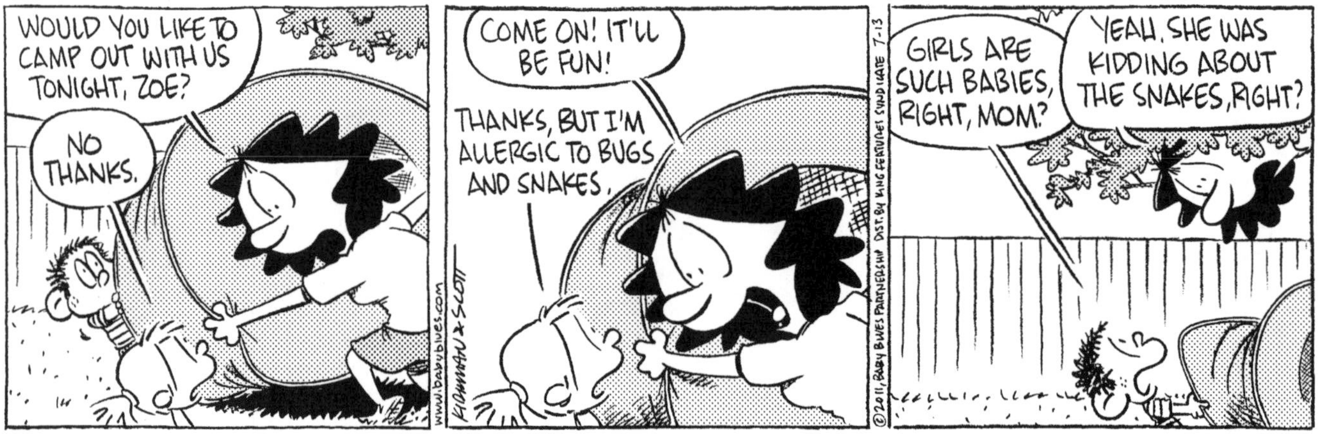
WOULD YOU LIKE TO CAMP OUT WITH US TONIGHT, ZOE?
NO THANKS.
www.babyblues.com
KIRKMAN & SCOTT
COME ON! IT'LL BE FUN!
THANKS, BUT I'M ALLERGIC TO BUGS AND SNAKES.
7-13
© 2011, BABY BLUES PARTNERSHIP DIST. BY KING FEATURES SYNDICATE
GIRLS ARE SUCH BABIES, RIGHT, MOM?
YEAH. SHE WAS KIDDING ABOUT THE SNAKES, RIGHT?

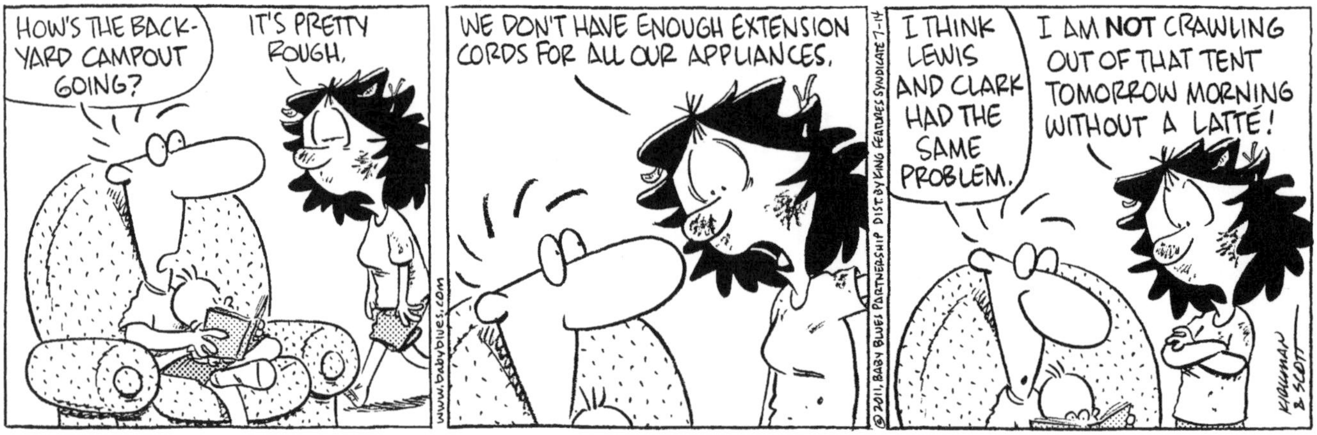
HOW'S THE BACK-YARD CAMPOUT GOING?
IT'S PRETTY ROUGH.
www.babyblues.com
WE DON'T HAVE ENOUGH EXTENSION CORDS FOR ALL OUR APPLIANCES.
7-14
© 2011, BABY BLUES PARTNERSHIP DIST. BY KING FEATURES SYNDICATE
I THINK LEWIS AND CLARK HAD THE SAME PROBLEM.
I AM NOT CRAWLING OUT OF THAT TENT TOMORROW MORNING WITHOUT A LATTÉ!
KIRKMAN & SCOTT

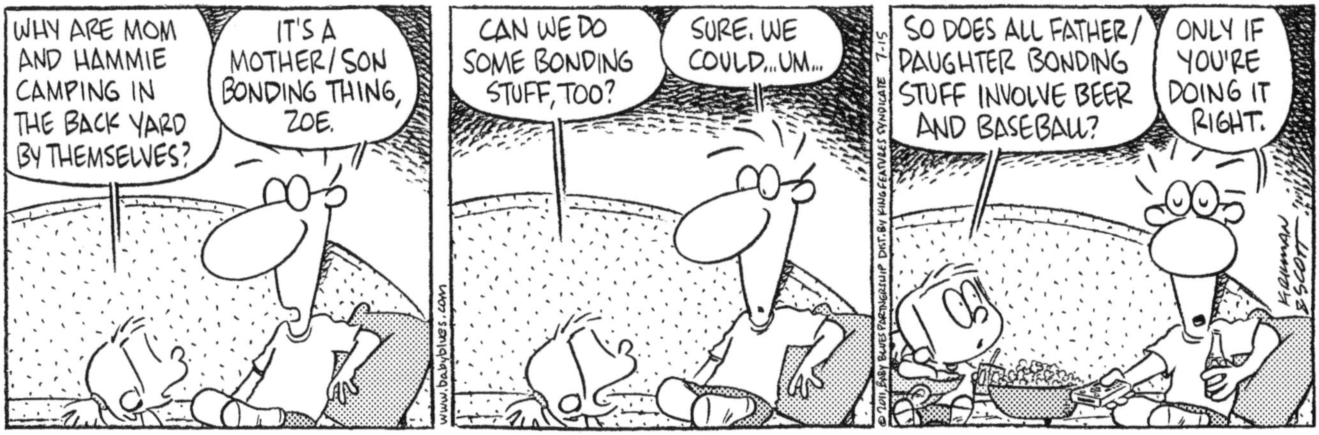
WHY ARE MOM AND HAMMIE CAMPING IN THE BACK YARD BY THEMSELVES?
IT'S A MOTHER/SON BONDING THING, ZOE.
CAN WE DO SOME BONDING STUFF, TOO?
SURE. WE COULD...UM...
SO DOES ALL FATHER/DAUGHTER BONDING STUFF INVOLVE BEER AND BASEBALL?
ONLY IF YOU'RE DOING IT RIGHT.
www.babyblues.com
©2011, BABY BLUES PARTNERSHIP DIST. BY KING FEATURES SYNDICATE
7-15
KIRKMAN & SCOTT

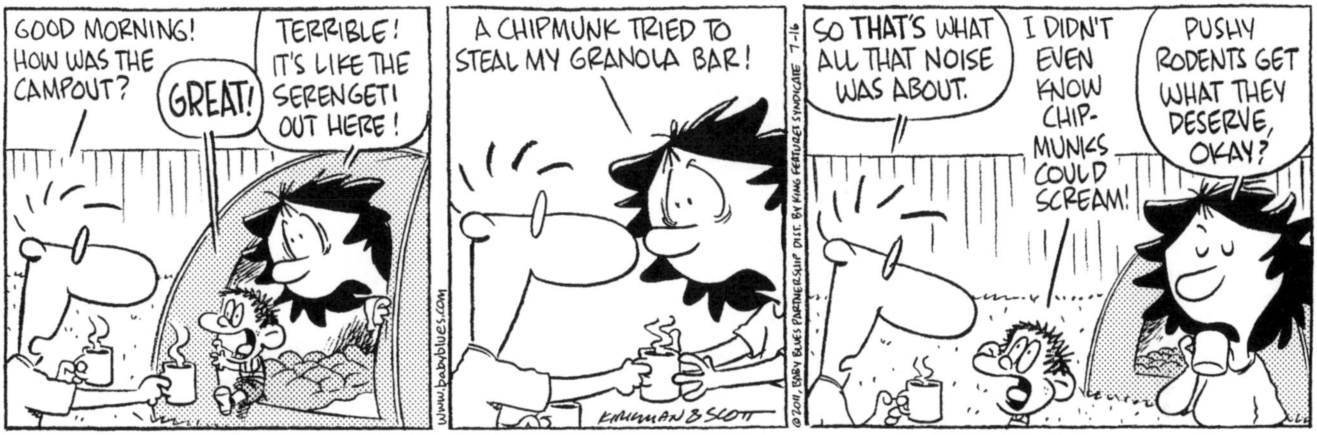
GOOD MORNING! HOW WAS THE CAMPOUT?
GREAT!
TERRIBLE! IT'S LIKE THE SERENGETI OUT HERE!
A CHIPMUNK TRIED TO STEAL MY GRANOLA BAR!
SO THAT'S WHAT ALL THAT NOISE WAS ABOUT.
I DIDN'T EVEN KNOW CHIPMUNKS COULD SCREAM!
PUSHY RODENTS GET WHAT THEY DESERVE, OKAY?
www.babyblues.com
©2011, BABY BLUES PARTNERSHIP DIST. BY KING FEATURES SYNDICATE
7-16
KIRKMAN & SCOTT

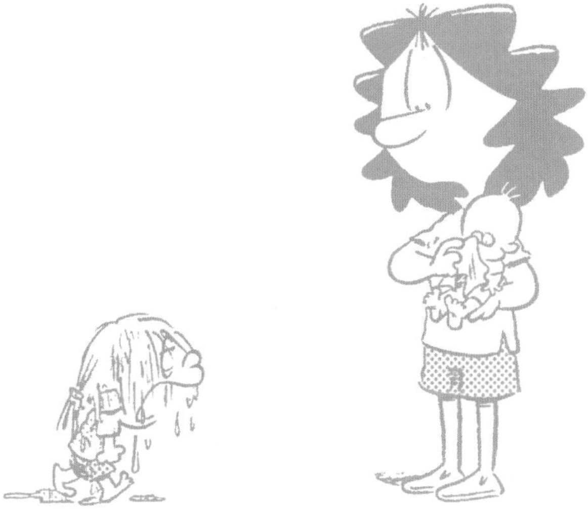

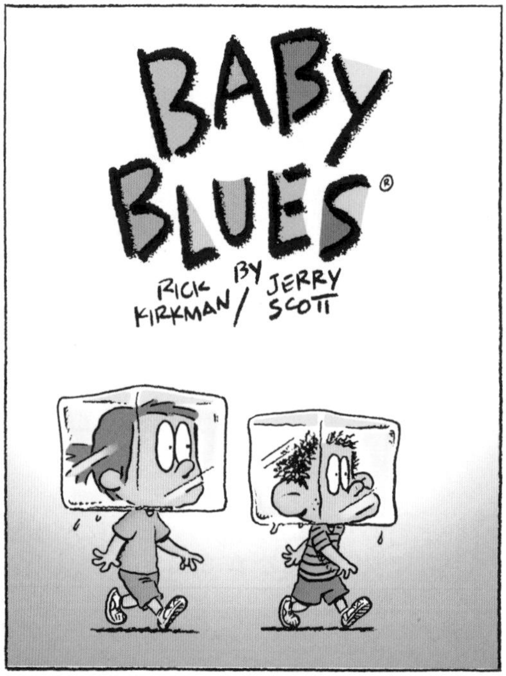
BABY BLUES®
BY RICK KIRKMAN / JERRY SCOTT

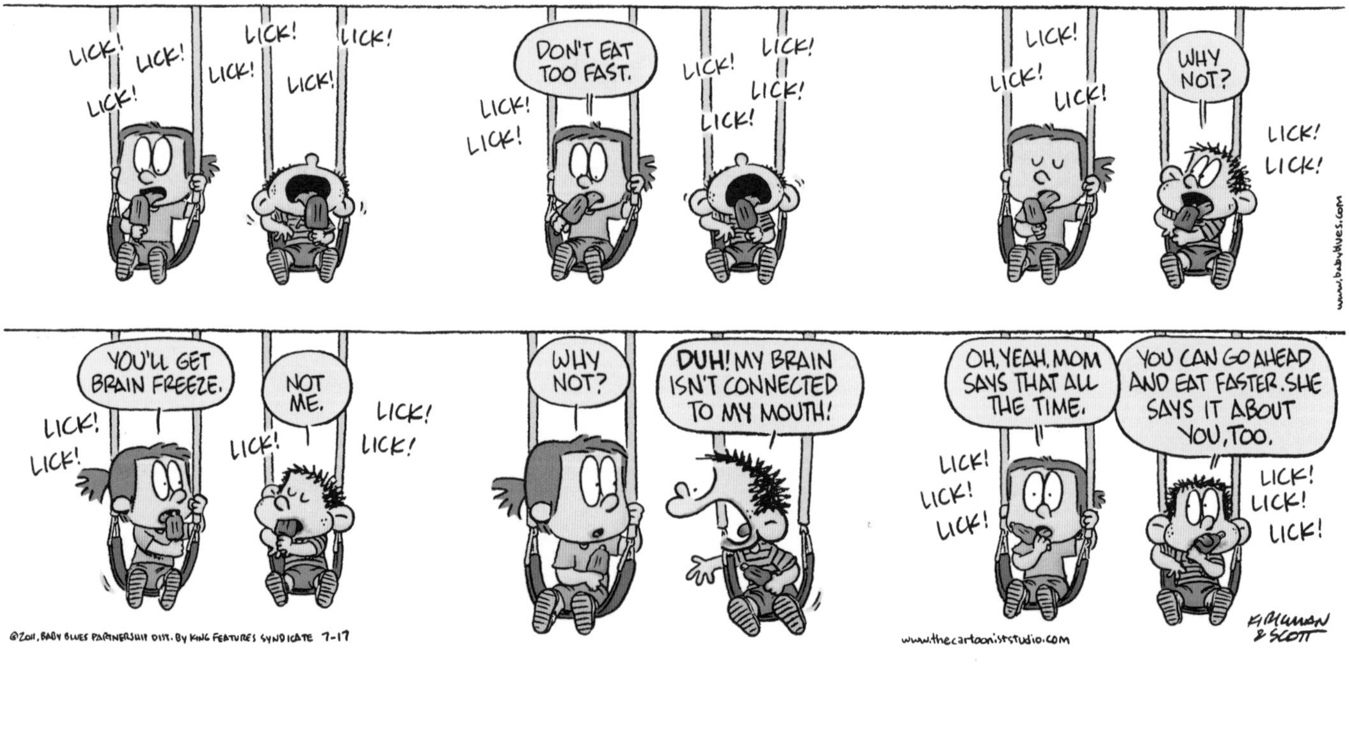
LICK! LICK! LICK!
LICK! LICK! LICK!
LICK! LICK!
DON'T EAT TOO FAST.
LICK! LICK! LICK! LICK!
LICK! LICK! LICK!
WHY NOT?
LICK! LICK!
www.babyblues.com
LICK! LICK!
YOU'LL GET BRAIN FREEZE.
LICK!
NOT ME.
LICK! LICK!
WHY NOT?
DUH! MY BRAIN ISN'T CONNECTED TO MY MOUTH!
LICK! LICK! LICK!
OH, YEAH, MOM SAYS THAT ALL THE TIME.
YOU CAN GO AHEAD AND EAT FASTER. SHE SAYS IT ABOUT YOU, TOO.
LICK! LICK! LICK!
©2011, BABY BLUES PARTNERSHIP DIST. BY KING FEATURES SYNDICATE 7-17
www.thecartoonistsstudio.com
KIRKMAN & SCOTT

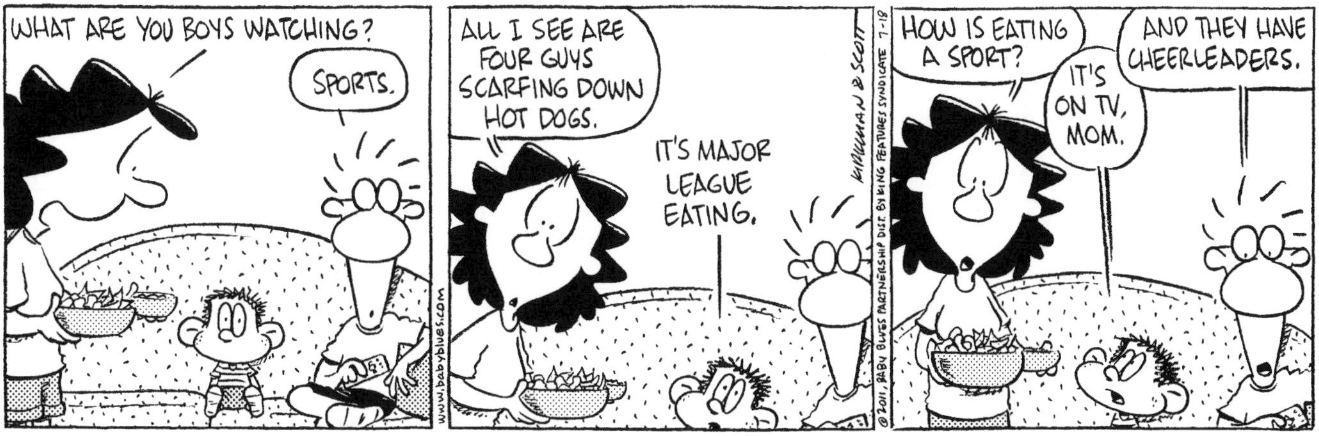
WHAT ARE YOU BOYS WATCHING?
SPORTS.
ALL I SEE ARE FOUR GUYS SCARFING DOWN HOT DOGS.
IT'S MAJOR LEAGUE EATING.
HOW IS EATING A SPORT?
IT'S ON TV, MOM.
AND THEY HAVE CHEERLEADERS.

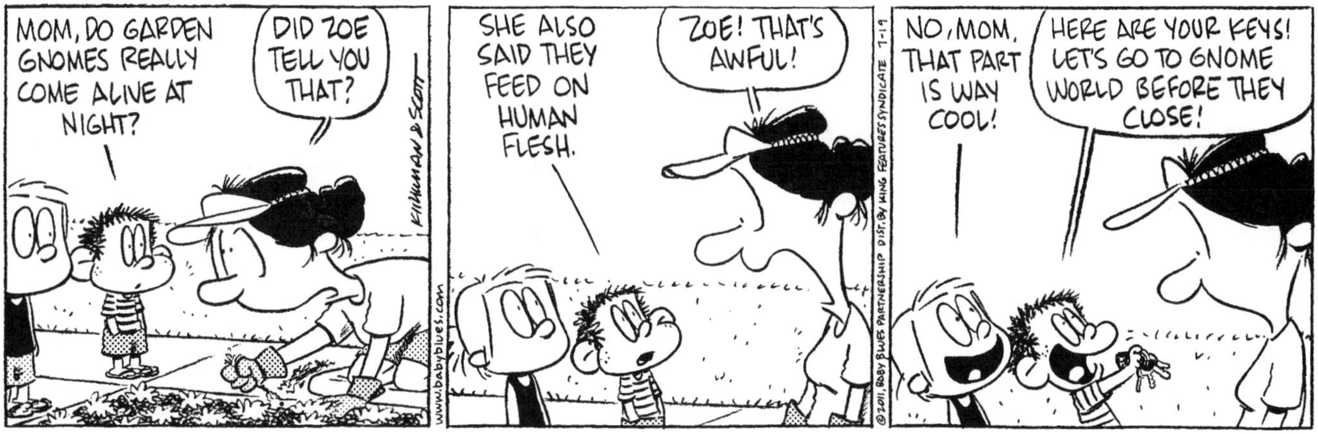
MOM, DO GARDEN GNOMES REALLY COME ALIVE AT NIGHT?
DID ZOE TELL YOU THAT?
SHE ALSO SAID THEY FEED ON HUMAN FLESH.
ZOE! THAT'S AWFUL!
NO, MOM. THAT PART IS WAY COOL!
HERE ARE YOUR KEYS! LET'S GO TO GNOME WORLD BEFORE THEY CLOSE!

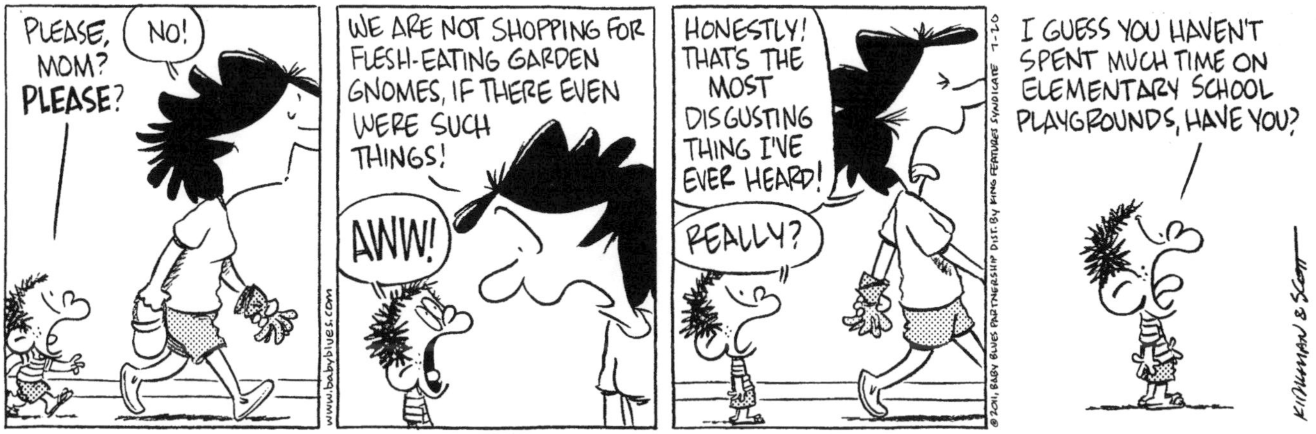
PLEASE, MOM? **PLEASE**?
NO!
WE ARE NOT SHOPPING FOR FLESH-EATING GARDEN GNOMES, IF THERE EVEN WERE SUCH THINGS!
AWW!
HONESTLY! THAT'S THE MOST DISGUSTING THING I'VE EVER HEARD!
REALLY?
I GUESS YOU HAVEN'T SPENT MUCH TIME ON ELEMENTARY SCHOOL PLAYGROUNDS, HAVE YOU?

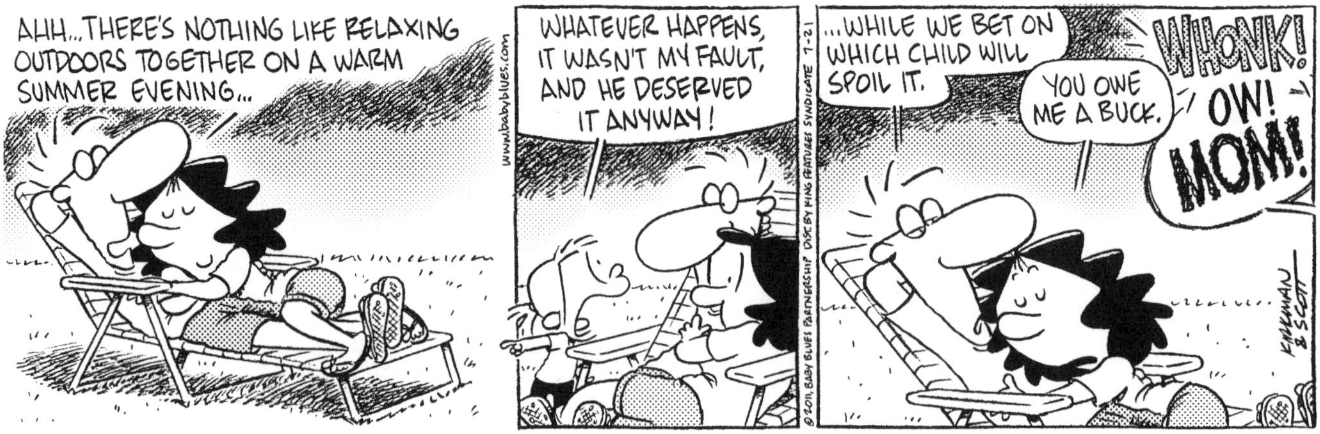
AHH... THERE'S NOTHING LIKE RELAXING OUTDOORS TOGETHER ON A WARM SUMMER EVENING...
WHATEVER HAPPENS, IT WASN'T MY FAULT, AND HE DESERVED IT ANYWAY!
...WHILE WE BET ON WHICH CHILD WILL SPOIL IT.
YOU OWE ME A BUCK.
WHONK!
OW!
MOM!
www.babyblues.com
© 2011, BABY BLUES PARTNERSHIP DIST. BY KING FEATURES SYNDICATE 7-21
KIRKMAN & SCOTT

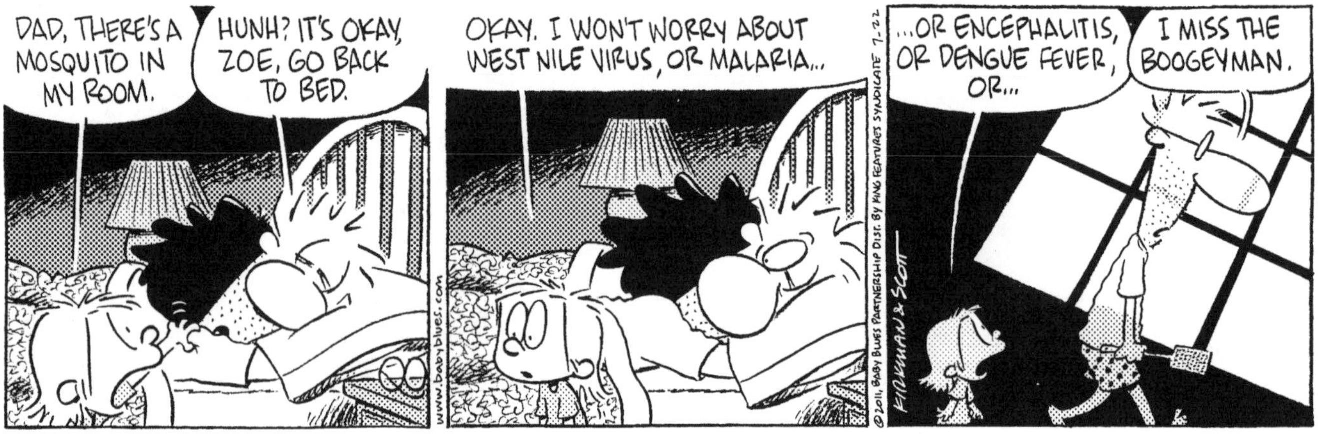
DAD, THERE'S A MOSQUITO IN MY ROOM.
HUNH? IT'S OKAY, ZOE, GO BACK TO BED.
OKAY. I WON'T WORRY ABOUT WEST NILE VIRUS, OR MALARIA...
...OR ENCEPHALITIS, OR DENGUE FEVER, OR...
I MISS THE BOOGEYMAN.
www.babyblues.com
© 2011, BABY BLUES PARTNERSHIP DIST. BY KING FEATURES SYNDICATE 7-22
KIRKMAN & SCOTT

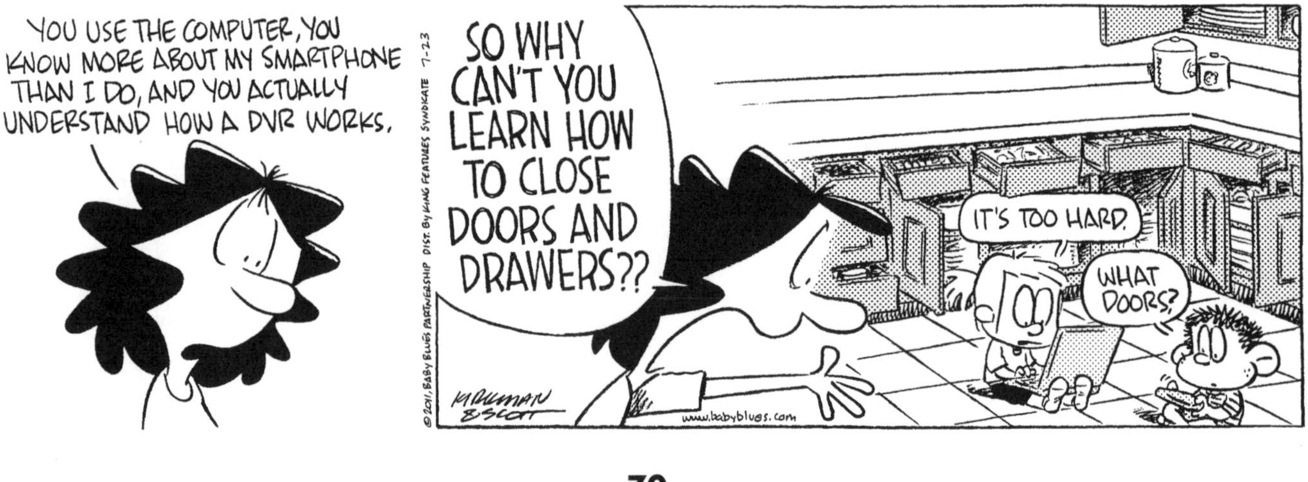
YOU USE THE COMPUTER, YOU KNOW MORE ABOUT MY SMARTPHONE THAN I DO, AND YOU ACTUALLY UNDERSTAND HOW A DVR WORKS.
SO WHY CAN'T YOU LEARN HOW TO CLOSE DOORS AND DRAWERS??
IT'S TOO HARD.
WHAT DOORS?
© 2011, BABY BLUES PARTNERSHIP DIST. BY KING FEATURES SYNDICATE 7-23
KIRKMAN & SCOTT
www.babyblues.com

BABY BLUES®
BY RICK KIRKMAN / JERRY SCOTT

GOO.
MA-BA-BA.
NAMB. NAMB. NAMB.
PBBBTH!
SHRIEK!!!
THREE ACROSS. TWO DEEP.
BEAT THAT.
©2011, BABY BLUES PARTNERSHIP DIST. BY KING FEATURES SYNDICATE www.babyblues.com
KIRKMAN & SCOTT 7-24

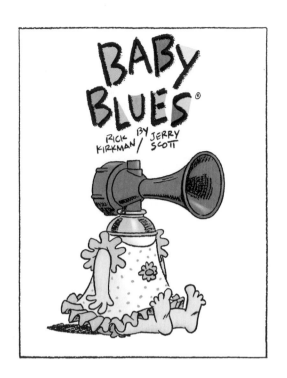

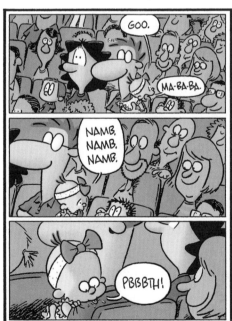

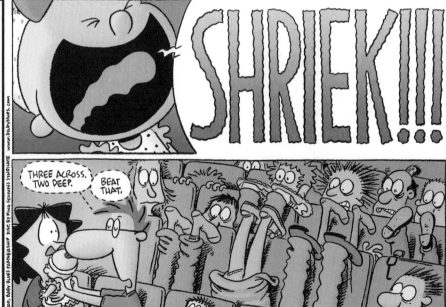

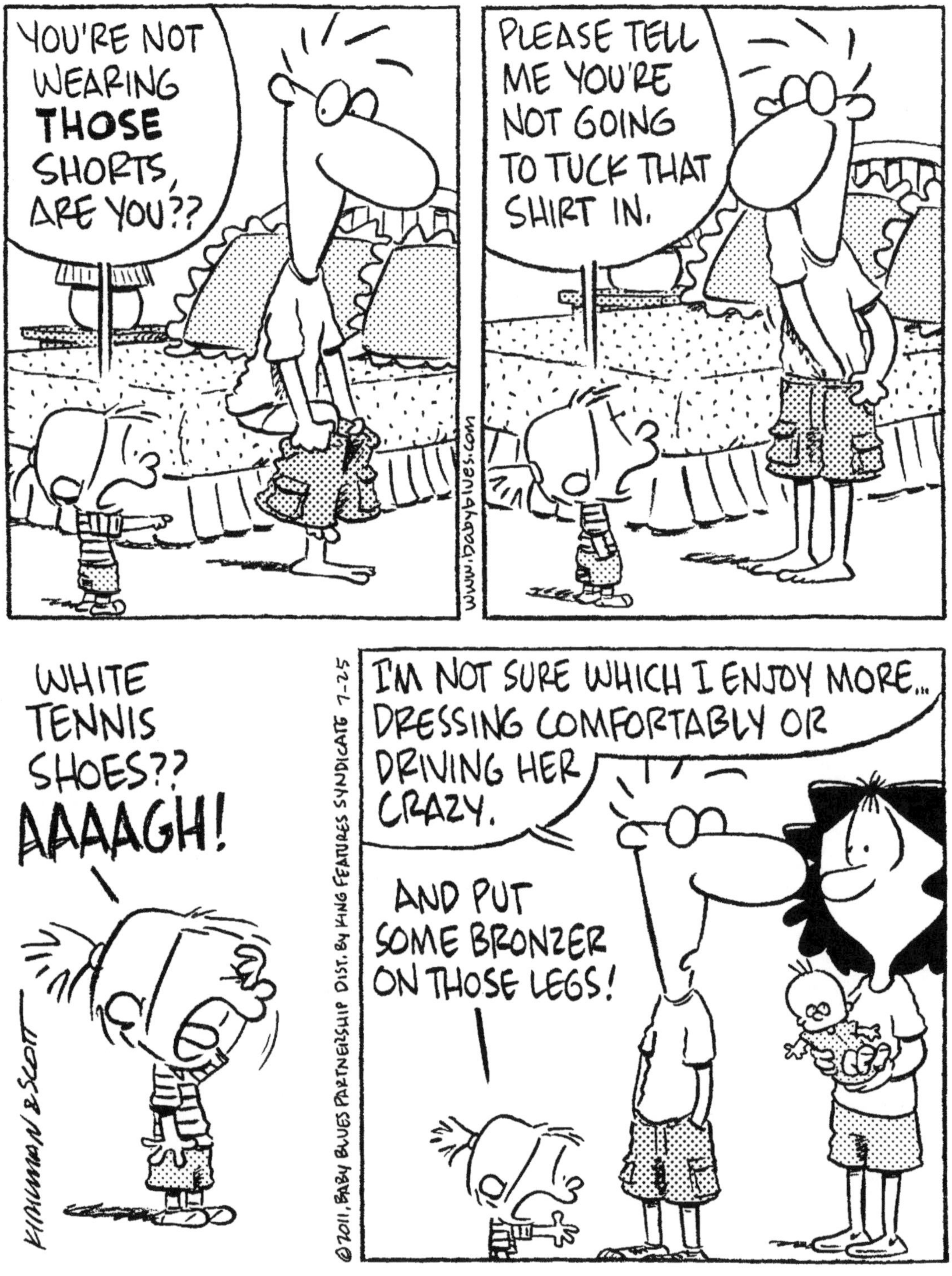
YOU'RE NOT WEARING **THOSE** SHORTS, ARE YOU??
www.babyblues.com
PLEASE TELL ME YOU'RE NOT GOING TO TUCK THAT SHIRT IN.
WHITE TENNIS SHOES?? AAAAGH!
KIRKMAN & SCOTT
©2011, BABY BLUES PARTNERSHIP DIST. BY KING FEATURES SYNDICATE 7-25
I'M NOT SURE WHICH I ENJOY MORE... DRESSING COMFORTABLY OR DRIVING HER CRAZY.
AND PUT SOME BRONZER ON THOSE LEGS!

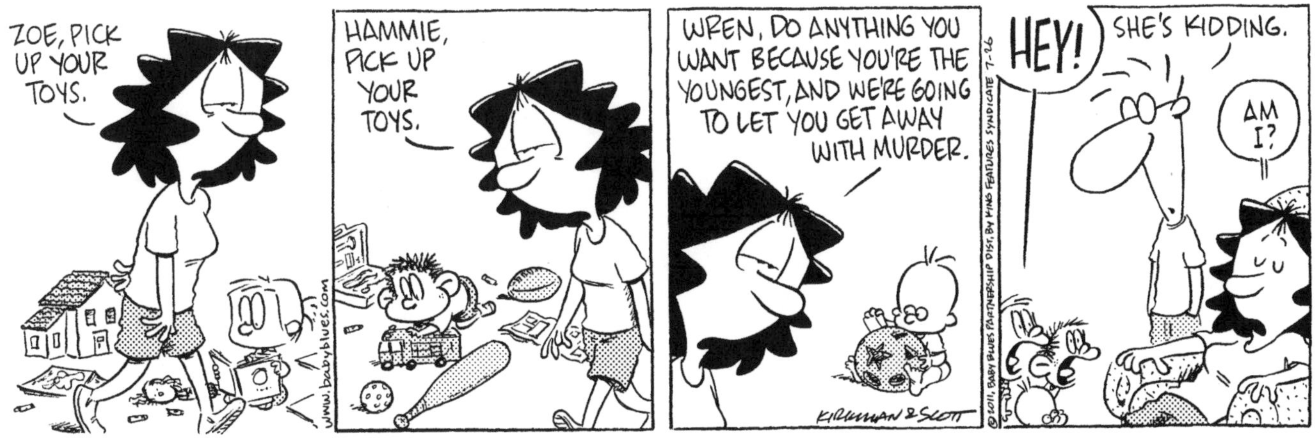
ZOE, PICK UP YOUR TOYS.
HAMMIE, PICK UP YOUR TOYS.
WREN, DO ANYTHING YOU WANT BECAUSE YOU'RE THE YOUNGEST, AND WE'RE GOING TO LET YOU GET AWAY WITH MURDER.
HEY!
SHE'S KIDDING.
AM I?
www.babyblues.com
KIRKMAN & SCOTT
© 2011, BABY BLUES PARTNERSHIP DIST. BY KING FEATURES SYNDICATE 7-26

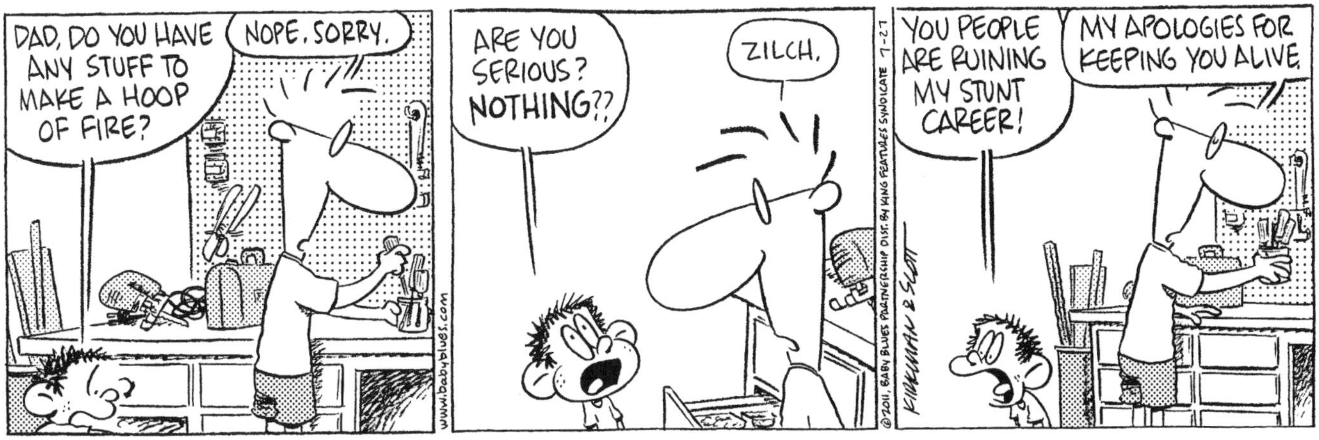
DAD, DO YOU HAVE ANY STUFF TO MAKE A HOOP OF FIRE?
NOPE. SORRY.
ARE YOU SERIOUS? NOTHING??
ZILCH.
YOU PEOPLE ARE RUINING MY STUNT CAREER!
MY APOLOGIES FOR KEEPING YOU ALIVE.
www.babyblues.com
KIRKMAN & SCOTT
© 2011, BABY BLUES PARTNERSHIP DIST. BY KING FEATURES SYNDICATE 7-27

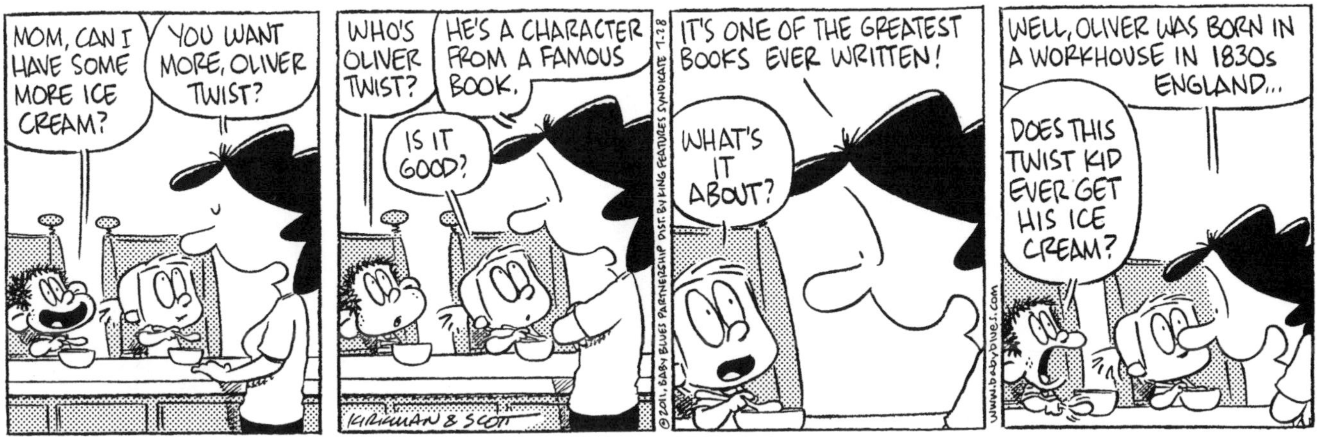
MOM, CAN I HAVE SOME MORE ICE CREAM?
YOU WANT MORE, OLIVER TWIST?
WHO'S OLIVER TWIST?
HE'S A CHARACTER FROM A FAMOUS BOOK.
IS IT GOOD?
IT'S ONE OF THE GREATEST BOOKS EVER WRITTEN!
WHAT'S IT ABOUT?
WELL, OLIVER WAS BORN IN A WORKHOUSE IN 1830s ENGLAND...
DOES THIS TWIST KID EVER GET HIS ICE CREAM?
KIRKMAN & SCOTT
© 2011, BABY BLUES PARTNERSHIP DIST. BY KING FEATURES SYNDICATE 7-28
www.babyblues.com

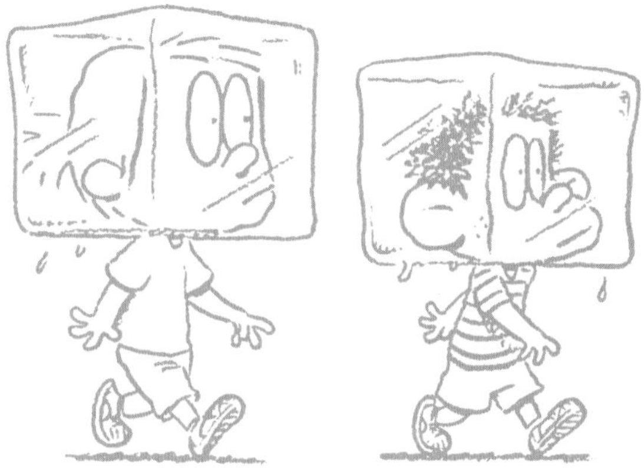

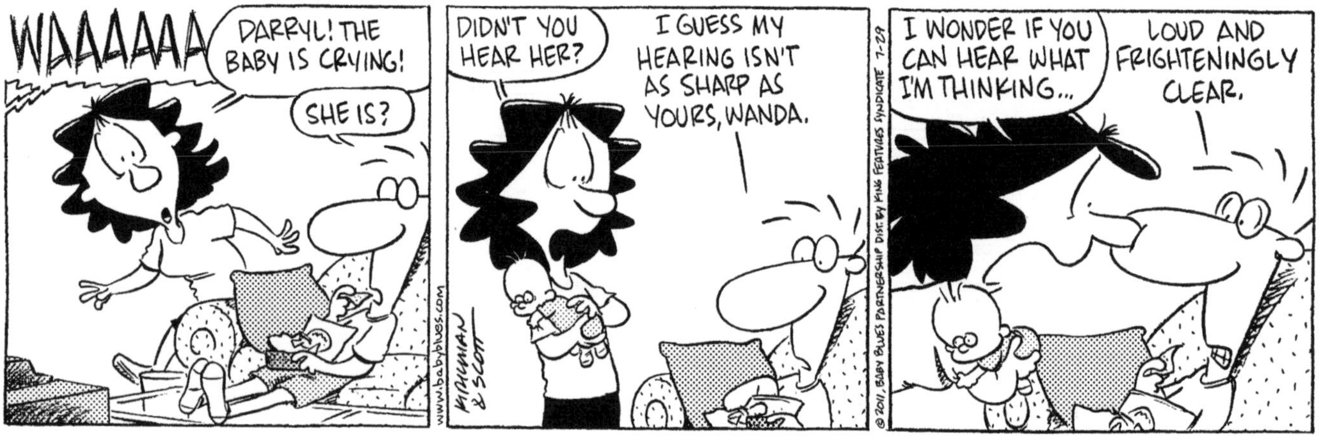
WAAAAAA
DARRYL! THE BABY IS CRYING!
SHE IS?
www.babyblues.com
KIRKMAN & SCOTT
DIDN'T YOU HEAR HER?
I GUESS MY HEARING ISN'T AS SHARP AS YOURS, WANDA.
© 2011, BABY BLUES PARTNERSHIP DIST. BY KING FEATURES SYNDICATE 7-29
I WONDER IF YOU CAN HEAR WHAT I'M THINKING...
LOUD AND FRIGHTENINGLY CLEAR.

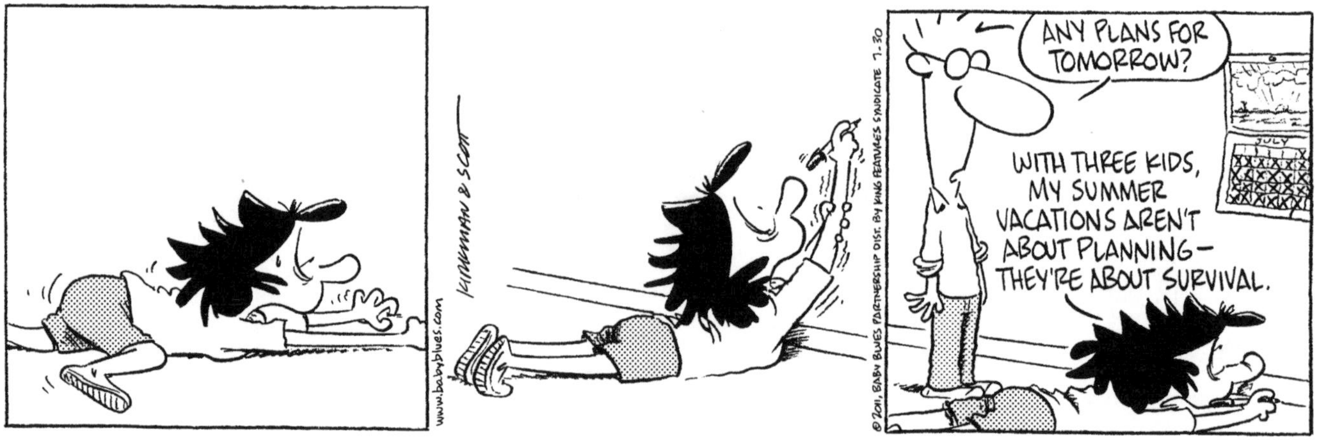
www.babyblues.com
KIRKMAN & SCOTT
© 2011, BABY BLUES PARTNERSHIP DIST. BY KING FEATURES SYNDICATE 7-30
ANY PLANS FOR TOMORROW?
WITH THREE KIDS, MY SUMMER VACATIONS AREN'T ABOUT PLANNING– THEY'RE ABOUT SURVIVAL.
JULY

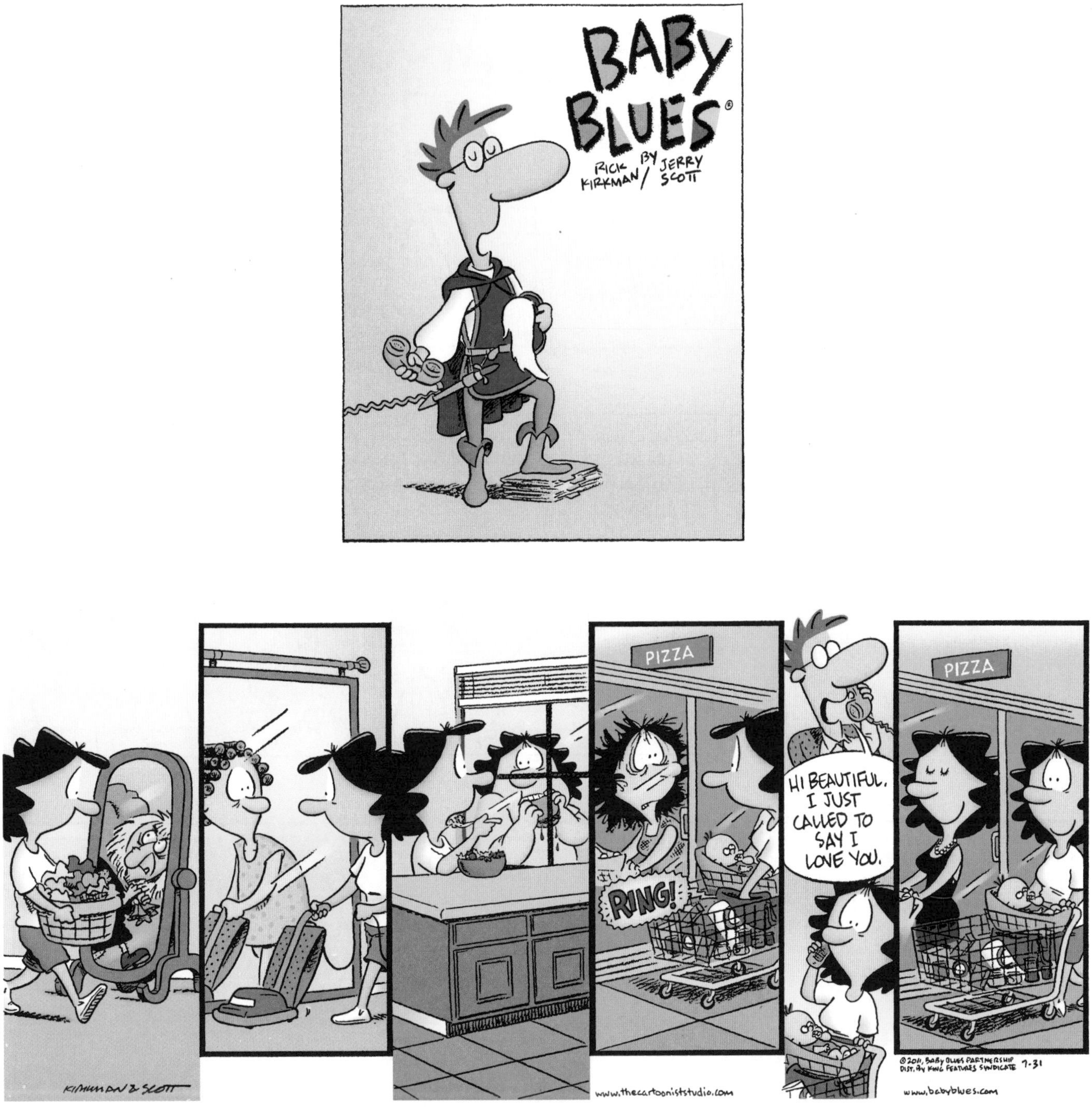
BABY BLUES®
RICK KIRKMAN / BY JERRY SCOTT
PIZZA
RING!
HI BEAUTIFUL. I JUST CALLED TO SAY I LOVE YOU.
PIZZA
KIRKMAN & SCOTT
www.thecartoonniststudio.com
©2011, BABY BLUES PARTNERSHIP DIST. BY KING FEATURES SYNDICATE 7-31
www.babyblues.com

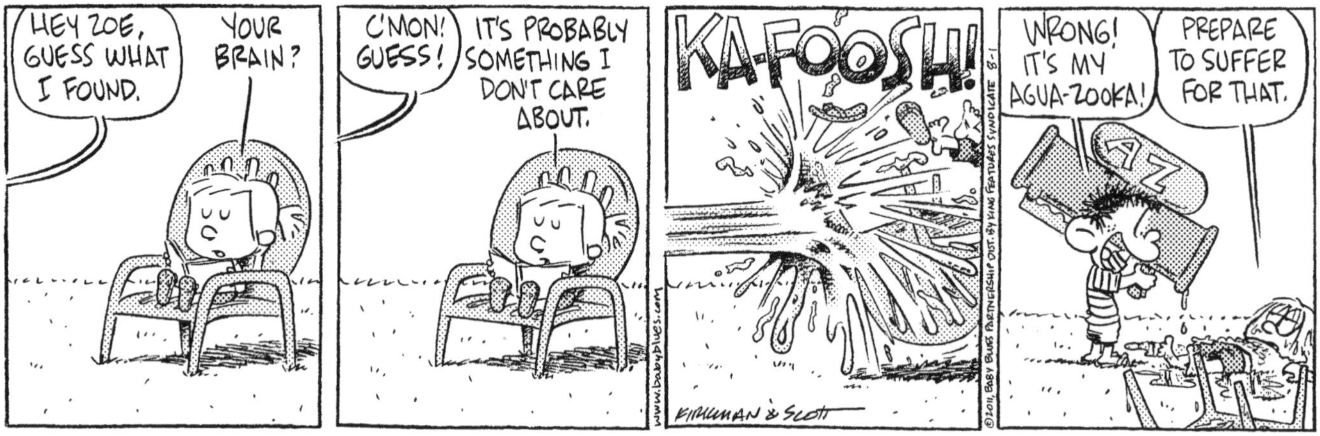
HEY ZOE, GUESS WHAT I FOUND.
YOUR BRAIN?
C'MON! GUESS!
IT'S PROBABLY SOMETHING I DON'T CARE ABOUT.
KA-FOOSH!
WRONG! IT'S MY AGUA-ZOOKA!
PREPARE TO SUFFER FOR THAT.
KIRKMAN & SCOTT
www.babyblues.com
©2011, BABY BLUES PARTNERSHIP DIST. BY KING FEATURES SYNDICATE 8-1

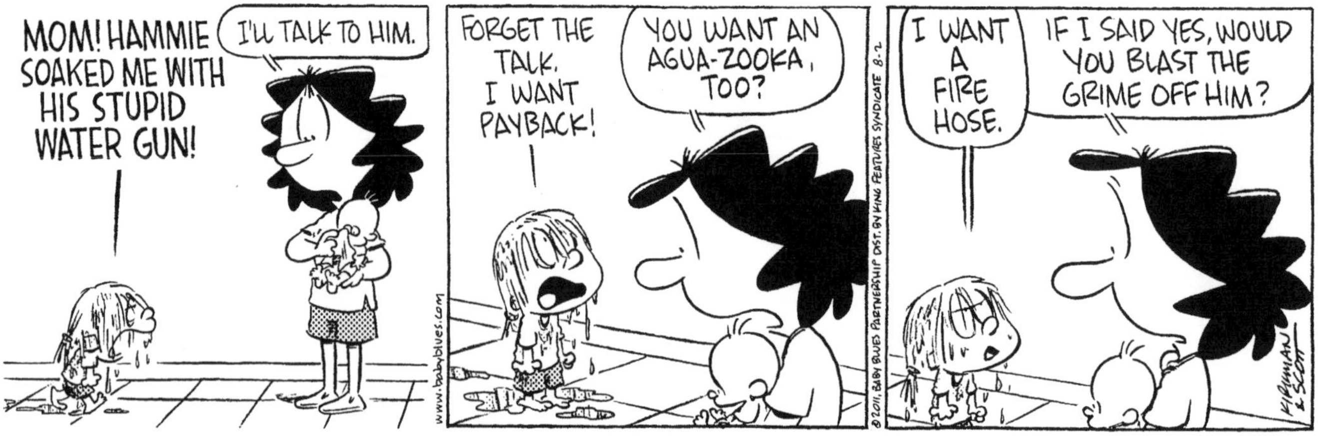
MOM! HAMMIE SOAKED ME WITH HIS STUPID WATER GUN!
I'LL TALK TO HIM.
FORGET THE TALK. I WANT PAYBACK!
YOU WANT AN AGUA-ZOOKA, TOO?
I WANT A FIRE HOSE.
IF I SAID YES, WOULD YOU BLAST THE GRIME OFF HIM?
www.babyblues.com
©2011, BABY BLUES PARTNERSHIP DIST. BY KING FEATURES SYNDICATE 8-2
KIRKMAN & SCOTT

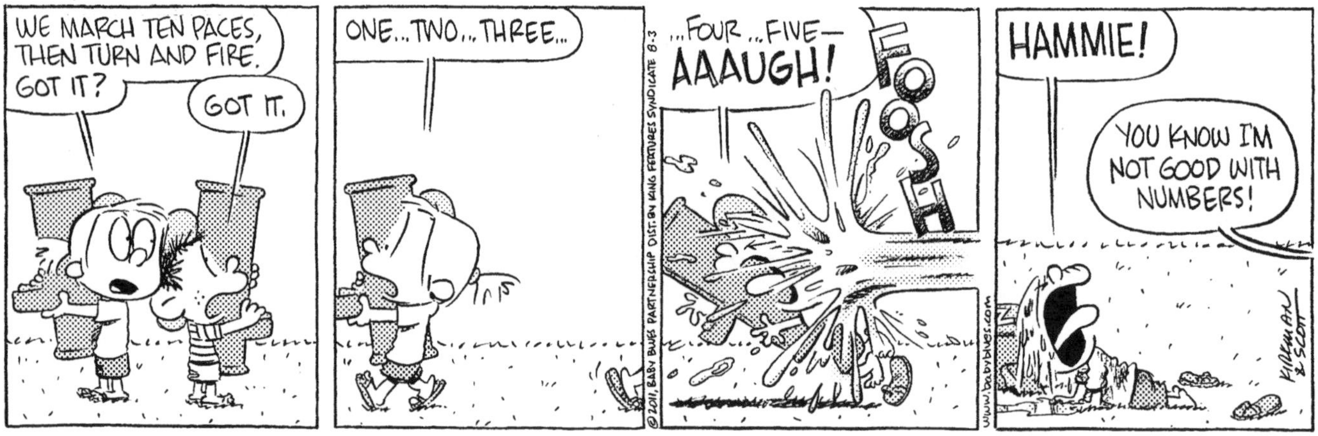
WE MARCH TEN PACES, THEN TURN AND FIRE. GOT IT?
GOT IT.
ONE... TWO... THREE...
...FOUR ...FIVE—
AAAUGH!
FOOSH
HAMMIE!
YOU KNOW I'M NOT GOOD WITH NUMBERS!
©2011, BABY BLUES PARTNERSHIP DIST. BY KING FEATURES SYNDICATE 8-3
www.babyblues.com
KIRKMAN & SCOTT

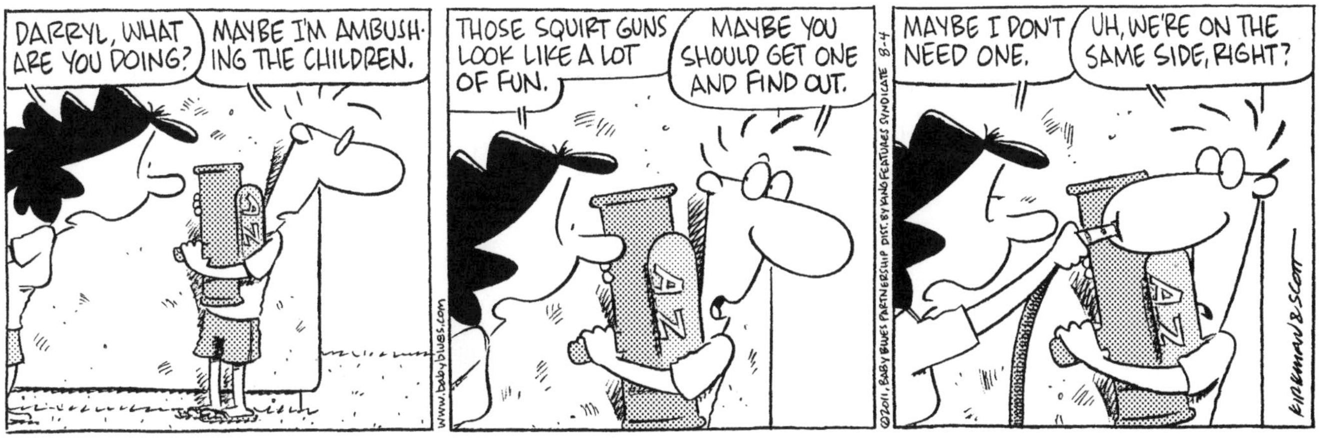
DARRYL, WHAT ARE YOU DOING?
MAYBE I'M AMBUSHING THE CHILDREN.
THOSE SQUIRT GUNS LOOK LIKE A LOT OF FUN.
MAYBE YOU SHOULD GET ONE AND FIND OUT.
MAYBE I DON'T NEED ONE.
UH, WE'RE ON THE SAME SIDE, RIGHT?
www.babyblues.com
©2011, BABY BLUES PARTNERSHIP DIST. BY KING FEATURES SYNDICATE 8-4
KIRKMAN & SCOTT

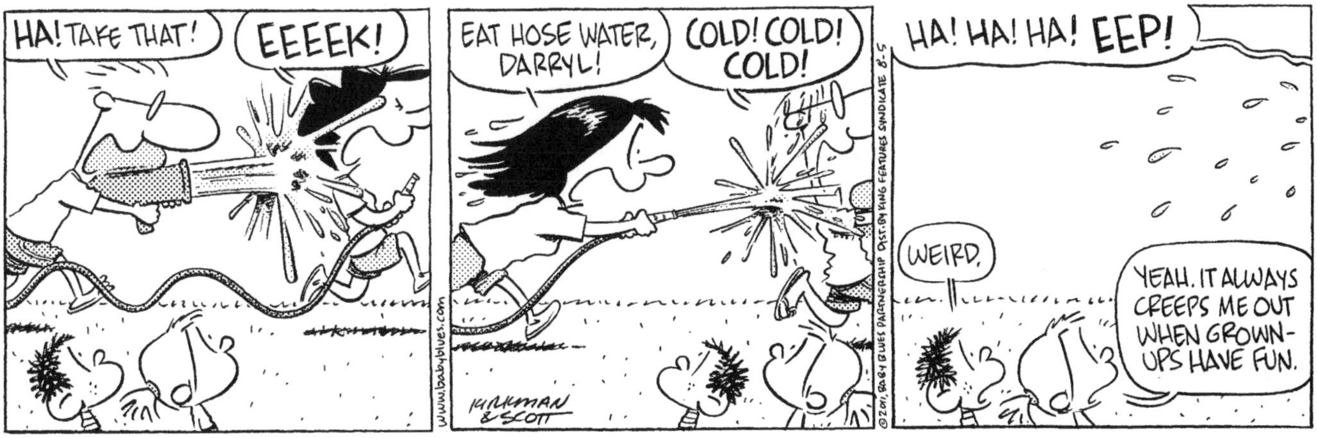
HA! TAKE THAT!
EEEEK!
EAT HOSE WATER, DARRYL!
COLD! COLD! COLD!
HA! HA! HA! EEP!
WEIRD.
YEAH. IT ALWAYS CREEPS ME OUT WHEN GROWN-UPS HAVE FUN.
www.babyblues.com
KIRKMAN & SCOTT
©2011, BABY BLUES PARTNERSHIP DIST. BY KING FEATURES SYNDICATE 8-5

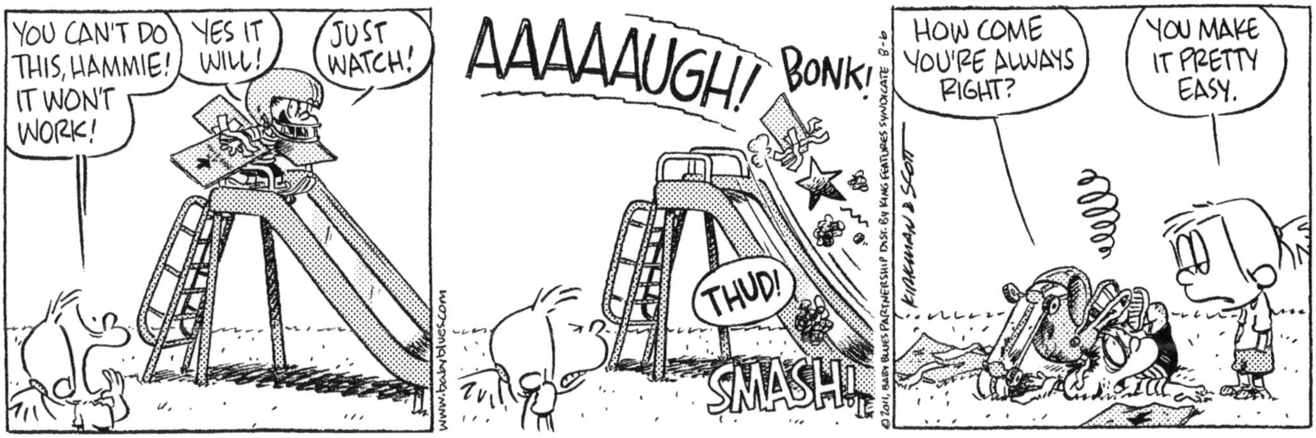
YOU CAN'T DO THIS, HAMMIE! IT WON'T WORK!
YES IT WILL!
JUST WATCH!
AAAAAUGH!
BONK!
THUD!
SMASH!
HOW COME YOU'RE ALWAYS RIGHT?
YOU MAKE IT PRETTY EASY.
www.babyblues.com
©2011, BABY BLUES PARTNERSHIP DIST. BY KING FEATURES SYNDICATE 8-6
KIRKMAN & SCOTT

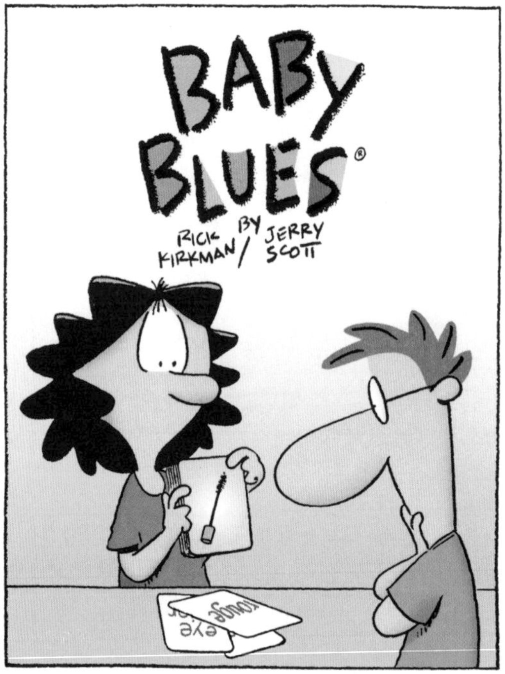

BABY BLUES®
BY RICK KIRKMAN / JERRY SCOTT

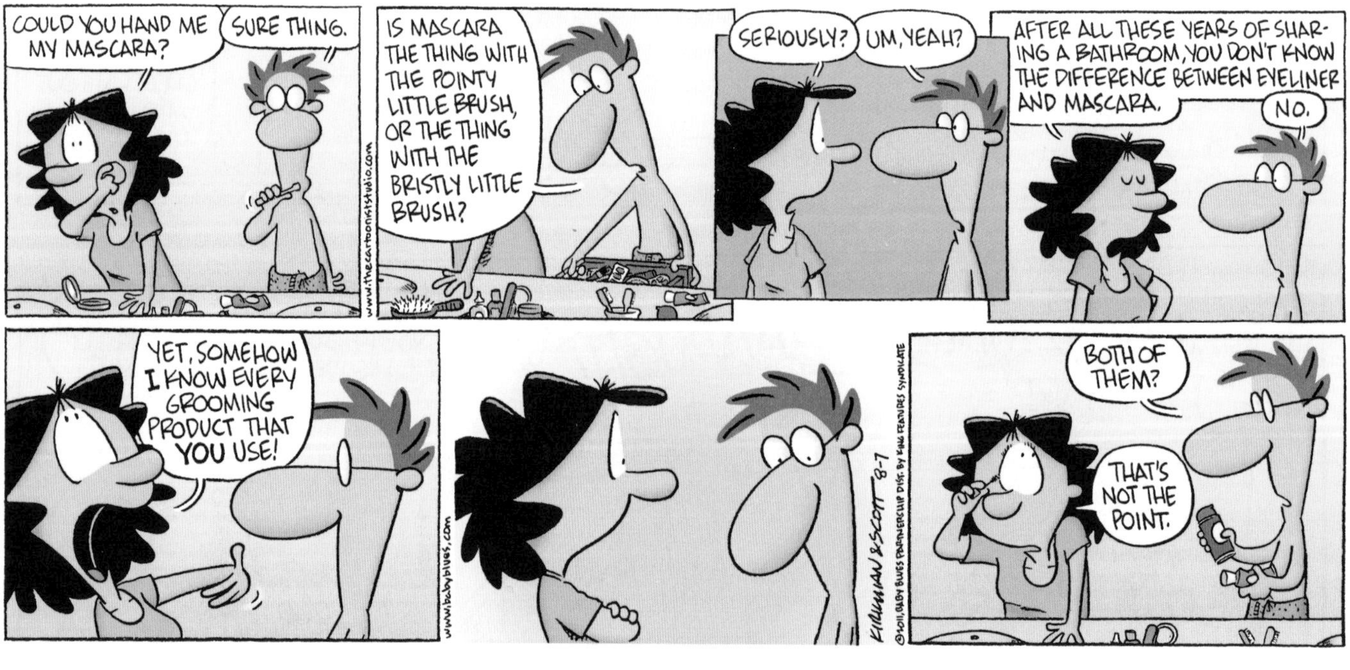

COULD YOU HAND ME MY MASCARA?
SURE THING.
www.thecartoonistsstudio.com
IS MASCARA THE THING WITH THE POINTY LITTLE BRUSH, OR THE THING WITH THE BRISTLY LITTLE BRUSH?
SERIOUSLY?
UM, YEAH?
AFTER ALL THESE YEARS OF SHARING A BATHROOM, YOU DON'T KNOW THE DIFFERENCE BETWEEN EYELINER AND MASCARA.
NO.
YET, SOMEHOW I KNOW EVERY GROOMING PRODUCT THAT YOU USE!
www.babyblues.com
KIRKMAN & SCOTT 8-7
©2011, BABY BLUES PARTNERSHIP DIST. BY KING FEATURES SYNDICATE
BOTH OF THEM?
THAT'S NOT THE POINT.

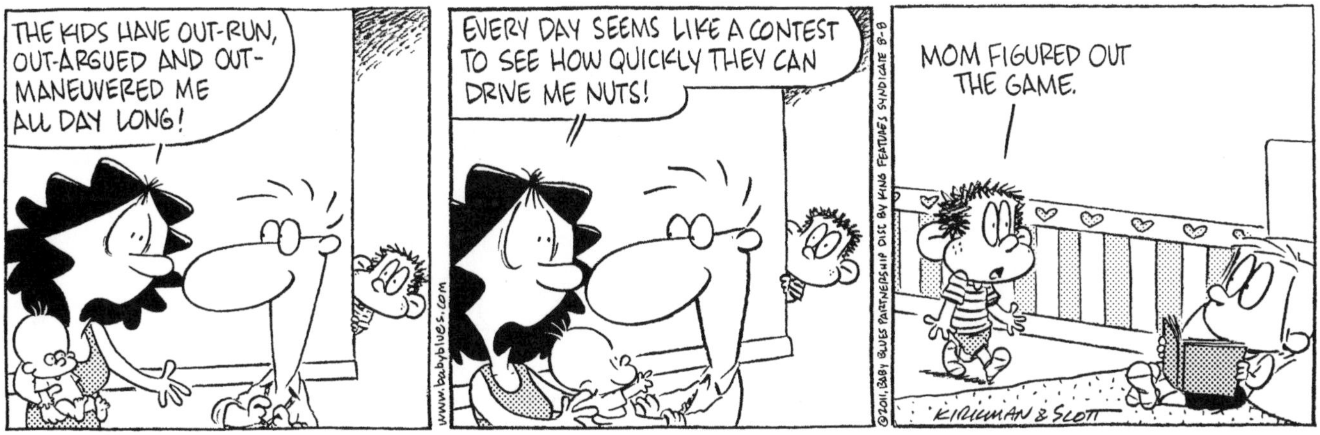
THE KIDS HAVE OUT-RUN, OUT-ARGUED AND OUT-MANEUVERED ME ALL DAY LONG!
www.babyblues.com
EVERY DAY SEEMS LIKE A CONTEST TO SEE HOW QUICKLY THEY CAN DRIVE ME NUTS!
©2011, BABY BLUES PARTNERSHIP DIST. BY KING FEATURES SYNDICATE 8-8
MOM FIGURED OUT THE GAME.
KIRKMAN & SCOTT

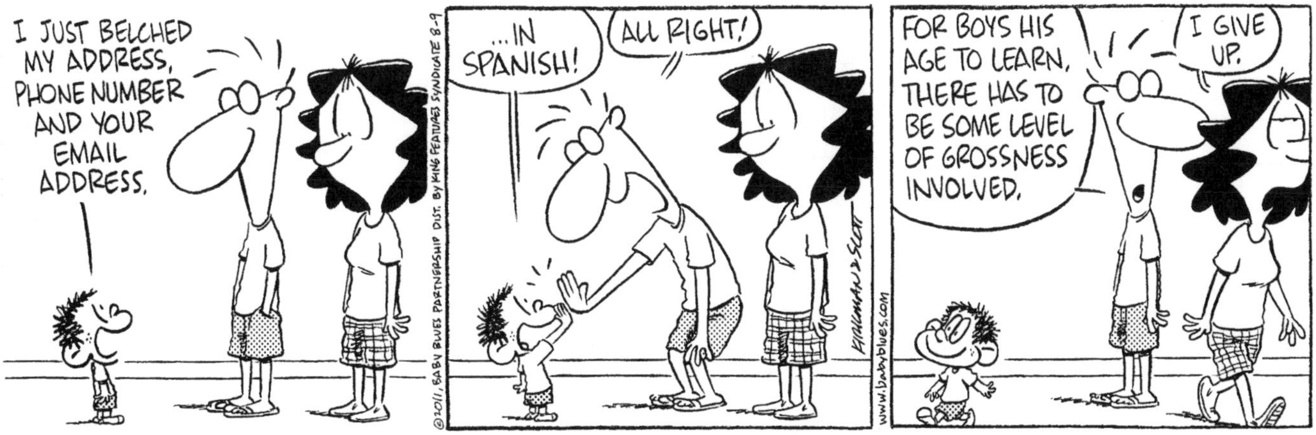
I JUST BELCHED MY ADDRESS, PHONE NUMBER AND YOUR EMAIL ADDRESS.
©2011, BABY BLUES PARTNERSHIP DIST. BY KING FEATURES SYNDICATE 8-9
...IN SPANISH!
ALL RIGHT!
KIRKMAN & SCOTT
www.babyblues.com
FOR BOYS HIS AGE TO LEARN, THERE HAS TO BE SOME LEVEL OF GROSSNESS INVOLVED.
I GIVE UP.

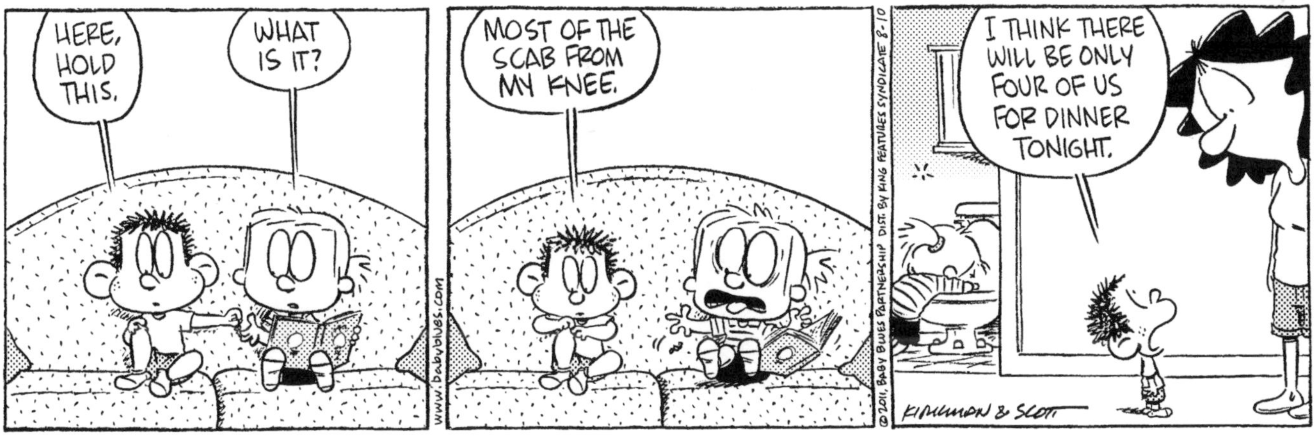
HERE, HOLD THIS.
WHAT IS IT?
www.babyblues.com
MOST OF THE SCAB FROM MY KNEE.
©2011, BABY BLUES PARTNERSHIP DIST. BY KING FEATURES SYNDICATE 8-10
I THINK THERE WILL BE ONLY FOUR OF US FOR DINNER TONIGHT.
KIRKMAN & SCOTT

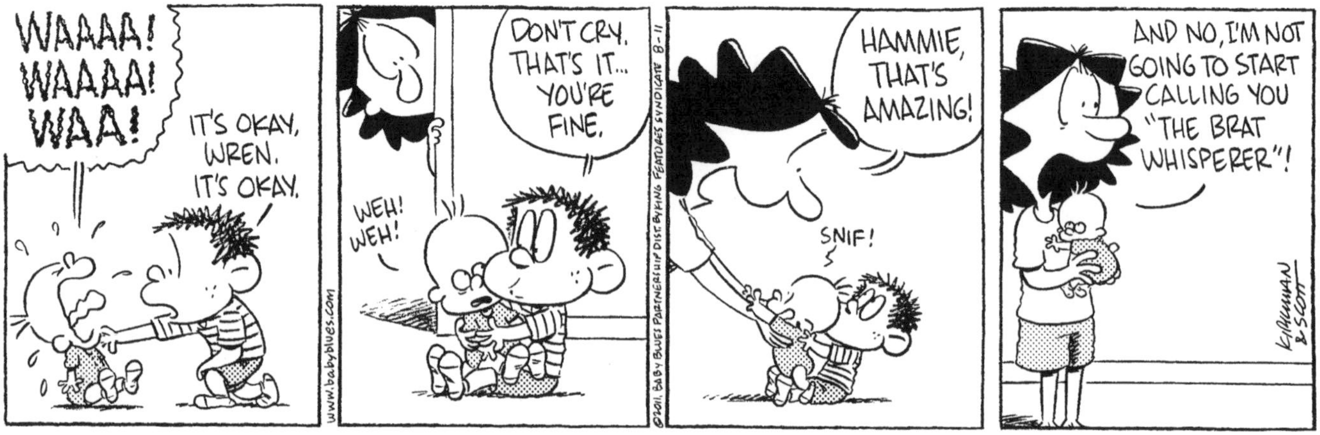
WAAAA! WAAAA! WAA!
IT'S OKAY, WREN. IT'S OKAY.
www.babyblues.com
DON'T CRY. THAT'S IT... YOU'RE FINE.
WEH! WEH!
©2011, BABY BLUES PARTNERSHIP DIST. BY KING FEATURES SYNDICATE 8-11
HAMMIE, THAT'S AMAZING!
SNIF!
AND NO, I'M NOT GOING TO START CALLING YOU "THE BRAT WHISPERER"!
KIRKMAN & SCOTT

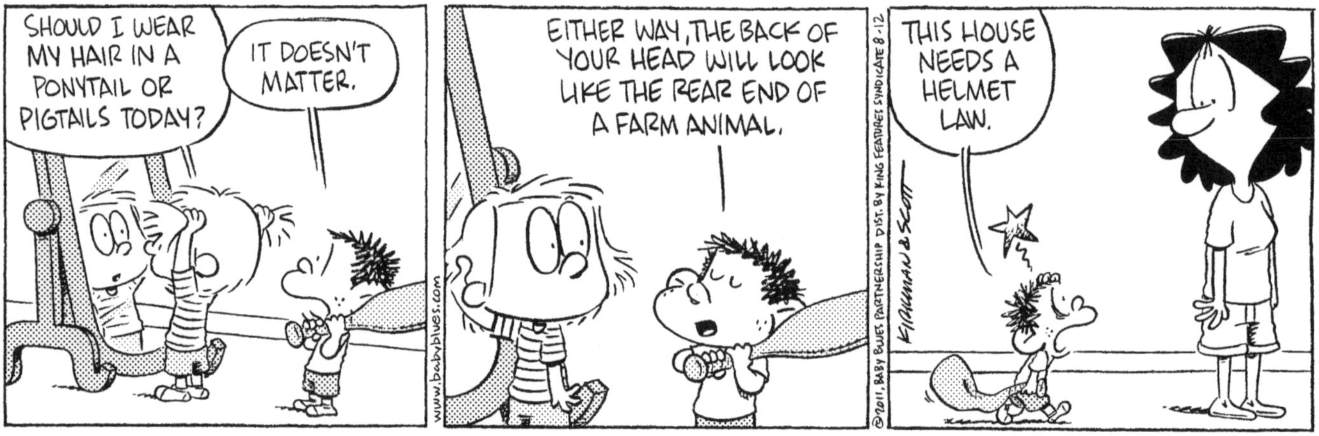
SHOULD I WEAR MY HAIR IN A PONYTAIL OR PIGTAILS TODAY?
IT DOESN'T MATTER.
www.babyblues.com
EITHER WAY, THE BACK OF YOUR HEAD WILL LOOK LIKE THE REAR END OF A FARM ANIMAL.
©2011, BABY BLUES PARTNERSHIP DIST. BY KING FEATURES SYNDICATE 8-12
THIS HOUSE NEEDS A HELMET LAW.
KIRKMAN & SCOTT

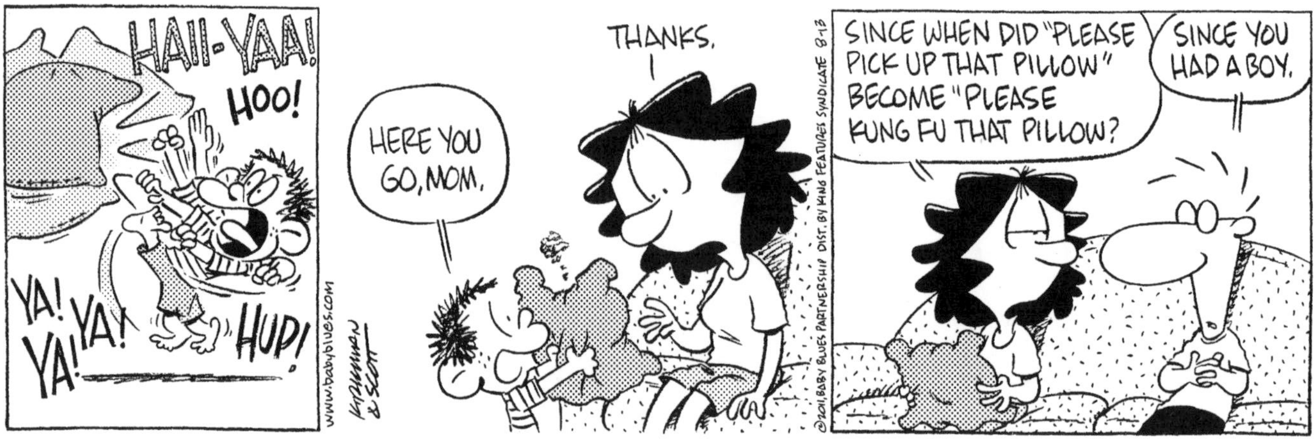
HAII-YAA!
HOO!
YA! YA! YA!
HUP!
www.babyblues.com
KIRKMAN & SCOTT
HERE YOU GO, MOM.
THANKS.
©2011, BABY BLUES PARTNERSHIP DIST. BY KING FEATURES SYNDICATE 8-13
SINCE WHEN DID "PLEASE PICK UP THAT PILLOW" BECOME "PLEASE KUNG FU THAT PILLOW?
SINCE YOU HAD A BOY.

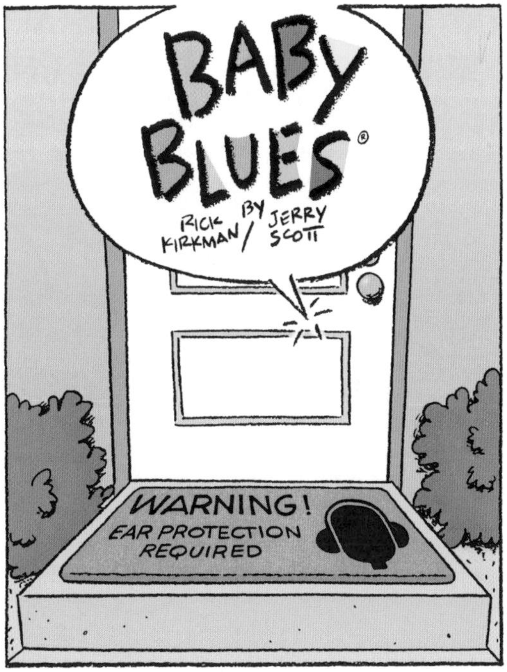
BABY BLUES®
BY RICK KIRKMAN / JERRY SCOTT
WARNING! EAR PROTECTION REQUIRED

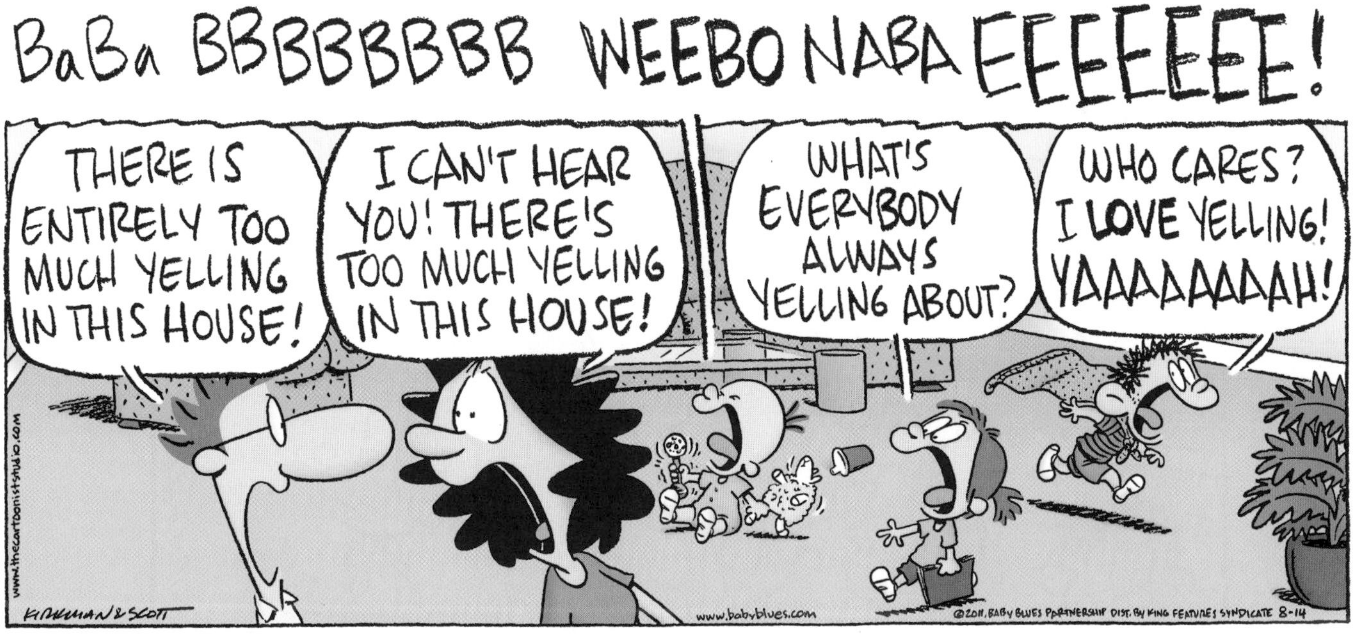
BaBa BBBBBBBB WEEBO NABA EEEEEEEE!
THERE IS ENTIRELY TOO MUCH YELLING IN THIS HOUSE!
I CAN'T HEAR YOU! THERE'S TOO MUCH YELLING IN THIS HOUSE!
WHAT'S EVERYBODY ALWAYS YELLING ABOUT?
WHO CARES? I LOVE YELLING! YAAAAAAAAH!
KIRKMAN & SCOTT
www.thecartoonistsstudio.com
www.babyblues.com
©2011, BABY BLUES PARTNERSHIP DIST. BY KING FEATURES SYNDICATE 8-14

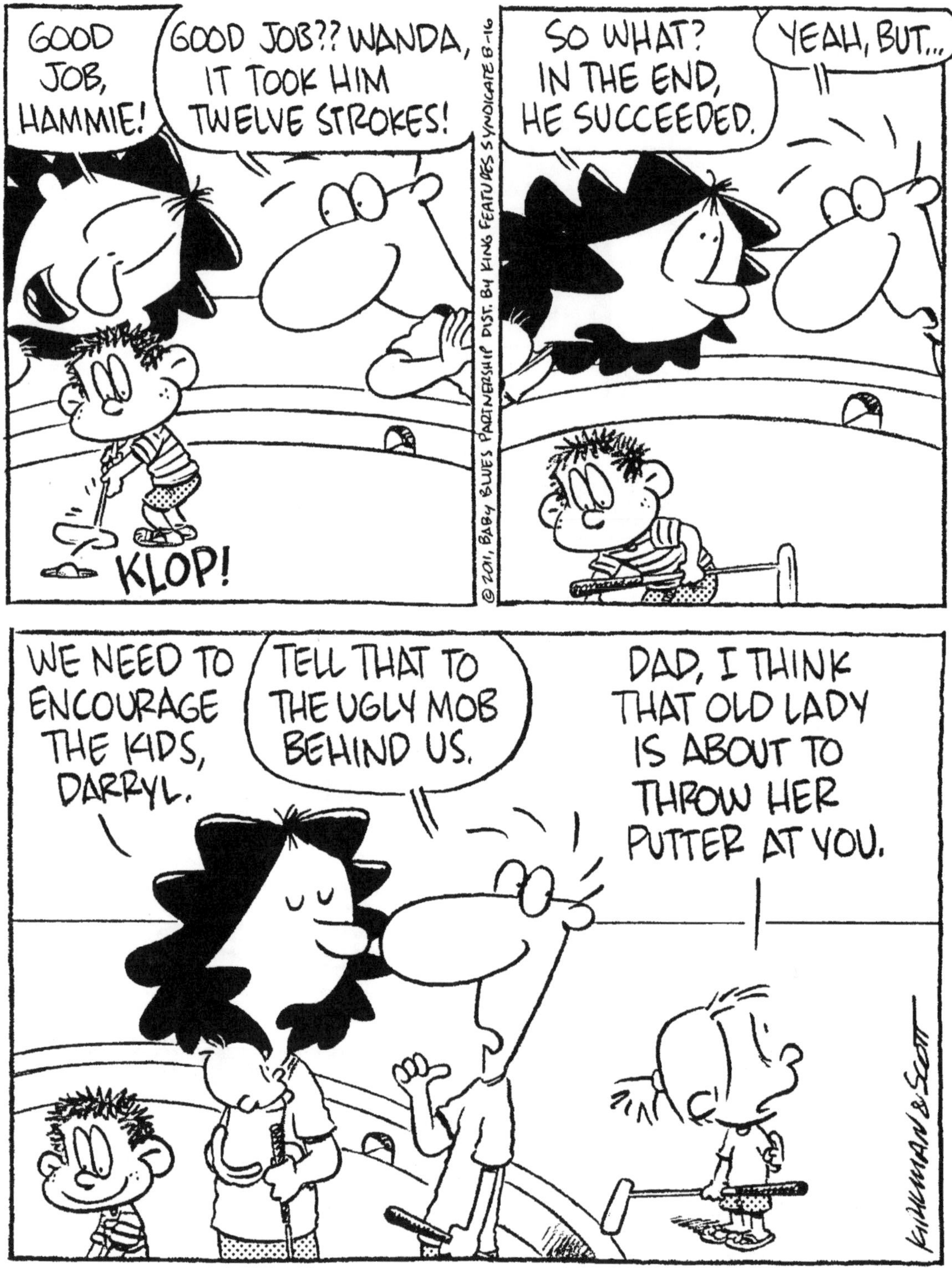
GOOD JOB, HAMMIE!
GOOD JOB?? WANDA, IT TOOK HIM TWELVE STROKES!
KLOP!
© 2011, BABY BLUES PARTNERSHIP DIST. BY KING FEATURES SYNDICATE 8-16
SO WHAT? IN THE END, HE SUCCEEDED.
YEAH, BUT...
WE NEED TO ENCOURAGE THE KIDS, DARRYL.
TELL THAT TO THE UGLY MOB BEHIND US.
DAD, I THINK THAT OLD LADY IS ABOUT TO THROW HER PUTTER AT YOU.
KIRKMAN & SCOTT

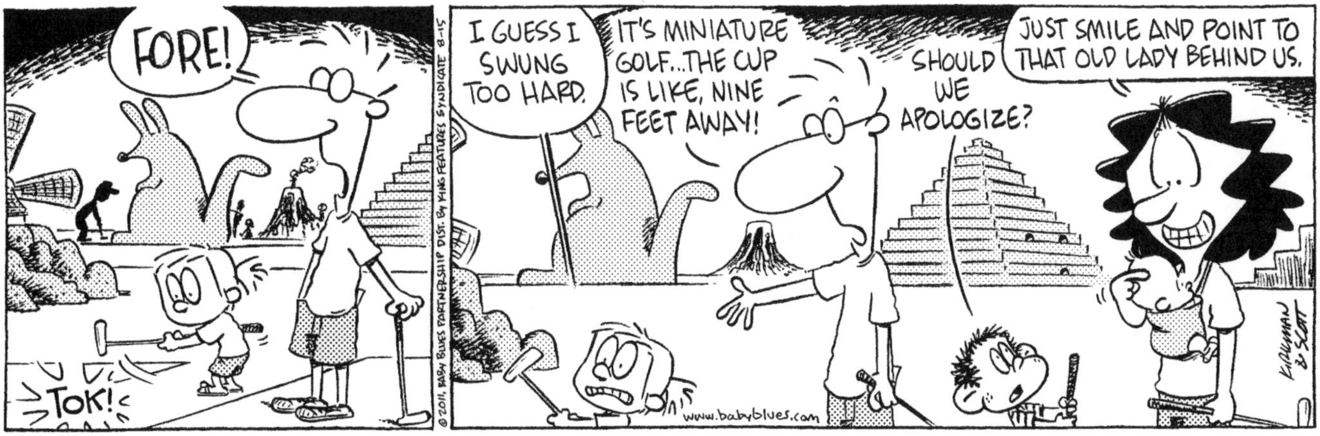
FORE!
TOK!
©2011, BABY BLUES PARTNERSHIP DIST. BY KING FEATURES SYNDICATE 8-15
I GUESS I SWUNG TOO HARD.
IT'S MINIATURE GOLF...THE CUP IS LIKE, NINE FEET AWAY!
SHOULD WE APOLOGIZE?
JUST SMILE AND POINT TO THAT OLD LADY BEHIND US.
www.babyblues.com
KIRKMAN & SCOTT

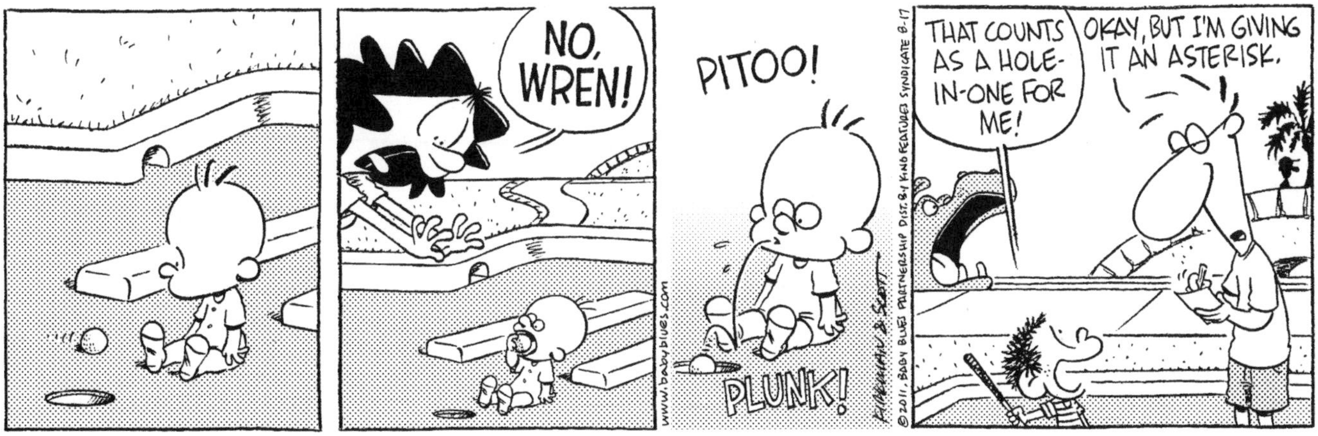
NO, WREN!
www.babyblues.com
PITOO!
PLUNK!
KIRKMAN & SCOTT
©2011, BABY BLUES PARTNERSHIP DIST. BY KING FEATURES SYNDICATE 8-17
THAT COUNTS AS A HOLE-IN-ONE FOR ME!
OKAY, BUT I'M GIVING IT AN ASTERISK.

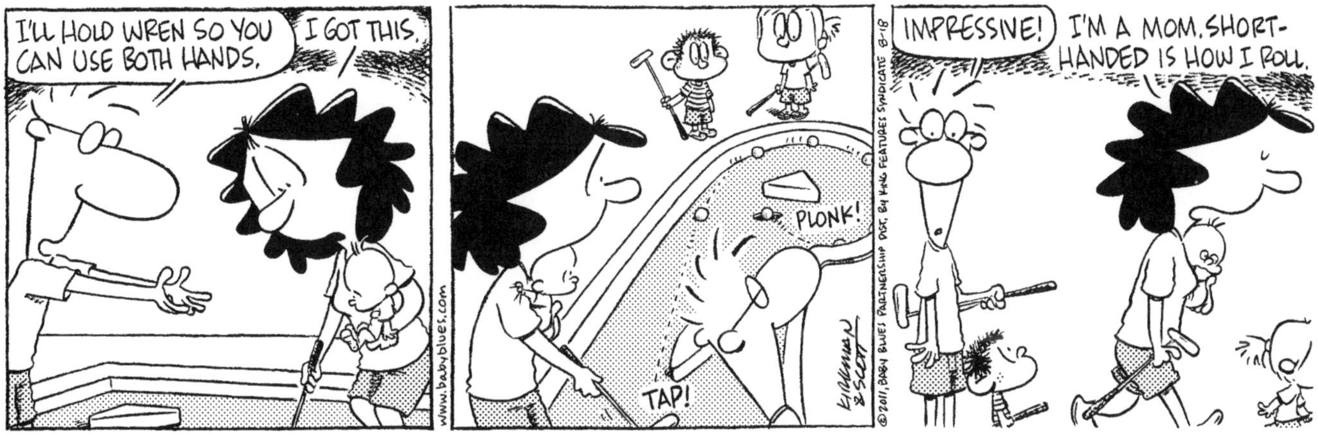
I'LL HOLD WREN SO YOU CAN USE BOTH HANDS.
I GOT THIS.
www.babyblues.com
PLONK!
TAP!
KIRKMAN & SCOTT
©2011, BABY BLUES PARTNERSHIP DIST. BY KING FEATURES SYNDICATE 8-18
IMPRESSIVE!
I'M A MOM. SHORT-HANDED IS HOW I ROLL.

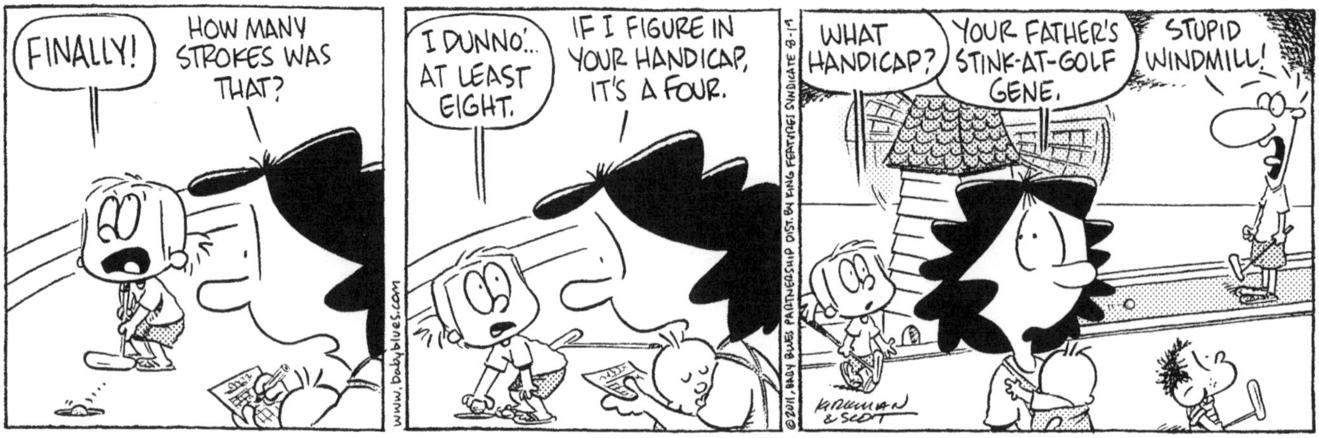
FINALLY!
HOW MANY STROKES WAS THAT?
www.babyblues.com
I DUNNO... AT LEAST EIGHT.
IF I FIGURE IN YOUR HANDICAP, IT'S A FOUR.
©2011, BABY BLUES PARTNERSHIP DIST. BY KING FEATURES SYNDICATE 8-19
WHAT HANDICAP?
YOUR FATHER'S STINK-AT-GOLF GENE.
STUPID WINDMILL!
KIRKMAN & SCOTT

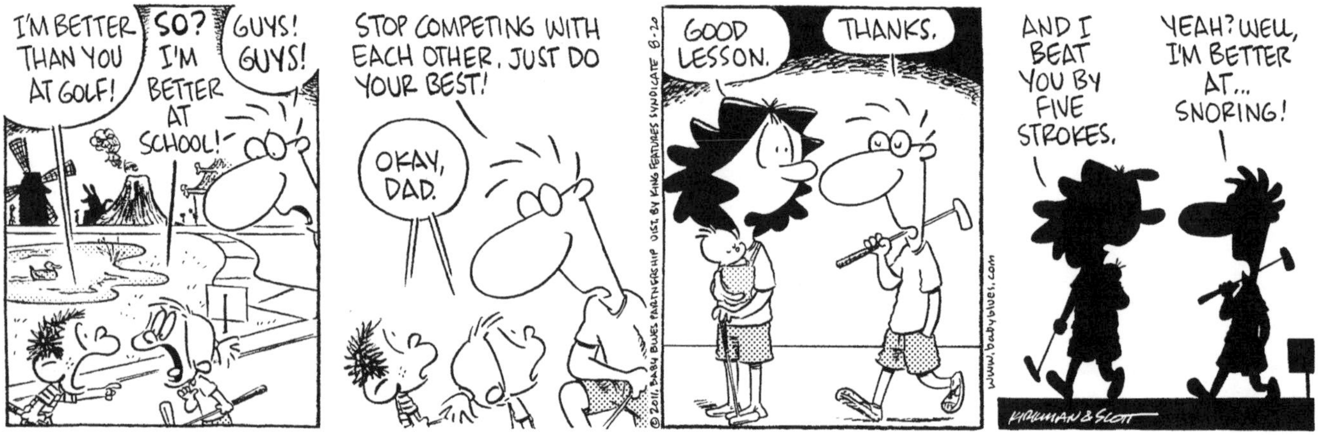
I'M BETTER THAN YOU AT GOLF!
SO? I'M BETTER AT SCHOOL!
GUYS! GUYS!
STOP COMPETING WITH EACH OTHER. JUST DO YOUR BEST!
OKAY, DAD.
©2011, BABY BLUES PARTNERSHIP DIST. BY KING FEATURES SYNDICATE 8-20
GOOD LESSON.
THANKS.
www.babyblues.com
AND I BEAT YOU BY FIVE STROKES.
YEAH? WELL, I'M BETTER AT... SNORING!
KIRKMAN & SCOTT

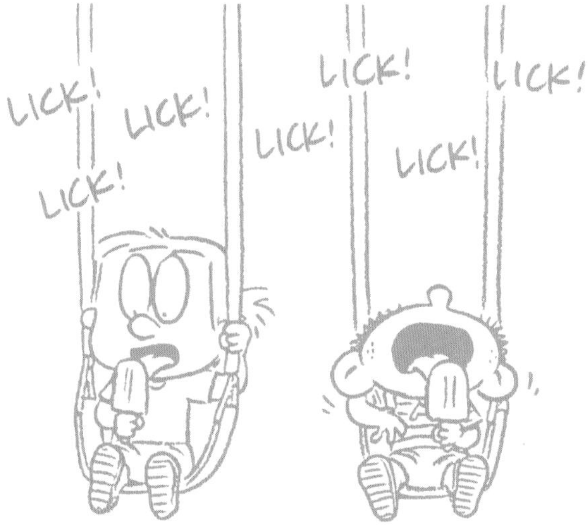
LICK!
LICK!
LICK!
LICK!
LICK!
LICK!
LICK!

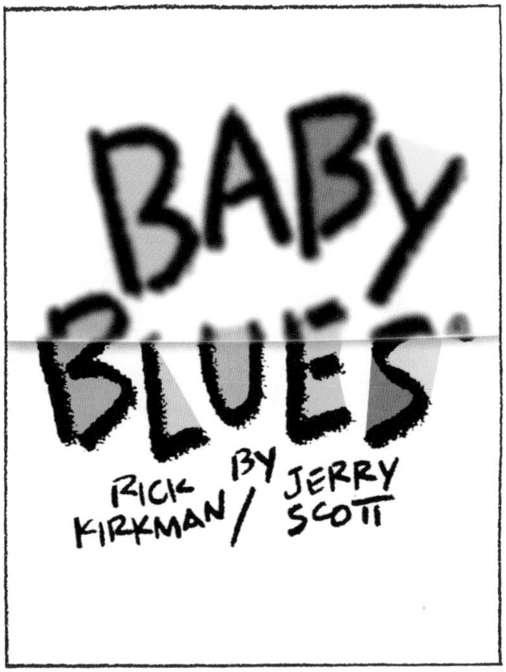
BABY BLUES
BY
RICK KIRKMAN / JERRY SCOTT

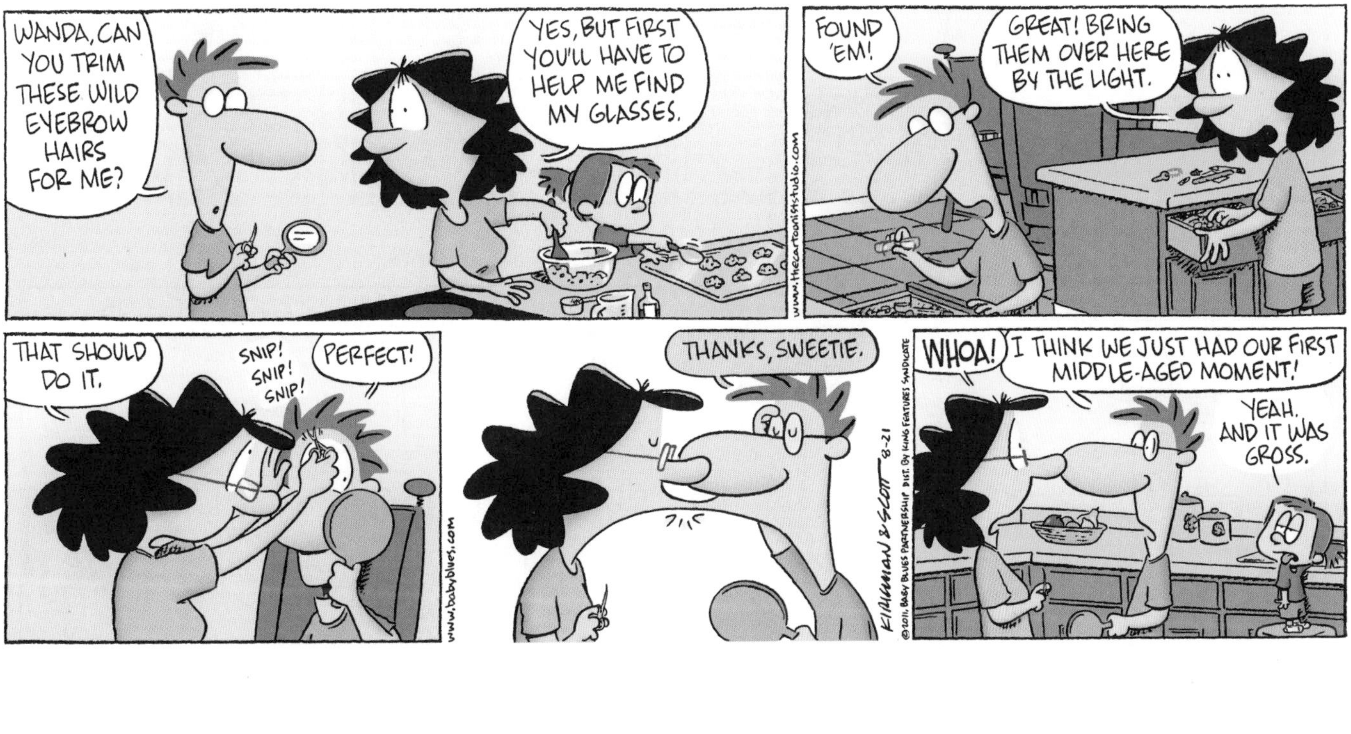
WANDA, CAN YOU TRIM THESE WILD EYEBROW HAIRS FOR ME?
YES, BUT FIRST YOU'LL HAVE TO HELP ME FIND MY GLASSES.
www.thecartoonistsstudio.com
FOUND 'EM!
GREAT! BRING THEM OVER HERE BY THE LIGHT.
THAT SHOULD DO IT.
SNIP! SNIP! SNIP!
PERFECT!
www.babyblues.com
THANKS, SWEETIE.
KIRKMAN & SCOTT 8-21
© 2011, BABY BLUES PARTNERSHIP DIST. BY KING FEATURES SYNDICATE
WHOA!
I THINK WE JUST HAD OUR FIRST MIDDLE-AGED MOMENT!
YEAH. AND IT WAS GROSS.

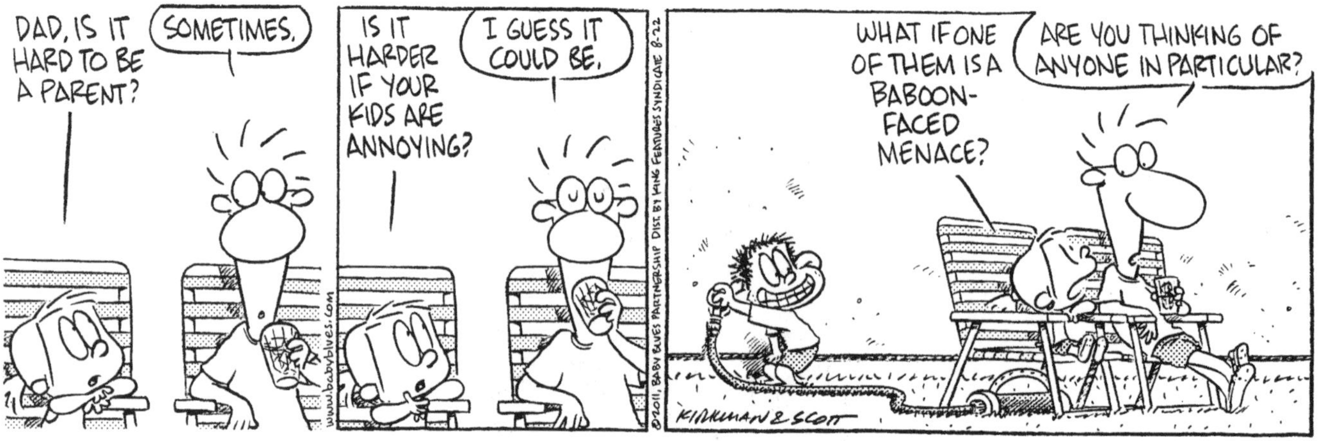
DAD, IS IT HARD TO BE A PARENT?
SOMETIMES.
IS IT HARDER IF YOUR KIDS ARE ANNOYING?
I GUESS IT COULD BE.
WHAT IF ONE OF THEM IS A BABOON-FACED MENACE?
ARE YOU THINKING OF ANYONE IN PARTICULAR?
www.babyblues.com
©2011, BABY BLUES PARTNERSHIP DIST. BY KING FEATURES SYNDICATE 8-22
KIRKMAN & SCOTT

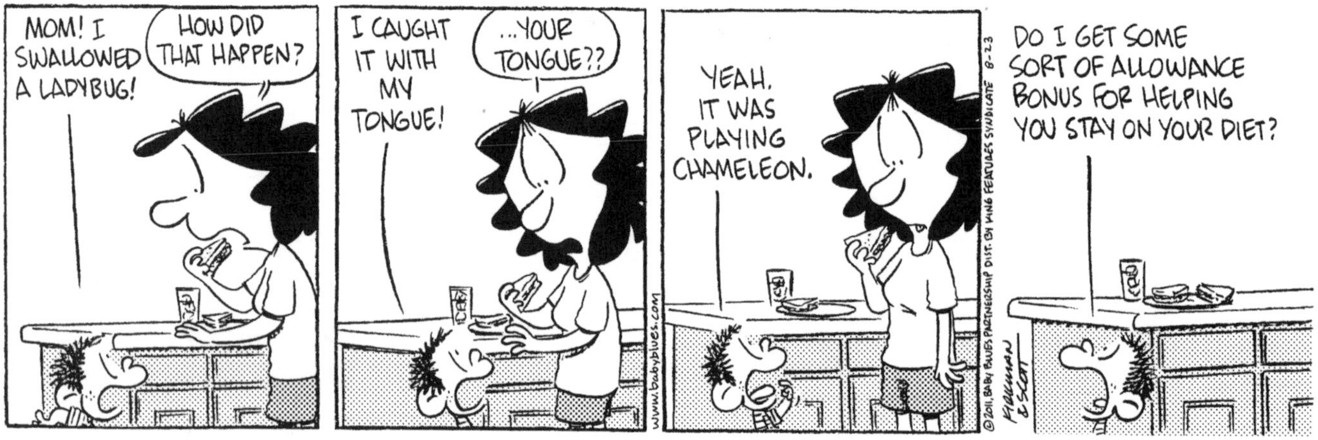
MOM! I SWALLOWED A LADYBUG!
HOW DID THAT HAPPEN?
I CAUGHT IT WITH MY TONGUE!
...YOUR TONGUE??
YEAH. IT WAS PLAYING CHAMELEON.
DO I GET SOME SORT OF ALLOWANCE BONUS FOR HELPING YOU STAY ON YOUR DIET?
www.babyblues.com
©2011, BABY BLUES PARTNERSHIP DIST. BY KING FEATURES SYNDICATE 8-23
KIRKMAN & SCOTT

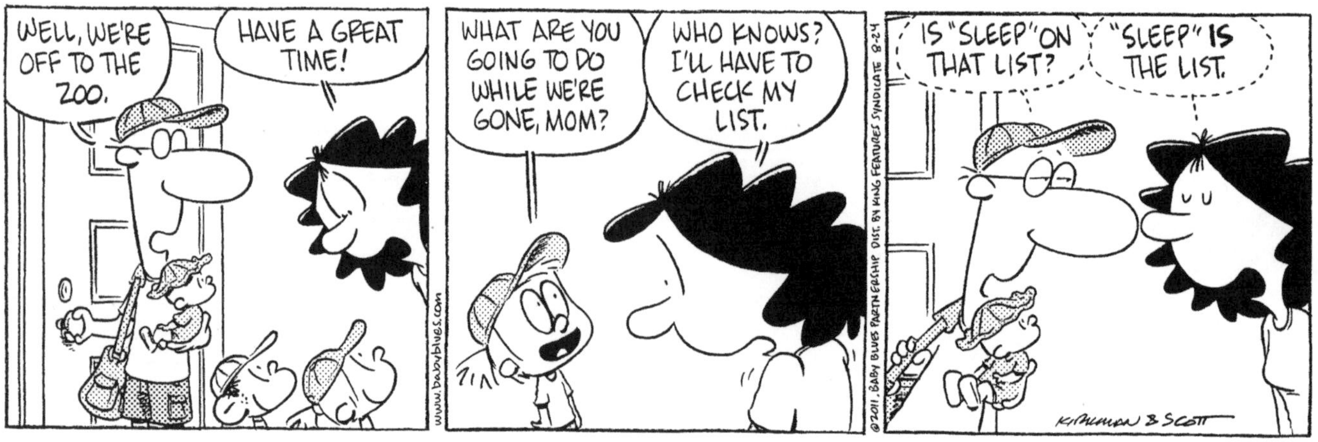
WELL, WE'RE OFF TO THE ZOO.
HAVE A GREAT TIME!
WHAT ARE YOU GOING TO DO WHILE WE'RE GONE, MOM?
WHO KNOWS? I'LL HAVE TO CHECK MY LIST.
IS "SLEEP" ON THAT LIST?
"SLEEP" IS THE LIST.
www.babyblues.com
©2011, BABY BLUES PARTNERSHIP DIST. BY KING FEATURES SYNDICATE 8-24
KIRKMAN & SCOTT

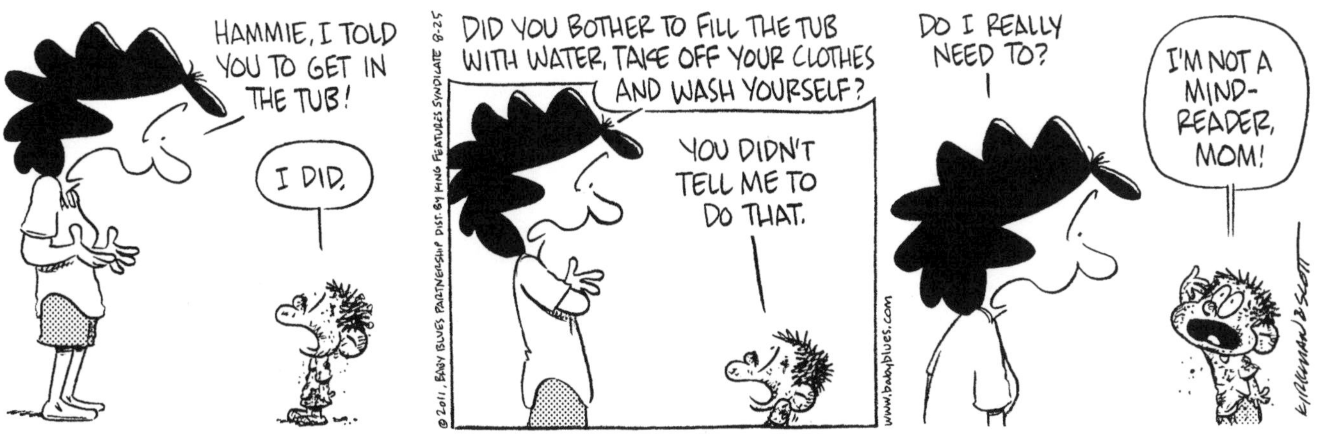
HAMMIE, I TOLD YOU TO GET IN THE TUB!
I DID.
© 2011, BABY BLUES PARTNERSHIP DIST. BY KING FEATURES SYNDICATE 8-25
DID YOU BOTHER TO FILL THE TUB WITH WATER, TAKE OFF YOUR CLOTHES AND WASH YOURSELF?
YOU DIDN'T TELL ME TO DO THAT.
www.babyblues.com
DO I REALLY NEED TO?
I'M NOT A MIND-READER, MOM!
KIRKMAN & SCOTT

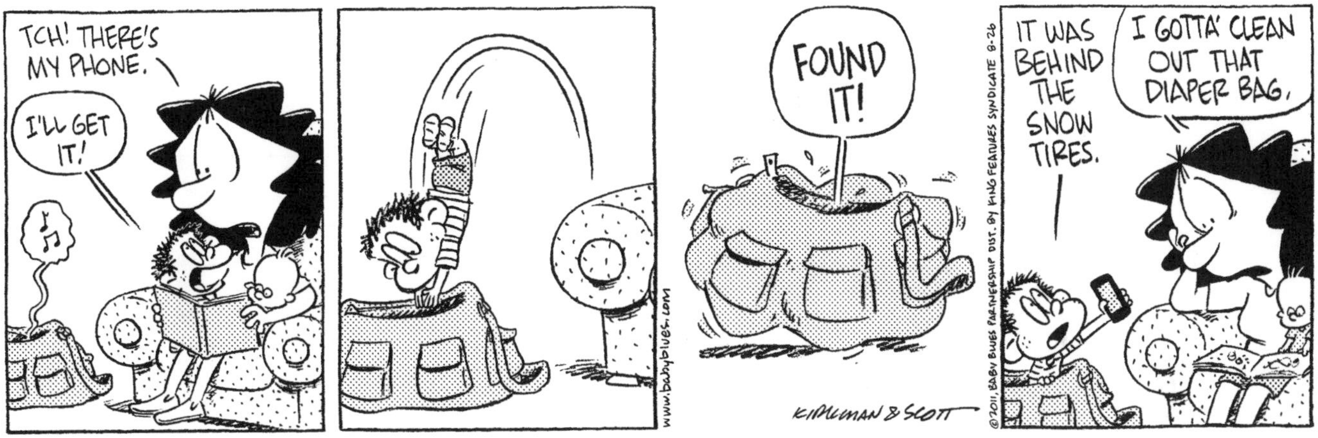
TCH! THERE'S MY PHONE.
I'LL GET IT!
www.babyblues.com
FOUND IT!
KIRKMAN & SCOTT
© 2011, BABY BLUES PARTNERSHIP DIST. BY KING FEATURES SYNDICATE 8-26
IT WAS BEHIND THE SNOW TIRES.
I GOTTA' CLEAN OUT THAT DIAPER BAG.

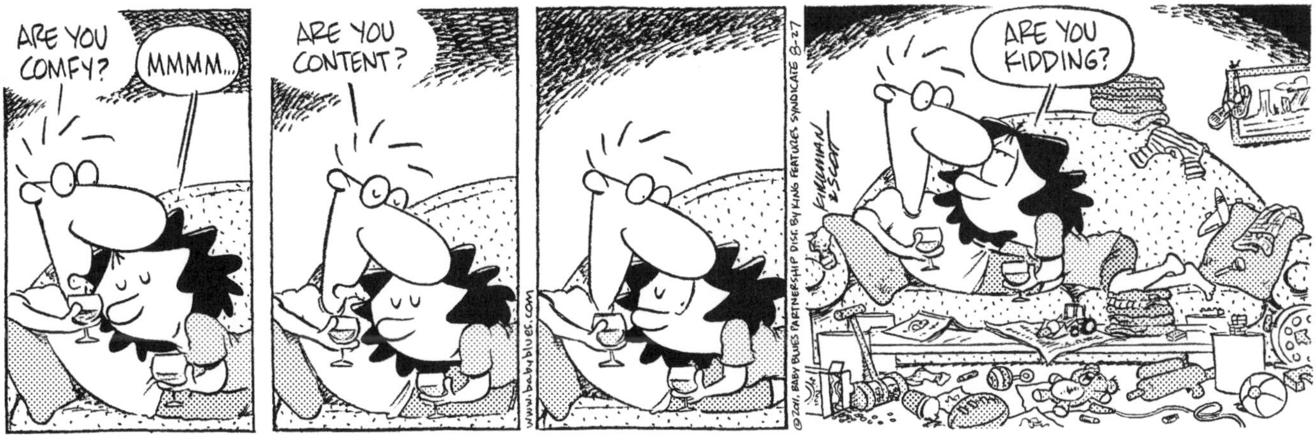
ARE YOU COMFY?
MMMM...
ARE YOU CONTENT?
www.babyblues.com
© 2011, BABY BLUES PARTNERSHIP DIST. BY KING FEATURES SYNDICATE 8-27
KIRKMAN & SCOTT
ARE YOU KIDDING?

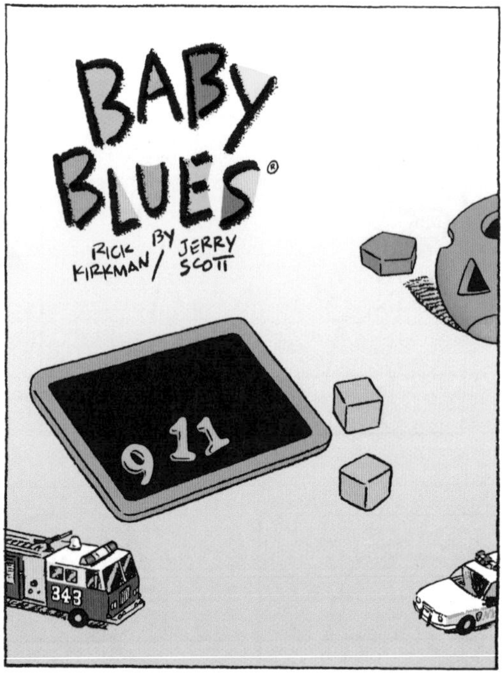
BABY BLUES®
RICK KIRKMAN / BY JERRY SCOTT
9 11
343

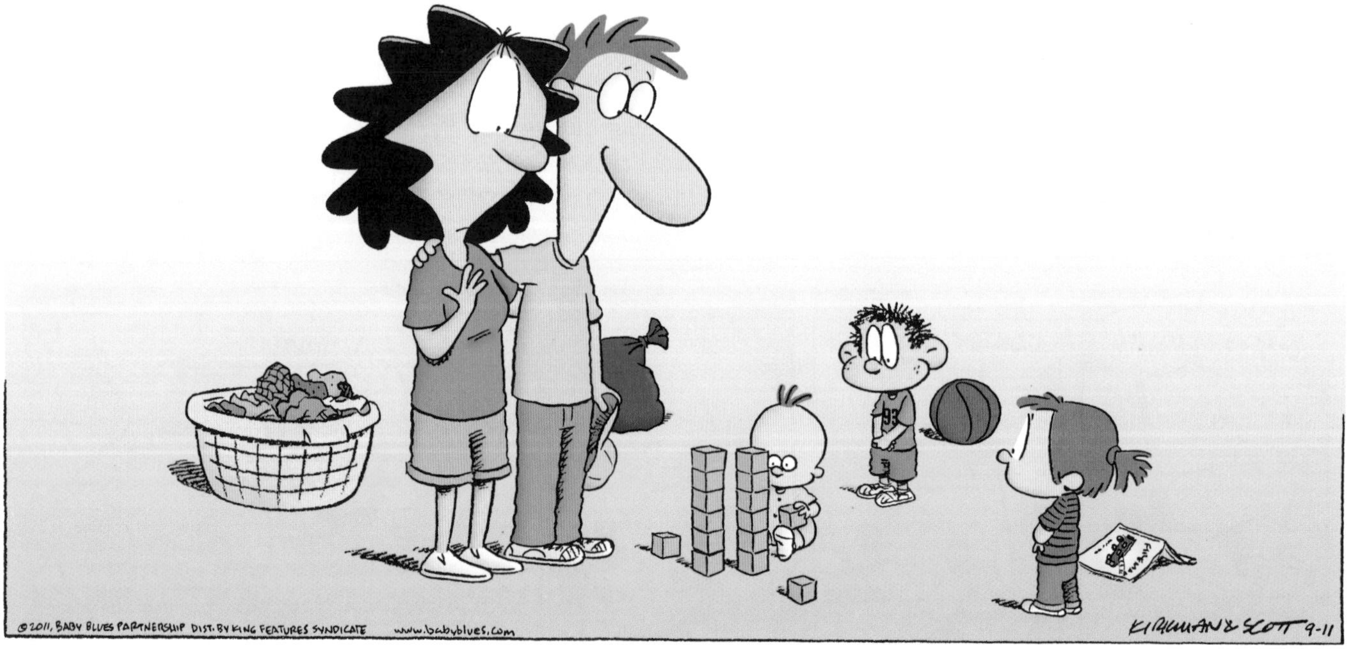
93
©2011, BABY BLUES PARTNERSHIP DIST. BY KING FEATURES SYNDICATE
www.babyblues.com
KIRKMAN & SCOTT 9-11

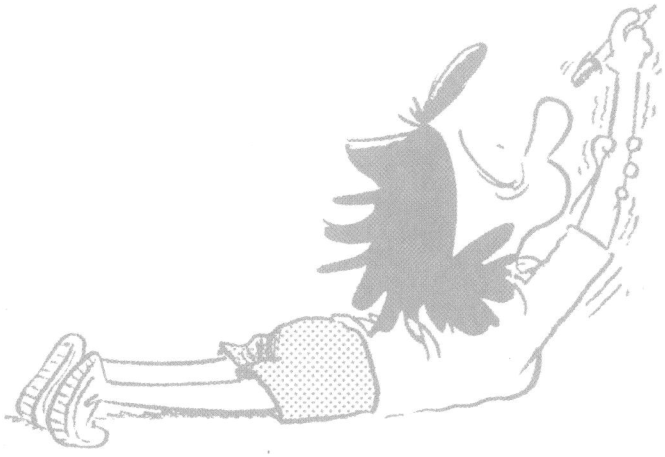

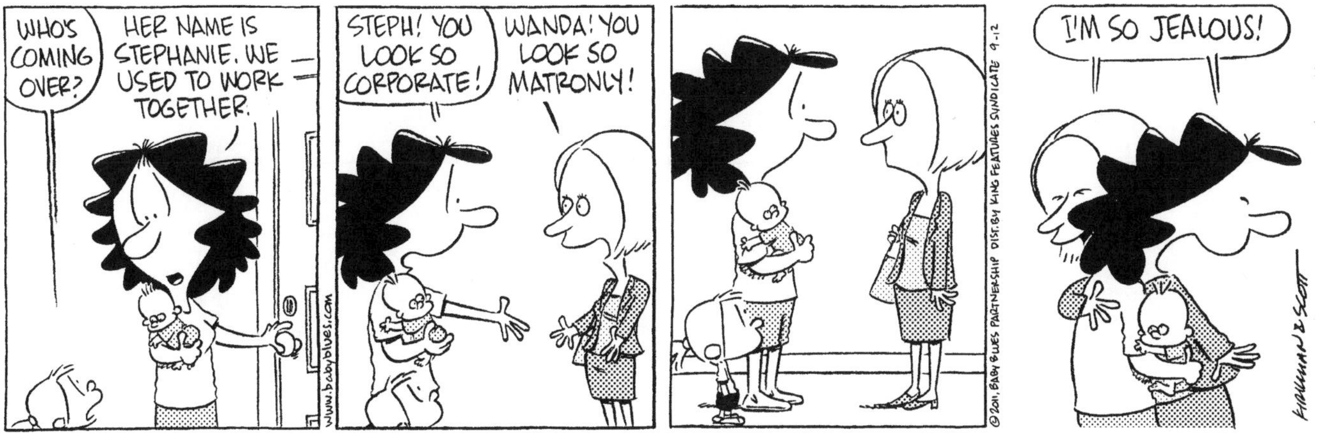
WHO'S COMING OVER?
HER NAME IS STEPHANIE. WE USED TO WORK TOGETHER.
www.babyblues.com
STEPH! YOU LOOK SO CORPORATE!
WANDA! YOU LOOK SO MATRONLY!
©2011, BABY BLUES PARTNERSHIP DIST. BY KING FEATURES SYNDICATE 9-12
I'M SO JEALOUS!
KIRKMAN & SCOTT

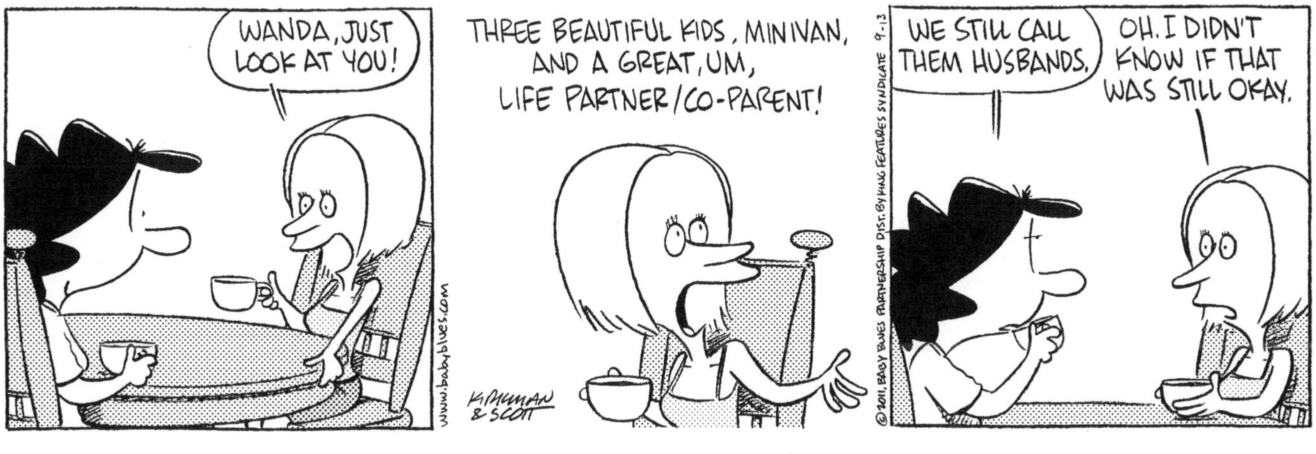
WANDA, JUST LOOK AT YOU!
www.babyblues.com
THREE BEAUTIFUL KIDS, MINIVAN, AND A GREAT, UM, LIFE PARTNER/CO-PARENT!
KIRKMAN & SCOTT
©2011, BABY BLUES PARTNERSHIP DIST. BY KING FEATURES SYNDICATE 9-13
WE STILL CALL THEM HUSBANDS.
OH. I DIDN'T KNOW IF THAT WAS STILL OKAY.

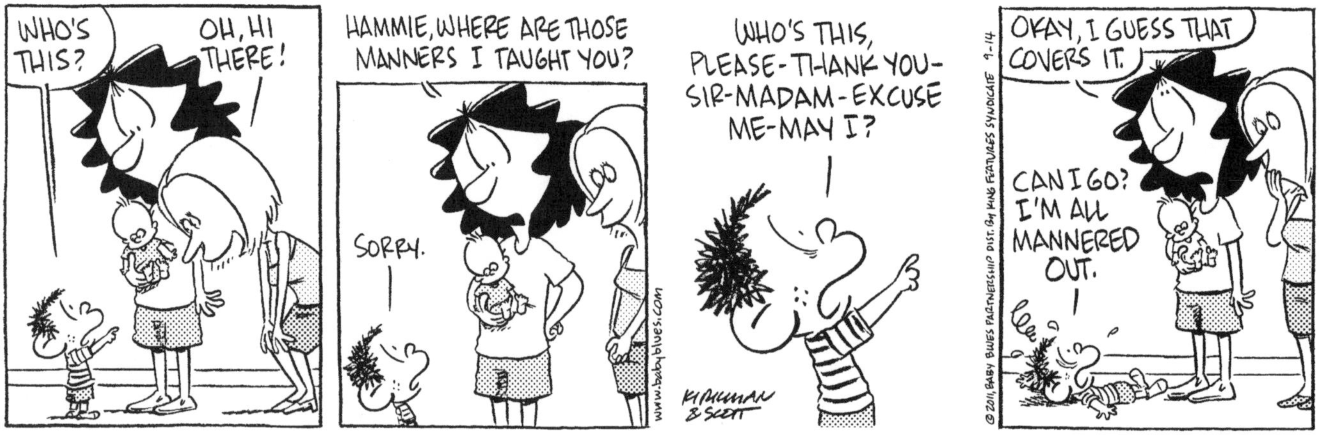
WHO'S THIS?
OH, HI THERE!
HAMMIE, WHERE ARE THOSE MANNERS I TAUGHT YOU?
SORRY.
www.babyblues.com
WHO'S THIS, PLEASE-THANK YOU-SIR-MADAM-EXCUSE ME-MAY I?
KIRKMAN & SCOTT
© 2011, BABY BLUES PARTNERSHIP DIST. BY KING FEATURES SYNDICATE 9-14
OKAY, I GUESS THAT COVERS IT.
CAN I GO? I'M ALL MANNERED OUT.

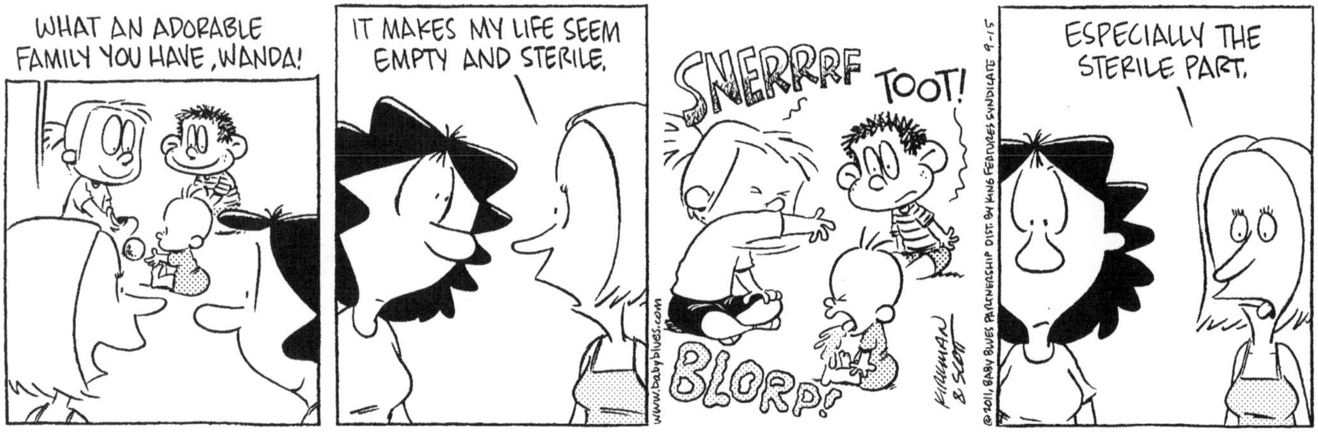
WHAT AN ADORABLE FAMILY YOU HAVE, WANDA!
IT MAKES MY LIFE SEEM EMPTY AND STERILE.
www.babyblues.com
SNERRRF
TOOT!
BLORP!
KIRKMAN & SCOTT
© 2011, BABY BLUES PARTNERSHIP DIST. BY KING FEATURES SYNDICATE 9-15
ESPECIALLY THE STERILE PART.

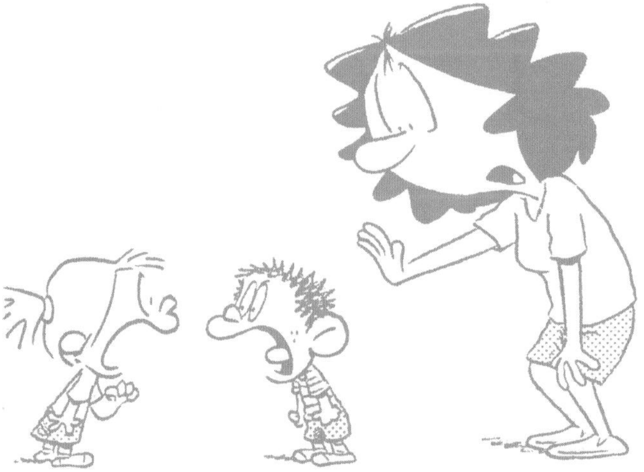

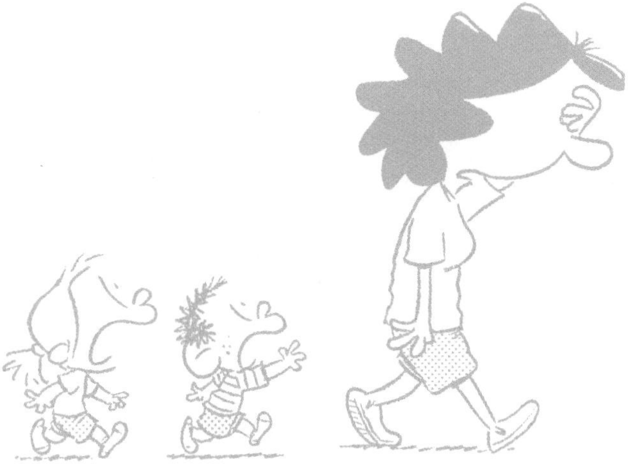

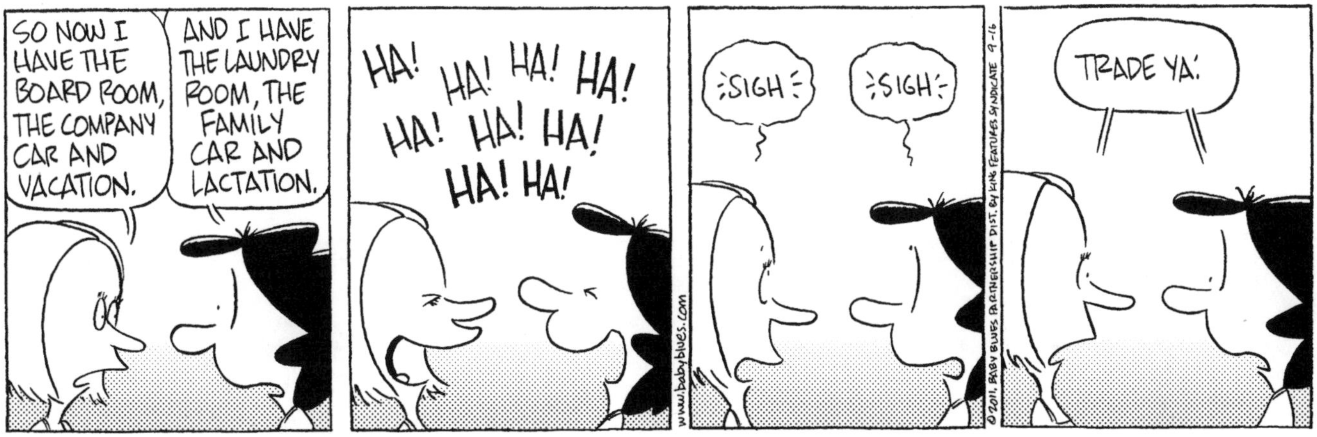
SO NOW I HAVE THE BOARD ROOM, THE COMPANY CAR AND VACATION.
AND I HAVE THE LAUNDRY ROOM, THE FAMILY CAR AND LACTATION.
HA! HA! HA! HA! HA! HA! HA! HA! HA!
SIGH
SIGH
TRADE YA.
www.babyblues.com
©2011, BABY BLUES PARTNERSHIP DIST. BY KING FEATURES SYNDICATE 9-16

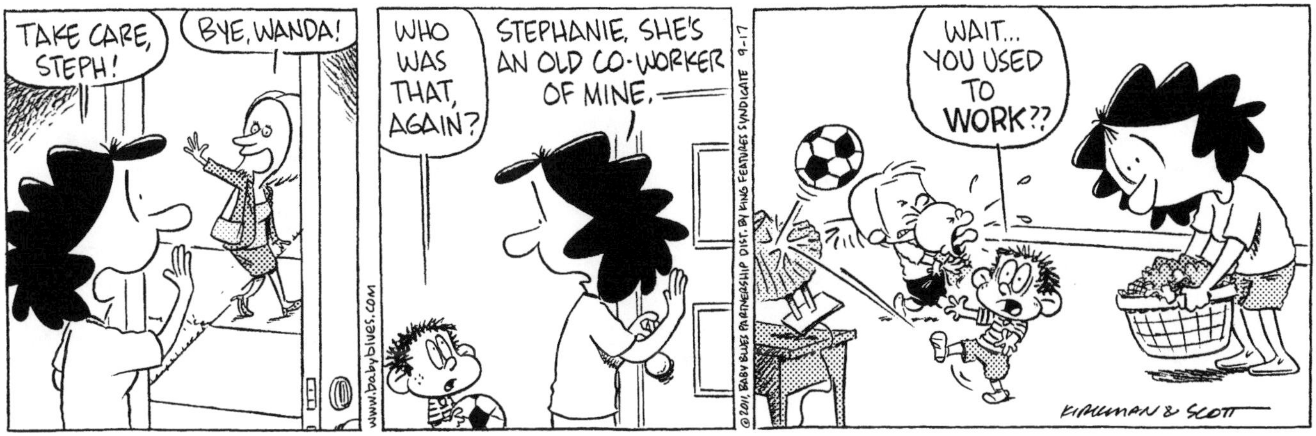
TAKE CARE, STEPH!
BYE, WANDA!
WHO WAS THAT, AGAIN?
STEPHANIE. SHE'S AN OLD CO-WORKER OF MINE.
WAIT... YOU USED TO WORK??
www.babyblues.com
©2011, BABY BLUES PARTNERSHIP DIST. BY KING FEATURES SYNDICATE 9-17
KIRKMAN & SCOTT

BABY BLUES®
BY RICK KIRKMAN / JERRY SCOTT

THERE'S THE BIG DIPPER, KIDS.
THE BIG WHAT??
ALL I SEE IS SKY.
RIGHT THERE, THE STARS THAT LOOK LIKE A WATER DIPPER.
WHAT'S A WATER DIPPER?
THAT'S JUST A BUNCH OF DOTS.
IT'S ALSO PART OF URSA MAJOR.
THERE'S AN ARMY GUY UP THERE? SERIOUSLY?
IS HE IN A SPACESHIP?
NO! NO! THOSE STARS FORM THE SHAPE OF A BEAR!
WHAT ARE YOU TALKING ABOUT?
BEARS DON'T JOIN THE ARMY, DAD.
IF THEY DID, MAYBE THIS WOULDN'T BE SO BORING.
HOW WAS THE STAR GAZING?
GALILEO WOULD WEEP.
www.babyblues.com
©2011, BABY BLUES PARTNERSHIP DIST. BY KING FEATURES SYNDICATE
KIRKMAN & SCOTT 9-18

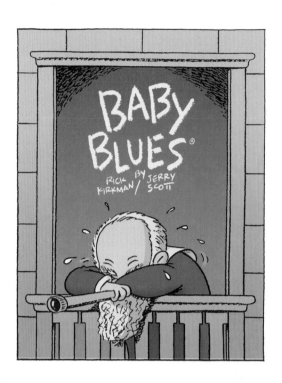

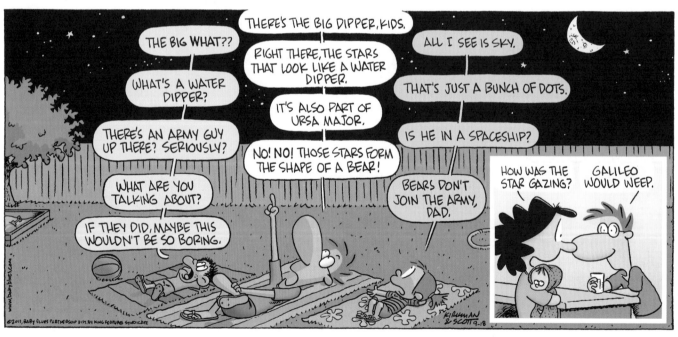

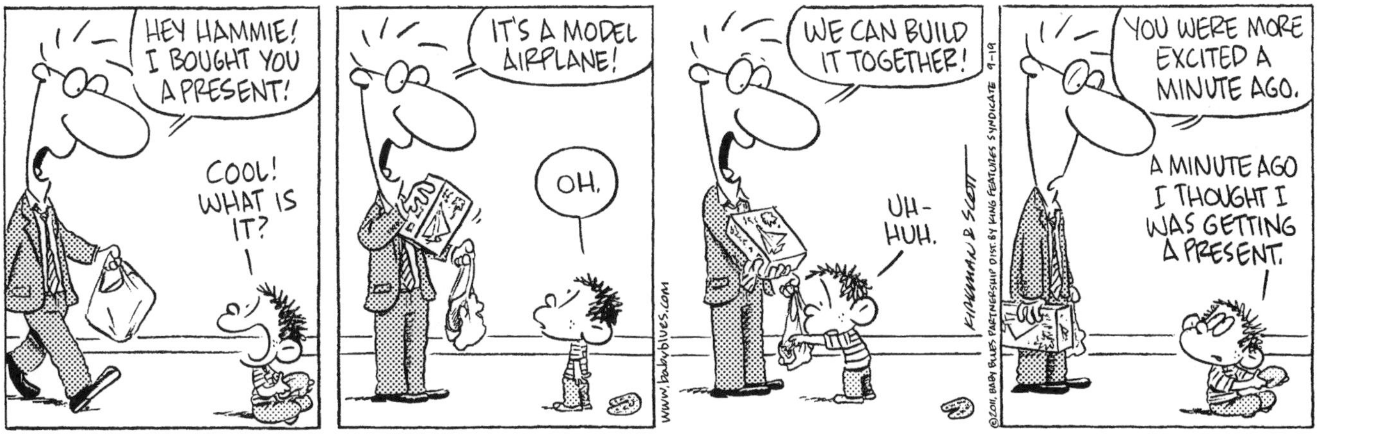
HEY HAMMIE! I BOUGHT YOU A PRESENT!
COOL! WHAT IS IT?
IT'S A MODEL AIRPLANE!
OH.
www.babyblues.com
WE CAN BUILD IT TOGETHER!
UH-HUH.
KIRKMAN & SCOTT
9-19
©2011, BABY BLUES PARTNERSHIP DIST. BY KING FEATURES SYNDICATE
YOU WERE MORE EXCITED A MINUTE AGO.
A MINUTE AGO I THOUGHT I WAS GETTING A PRESENT.

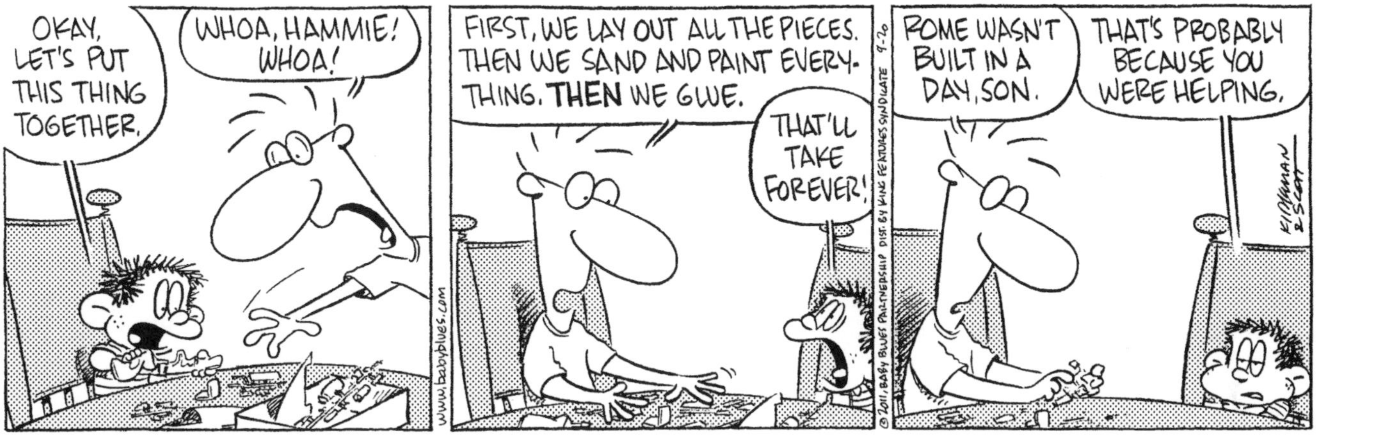
OKAY, LET'S PUT THIS THING TOGETHER.
WHOA, HAMMIE! WHOA!
www.babyblues.com
FIRST, WE LAY OUT ALL THE PIECES. THEN WE SAND AND PAINT EVERYTHING. THEN WE GLUE.
THAT'LL TAKE FOREVER!
9-20
©2011, BABY BLUES PARTNERSHIP DIST. BY KING FEATURES SYNDICATE
ROME WASN'T BUILT IN A DAY, SON.
THAT'S PROBABLY BECAUSE YOU WERE HELPING.
KIRKMAN & SCOTT

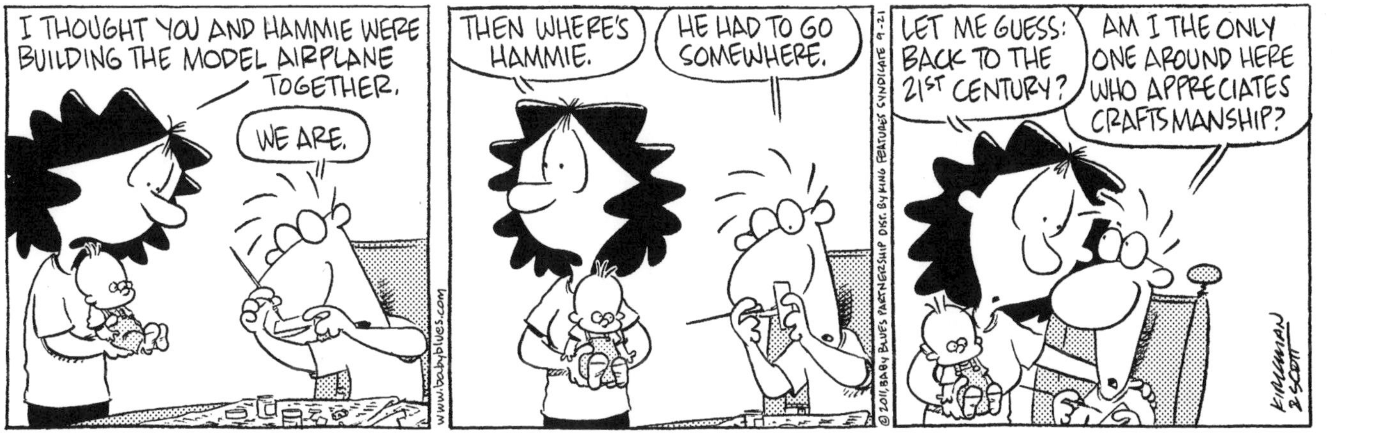
I THOUGHT YOU AND HAMMIE WERE BUILDING THE MODEL AIRPLANE TOGETHER.
WE ARE.
www.babyblues.com
THEN WHERE'S HAMMIE.
HE HAD TO GO SOMEWHERE.
9-21
©2011, BABY BLUES PARTNERSHIP DIST. BY KING FEATURES SYNDICATE
LET ME GUESS: BACK TO THE 21ST CENTURY?
AM I THE ONLY ONE AROUND HERE WHO APPRECIATES CRAFTSMANSHIP?
KIRKMAN & SCOTT

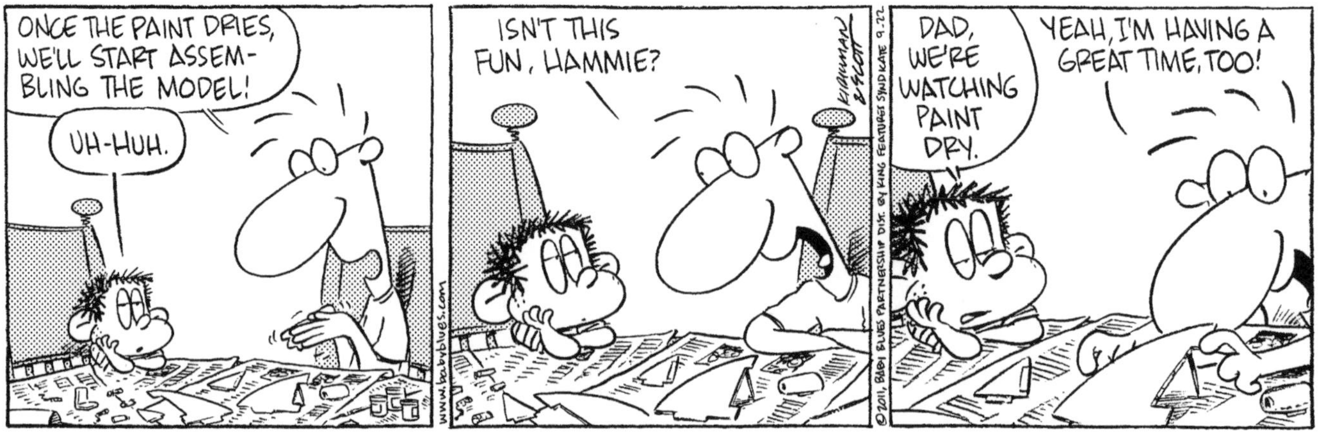
ONCE THE PAINT DRIES, WE'LL START ASSEMBLING THE MODEL!
UH-HUH.
ISN'T THIS FUN, HAMMIE?
DAD, WE'RE WATCHING PAINT DRY.
YEAH, I'M HAVING A GREAT TIME, TOO!
©2011, BABY BLUES PARTNERSHIP DIST. BY KING FEATURES SYNDICATE 9-22
www.babyblues.com

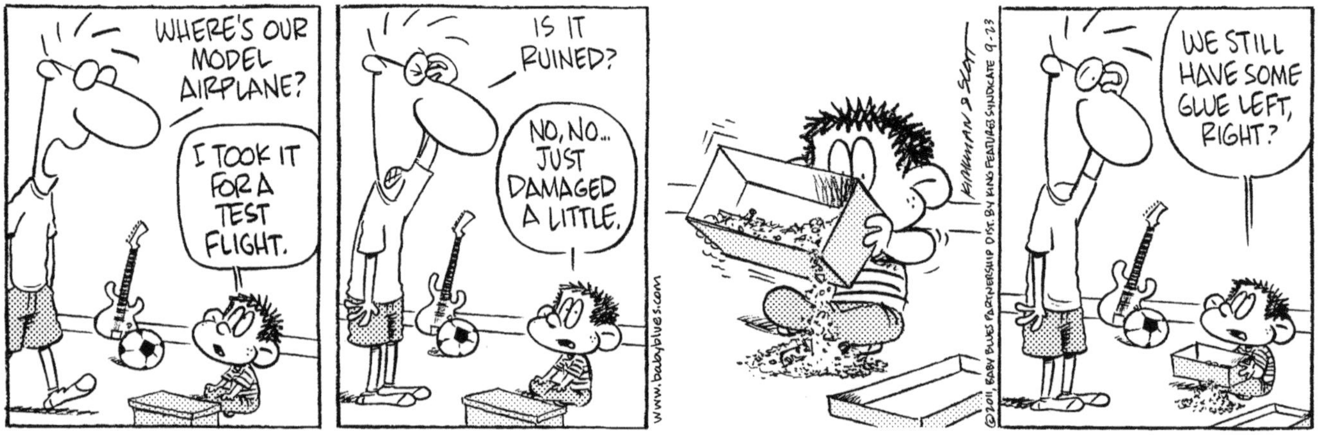
WHERE'S OUR MODEL AIRPLANE?
I TOOK IT FOR A TEST FLIGHT.
IS IT RUINED?
NO, NO... JUST DAMAGED A LITTLE.
WE STILL HAVE SOME GLUE LEFT, RIGHT?
©2011, BABY BLUES PARTNERSHIP DIST. BY KING FEATURES SYNDICATE 9-23
www.babyblues.com

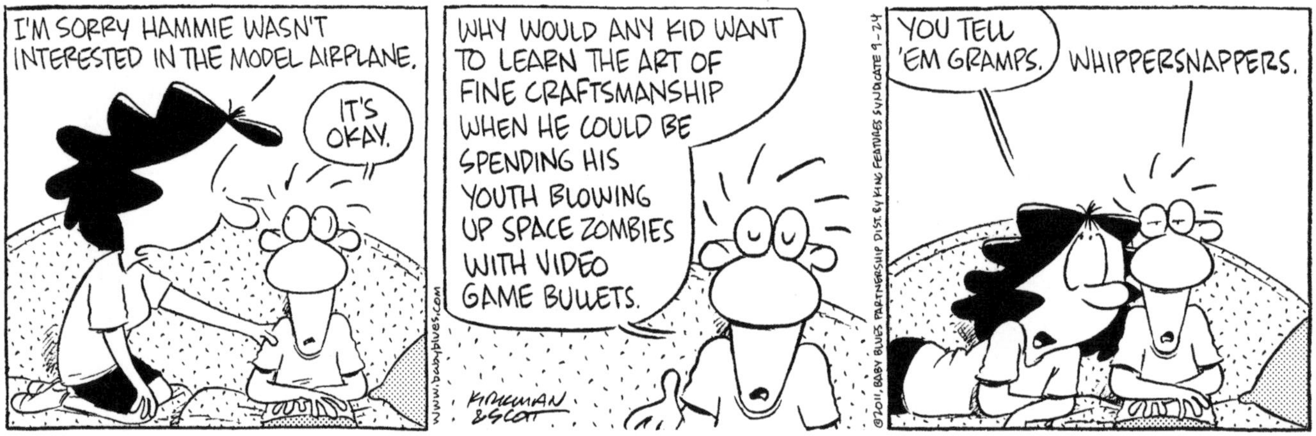
I'M SORRY HAMMIE WASN'T INTERESTED IN THE MODEL AIRPLANE.
IT'S OKAY.
WHY WOULD ANY KID WANT TO LEARN THE ART OF FINE CRAFTSMANSHIP WHEN HE COULD BE SPENDING HIS YOUTH BLOWING UP SPACE ZOMBIES WITH VIDEO GAME BULLETS.
YOU TELL 'EM GRAMPS.
WHIPPERSNAPPERS.
©2011, BABY BLUES PARTNERSHIP DIST. BY KING FEATURES SYNDICATE 9-24
www.babyblues.com

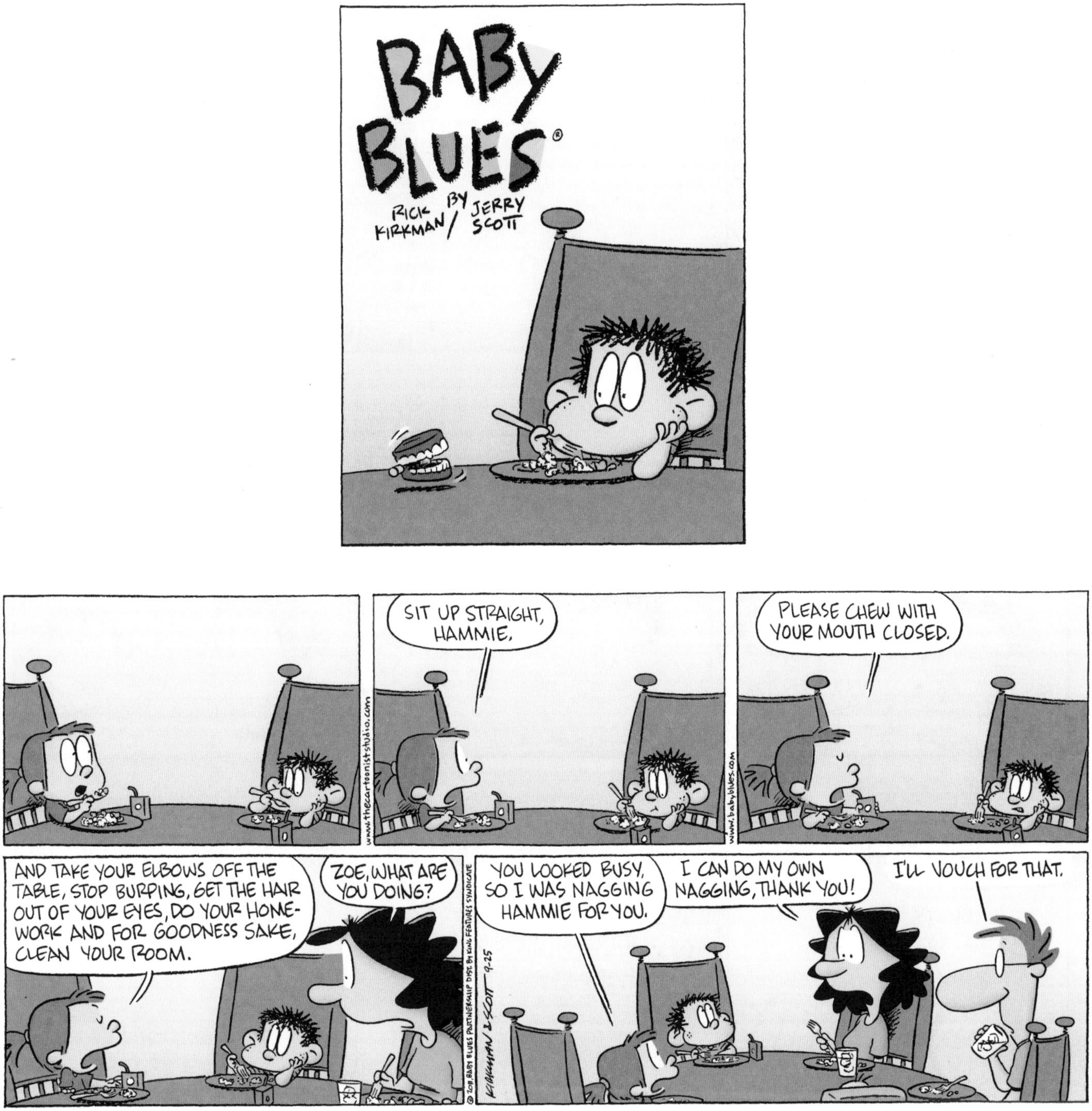
BABY BLUES®
BY RICK KIRKMAN / JERRY SCOTT
www.thecartoonniststudio.com
SIT UP STRAIGHT, HAMMIE.
PLEASE CHEW WITH YOUR MOUTH CLOSED.
www.babyblues.com
AND TAKE YOUR ELBOWS OFF THE TABLE, STOP BURPING, GET THE HAIR OUT OF YOUR EYES, DO YOUR HOME-WORK AND FOR GOODNESS SAKE, CLEAN YOUR ROOM.
ZOE, WHAT ARE YOU DOING?
© 2011, BABY BLUES PARTNERSHIP DIST. BY KING FEATURES SYNDICATE
KIRKMAN & SCOTT 9-25
YOU LOOKED BUSY, SO I WAS NAGGING HAMMIE FOR YOU.
I CAN DO MY OWN NAGGING, THANK YOU!
I'LL VOUCH FOR THAT.

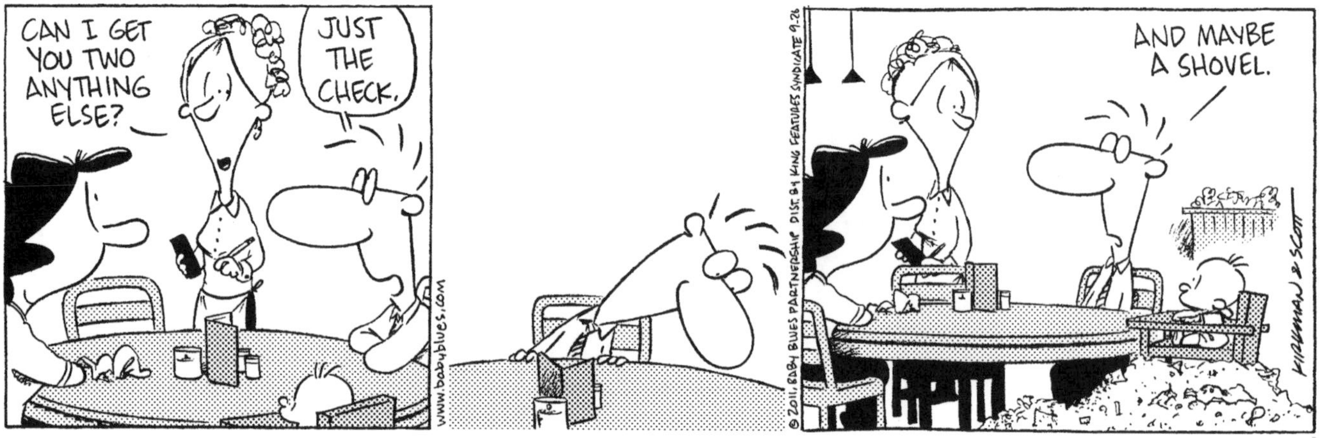
CAN I GET YOU TWO ANYTHING ELSE?
JUST THE CHECK.
www.babyblues.com
© 2011, BABY BLUES PARTNERSHIP DIST. BY KING FEATURES SYNDICATE 9-26
AND MAYBE A SHOVEL.
KIRKMAN & SCOTT

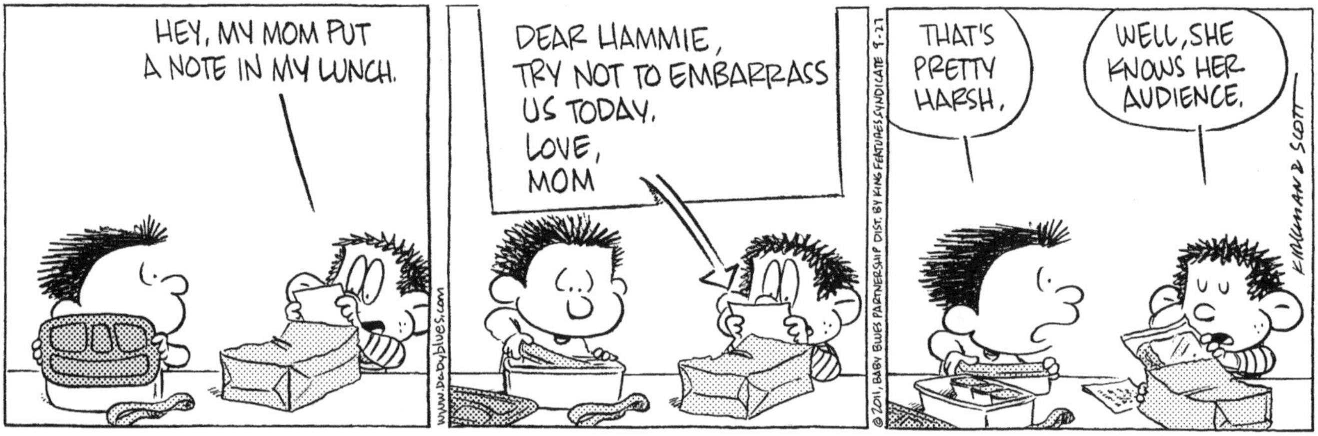
HEY, MY MOM PUT A NOTE IN MY LUNCH.
www.babyblues.com
DEAR HAMMIE, TRY NOT TO EMBARRASS US TODAY. LOVE, MOM
© 2011, BABY BLUES PARTNERSHIP DIST. BY KING FEATURES SYNDICATE 9-27
THAT'S PRETTY HARSH.
WELL, SHE KNOWS HER AUDIENCE.
KIRKMAN & SCOTT

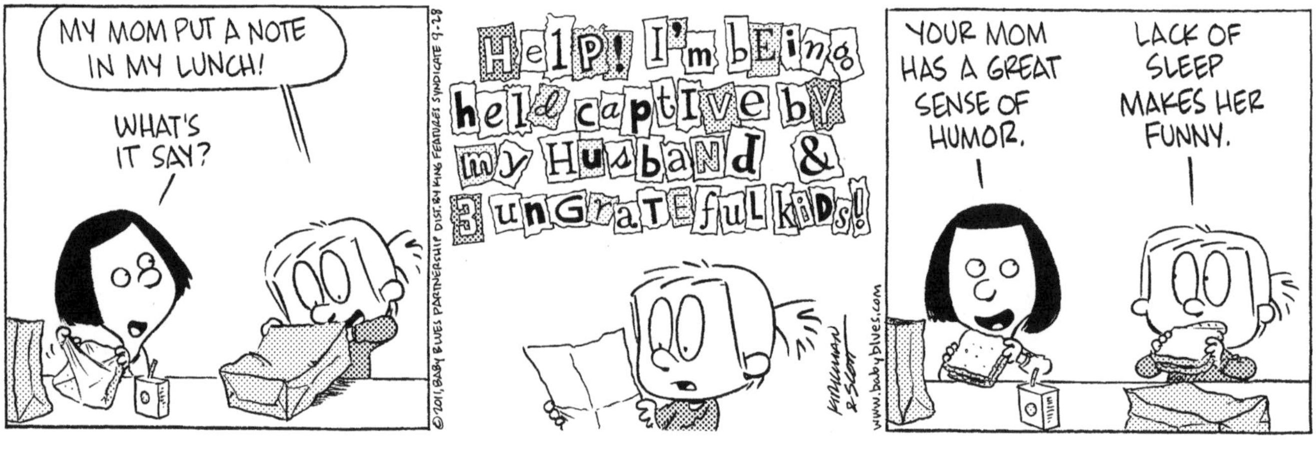
MY MOM PUT A NOTE IN MY LUNCH!
WHAT'S IT SAY?
© 2011, BABY BLUES PARTNERSHIP DIST. BY KING FEATURES SYNDICATE 9-28
HelP! I'm bEing held captive by my Husband & 3 unGrateful kiDs!
KIRKMAN & SCOTT
www.babyblues.com
YOUR MOM HAS A GREAT SENSE OF HUMOR.
LACK OF SLEEP MAKES HER FUNNY.

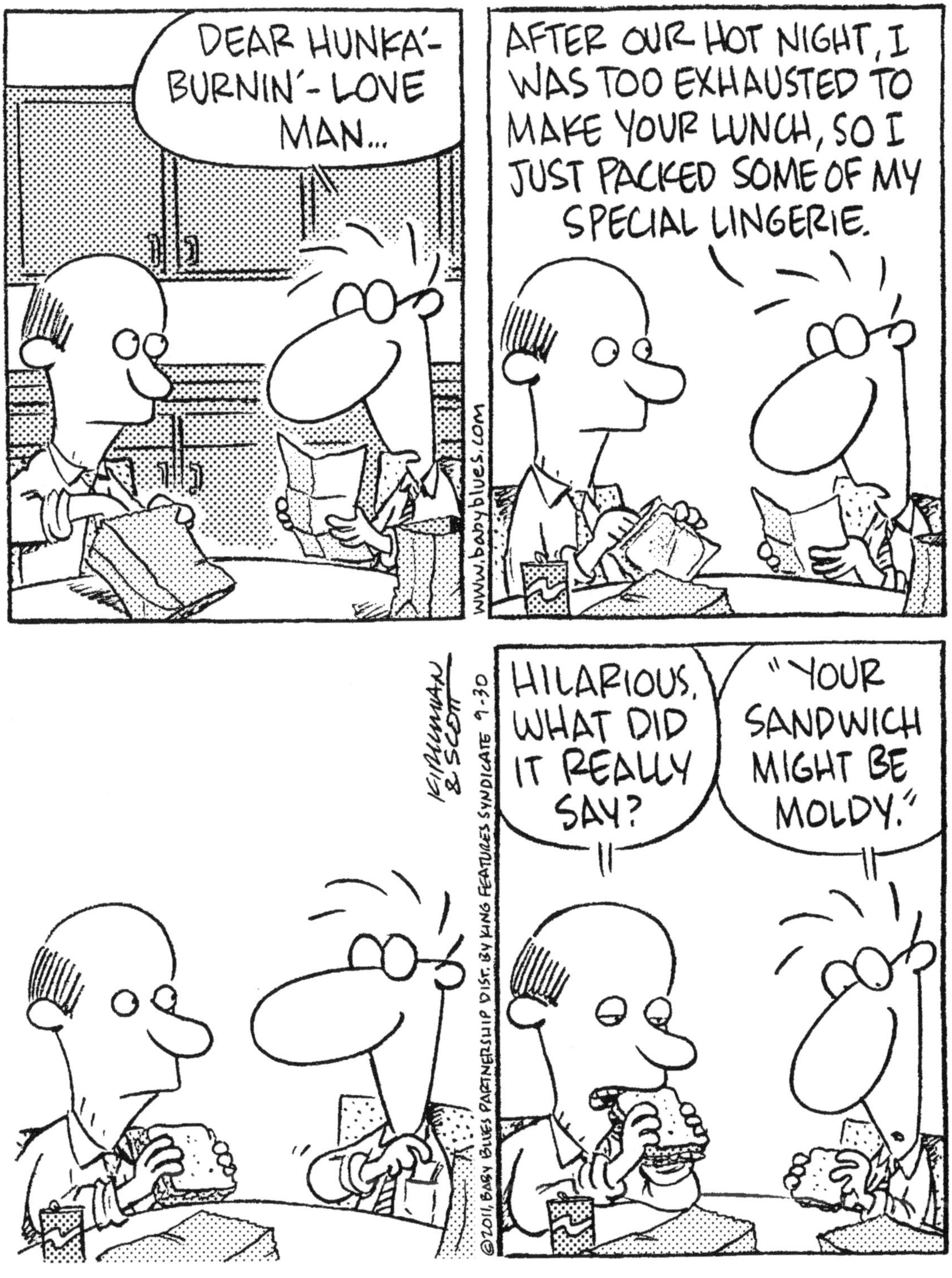
DEAR HUNKA'-BURNIN'-LOVE MAN...
AFTER OUR HOT NIGHT, I WAS TOO EXHAUSTED TO MAKE YOUR LUNCH, SO I JUST PACKED SOME OF MY SPECIAL LINGERIE.
HILARIOUS. WHAT DID IT REALLY SAY?
"YOUR SANDWICH MIGHT BE MOLDY."
www.babyblues.com
KIRKMAN & SCOTT 9-30
©2011, BABY BLUES PARTNERSHIP DIST. BY KING FEATURES SYNDICATE

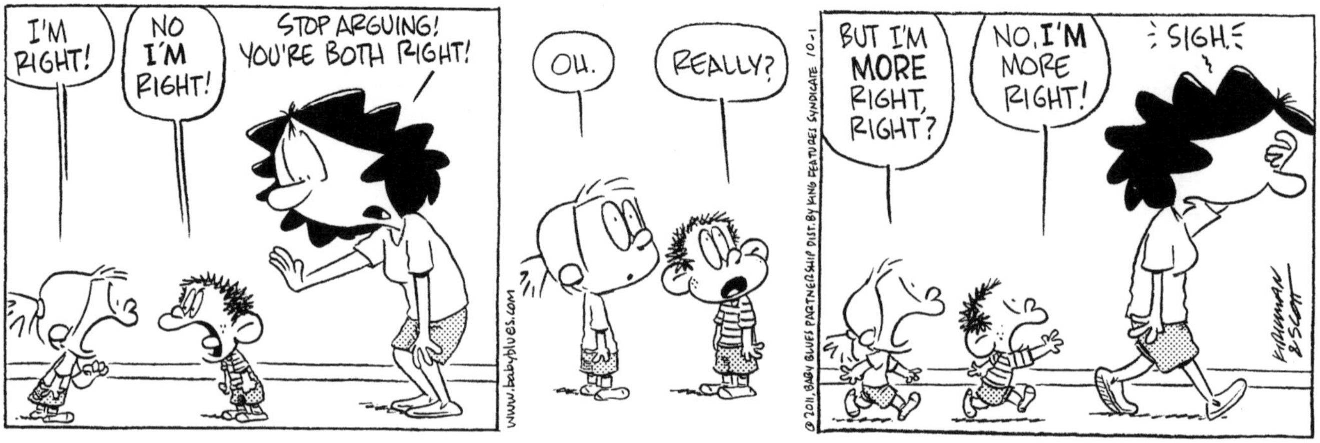
I'M RIGHT!
NO I'M RIGHT!
STOP ARGUING! YOU'RE BOTH RIGHT!
www.babyblues.com
OH.
REALLY?
© 2011, BABY BLUES PARTNERSHIP DIST. BY KING FEATURES SYNDICATE 10-1
BUT I'M MORE RIGHT, RIGHT?
NO, I'M MORE RIGHT!
SIGH.
KIRKMAN & SCOTT

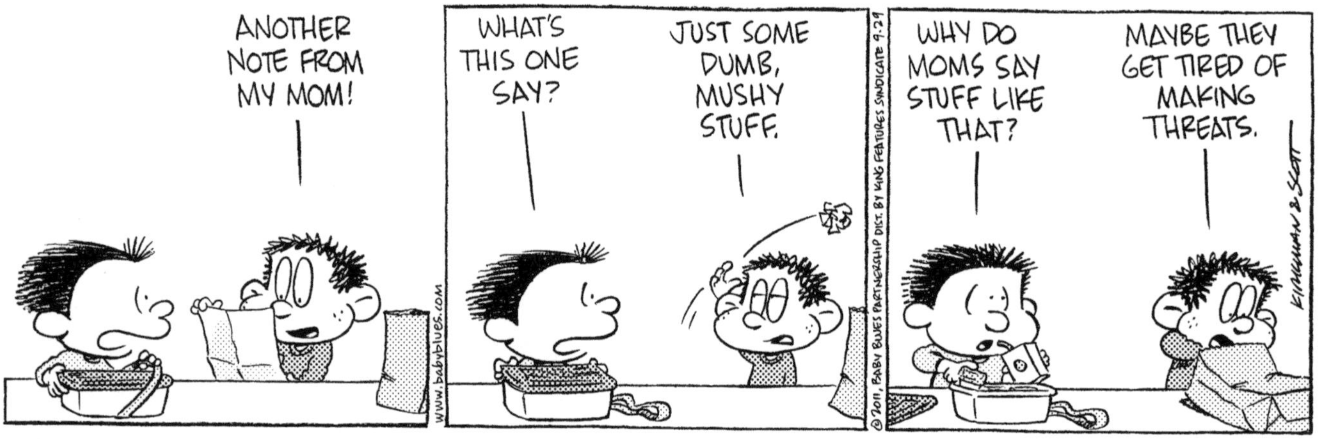
ANOTHER NOTE FROM MY MOM!
www.babyblues.com
WHAT'S THIS ONE SAY?
JUST SOME DUMB, MUSHY STUFF.
© 2011, BABY BLUES PARTNERSHIP DIST. BY KING FEATURES SYNDICATE 9-29
WHY DO MOMS SAY STUFF LIKE THAT?
MAYBE THEY GET TIRED OF MAKING THREATS.
KIRKMAN & SCOTT

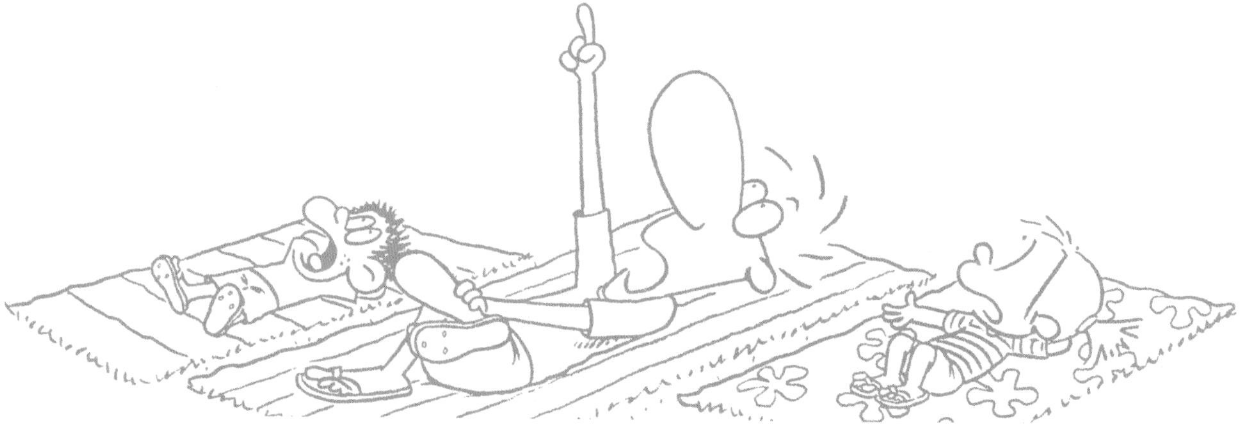

BABY BLUES®

BY RICK KIRKMAN / JERRY SCOTT

WE SHOULD CLEAN OUT THE DIAPER BAG MORE OFTEN.
IS THIS A BREAST PUMP OR THAT THING THAT FELL OFF THE MINIVAN LAST YEAR?
www.thecartoonniststudio.com
www.babyblues.com
©2011, BABY BLUES PARTNERSHIP DIST. BY KING FEATURES SYNDICATE
KIRKMAN & SCOTT 10-2

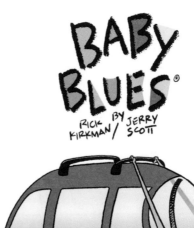

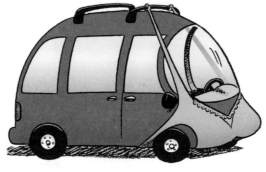

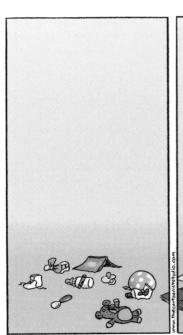

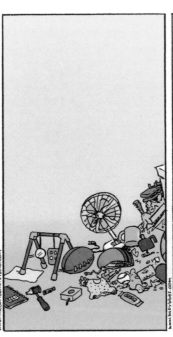

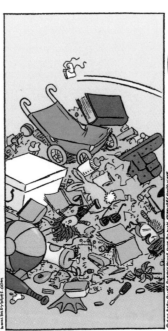

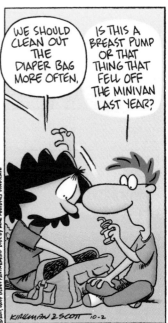

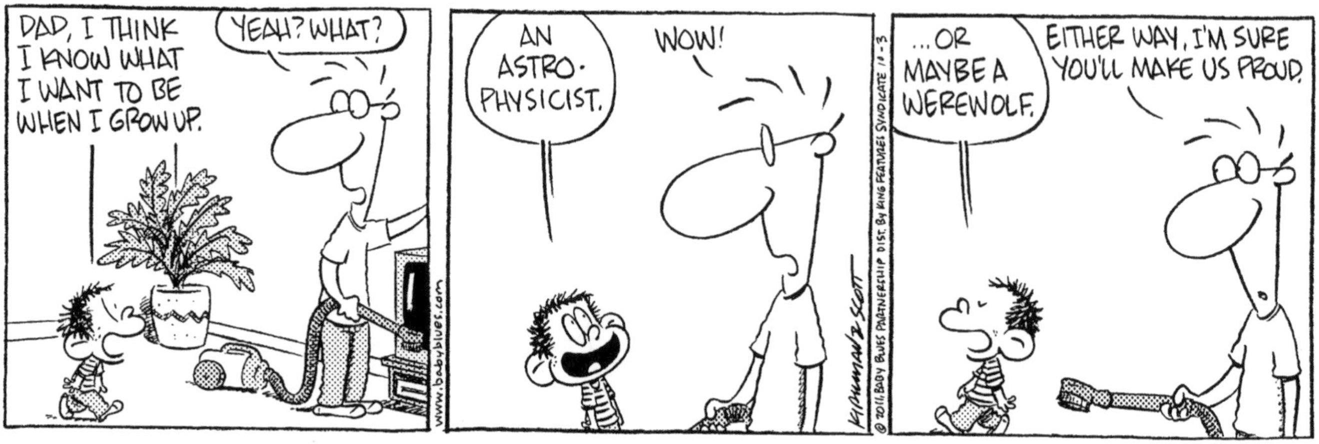
DAD, I THINK I KNOW WHAT I WANT TO BE WHEN I GROW UP.
YEAH? WHAT?
AN ASTRO-PHYSICIST.
WOW!
...OR MAYBE A WEREWOLF.
EITHER WAY, I'M SURE YOU'LL MAKE US PROUD.
www.babyblues.com
KIRKMAN & SCOTT
© 2011, BABY BLUES PARTNERSHIP DIST. BY KING FEATURES SYNDICATE 10-3

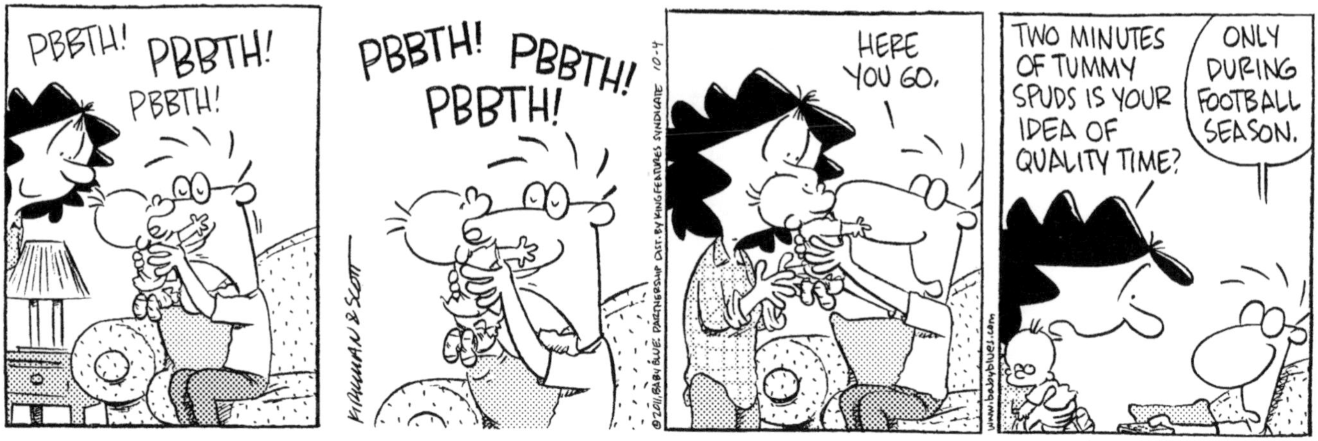
PBBTH! PBBTH! PBBTH!
PBBTH! PBBTH! PBBTH!
KIRKMAN & SCOTT
© 2011, BABY BLUES PARTNERSHIP DIST. BY KING FEATURES SYNDICATE 10-4
HERE YOU GO.
TWO MINUTES OF TUMMY SPUDS IS YOUR IDEA OF QUALITY TIME?
ONLY DURING FOOTBALL SEASON.
www.babyblues.com

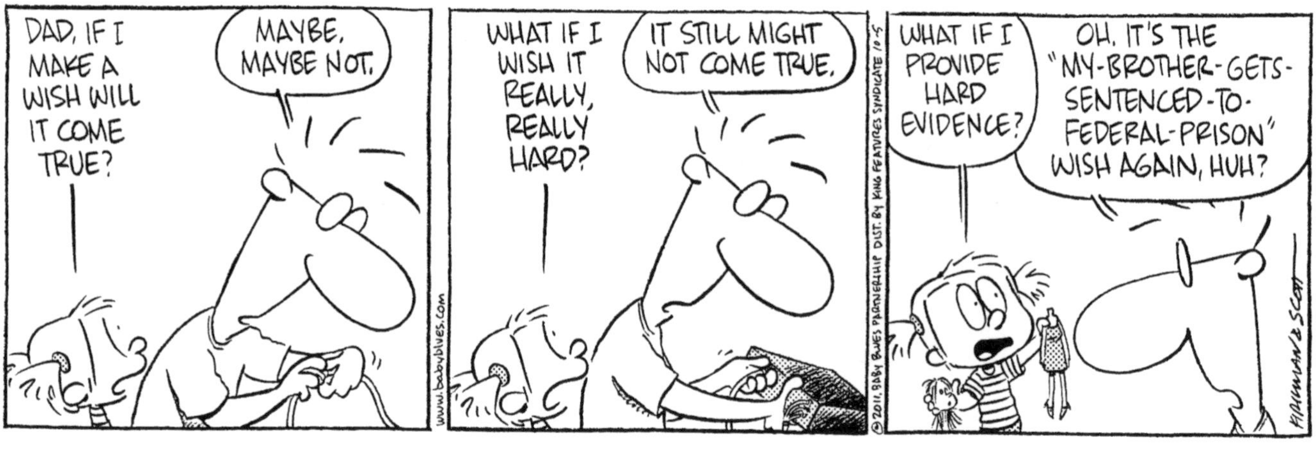
DAD, IF I MAKE A WISH WILL IT COME TRUE?
MAYBE, MAYBE NOT.
www.babyblues.com
WHAT IF I WISH IT REALLY, REALLY HARD?
IT STILL MIGHT NOT COME TRUE.
© 2011, BABY BLUES PARTNERSHIP DIST. BY KING FEATURES SYNDICATE 10-5
WHAT IF I PROVIDE HARD EVIDENCE?
OH, IT'S THE "MY-BROTHER-GETS-SENTENCED-TO-FEDERAL-PRISON" WISH AGAIN, HUH?
KIRKMAN & SCOTT

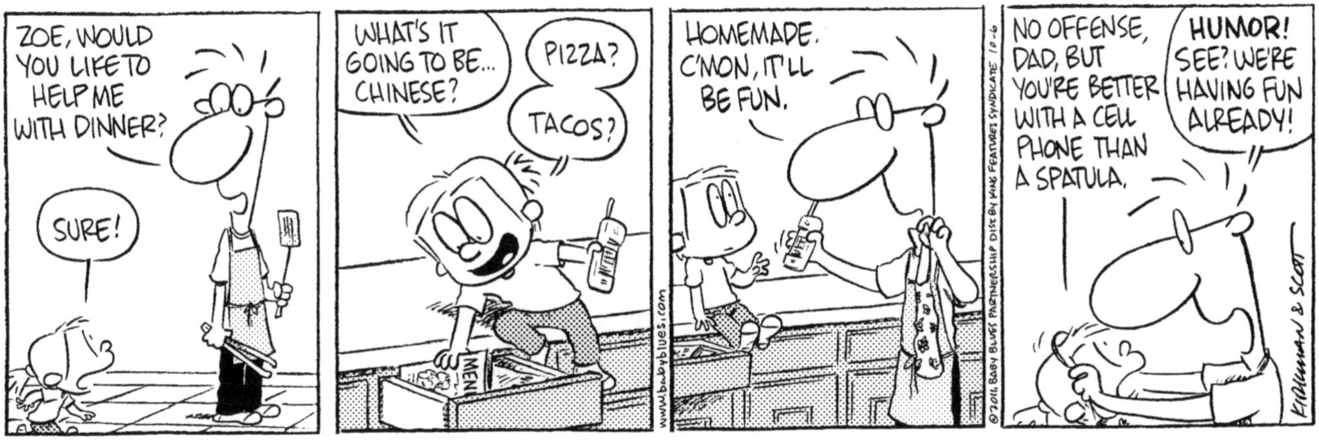
ZOE, WOULD YOU LIKE TO HELP ME WITH DINNER?
SURE!
WHAT'S IT GOING TO BE... CHINESE?
PIZZA?
TACOS?
www.babyblues.com
HOMEMADE. C'MON, IT'LL BE FUN.
© 2011, BABY BLUES PARTNERSHIP DIST. BY KING FEATURES SYNDICATE 10-6
NO OFFENSE, DAD, BUT YOU'RE BETTER WITH A CELL PHONE THAN A SPATULA.
HUMOR! SEE? WE'RE HAVING FUN ALREADY!
KIRKMAN & SCOTT

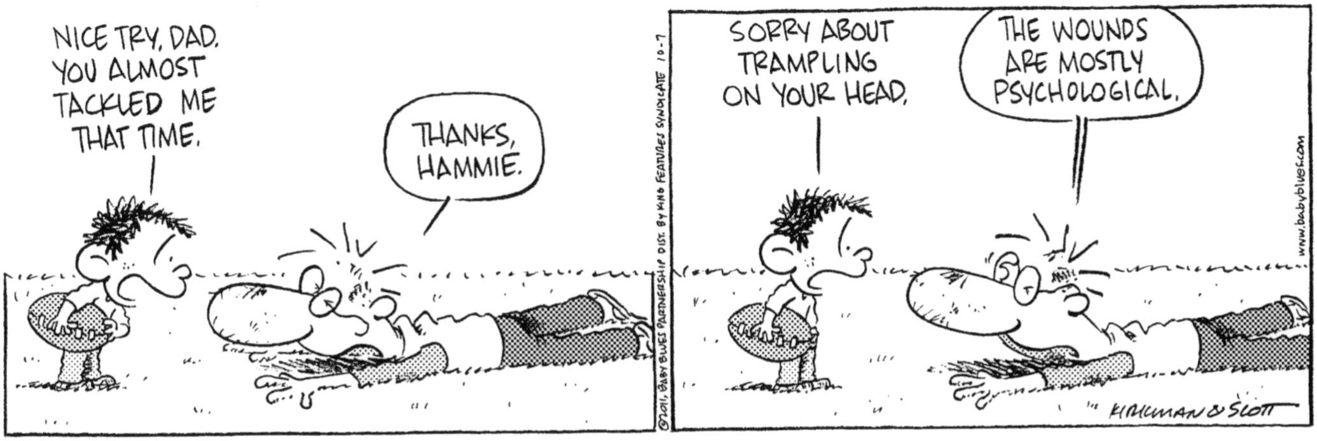
NICE TRY, DAD. YOU ALMOST TACKLED ME THAT TIME.
THANKS, HAMMIE.
© 2011, BABY BLUES PARTNERSHIP DIST. BY KING FEATURES SYNDICATE 10-7
SORRY ABOUT TRAMPLING ON YOUR HEAD.
THE WOUNDS ARE MOSTLY PSYCHOLOGICAL.
www.babyblues.com
KIRKMAN & SCOTT

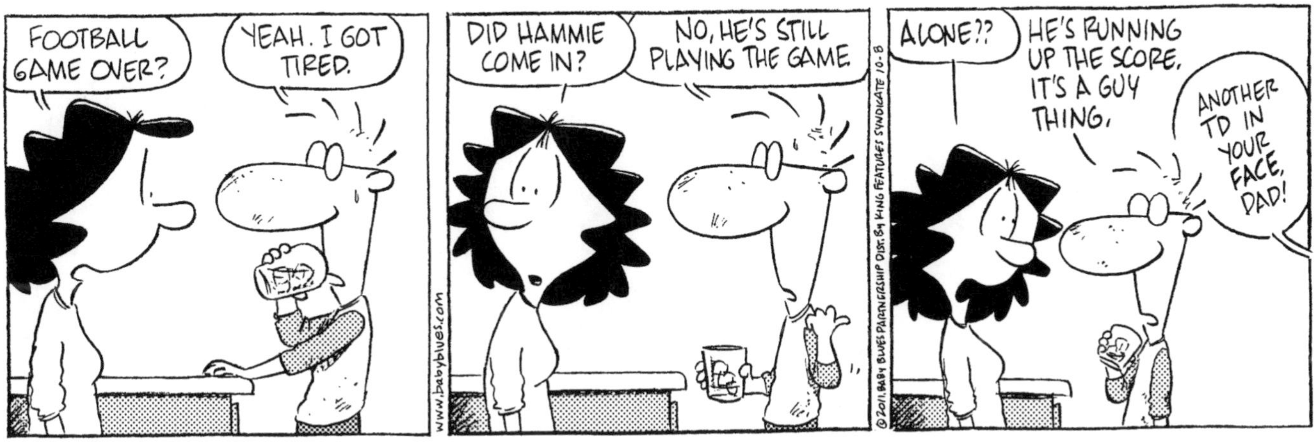
FOOTBALL GAME OVER?
YEAH. I GOT TIRED.
www.babyblues.com
DID HAMMIE COME IN?
NO, HE'S STILL PLAYING THE GAME.
© 2011, BABY BLUES PARTNERSHIP DIST. BY KING FEATURES SYNDICATE 10-8
ALONE??
HE'S RUNNING UP THE SCORE. IT'S A GUY THING.
ANOTHER TD IN YOUR **FACE**, DAD!

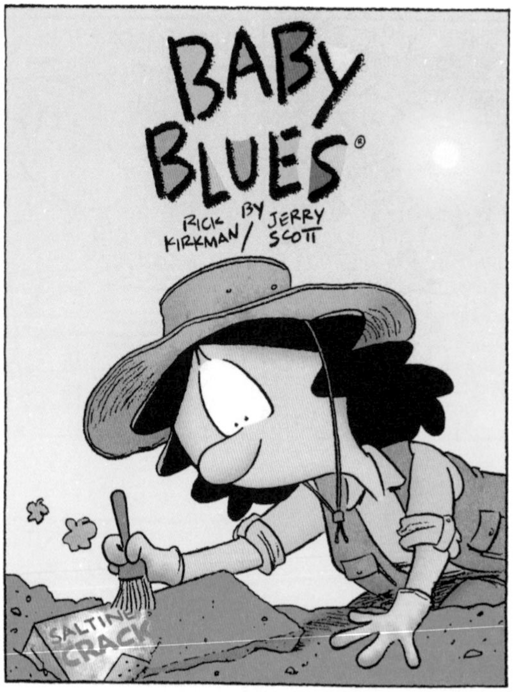
BABY BLUES®
BY RICK KIRKMAN / JERRY SCOTT
SALTINE CRACK

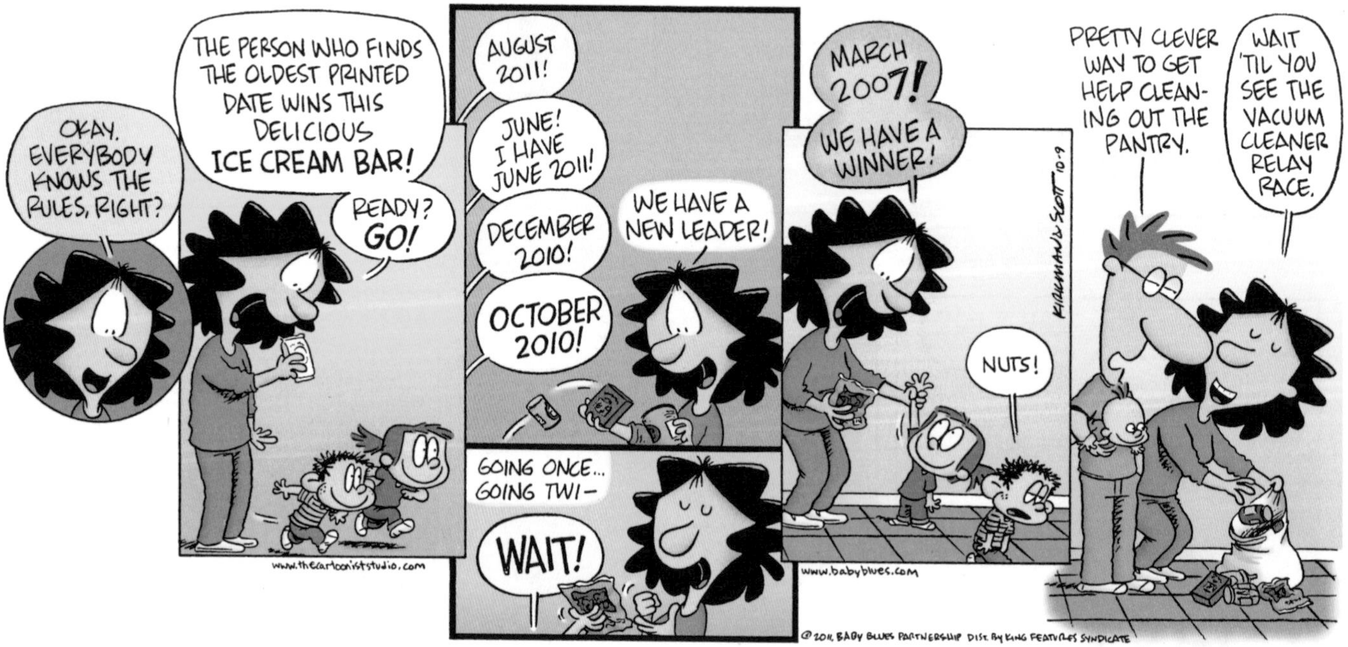
OKAY. EVERYBODY KNOWS THE RULES, RIGHT?
THE PERSON WHO FINDS THE OLDEST PRINTED DATE WINS THIS DELICIOUS ICE CREAM BAR!
READY? GO!
www.thecartooniststudio.com
AUGUST 2011!
JUNE! I HAVE JUNE 2011!
DECEMBER 2010!
OCTOBER 2010!
WE HAVE A NEW LEADER!
GOING ONCE... GOING TWI–
WAIT!
MARCH 2007!
WE HAVE A WINNER!
NUTS!
KIRKMAN & SCOTT 10-9
www.babyblues.com
PRETTY CLEVER WAY TO GET HELP CLEAN-ING OUT THE PANTRY.
WAIT 'TIL YOU SEE THE VACUUM CLEANER RELAY RACE.
©2011, BABY BLUES PARTNERSHIP DIST. BY KING FEATURES SYNDICATE

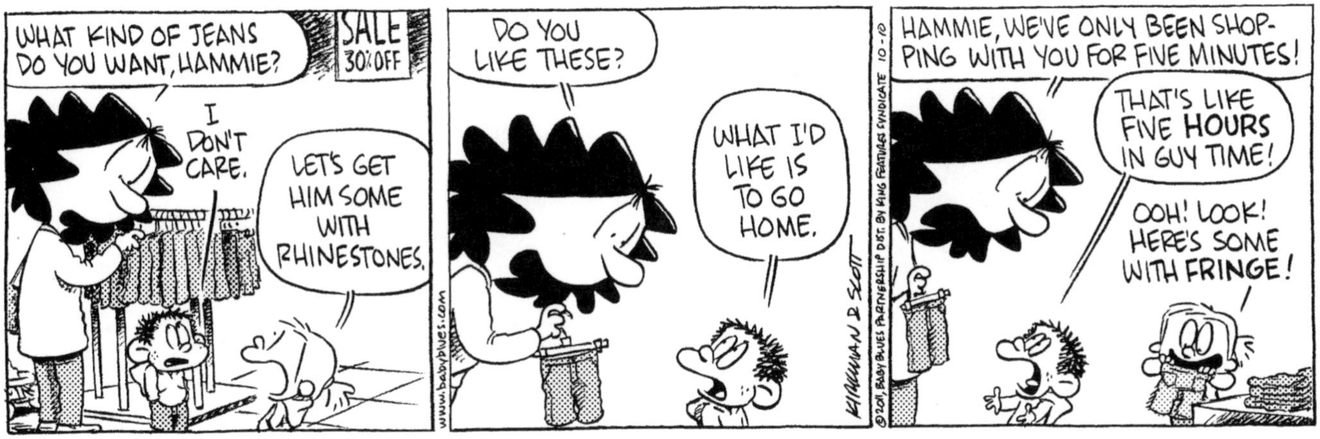
WHAT KIND OF JEANS DO YOU WANT, HAMMIE?
SALE 30% OFF
I DON'T CARE.
LET'S GET HIM SOME WITH RHINESTONES.
www.babyblues.com
DO YOU LIKE THESE?
WHAT I'D LIKE IS TO GO HOME.
KIRKMAN & SCOTT
©2011, BABY BLUES PARTNERSHIP DIST. BY KING FEATURES SYNDICATE 10-10
HAMMIE, WE'VE ONLY BEEN SHOPPING WITH YOU FOR FIVE MINUTES!
THAT'S LIKE FIVE **HOURS** IN GUY TIME!
OOH! LOOK! HERE'S SOME WITH **FRINGE**!

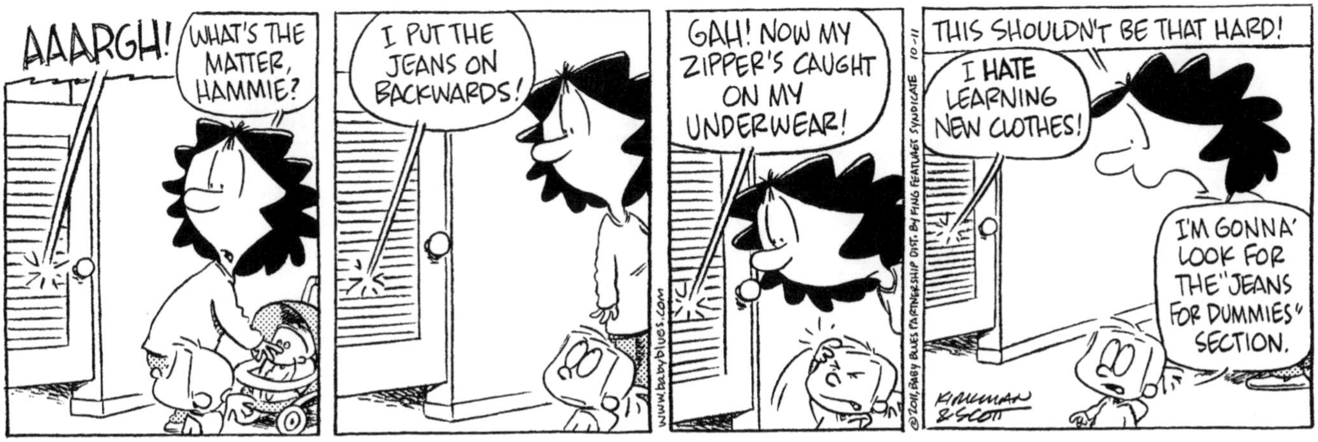
AAARGH!
WHAT'S THE MATTER, HAMMIE?
I PUT THE JEANS ON BACKWARDS!
www.babyblues.com
GAH! NOW MY ZIPPER'S CAUGHT ON MY UNDERWEAR!
©2011, BABY BLUES PARTNERSHIP DIST. BY KING FEATURES SYNDICATE 10-11
THIS SHOULDN'T BE THAT HARD!
I **HATE** LEARNING NEW CLOTHES!
I'M GONNA' LOOK FOR THE "JEANS FOR DUMMIES" SECTION.
KIRKMAN & SCOTT

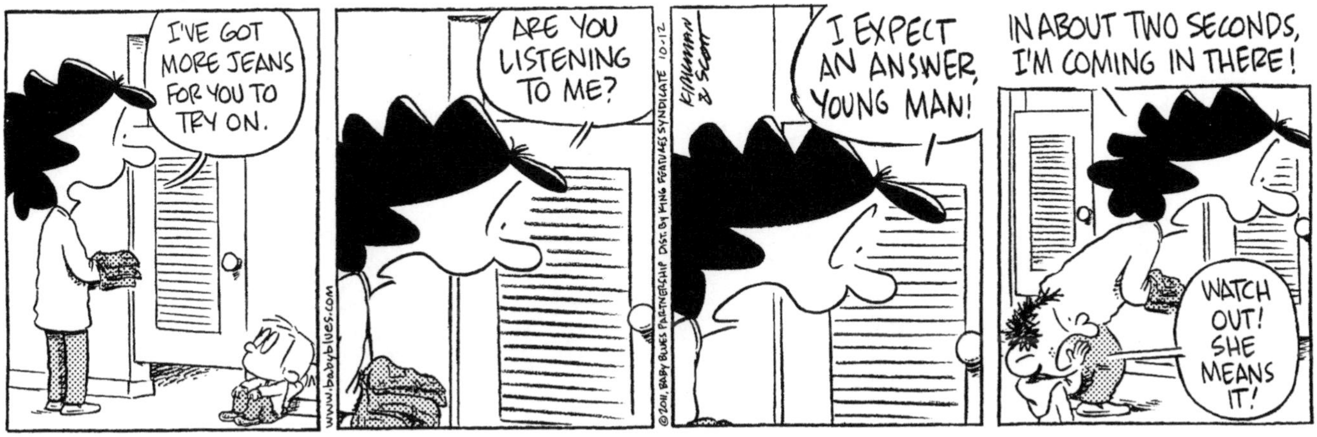
I'VE GOT MORE JEANS FOR YOU TO TRY ON.
www.babyblues.com
ARE YOU LISTENING TO ME?
©2011, BABY BLUES PARTNERSHIP DIST. BY KING FEATURES SYNDICATE 10-12
KIRKMAN & SCOTT
I EXPECT AN ANSWER, YOUNG MAN!
IN ABOUT TWO SECONDS, I'M COMING IN THERE!
WATCH OUT! SHE MEANS IT!

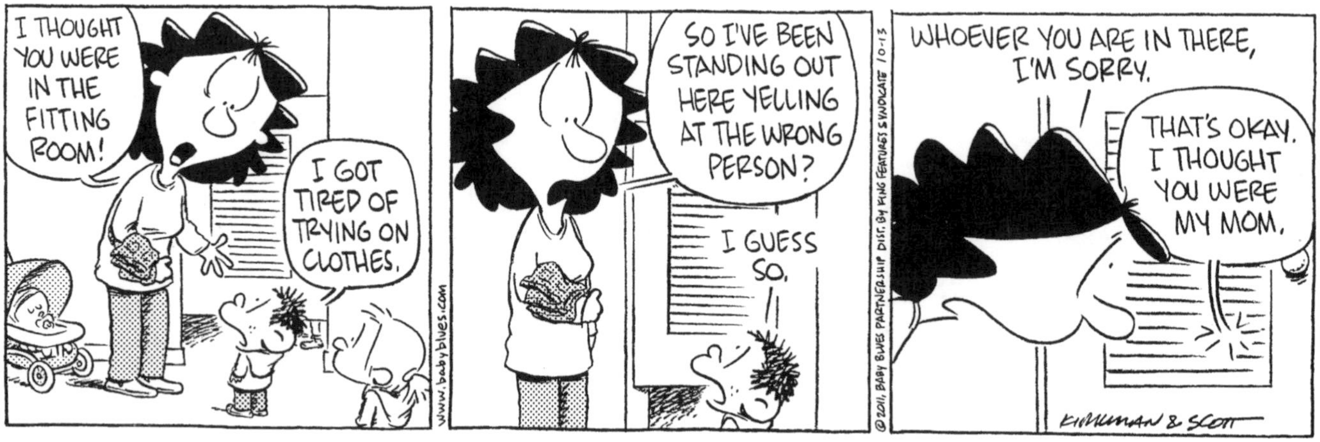
I THOUGHT YOU WERE IN THE FITTING ROOM!
I GOT TIRED OF TRYING ON CLOTHES.
www.babyblues.com
SO I'VE BEEN STANDING OUT HERE YELLING AT THE WRONG PERSON?
I GUESS SO.
© 2011, BABY BLUES PARTNERSHIP DIST. BY KING FEATURES SYNDICATE 10-13
WHOEVER YOU ARE IN THERE, I'M SORRY.
THAT'S OKAY. I THOUGHT YOU WERE MY MOM.
KIRKMAN & SCOTT

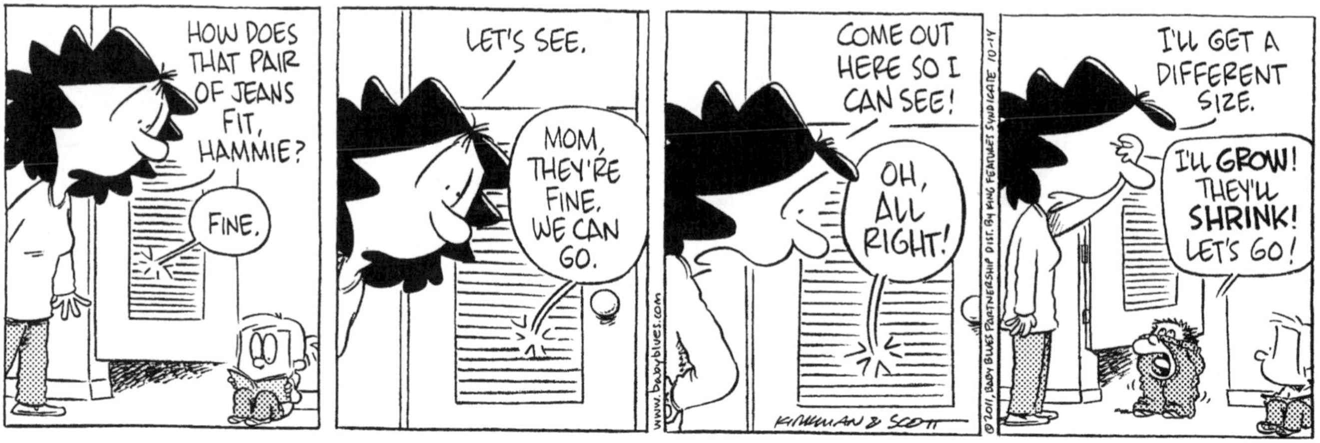
HOW DOES THAT PAIR OF JEANS FIT, HAMMIE?
FINE.
LET'S SEE.
MOM, THEY'RE FINE. WE CAN GO.
www.babyblues.com
COME OUT HERE SO I CAN SEE!
OH, ALL RIGHT!
KIRKMAN & SCOTT
© 2011, BABY BLUES PARTNERSHIP DIST. BY KING FEATURES SYNDICATE 10-14
I'LL GET A DIFFERENT SIZE.
I'LL GROW! THEY'LL SHRINK! LET'S GO!

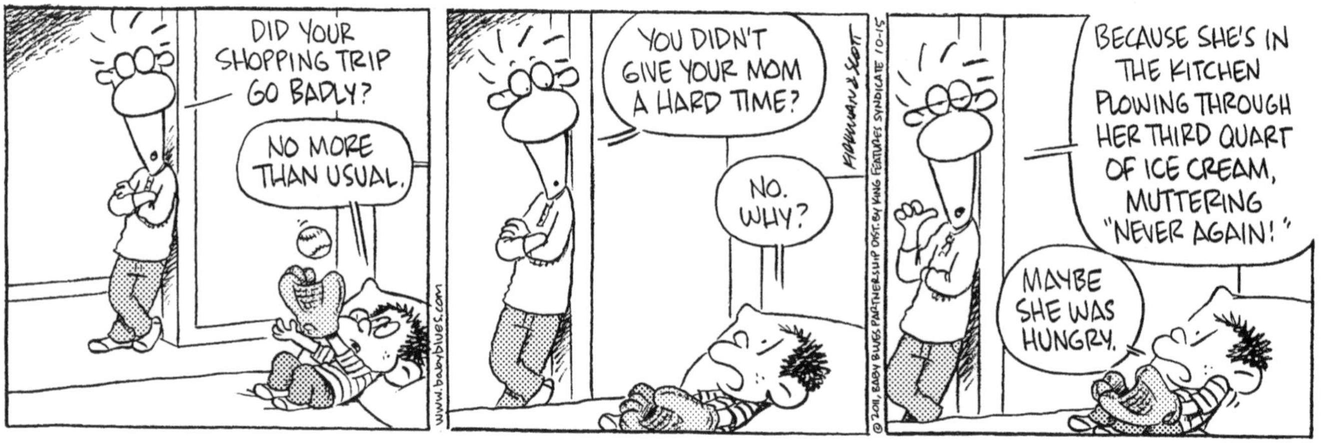
DID YOUR SHOPPING TRIP GO BADLY?
NO MORE THAN USUAL.
www.babyblues.com
YOU DIDN'T GIVE YOUR MOM A HARD TIME?
NO. WHY?
KIRKMAN & SCOTT 10-15
© 2011, BABY BLUES PARTNERSHIP DIST. BY KING FEATURES SYNDICATE
BECAUSE SHE'S IN THE KITCHEN PLOWING THROUGH HER THIRD QUART OF ICE CREAM, MUTTERING "NEVER AGAIN!"
MAYBE SHE WAS HUNGRY.

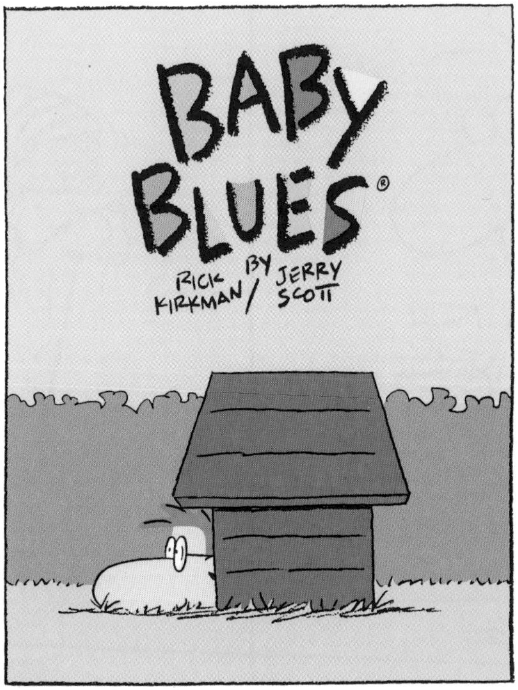
BABY BLUES®
BY RICK KIRKMAN / JERRY SCOTT

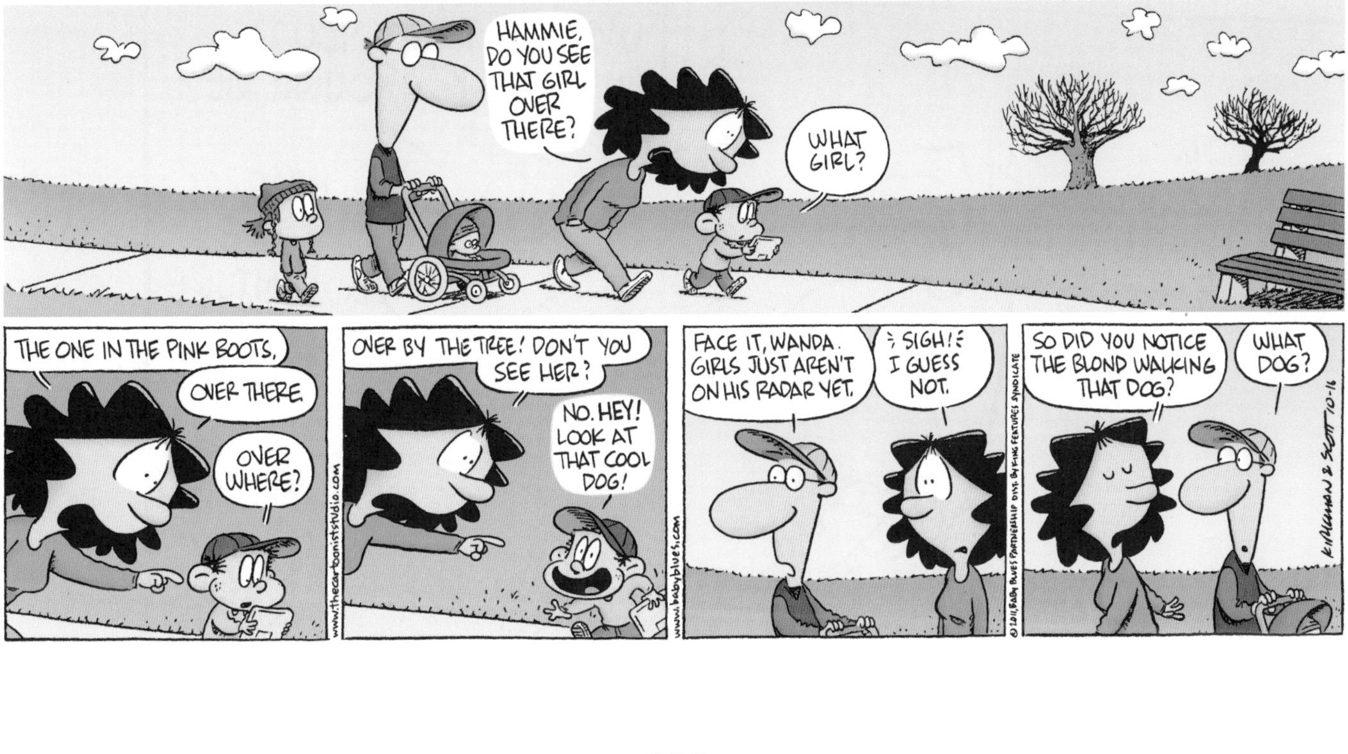
HAMMIE, DO YOU SEE THAT GIRL OVER THERE?
WHAT GIRL?
THE ONE IN THE PINK BOOTS.
OVER THERE.
OVER WHERE?
www.thecartoonistsstudio.com
OVER BY THE TREE! DON'T YOU SEE HER?
NO. HEY! LOOK AT THAT COOL DOG!
www.babyblues.com
FACE IT, WANDA. GIRLS JUST AREN'T ON HIS RADAR YET.
SIGH! I GUESS NOT.
© 2011, BABY BLUES PARTNERSHIP DIST. BY KING FEATURES SYNDICATE
SO DID YOU NOTICE THE BLOND WALKING THAT DOG?
WHAT DOG?
KIRKMAN & SCOTT 10-16

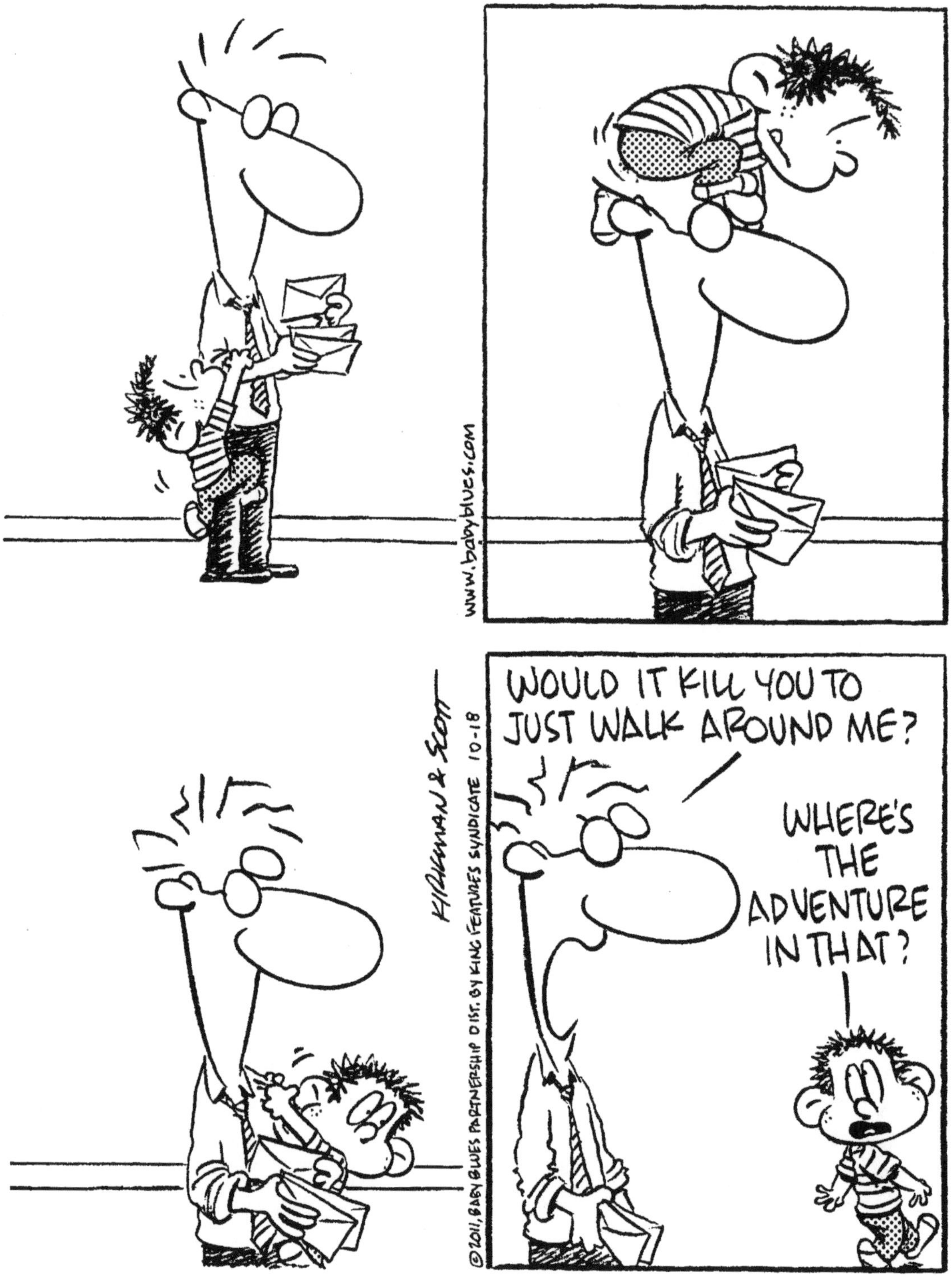
www.babyblues.com
KIRKMAN & SCOTT
©2011, BABY BLUES PARTNERSHIP DIST. BY KING FEATURES SYNDICATE 10-18
WOULD IT KILL YOU TO JUST WALK AROUND ME?
WHERE'S THE ADVENTURE IN THAT?

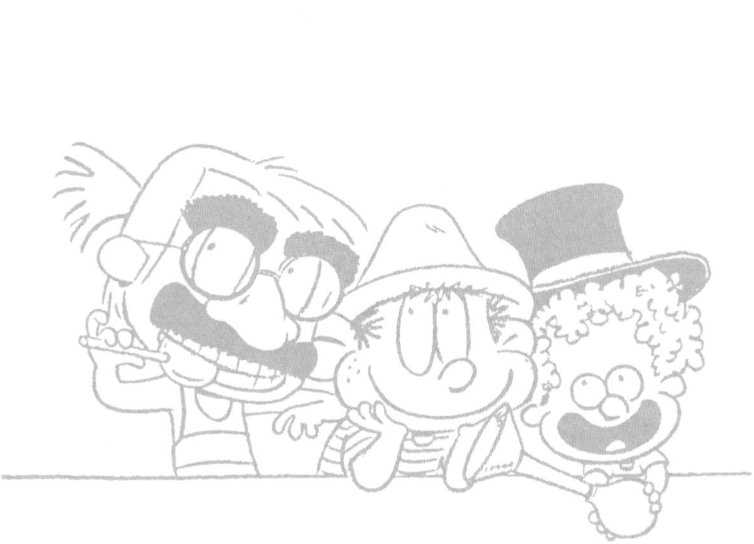

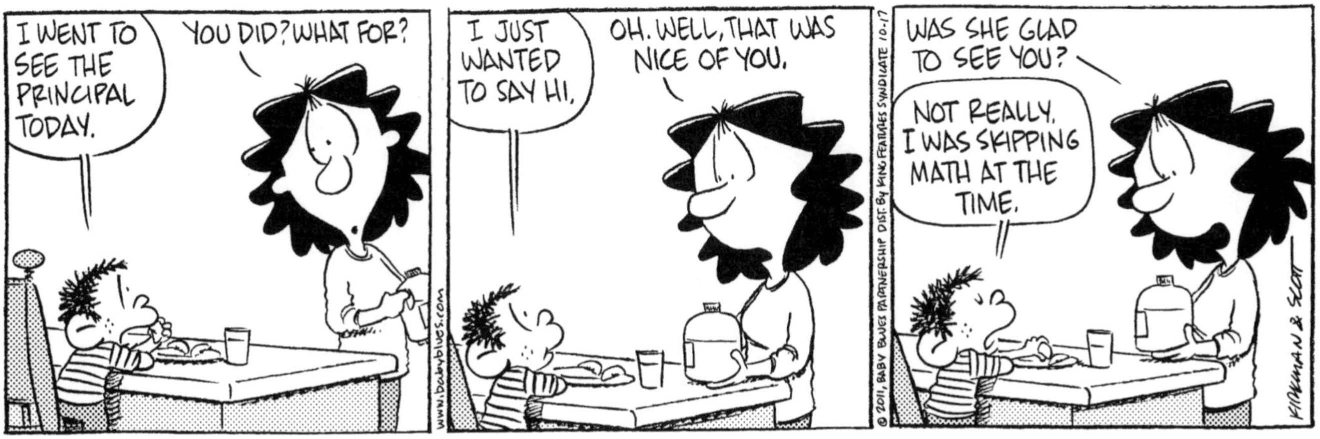

I WENT TO SEE THE PRINCIPAL TODAY.
YOU DID? WHAT FOR?
www.babyblues.com
I JUST WANTED TO SAY HI.
OH. WELL, THAT WAS NICE OF YOU.
© 2011, BABY BLUES PARTNERSHIP DIST. BY KING FEATURES SYNDICATE 10-17
WAS SHE GLAD TO SEE YOU?
NOT REALLY. I WAS SKIPPING MATH AT THE TIME.
KIRKMAN & SCOTT

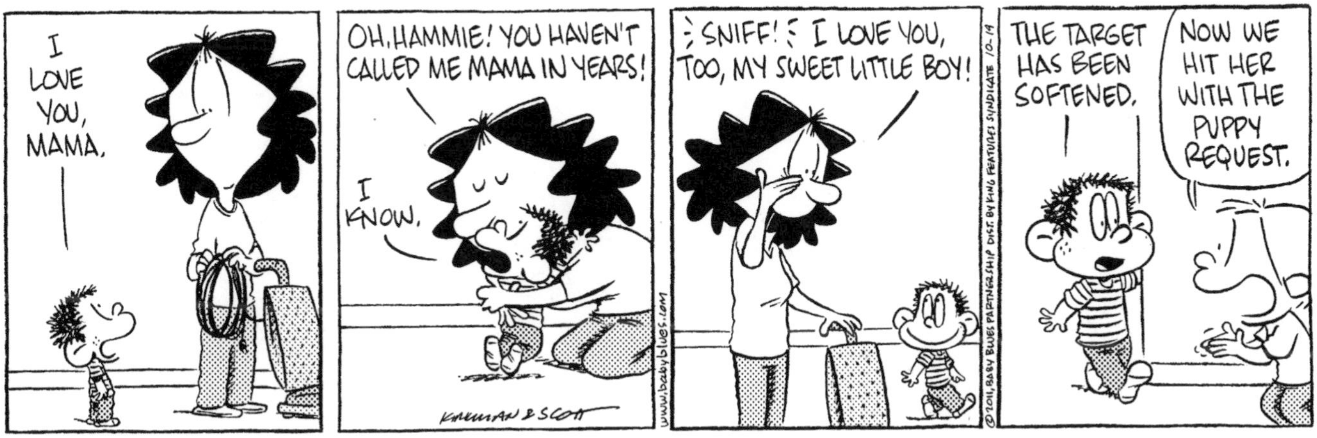

I LOVE YOU, MAMA.
OH, HAMMIE! YOU HAVEN'T CALLED ME MAMA IN YEARS!
I KNOW.
KIRKMAN & SCOTT
www.babyblues.com
SNIFF! I LOVE YOU, TOO, MY SWEET LITTLE BOY!
© 2011, BABY BLUES PARTNERSHIP DIST. BY KING FEATURES SYNDICATE 10-19
THE TARGET HAS BEEN SOFTENED.
NOW WE HIT HER WITH THE PUPPY REQUEST.

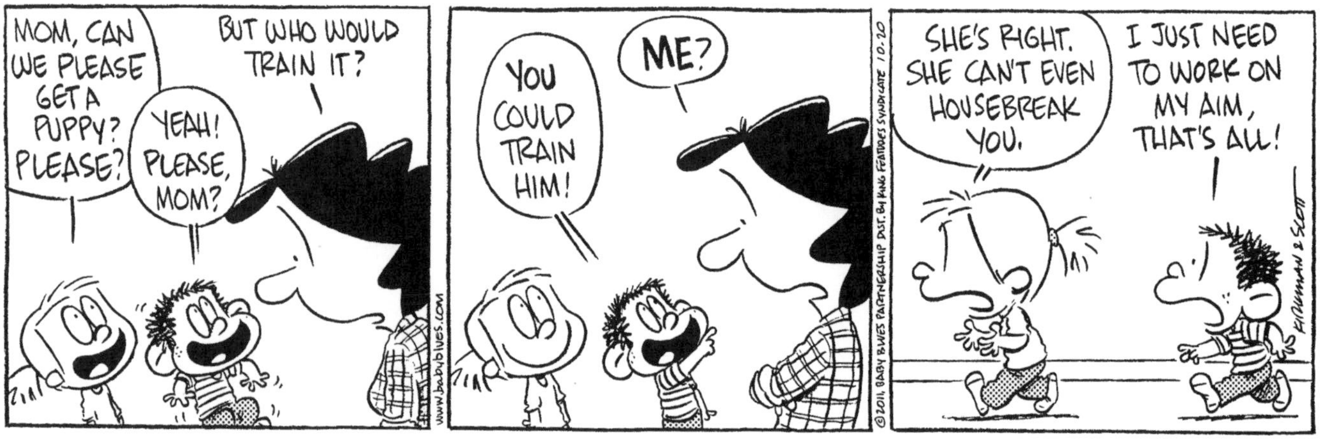
MOM, CAN WE PLEASE GET A PUPPY? PLEASE?
YEAH! PLEASE, MOM?
BUT WHO WOULD TRAIN IT?
YOU COULD TRAIN HIM!
ME?
SHE'S RIGHT. SHE CAN'T EVEN HOUSEBREAK YOU.
I JUST NEED TO WORK ON MY AIM, THAT'S ALL!

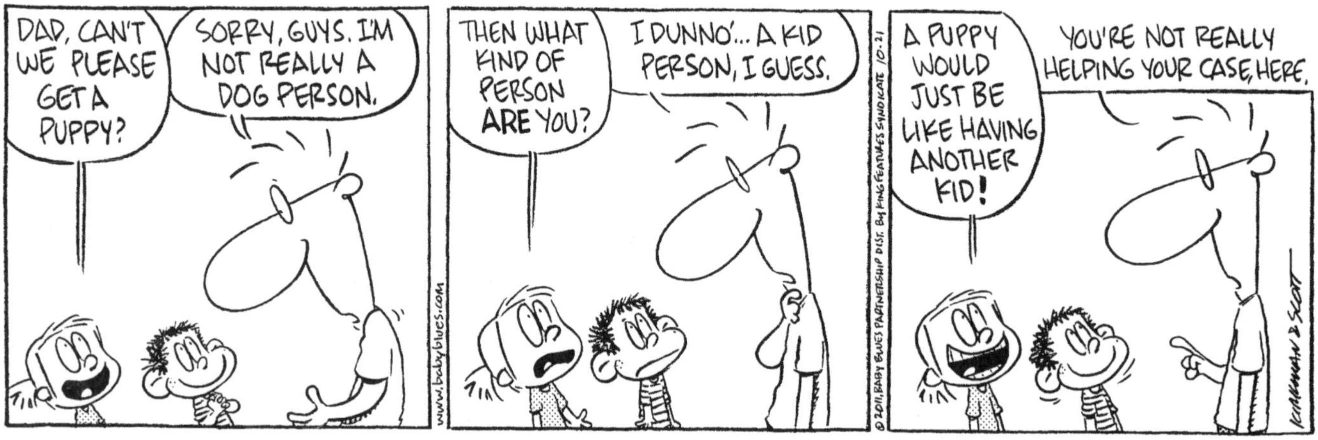
DAD, CAN'T WE PLEASE GET A PUPPY?
SORRY, GUYS. I'M NOT REALLY A DOG PERSON.
THEN WHAT KIND OF PERSON ARE YOU?
I DUNNO... A KID PERSON, I GUESS.
A PUPPY WOULD JUST BE LIKE HAVING ANOTHER KID!
YOU'RE NOT REALLY HELPING YOUR CASE, HERE.

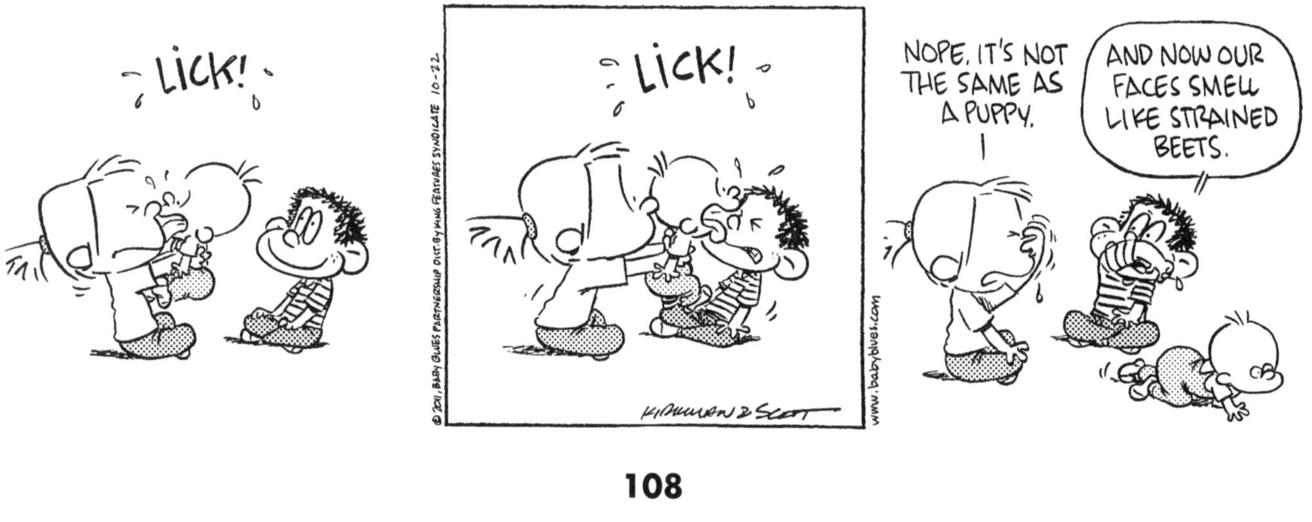
LICK!
LICK!
NOPE. IT'S NOT THE SAME AS A PUPPY.
AND NOW OUR FACES SMELL LIKE STRAINED BEETS.

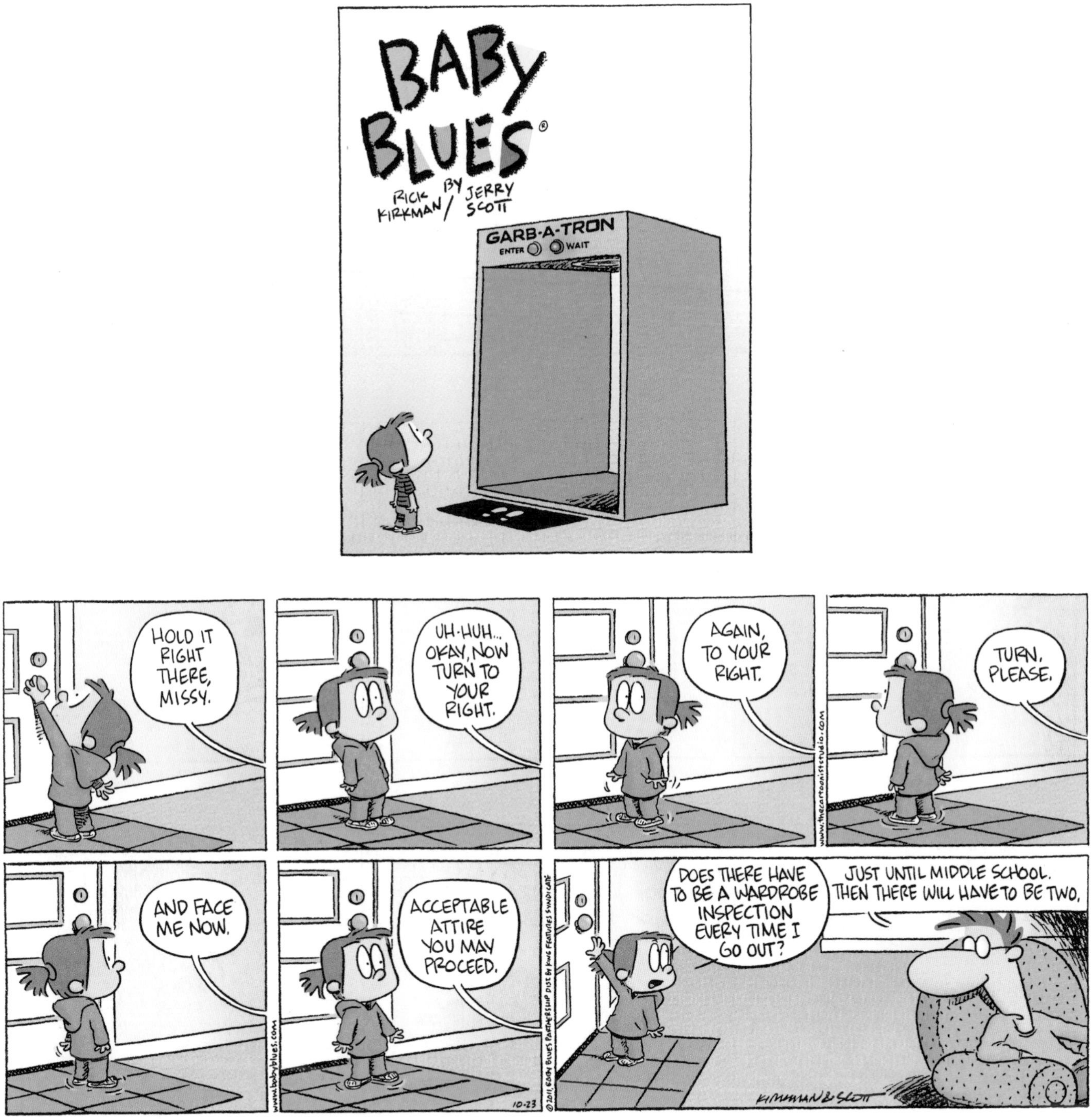
BABY BLUES®
BY RICK KIRKMAN / JERRY SCOTT
GARB-A-TRON
ENTER WAIT
HOLD IT RIGHT THERE, MISSY.
UH-HUH... OKAY, NOW TURN TO YOUR RIGHT.
AGAIN, TO YOUR RIGHT.
www.thecartooniststudio.com
TURN, PLEASE.
AND FACE ME NOW.
www.babyblues.com
ACCEPTABLE ATTIRE YOU MAY PROCEED.
10-23
©2011, BABY BLUES PARTNERSHIP DIST BY KING FEATURES SYNDICATE
DOES THERE HAVE TO BE A WARDROBE INSPECTION EVERY TIME I GO OUT?
JUST UNTIL MIDDLE SCHOOL. THEN THERE WILL HAVE TO BE TWO.
KIRKMAN & SCOTT

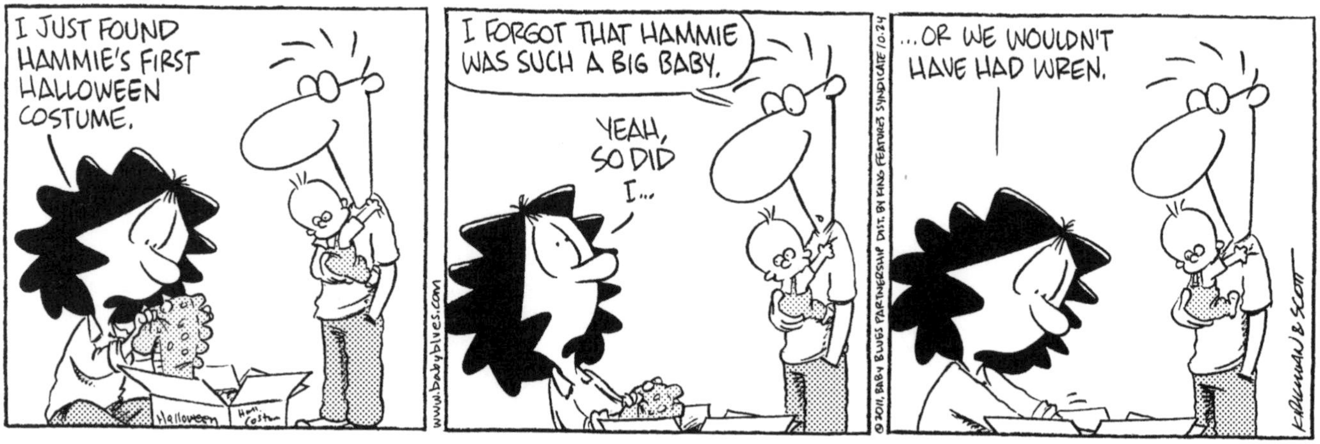
I JUST FOUND HAMMIE'S FIRST HALLOWEEN COSTUME.
Halloween
I FORGOT THAT HAMMIE WAS SUCH A BIG BABY.
YEAH, SO DID I...
...OR WE WOULDN'T HAVE HAD WREN.
www.babyblues.com
© 2011, BABY BLUES PARTNERSHIP DIST. BY KING FEATURES SYNDICATE 10·24
KIRKMAN & SCOTT

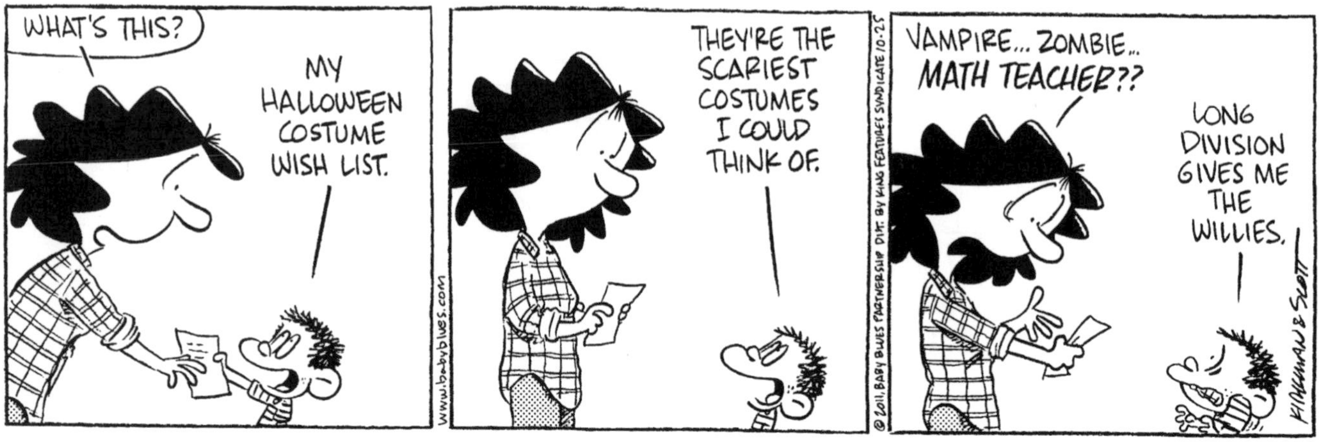
WHAT'S THIS?
MY HALLOWEEN COSTUME WISH LIST.
THEY'RE THE SCARIEST COSTUMES I COULD THINK OF.
VAMPIRE... ZOMBIE... MATH TEACHER??
LONG DIVISION GIVES ME THE WILLIES.
www.babyblues.com
© 2011, BABY BLUES PARTNERSHIP DIST. BY KING FEATURES SYNDICATE 10·25
KIRKMAN & SCOTT

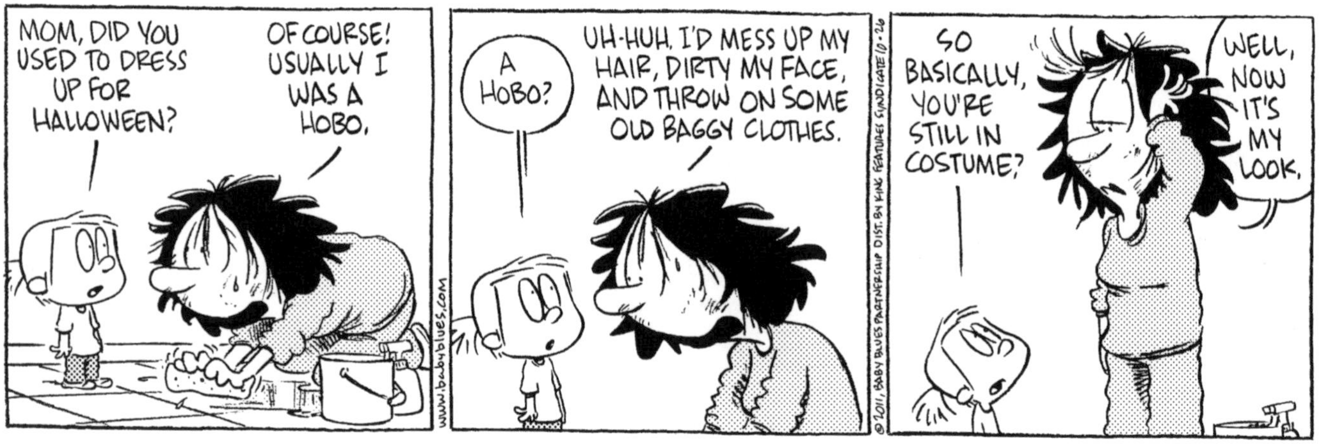
MOM, DID YOU USED TO DRESS UP FOR HALLOWEEN?
OF COURSE! USUALLY I WAS A HOBO.
A HOBO?
UH-HUH. I'D MESS UP MY HAIR, DIRTY MY FACE, AND THROW ON SOME OLD BAGGY CLOTHES.
SO BASICALLY, YOU'RE STILL IN COSTUME?
WELL, NOW IT'S MY LOOK.
www.babyblues.com
© 2011, BABY BLUES PARTNERSHIP DIST. BY KING FEATURES SYNDICATE 10·26

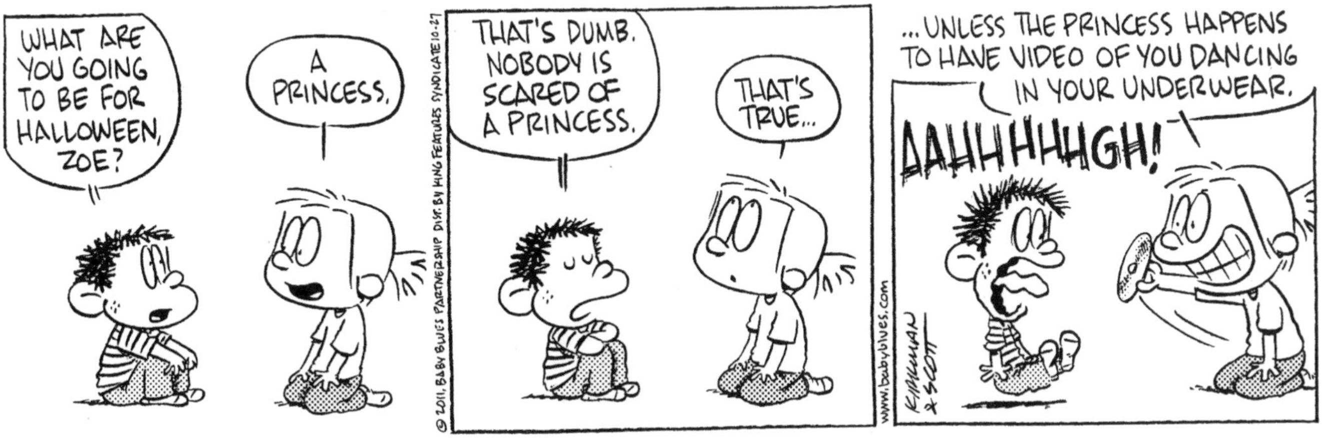
WHAT ARE YOU GOING TO BE FOR HALLOWEEN, ZOE?
A PRINCESS.
© 2011, BABY BLUES PARTNERSHIP DIST. BY KING FEATURES SYNDICATE 10-27
THAT'S DUMB. NOBODY IS SCARED OF A PRINCESS.
THAT'S TRUE...
www.babyblues.com
...UNLESS THE PRINCESS HAPPENS TO HAVE VIDEO OF YOU DANCING IN YOUR UNDERWEAR.
AAHHHHHGH!
KIRKMAN & SCOTT

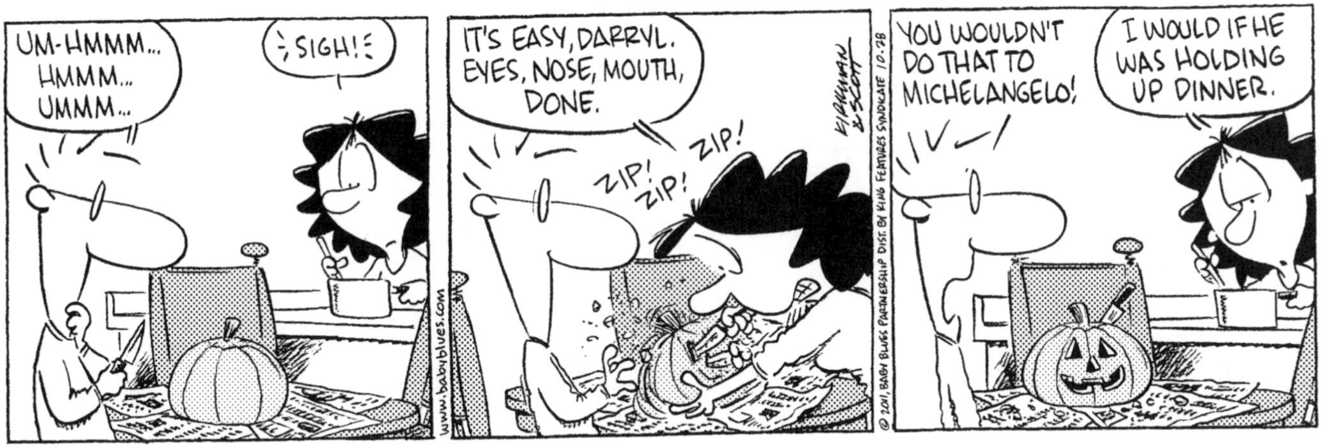
UM-HMMM... HMMM... UMMM...
SIGH!
www.babyblues.com
IT'S EASY, DARRYL. EYES, NOSE, MOUTH, DONE.
ZIP! ZIP! ZIP!
KIRKMAN & SCOTT 10-28
© 2011, BABY BLUES PARTNERSHIP DIST. BY KING FEATURES SYNDICATE
YOU WOULDN'T DO THAT TO MICHELANGELO!
I WOULD IF HE WAS HOLDING UP DINNER.

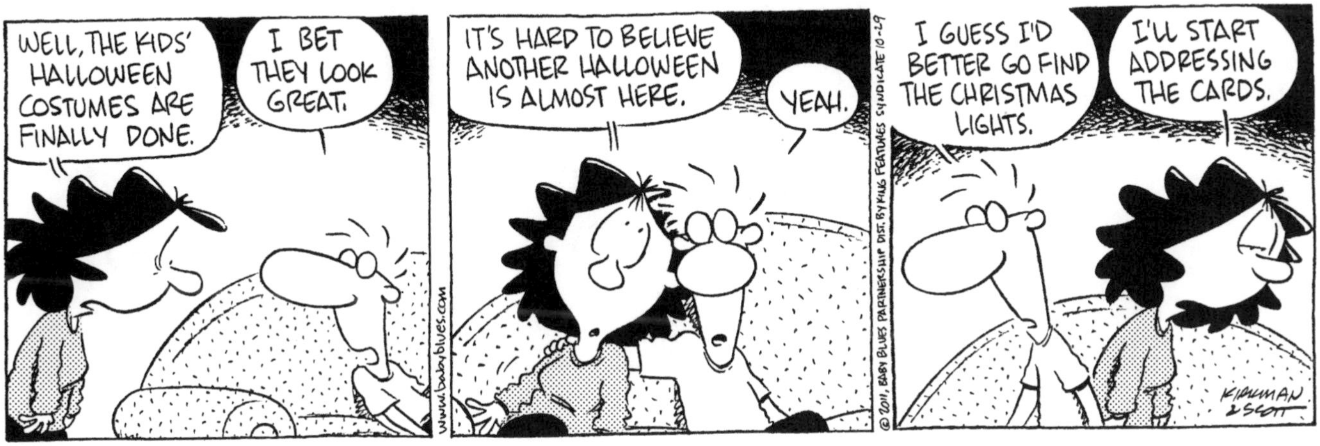
WELL, THE KIDS' HALLOWEEN COSTUMES ARE FINALLY DONE.
I BET THEY LOOK GREAT.
www.babyblues.com
IT'S HARD TO BELIEVE ANOTHER HALLOWEEN IS ALMOST HERE.
YEAH.
© 2011, BABY BLUES PARTNERSHIP DIST. BY KING FEATURES SYNDICATE 10-29
I GUESS I'D BETTER GO FIND THE CHRISTMAS LIGHTS.
I'LL START ADDRESSING THE CARDS.
KIRKMAN & SCOTT

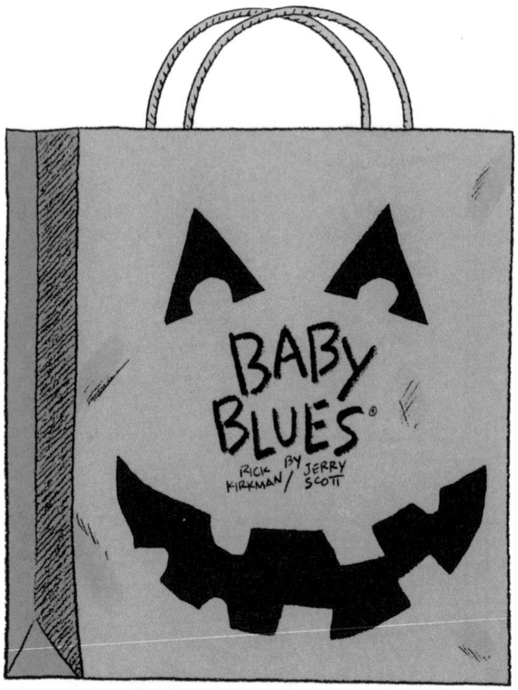
BABY BLUES®
BY
RICK KIRKMAN / JERRY SCOTT

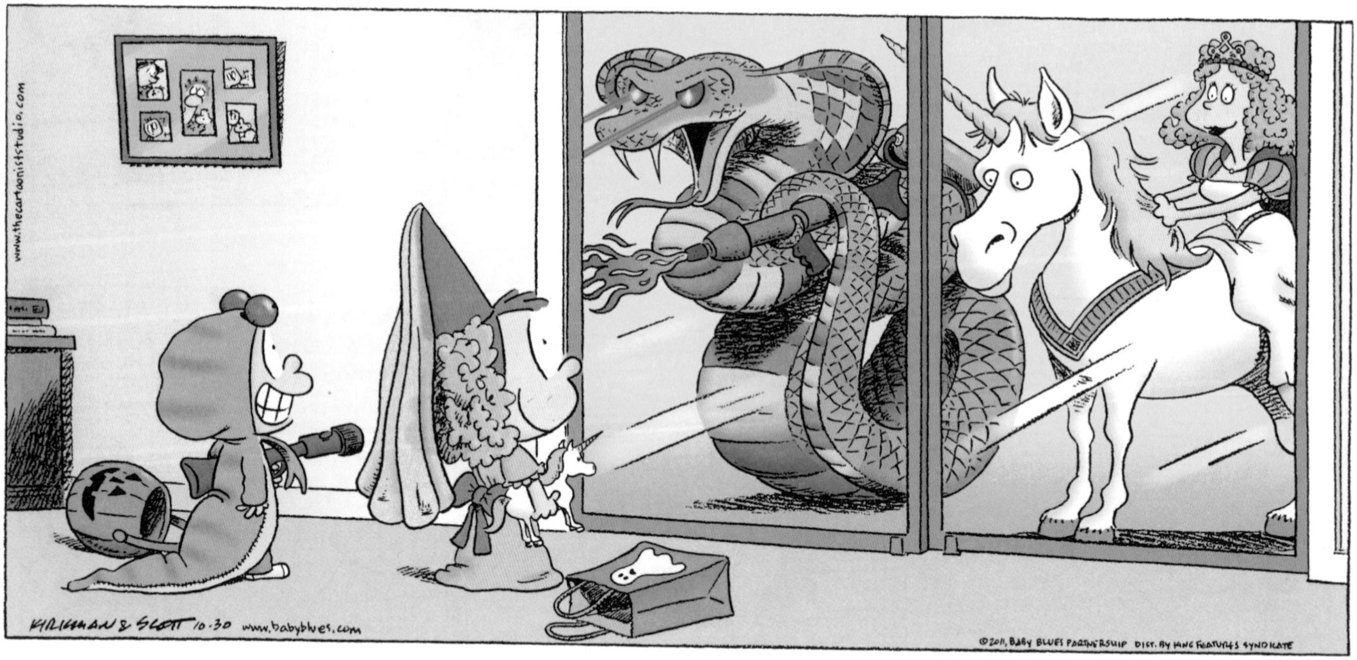
www.thecartoonniststudio.com
KIRKMAN & SCOTT 10-30 www.babyblues.com
©2011, BABY BLUES PARTNERSHIP DIST. BY KING FEATURES SYNDICATE

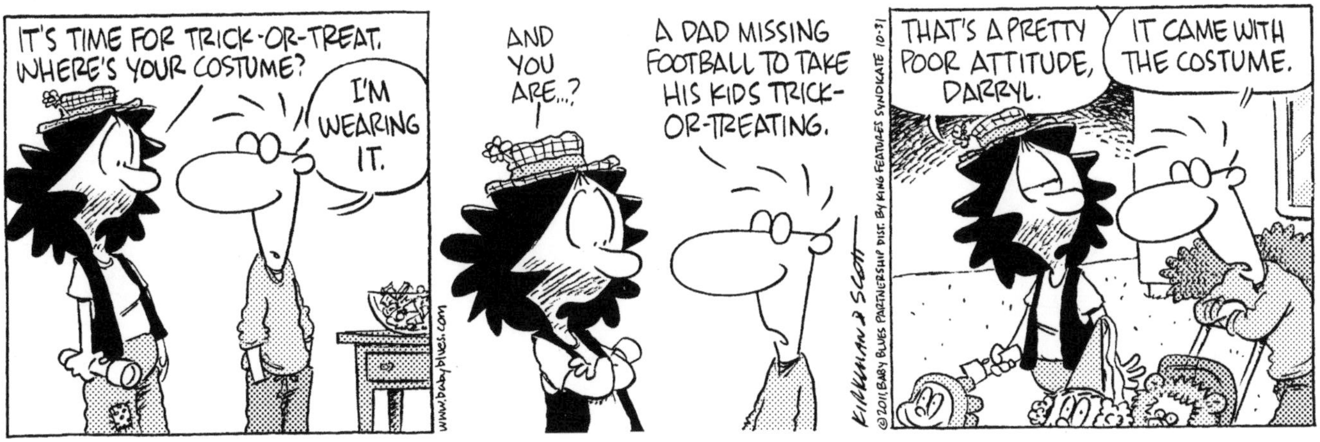
IT'S TIME FOR TRICK-OR-TREAT. WHERE'S YOUR COSTUME?
I'M WEARING IT.
www.babyblues.com
AND YOU ARE...?
A DAD MISSING FOOTBALL TO TAKE HIS KIDS TRICK-OR-TREATING.
KIRKMAN & SCOTT
©2011, BABY BLUES PARTNERSHIP DIST. BY KING FEATURES SYNDICATE 10-31
THAT'S A PRETTY POOR ATTITUDE, DARRYL.
IT CAME WITH THE COSTUME.

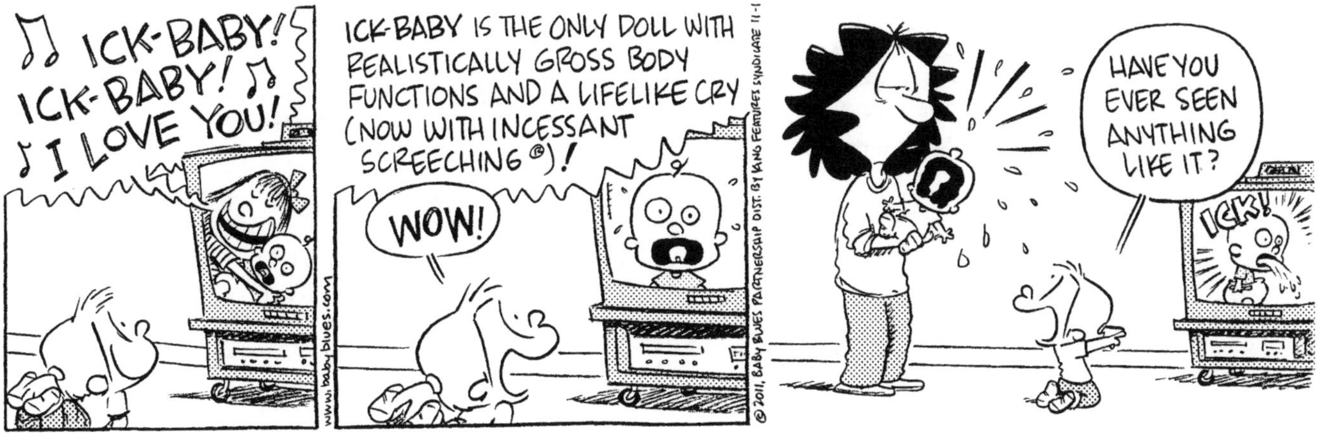
ICK-BABY! ICK-BABY! I LOVE YOU!
www.babyblues.com
ICK-BABY IS THE ONLY DOLL WITH REALISTICALLY GROSS BODY FUNCTIONS AND A LIFELIKE CRY (NOW WITH INCESSANT SCREECHING®)!
WOW!
©2011, BABY BLUES PARTNERSHIP DIST. BY KING FEATURES SYNDICATE 11-1
HAVE YOU EVER SEEN ANYTHING LIKE IT?
ICK!

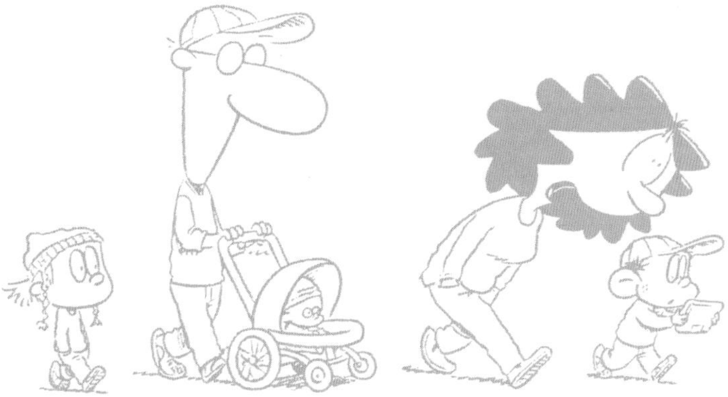

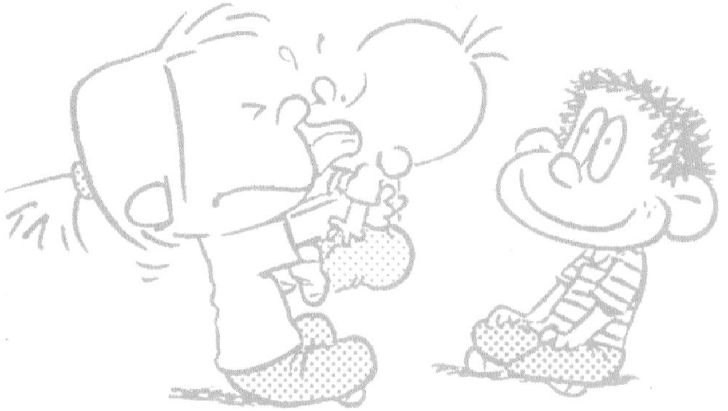

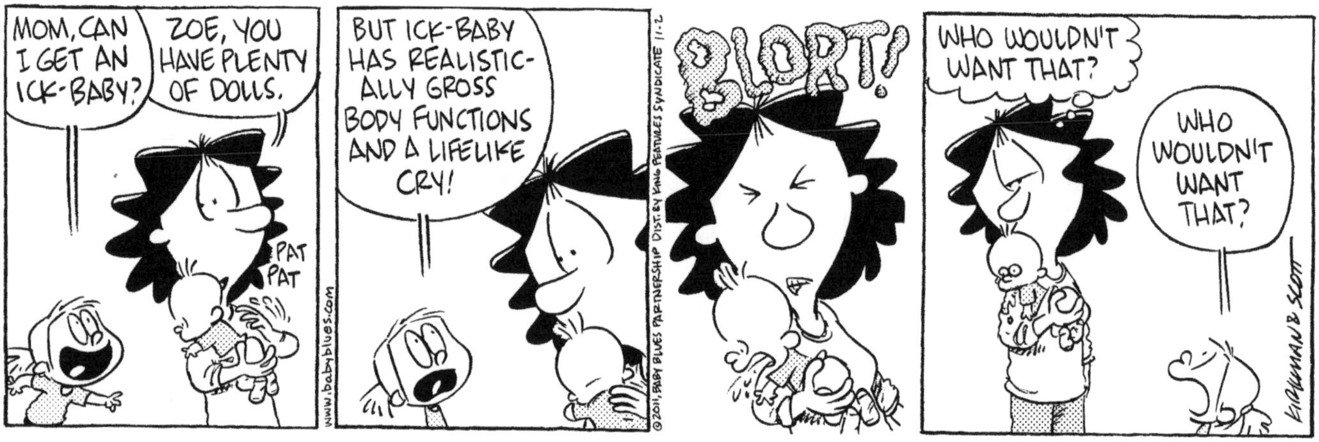
MOM, CAN I GET AN ICK-BABY?
ZOE, YOU HAVE PLENTY OF DOLLS.
PAT PAT
www.babyblues.com
BUT ICK-BABY HAS REALISTIC-ALLY GROSS BODY FUNCTIONS AND A LIFELIKE CRY!
©2011, BABY BLUES PARTNERSHIP DIST. BY KING FEATURES SYNDICATE 11-2
BLORT!
WHO WOULDN'T WANT THAT?
WHO WOULDN'T WANT THAT?
KIRKMAN & SCOTT

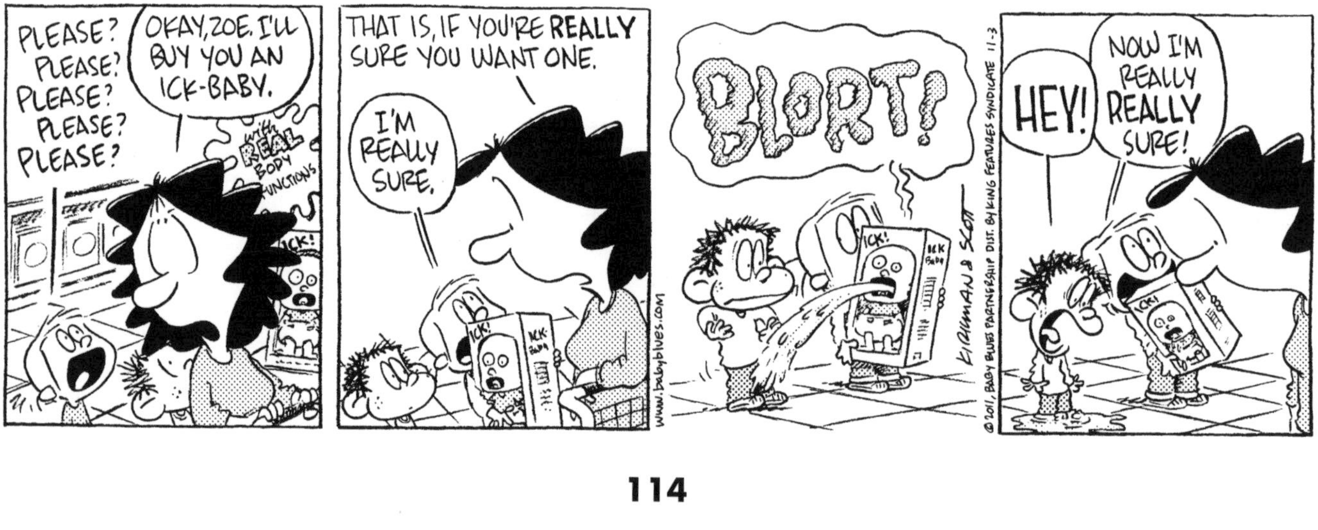
PLEASE? PLEASE? PLEASE? PLEASE? PLEASE?
OKAY, ZOE. I'LL BUY YOU AN ICK-BABY.
with REAL BODY FUNCTIONS
ICK!
THAT IS, IF YOU'RE **REALLY** SURE YOU WANT ONE.
I'M REALLY SURE.
ICK!
www.babyblues.com
BLORT!
ICK!
KIRKMAN & SCOTT
©2011, BABY BLUES PARTNERSHIP DIST. BY KING FEATURES SYNDICATE 11-3
HEY!
NOW I'M REALLY **REALLY** SURE!
ICK!

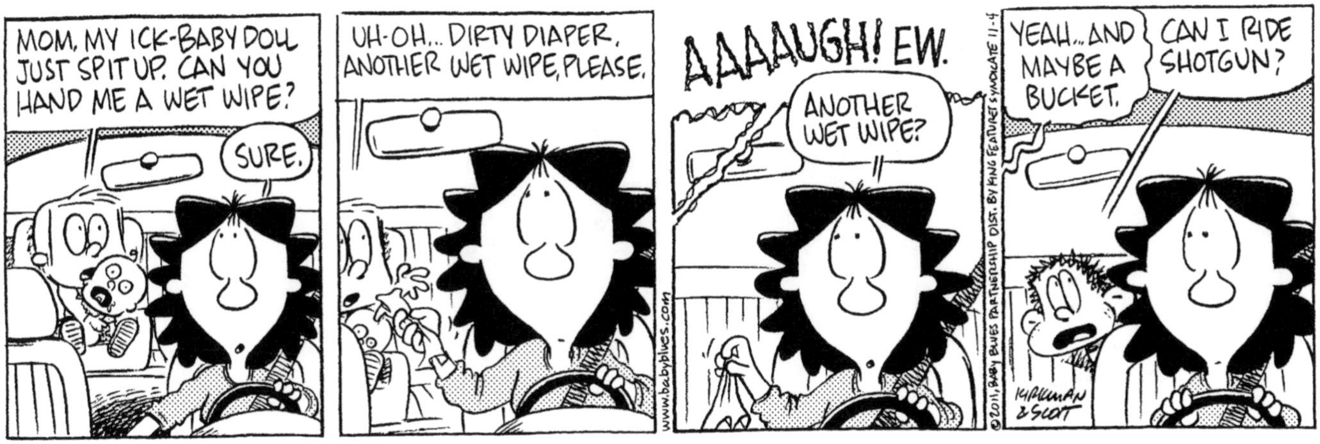
MOM, MY ICK-BABY DOLL JUST SPIT UP. CAN YOU HAND ME A WET WIPE?
SURE.
UH-OH... DIRTY DIAPER. ANOTHER WET WIPE, PLEASE.
www.babyblues.com
AAAAUGH! EW.
ANOTHER WET WIPE?
©2011, BABY BLUES PARTNERSHIP DIST. BY KING FEATURES SYNDICATE 11-4
YEAH... AND MAYBE A BUCKET.
CAN I RIDE SHOTGUN?
KIRKMAN & SCOTT

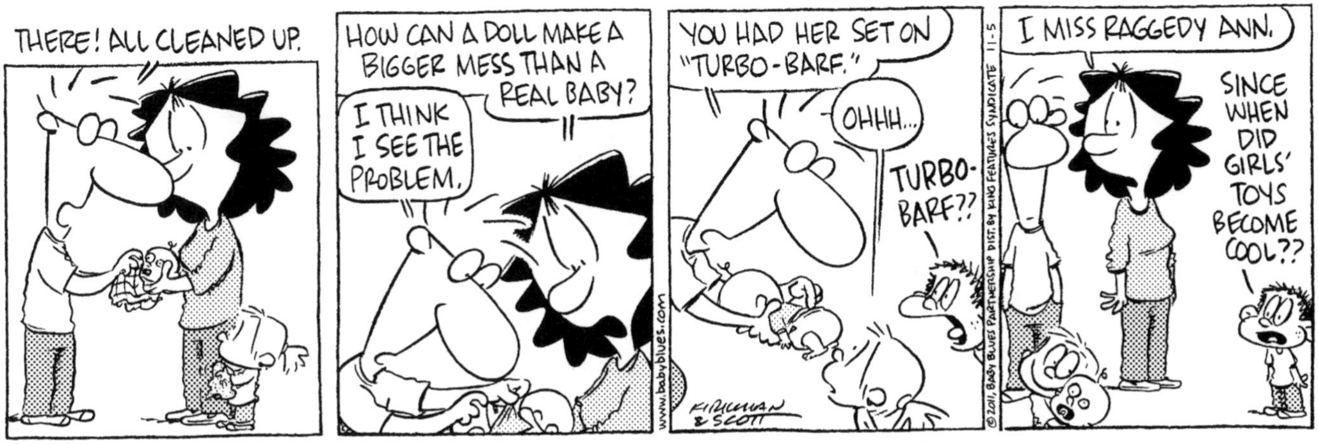
THERE! ALL CLEANED UP.
HOW CAN A DOLL MAKE A BIGGER MESS THAN A REAL BABY?
I THINK I SEE THE PROBLEM.
www.babyblues.com
YOU HAD HER SET ON "TURBO-BARF."
OHHH...
TURBO-BARF??
KIRKMAN & SCOTT
©2011, BABY BLUES PARTNERSHIP DIST. BY KING FEATURES SYNDICATE 11-5
I MISS RAGGEDY ANN.
SINCE WHEN DID GIRLS' TOYS BECOME COOL??

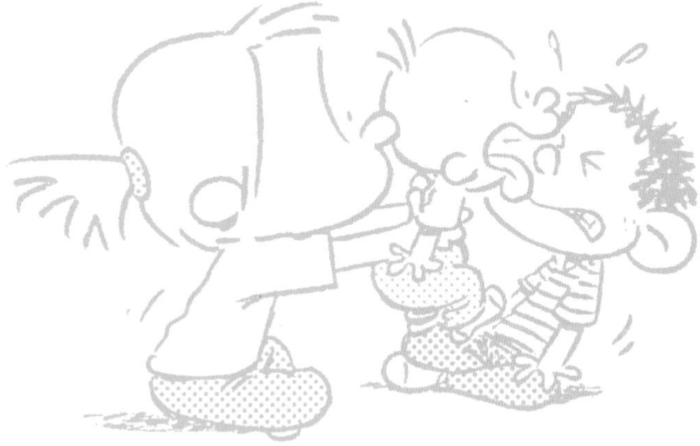

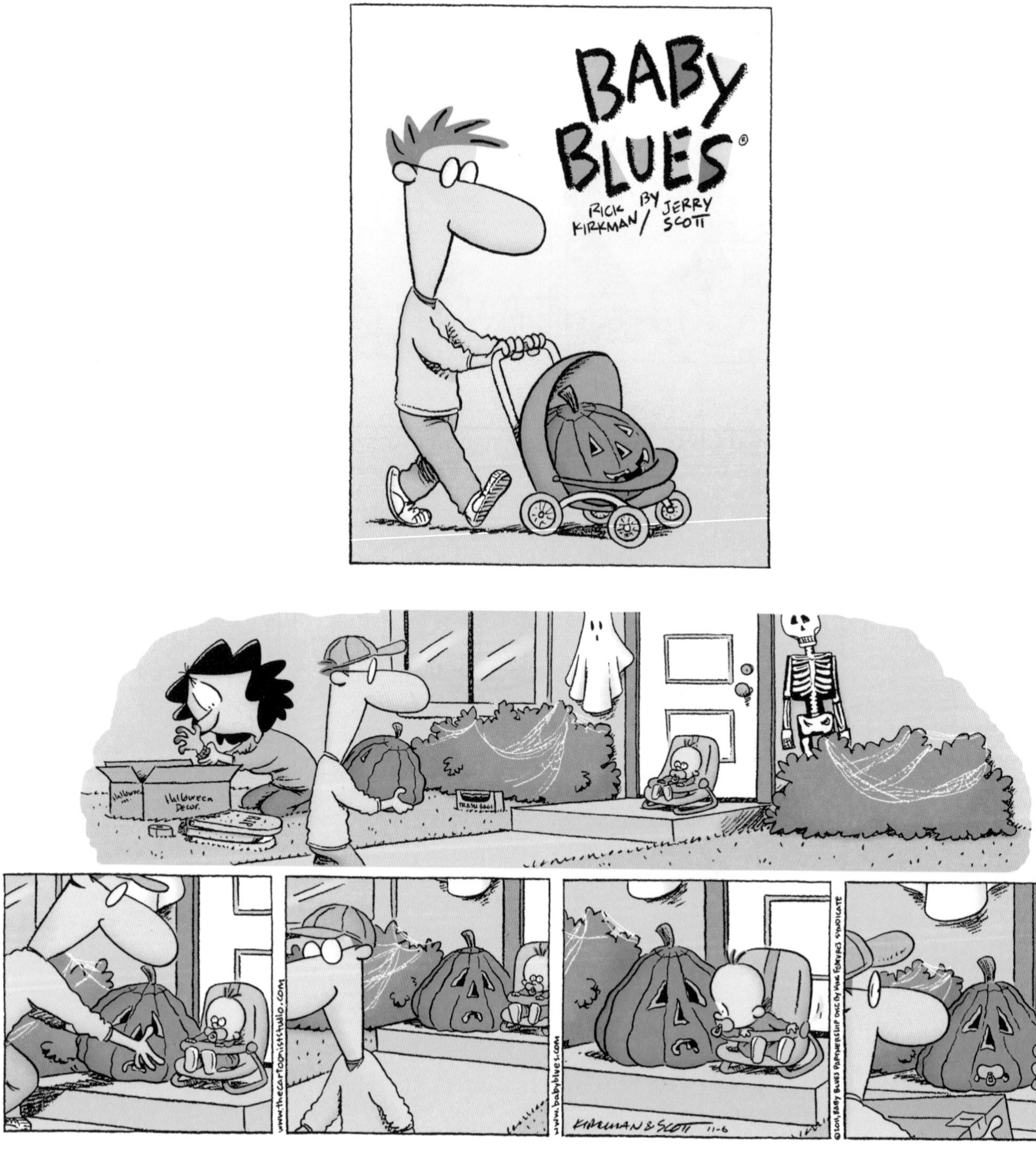
BABY BLUES®
BY RICK KIRKMAN / JERRY SCOTT
Halloween Decor.
RIP
TRASH BAGS
www.thecartoonniststudio.com
www.babyblues.com
KIRKMAN & SCOTT 11-6
©2011, BABY BLUES PARTNERSHIP DIST. BY KING FEATURES SYNDICATE

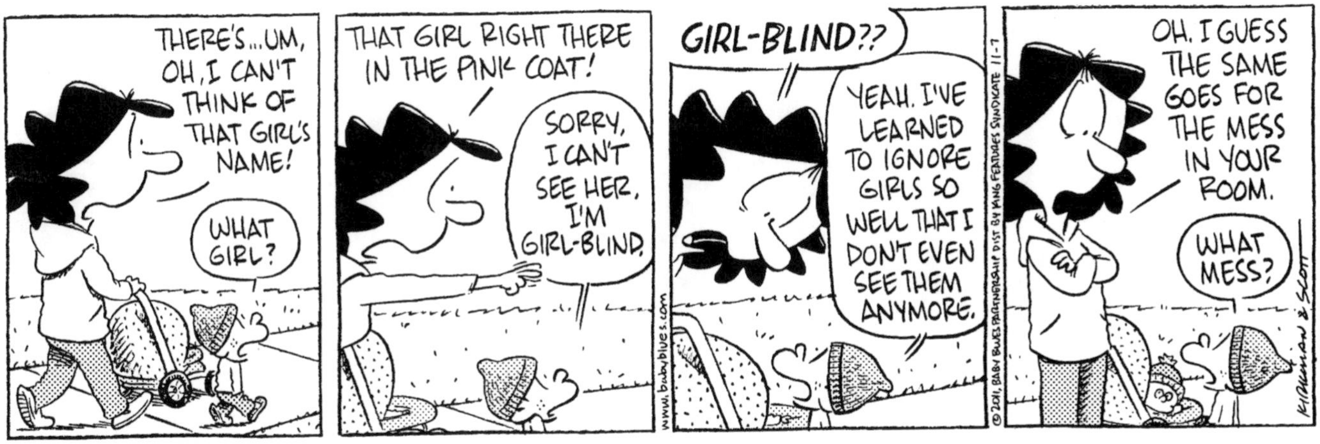
THERE'S...UM, OH, I CAN'T THINK OF THAT GIRL'S NAME!
WHAT GIRL?
THAT GIRL RIGHT THERE IN THE PINK COAT!
SORRY, I CAN'T SEE HER. I'M GIRL-BLIND.
GIRL-BLIND??
YEAH. I'VE LEARNED TO IGNORE GIRLS SO WELL THAT I DON'T EVEN SEE THEM ANYMORE.
OH. I GUESS THE SAME GOES FOR THE MESS IN YOUR ROOM.
WHAT MESS?
www.babyblues.com
© 2011, BABY BLUES PARTNERSHIP DIST. BY KING FEATURES SYNDICATE 11-7
KIRKMAN & SCOTT

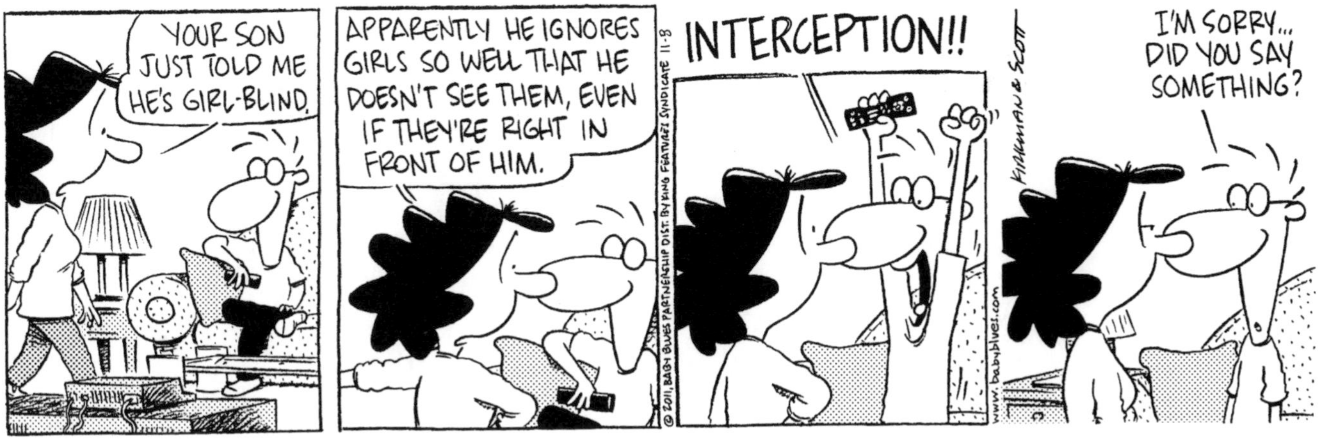
YOUR SON JUST TOLD ME HE'S GIRL-BLIND.
APPARENTLY HE IGNORES GIRLS SO WELL THAT HE DOESN'T SEE THEM, EVEN IF THEY'RE RIGHT IN FRONT OF HIM.
© 2011, BABY BLUES PARTNERSHIP DIST. BY KING FEATURES SYNDICATE 11-8
INTERCEPTION!!
KIRKMAN & SCOTT
www.babyblues.com
I'M SORRY... DID YOU SAY SOMETHING?

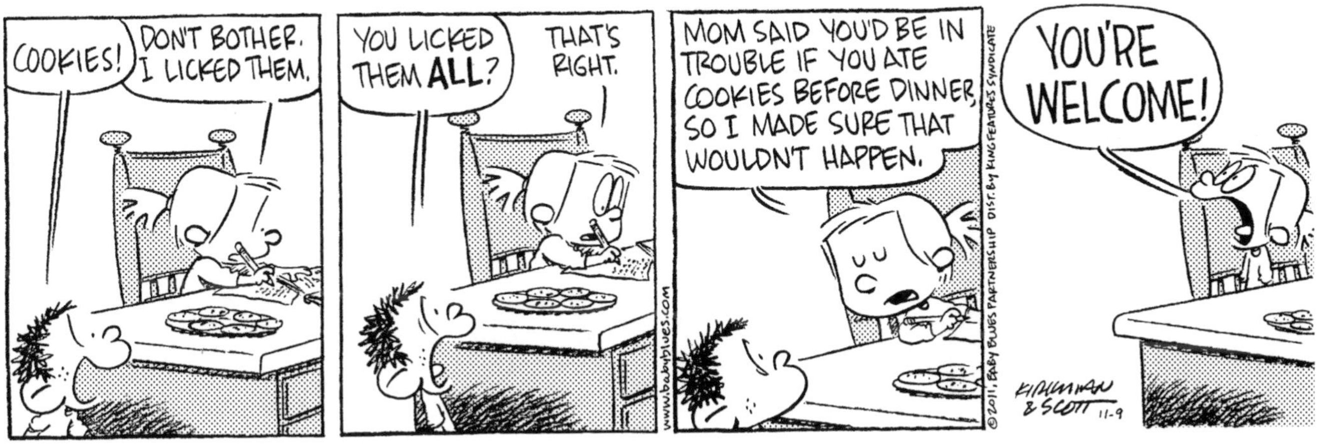
COOKIES!
DON'T BOTHER. I LICKED THEM.
YOU LICKED THEM ALL?
THAT'S RIGHT.
www.babyblues.com
MOM SAID YOU'D BE IN TROUBLE IF YOU ATE COOKIES BEFORE DINNER, SO I MADE SURE THAT WOULDN'T HAPPEN.
© 2011, BABY BLUES PARTNERSHIP DIST. BY KING FEATURES SYNDICATE
YOU'RE WELCOME!
KIRKMAN & SCOTT 11-9

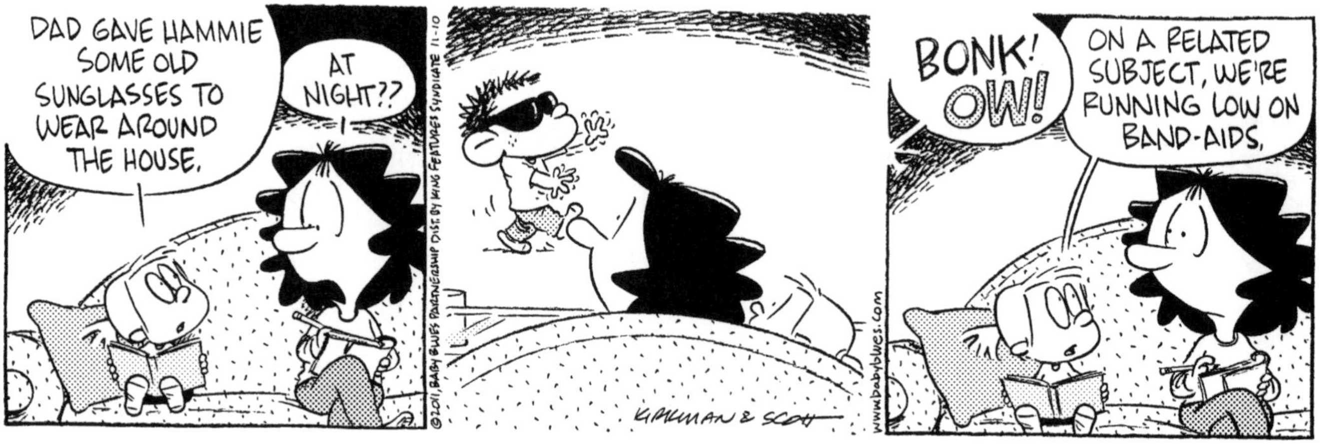
DAD GAVE HAMMIE SOME OLD SUNGLASSES TO WEAR AROUND THE HOUSE.
AT NIGHT??
©2011, BABY BLUES PARTNERSHIP DIST. BY KING FEATURES SYNDICATE 11-10
KIRKMAN & SCOTT
BONK! OW!
ON A RELATED SUBJECT, WE'RE RUNNING LOW ON BAND-AIDS.
www.babyblues.com

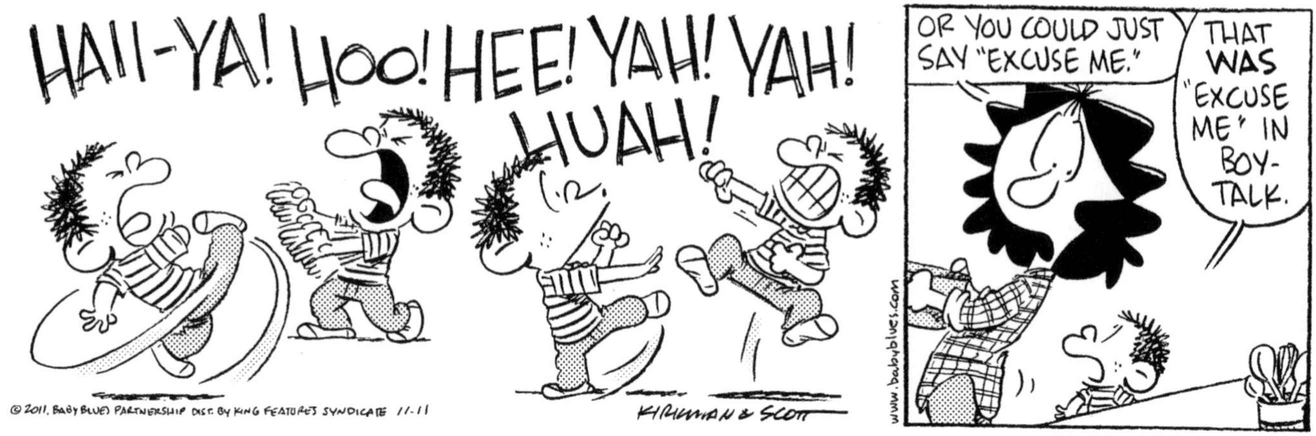
HAII-YA! HOO! HEE! YAH! YAH! HUAH!
© 2011, BABY BLUES PARTNERSHIP DIST. BY KING FEATURES SYNDICATE 11-11
KIRKMAN & SCOTT
OR YOU COULD JUST SAY "EXCUSE ME."
THAT **WAS** "EXCUSE ME" IN BOY-TALK.
www.babyblues.com

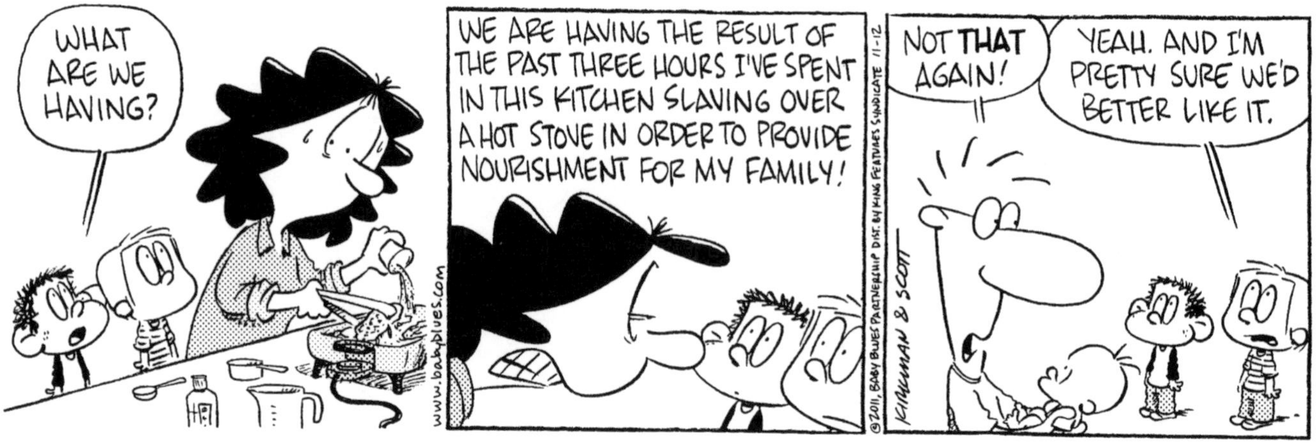
WHAT ARE WE HAVING?
www.babyblues.com
WE ARE HAVING THE RESULT OF THE PAST THREE HOURS I'VE SPENT IN THIS KITCHEN SLAVING OVER A HOT STOVE IN ORDER TO PROVIDE NOURISHMENT FOR MY FAMILY!
©2011, BABY BLUES PARTNERSHIP DIST. BY KING FEATURES SYNDICATE 11-12
KIRKMAN & SCOTT
NOT **THAT** AGAIN!
YEAH. AND I'M PRETTY SURE WE'D BETTER LIKE IT.

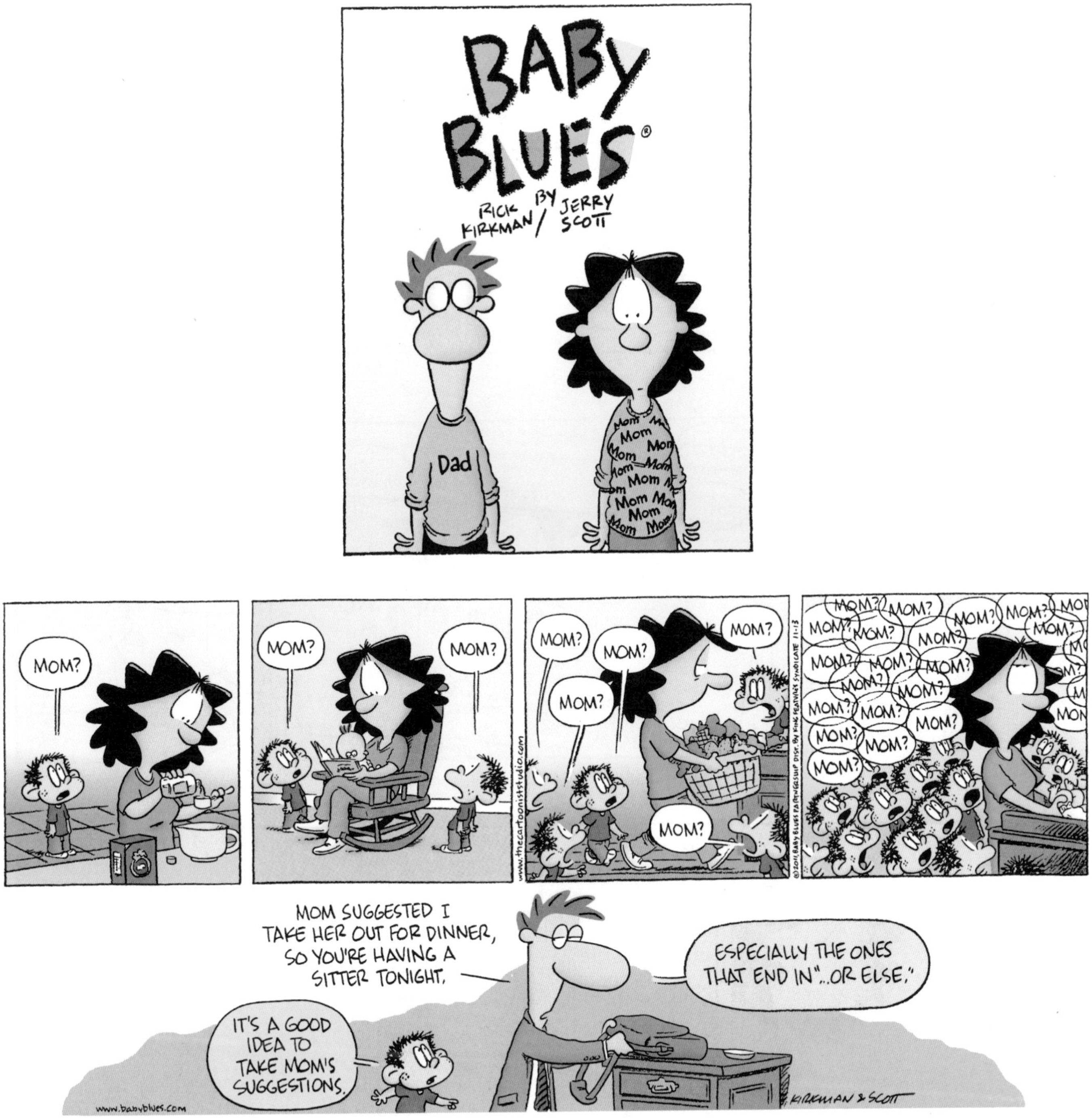

BABY BLUES®
BY RICK KIRKMAN / JERRY SCOTT
Dad
Mom
MOM?
MOM?
MOM?
www.thecartoonniststudio.com
MOM?
MOM?
MOM?
MOM?
MOM?
©2011, BABY BLUES PARTNERSHIP DIST. BY KING FEATURES SYNDICATE 11-13
MOM?
MOM SUGGESTED I TAKE HER OUT FOR DINNER, SO YOU'RE HAVING A SITTER TONIGHT.
IT'S A GOOD IDEA TO TAKE MOM'S SUGGESTIONS.
ESPECIALLY THE ONES THAT END IN "...OR ELSE."
www.babyblues.com
KIRKMAN & SCOTT

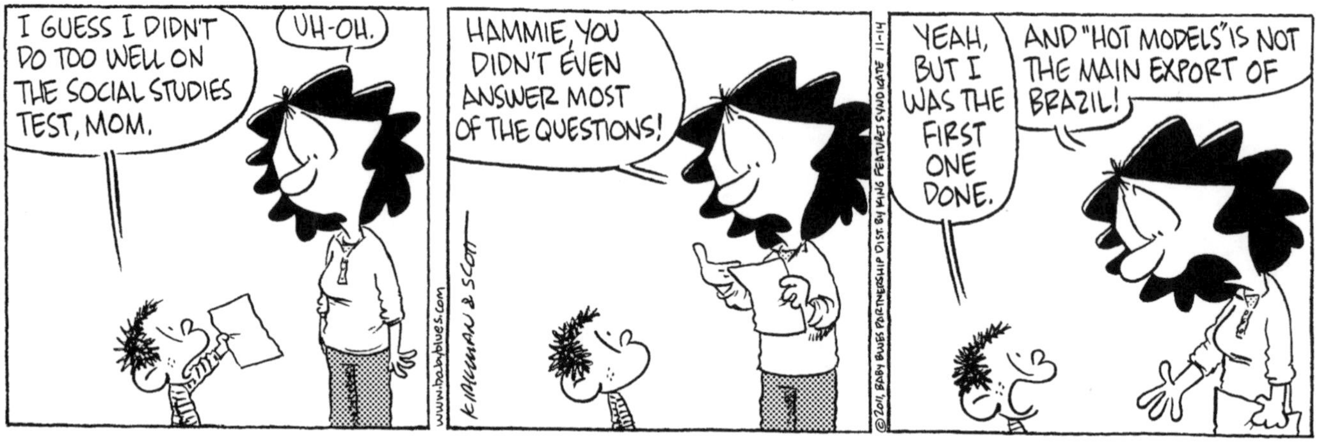
I GUESS I DIDN'T DO TOO WELL ON THE SOCIAL STUDIES TEST, MOM.
UH-OH.
www.babyblues.com
KIRKMAN & SCOTT
HAMMIE, YOU DIDN'T EVEN ANSWER MOST OF THE QUESTIONS!
© 2011, BABY BLUES PARTNERSHIP DIST. BY KING FEATURES SYNDICATE 11-14
YEAH, BUT I WAS THE FIRST ONE DONE.
AND "HOT MODELS" IS NOT THE MAIN EXPORT OF BRAZIL!

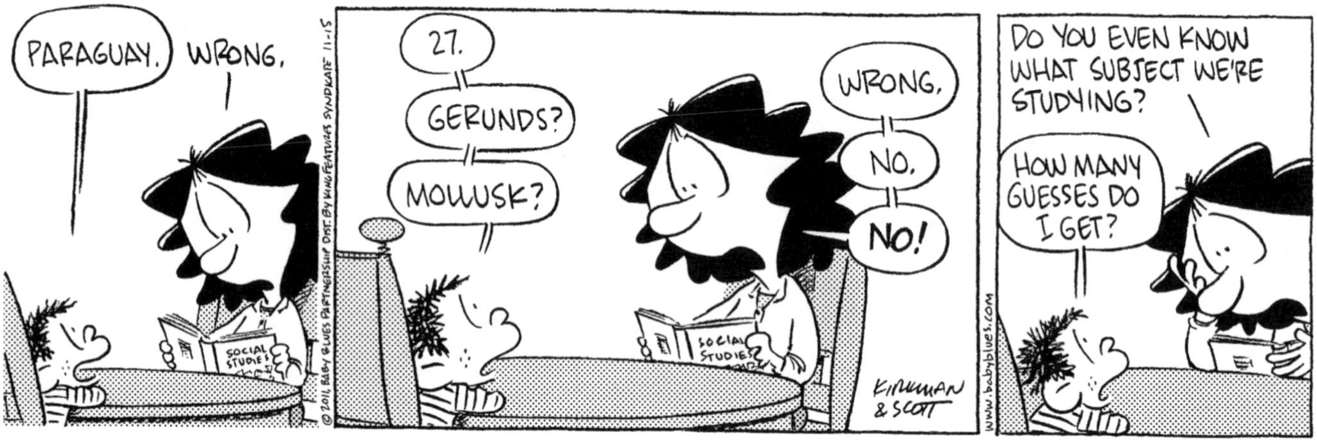
PARAGUAY.
WRONG.
© 2011, BABY BLUES PARTNERSHIP DIST. BY KING FEATURES SYNDICATE 11-15
SOCIAL STUDIES
27.
GERUNDS?
MOLLUSK?
WRONG.
NO.
NO!
KIRKMAN & SCOTT
www.babyblues.com
DO YOU EVEN KNOW WHAT SUBJECT WE'RE STUDYING?
HOW MANY GUESSES DO I GET?

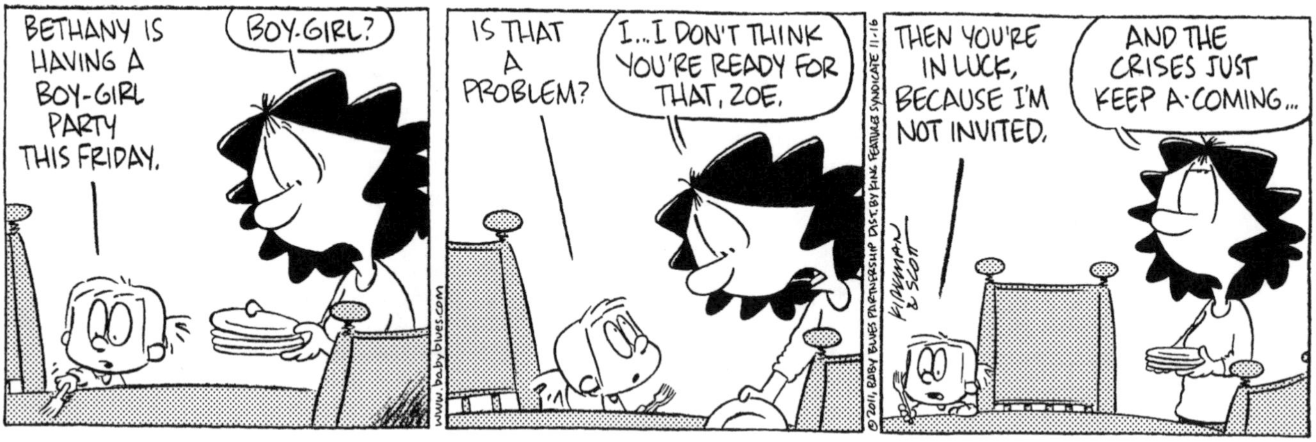
BETHANY IS HAVING A BOY-GIRL PARTY THIS FRIDAY.
BOY-GIRL?
www.babyblues.com
IS THAT A PROBLEM?
I...I DON'T THINK YOU'RE READY FOR THAT, ZOE.
KIRKMAN & SCOTT
© 2011, BABY BLUES PARTNERSHIP DIST. BY KING FEATURES SYNDICATE 11-16
THEN YOU'RE IN LUCK, BECAUSE I'M NOT INVITED.
AND THE CRISES JUST KEEP A-COMING...

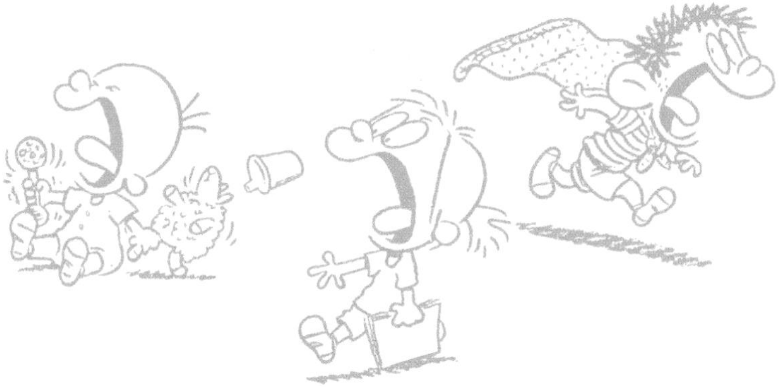

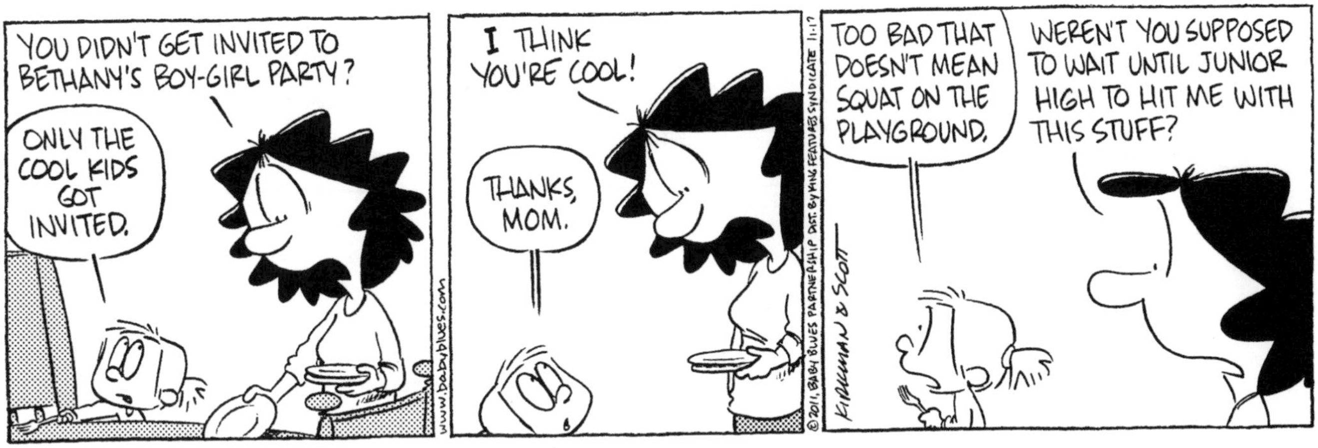
YOU DIDN'T GET INVITED TO BETHANY'S BOY-GIRL PARTY?
ONLY THE COOL KIDS GOT INVITED.
www.babyblues.com
I THINK YOU'RE COOL!
THANKS, MOM.
© 2011, BABY BLUES PARTNERSHIP DIST. BY KING FEATURES SYNDICATE 11-17
KIRKMAN & SCOTT
TOO BAD THAT DOESN'T MEAN SQUAT ON THE PLAYGROUND.
WEREN'T YOU SUPPOSED TO WAIT UNTIL JUNIOR HIGH TO HIT ME WITH THIS STUFF?

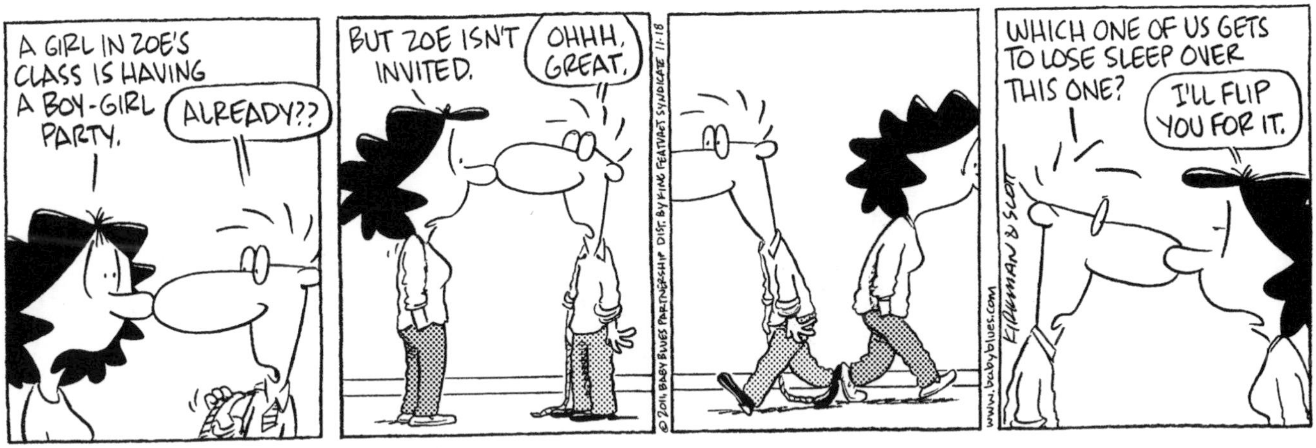
A GIRL IN ZOE'S CLASS IS HAVING A BOY-GIRL PARTY.
ALREADY??
BUT ZOE ISN'T INVITED.
OHHH, GREAT.
© 2011, BABY BLUES PARTNERSHIP DIST. BY KING FEATURES SYNDICATE 11-18
www.babyblues.com
KIRKMAN & SCOTT
WHICH ONE OF US GETS TO LOSE SLEEP OVER THIS ONE?
I'LL FLIP YOU FOR IT.

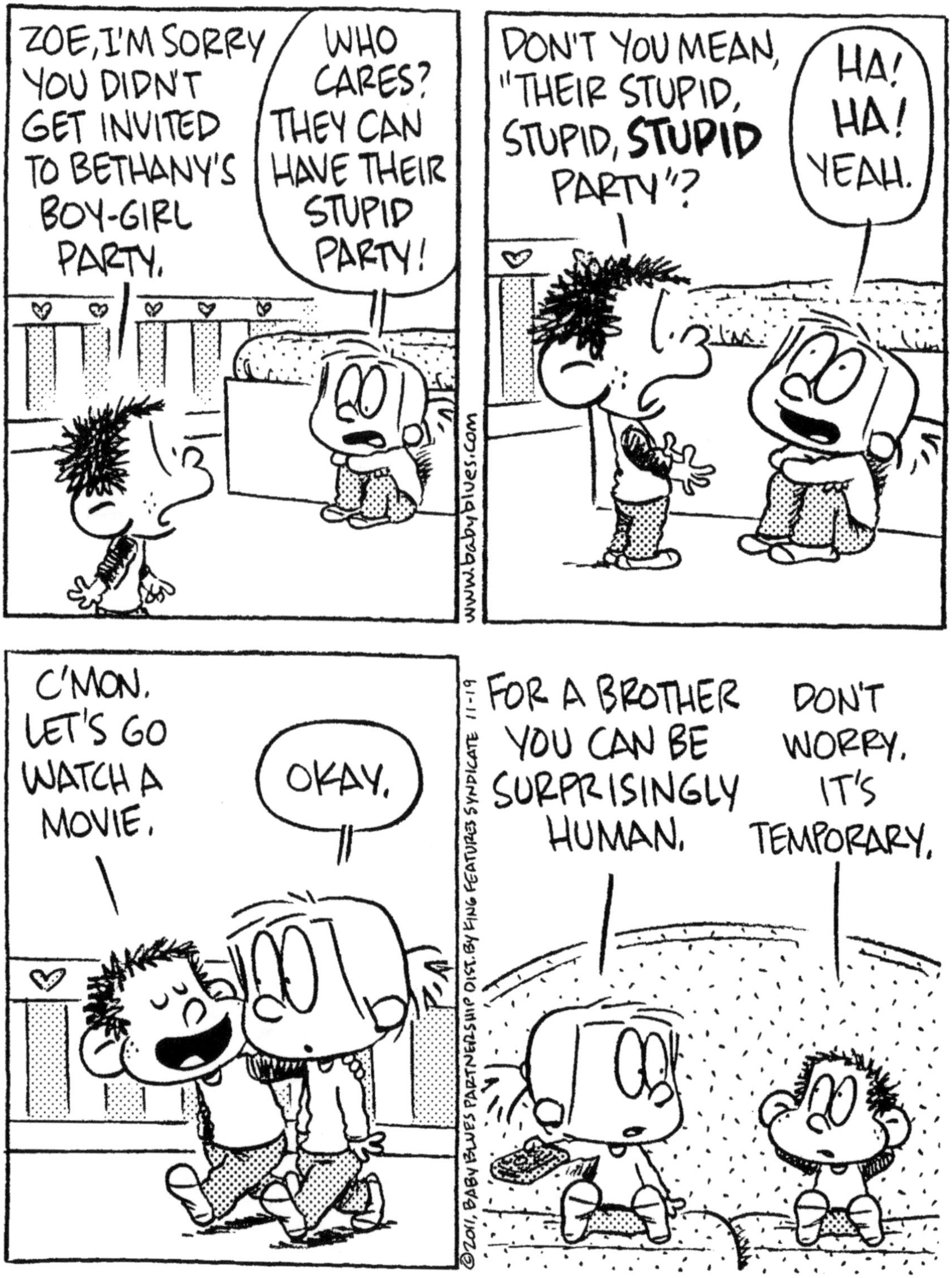
ZOE, I'M SORRY YOU DIDN'T GET INVITED TO BETHANY'S BOY-GIRL PARTY.
WHO CARES? THEY CAN HAVE THEIR STUPID PARTY!
www.babyblues.com
DON'T YOU MEAN, "THEIR STUPID, STUPID, STUPID PARTY"?
HA! HA! YEAH.
C'MON. LET'S GO WATCH A MOVIE.
OKAY.
©2011, BABY BLUES PARTNERSHIP DIST. BY KING FEATURES SYNDICATE 11-19
FOR A BROTHER YOU CAN BE SURPRISINGLY HUMAN.
DON'T WORRY. IT'S TEMPORARY.

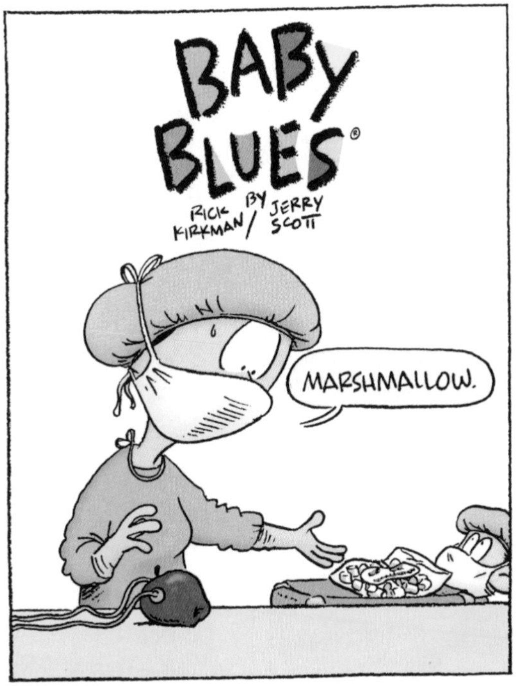
BABY BLUES®
BY RICK KIRKMAN / JERRY SCOTT
MARSHMALLOW.

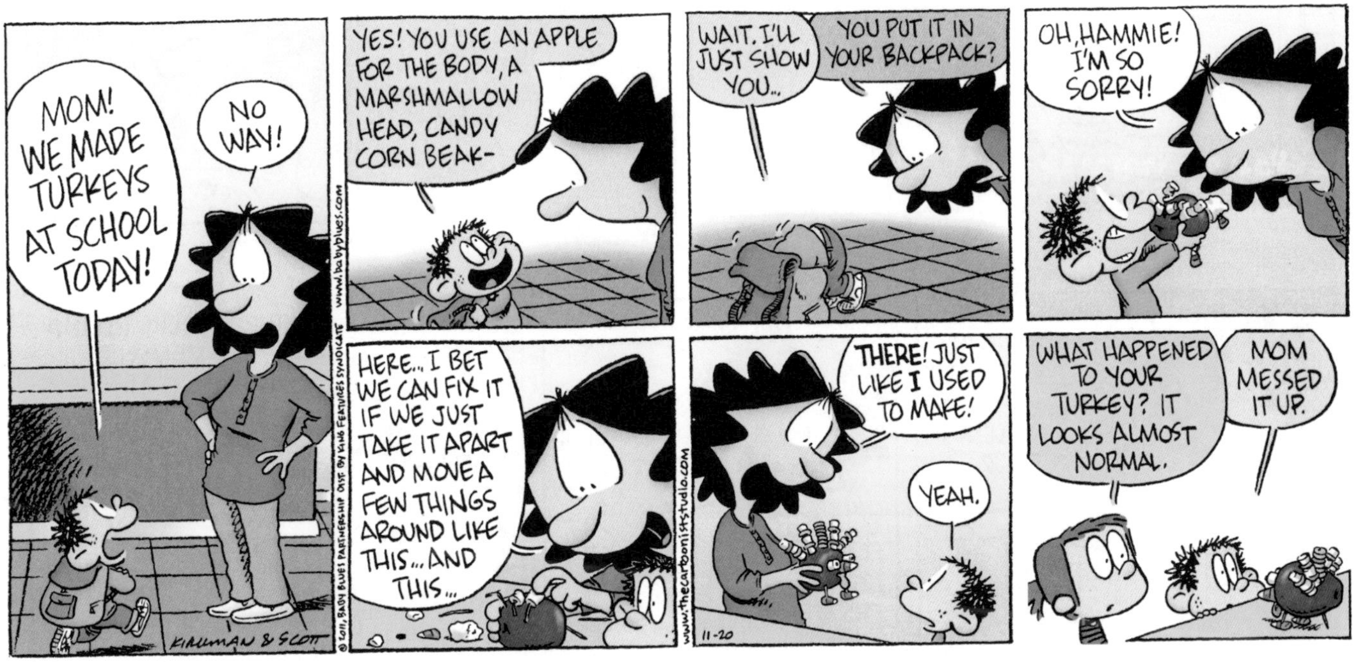
MOM! WE MADE TURKEYS AT SCHOOL TODAY!
NO WAY!
KIRKMAN & SCOTT
© 2011, BABY BLUES PARTNERSHIP DIST. BY KING FEATURES SYNDICATE www.babyblues.com
YES! YOU USE AN APPLE FOR THE BODY, A MARSHMALLOW HEAD, CANDY CORN BEAK-
WAIT. I'LL JUST SHOW YOU...
YOU PUT IT IN YOUR BACKPACK?
OH, HAMMIE! I'M SO SORRY!
HERE... I BET WE CAN FIX IT IF WE JUST TAKE IT APART AND MOVE A FEW THINGS AROUND LIKE THIS... AND THIS...
www.thecartoonistsstudio.com
11-20
THERE! JUST LIKE I USED TO MAKE!
YEAH.
WHAT HAPPENED TO YOUR TURKEY? IT LOOKS ALMOST NORMAL.
MOM MESSED IT UP.

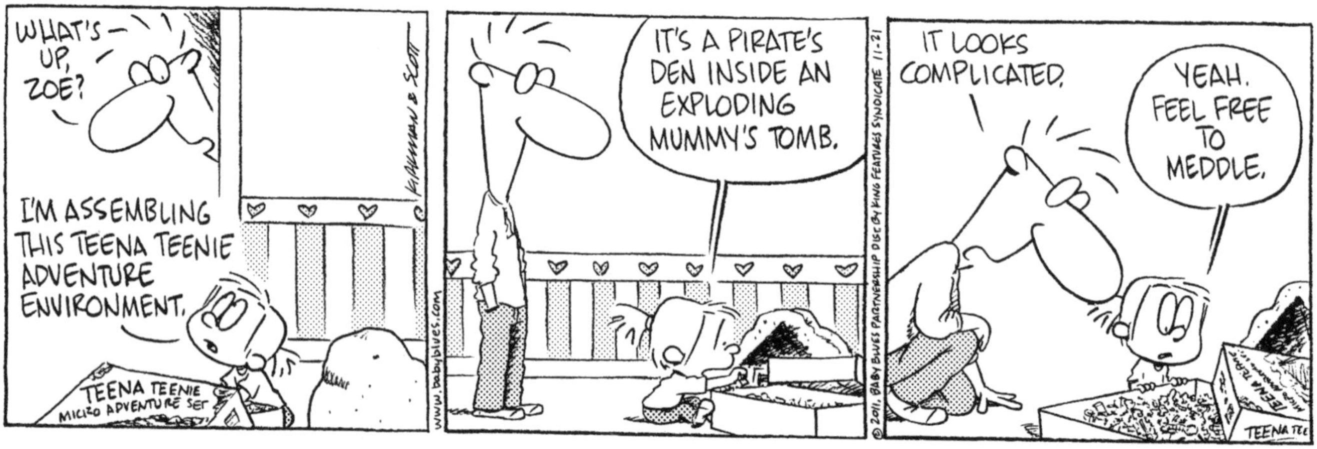
WHAT'S UP, ZOE?
I'M ASSEMBLING THIS TEENA TEENIE ADVENTURE ENVIRONMENT.
TEENA TEENIE MICRO ADVENTURE SET
KIRKMAN & SCOTT
www.babyblues.com
IT'S A PIRATE'S DEN INSIDE AN EXPLODING MUMMY'S TOMB.
© 2011, BABY BLUES PARTNERSHIP DIST. BY KING FEATURES SYNDICATE 11-21
IT LOOKS COMPLICATED.
YEAH. FEEL FREE TO MEDDLE.

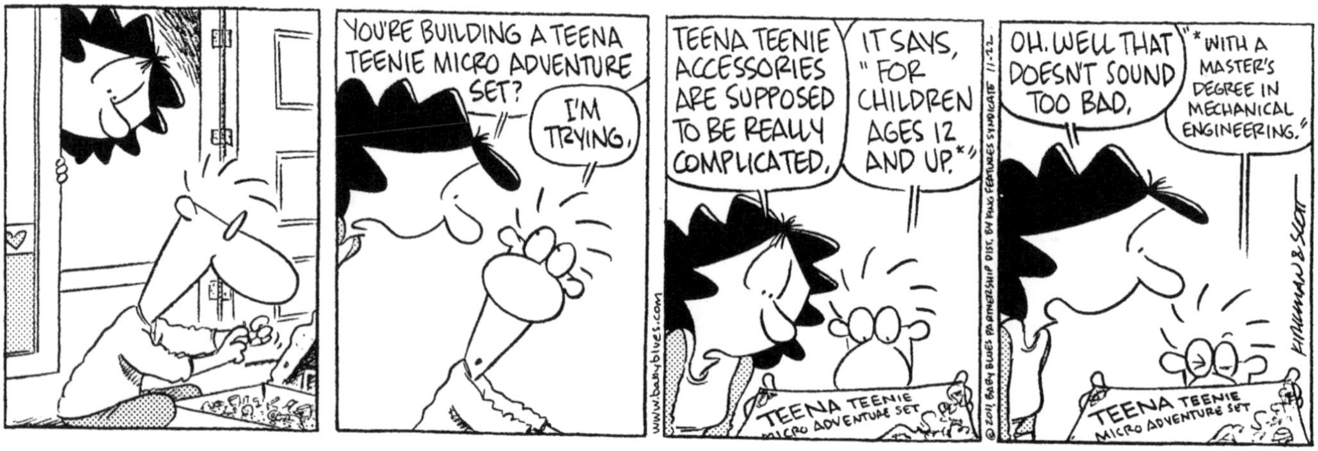
YOU'RE BUILDING A TEENA TEENIE MICRO ADVENTURE SET?
I'M TRYING.
www.babyblues.com
TEENA TEENIE ACCESSORIES ARE SUPPOSED TO BE REALLY COMPLICATED.
IT SAYS, "FOR CHILDREN AGES 12 AND UP."*
TEENA TEENIE MICRO ADVENTURE SET
© 2011, BABY BLUES PARTNERSHIP DIST. BY KING FEATURES SYNDICATE 11-22
OH. WELL THAT DOESN'T SOUND TOO BAD.
*WITH A MASTER'S DEGREE IN MECHANICAL ENGINEERING.
KIRKMAN & SCOTT
TEENA TEENIE MICRO ADVENTURE SET

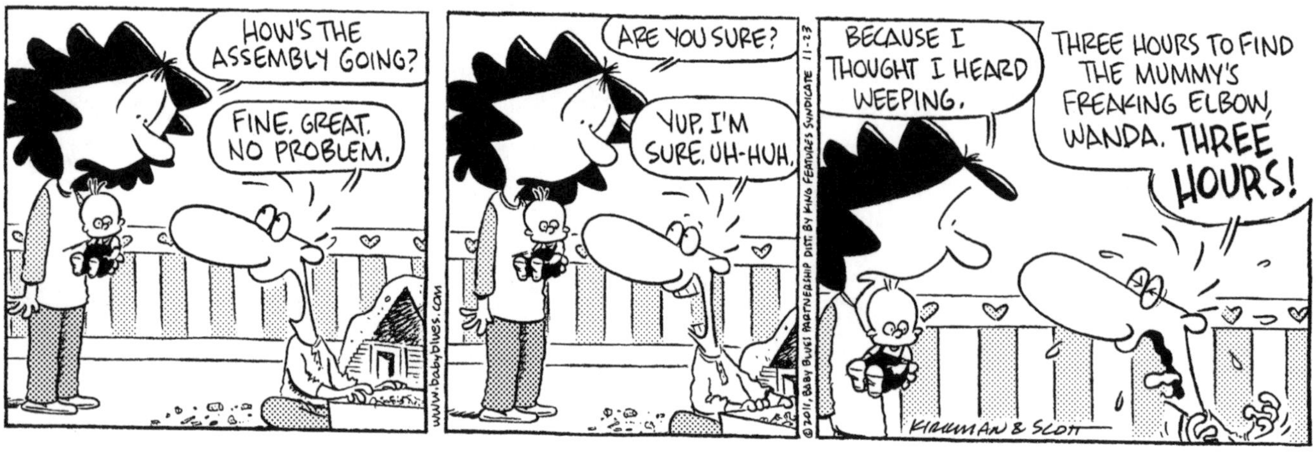
HOW'S THE ASSEMBLY GOING?
FINE. GREAT. NO PROBLEM.
www.babyblues.com
ARE YOU SURE?
YUP. I'M SURE. UH-HUH.
© 2011, BABY BLUES PARTNERSHIP DIST. BY KING FEATURES SYNDICATE 11-23
BECAUSE I THOUGHT I HEARD WEEPING.
THREE HOURS TO FIND THE MUMMY'S FREAKING ELBOW, WANDA. THREE HOURS!
KIRKMAN & SCOTT

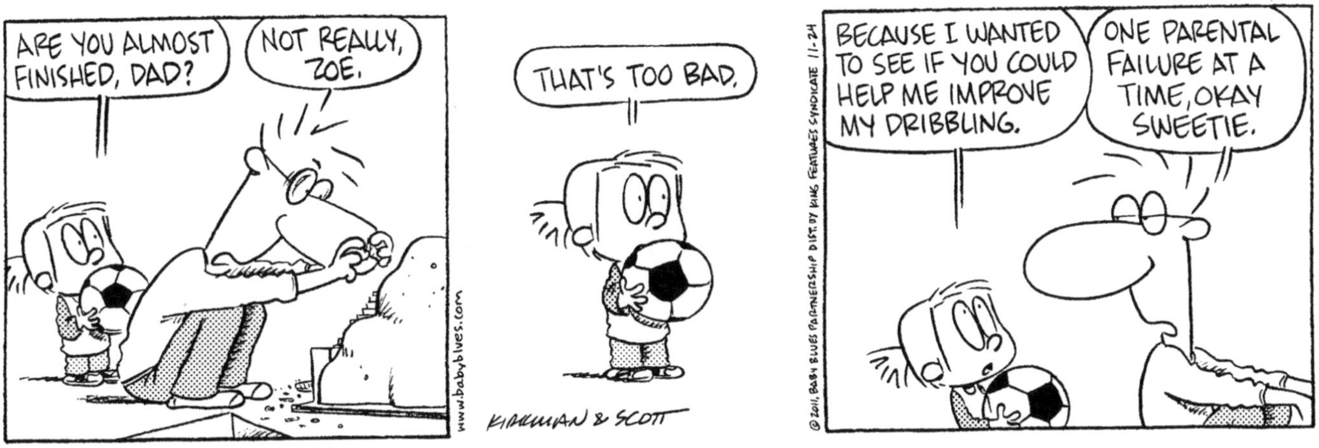
ARE YOU ALMOST FINISHED, DAD?
NOT REALLY, ZOE.
THAT'S TOO BAD.
BECAUSE I WANTED TO SEE IF YOU COULD HELP ME IMPROVE MY DRIBBLING.
ONE PARENTAL FAILURE AT A TIME, OKAY SWEETIE.
www.babyblues.com
KIRKMAN & SCOTT
© 2011, BABY BLUES PARTNERSHIP DIST. BY KING FEATURES SYNDICATE 11-24

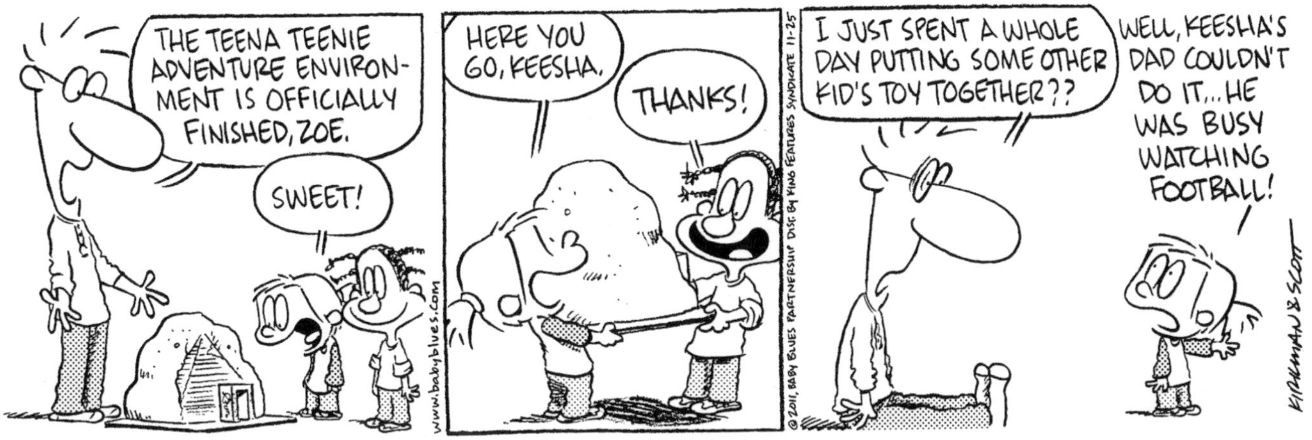
THE TEENA TEENIE ADVENTURE ENVIRONMENT IS OFFICIALLY FINISHED, ZOE.
SWEET!
HERE YOU GO, KEESHA.
THANKS!
I JUST SPENT A WHOLE DAY PUTTING SOME OTHER KID'S TOY TOGETHER??
WELL, KEESHA'S DAD COULDN'T DO IT... HE WAS BUSY WATCHING FOOTBALL!
www.babyblues.com
KIRKMAN & SCOTT
© 2011, BABY BLUES PARTNERSHIP DIST. BY KING FEATURES SYNDICATE 11-25

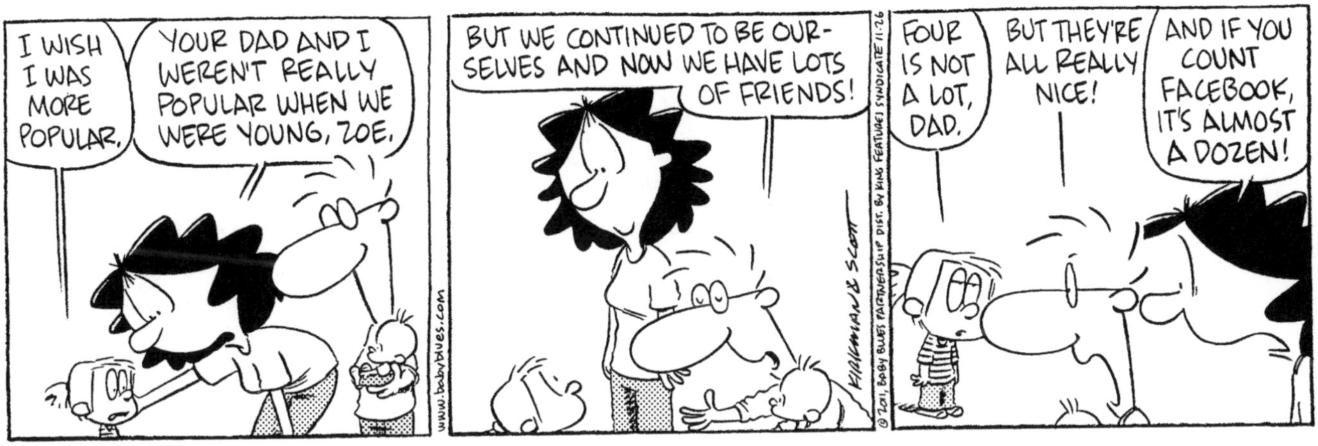
I WISH I WAS MORE POPULAR.
YOUR DAD AND I WEREN'T REALLY POPULAR WHEN WE WERE YOUNG, ZOE.
BUT WE CONTINUED TO BE OURSELVES AND NOW WE HAVE LOTS OF FRIENDS!
FOUR IS NOT A LOT, DAD.
BUT THEY'RE ALL REALLY NICE!
AND IF YOU COUNT FACEBOOK, IT'S ALMOST A DOZEN!
www.babyblues.com
KIRKMAN & SCOTT
© 2011, BABY BLUES PARTNERSHIP DIST. BY KING FEATURES SYNDICATE 11-26

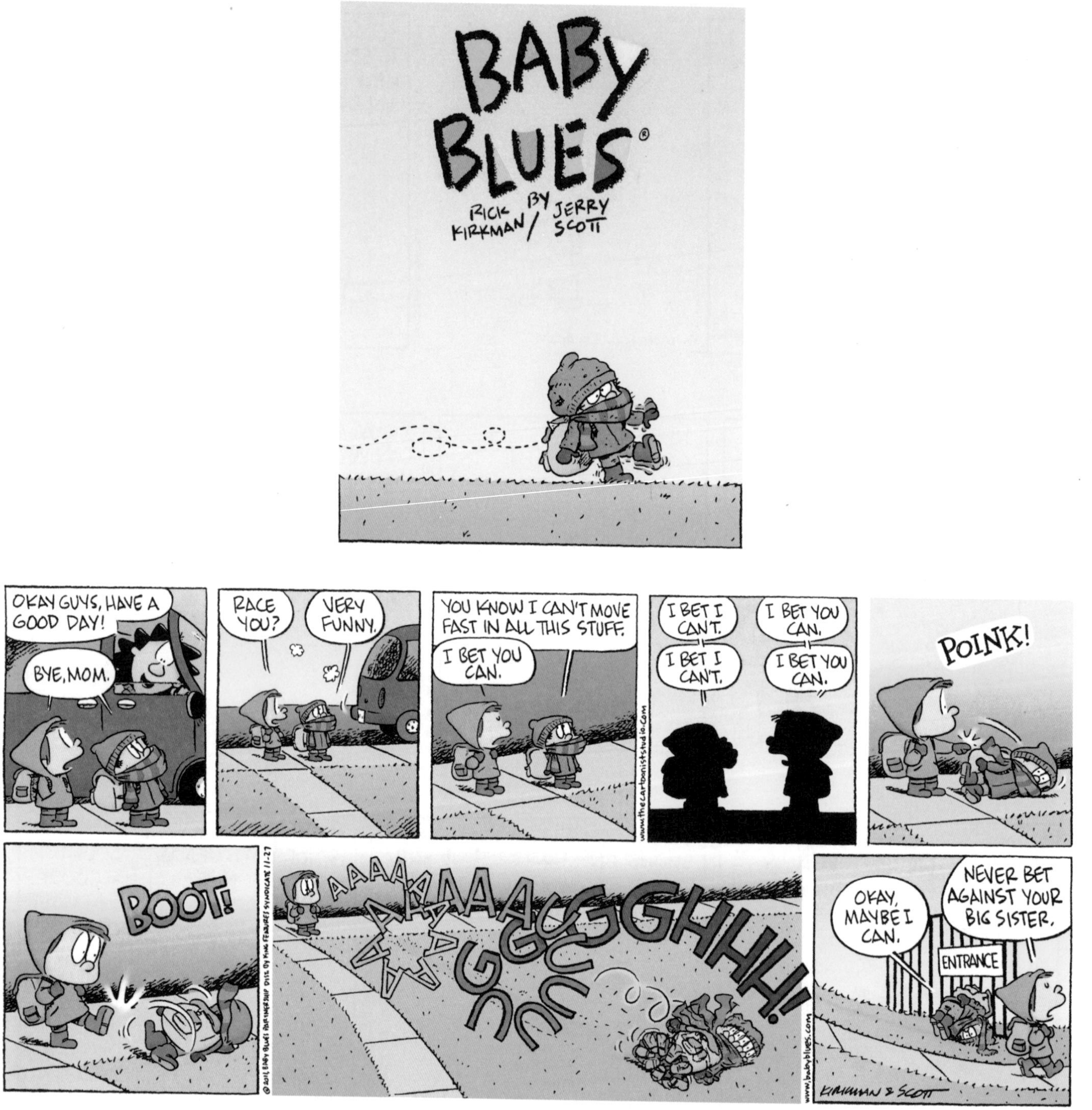
BABY BLUES®
BY RICK KIRKMAN / JERRY SCOTT
OKAY GUYS, HAVE A GOOD DAY!
BYE, MOM.
RACE YOU?
VERY FUNNY.
YOU KNOW I CAN'T MOVE FAST IN ALL THIS STUFF.
I BET YOU CAN.
www.thecartoonistsstudio.com
I BET I CAN'T.
I BET YOU CAN.
I BET I CAN'T.
I BET YOU CAN.
POINK!
BOOT!
AAAAAAAAAAAAAAAGGGGGGGHHH!
www.babyblues.com
OKAY, MAYBE I CAN.
NEVER BET AGAINST YOUR BIG SISTER.
ENTRANCE
KIRKMAN & SCOTT

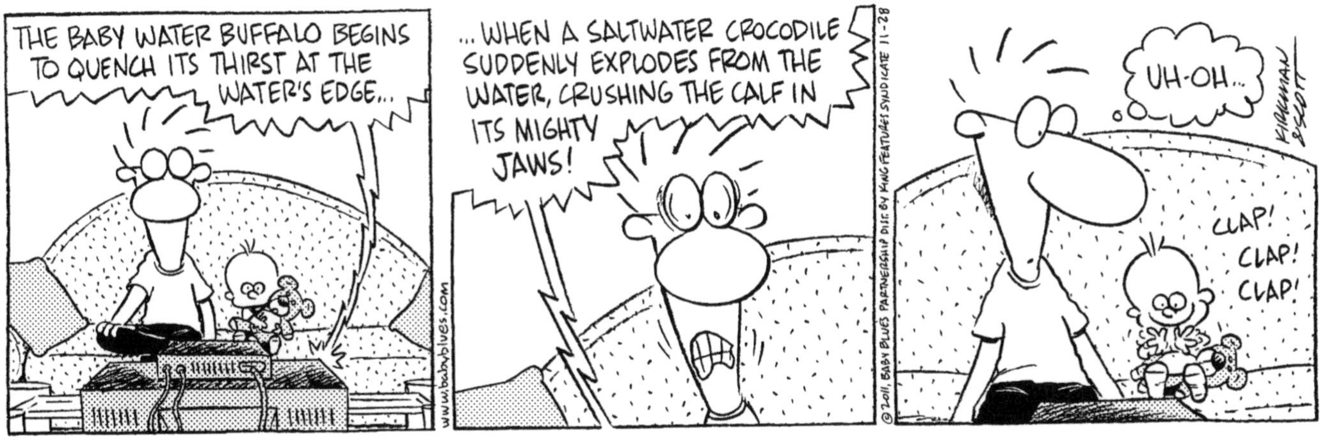
THE BABY WATER BUFFALO BEGINS TO QUENCH ITS THIRST AT THE WATER'S EDGE...
www.babyblues.com
...WHEN A SALTWATER CROCODILE SUDDENLY EXPLODES FROM THE WATER, CRUSHING THE CALF IN ITS MIGHTY JAWS!
© 2011, BABY BLUES PARTNERSHIP DIST. BY KING FEATURES SYNDICATE 11-28
UH-OH...
CLAP! CLAP! CLAP!
KIRKMAN & SCOTT

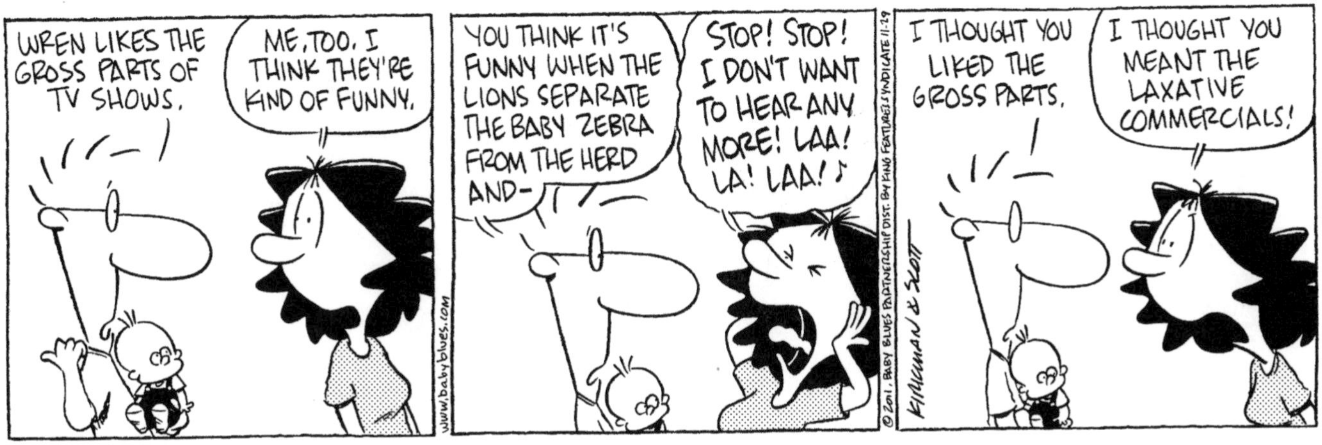
WREN LIKES THE GROSS PARTS OF TV SHOWS.
ME, TOO. I THINK THEY'RE KIND OF FUNNY.
www.babyblues.com
YOU THINK IT'S FUNNY WHEN THE LIONS SEPARATE THE BABY ZEBRA FROM THE HERD AND-
STOP! STOP! I DON'T WANT TO HEAR ANY MORE! LAA! LA! LAA! ♪
© 2011, BABY BLUES PARTNERSHIP DIST. BY KING FEATURES SYNDICATE 11-29
KIRKMAN & SCOTT
I THOUGHT YOU LIKED THE GROSS PARTS.
I THOUGHT YOU MEANT THE LAXATIVE COMMERCIALS!

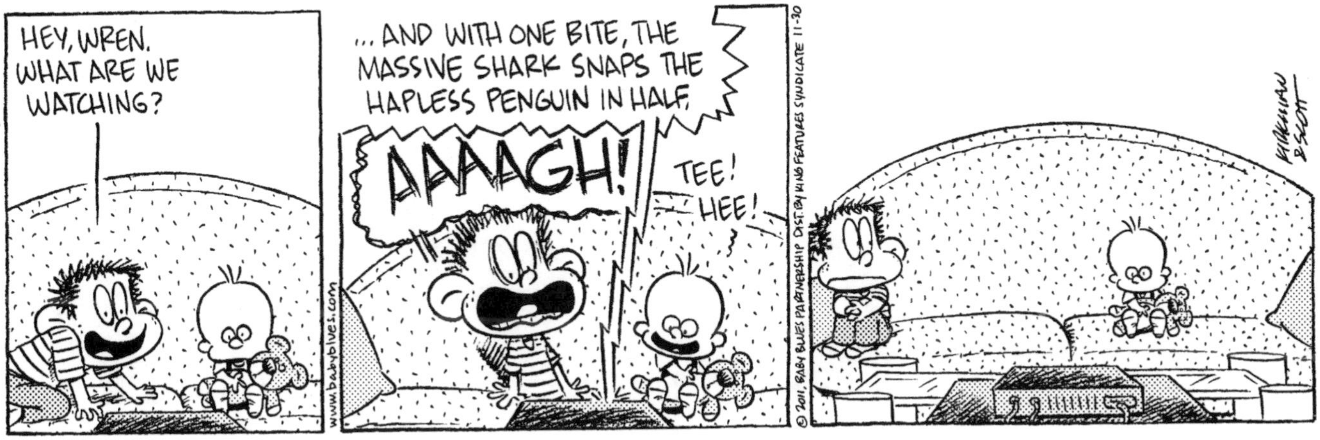
HEY, WREN. WHAT ARE WE WATCHING?
www.babyblues.com
...AND WITH ONE BITE, THE MASSIVE SHARK SNAPS THE HAPLESS PENGUIN IN HALF.
AAAAGH!
TEE! HEE!
© 2011, BABY BLUES PARTNERSHIP DIST. BY KING FEATURES SYNDICATE 11-30
KIRKMAN & SCOTT

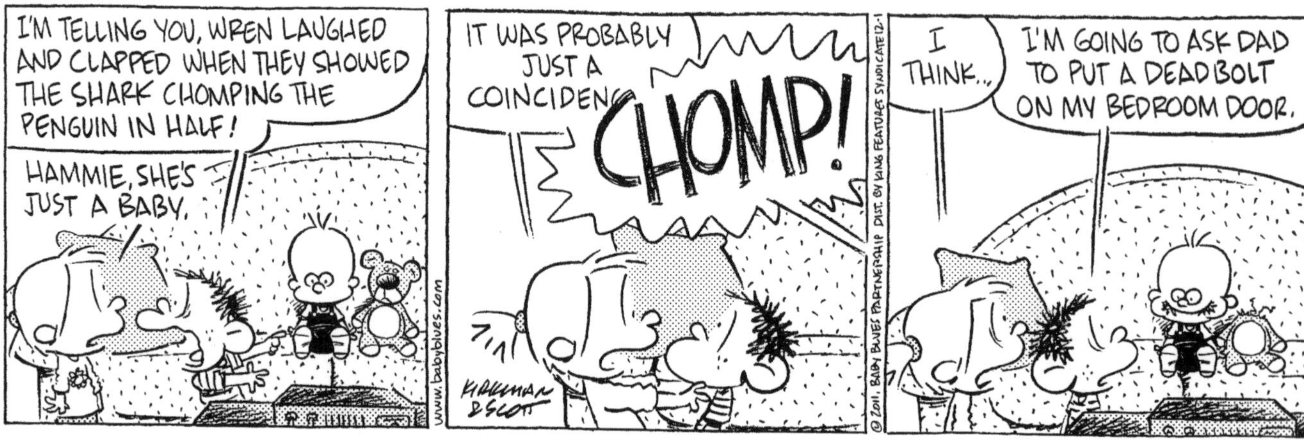
I'M TELLING YOU, WREN LAUGHED AND CLAPPED WHEN THEY SHOWED THE SHARK CHOMPING THE PENGUIN IN HALF!
HAMMIE, SHE'S JUST A BABY.
www.babyblues.com
IT WAS PROBABLY JUST A COINCIDEN
CHOMP!
KIRKMAN & SCOTT
© 2011, BABY BLUES PARTNERSHIP DIST. BY KING FEATURES SYNDICATE 12-1
I THINK...
I'M GOING TO ASK DAD TO PUT A DEADBOLT ON MY BEDROOM DOOR.

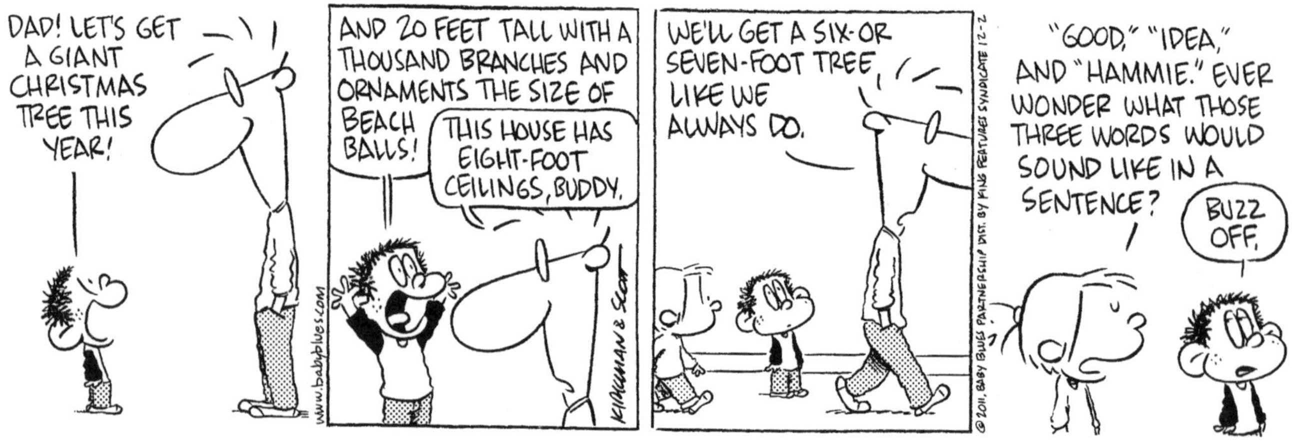
DAD! LET'S GET A GIANT CHRISTMAS TREE THIS YEAR!
www.babyblues.com
AND 20 FEET TALL WITH A THOUSAND BRANCHES AND ORNAMENTS THE SIZE OF BEACH BALLS!
THIS HOUSE HAS EIGHT-FOOT CEILINGS, BUDDY.
KIRKMAN & SCOTT
WE'LL GET A SIX- OR SEVEN-FOOT TREE, LIKE WE ALWAYS DO.
© 2011, BABY BLUES PARTNERSHIP DIST. BY KING FEATURES SYNDICATE 12-2
"GOOD," "IDEA," AND "HAMMIE." EVER WONDER WHAT THOSE THREE WORDS WOULD SOUND LIKE IN A SENTENCE?
BUZZ OFF.

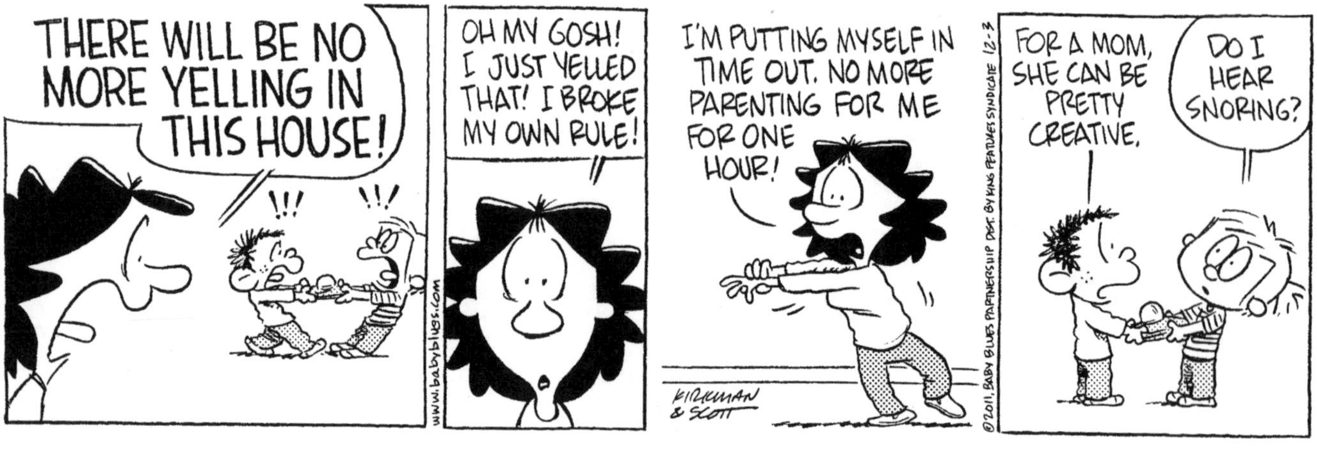
THERE WILL BE NO MORE YELLING IN THIS HOUSE!
!!!
!!!
www.babyblues.com
OH MY GOSH! I JUST YELLED THAT! I BROKE MY OWN RULE!
I'M PUTTING MYSELF IN TIME OUT. NO MORE PARENTING FOR ME FOR ONE HOUR!
KIRKMAN & SCOTT
© 2011, BABY BLUES PARTNERSHIP DIST. BY KING FEATURES SYNDICATE 12-3
FOR A MOM, SHE CAN BE PRETTY CREATIVE.
DO I HEAR SNORING?